Accountancy

A Career Guide

Accountancy Basics Concepts, History and Advancement, Branches of Accountancy, Common Types of Accounting Positions, Education, Qualifications, Salary Expectations, and More!

By Christopher Wright

Foreword

Accounting and accountancy is a vital part of everyday life, not only for the independent business person or money-maker, but also more importantly for big companies and corporations. The history of accounting and the recognition for the need to centralize the movement of finances can be traced back to 15,000 years ago, when math, money and writing came about formally into the lives of humans. Any business entity or household even, has some sort or form of accounting to accomplish to help balance finances and to sort out incoming and outgoing cash flow. It is considered as the language of business because accounting measures the results of an organization's financial and economic activities.

The process of accounting delivers this information to a host of viewers which is inclusive of creditors, investors, regulators and, of course, management. There are several fields of accounting which include, management accounting, external auditing, financial accounting, cost accounting and tax accounting. In order to support functions of accounting and activities related to it, accounting information systems have been designed.

The facilitation of accounting services are offered by accounting firms, standard-setters as well as professional accounting bodies of a particular jurisdiction to companies and entities needing their services. There are many forms of accounting needed in the world today that is relevant in all sorts of businesses, and we shall be discussing these, one by one, as we progress. You will find out what the branches of accounting are and what each of them represent and reveal. Accounting may seem tedious and repetitive to the unenlightened but it is in fact an exciting journey toward discovery, if you like, revealing important figures that matter in economic management and finances.

We shall touch upon important topics of accounting such as the history of accounting, the branches of accounting, and the best places to get an accounting education. We will also be discussing what is expected of a student of accounting as well as the experience one would need to gather in order to have a lucrative and lasting career in accounting. Delving into the topic of accounting and accountancy is our goal for this book so that you can get some guidance about this career path that revolves around numbers, information management and economics.

You will be able to know more about accountancy and being an accountant with this little book full of accounting knowledge, to arm and able you to create a very manageable career in the world of accounting and finances. Be in the know and find out what it takes for one to get into this business and this career that is not only useful but is relevant and needed in our day and age as it was in the past. Read on to find out more about what educational requirement is needed for a post in the financial sector, the history of the profession and much more!

Table of Contents

Chapter One: Introduction to Accountancy

Lots of people have misjudged accountancy to be one of the most boring professions to go into and this has been expressed time and again through jokes, puns, and stories passed on from one to another. And to solidify statements with random observations of people who deal with numbers, there have been countless references to accountants and accountancy being a boring, mundane job that many think is almost laughable. In order to understand the misguided conception and misinformation of many about this noble career, we've come up with a short book on guiding you to know accountancy better.

Accountancy goes back to thousands of years and can be detected in historical documentations to have been used by civilizations as far back as the ancient world existed. The little-known and unsung founding father of accounting was the Italian, Luca Pacioli, who was also the first to publish his writings on double-entry booking work and who formally brought about the introduction of accountancy to the Italian society. Luca Pacioli had never really ever gotten the credit that was due for him, and it's about time we talk about him a little bit more so that you can appreciate the subject that makes the world go 'round so to speak.

Accountancy is a practice that has been around for thousands of years and can be traced back to ancient Mesopotamia. Accounting came about and is associated with counting, writing, and ancient auditing systems used by the ancient Babylonians and Egyptians. A financial management manuscript was written by the Indian philosopher, economist and teacher, Chanakya. The financial management book titled "Arthashastra" it was first published in India. The Arthashastra contained detailed features on the upkeep of financial accounts for the Sovereign State of the Mauryan Empire (322 BCE-180 BCE).

It was in the nineteenth century when Scotland first produced the profession of chartered accountants in the country. Back then, the chartered accountants in Scotland were part of the same firms and associations as lawyers who offered accounting and legal services to their clients. It was during this time when accounting turned into a standard profession with professional organizations from England, in 1880, combined to form the Institute of Chartered Accountants in England and Wales.

In more recent years, the subject of accountancy was placed under bad light in the wake of the Enron debacle of 2002. The expose of the messy business with the company put the accounting profession in very bad light with the revelation of important and vital documents being shredded to hide anomalies. This was a big blow to the sector of people in the accounting field and it was indeed a bleak spell for many. But that is just one part of the history. During the course of you reading this book, you shall discover the rich history of accountancy a little bit more and will discover how building a career in accountancy can help you become a great contributor to society and its betterment.

Accountants are some of the most dedicated people to doing their job right. They are vital to many of us if we would just give a minute or two of thought to the work they provide. They are woven from a different sort of fabric, that, the knit of their personalities are geared toward making a positive difference, contributing to society in a substantial manner. Accountants come into their career with great expectations of themselves and the task they have been allotted.

Have you been thinking about starting a career in the finance sector? Perhaps you have been exposed to the profession through knowing people who have built their life's work crunching numbers. Your reasons may be as straightforward as you being keen on working with numbers. Or, you could have possibly heard about the stability of the profession and its lasting power of employability from family and friends.

Whatever your reasons are, you've come to the proper place to get to know more about the profession of accounting and what you would need to give and invest, time and money, in order to attain your goal of becoming a key player in the bigger picture of taxes and finances. We have also compiled recent statistical data that gives you a clearer picture of accounting and accountants in the workforce, their numbers, the foreseen employability of accountants, and the median annual wages earned by them.

Getting an Education

Going into accountancy, whether you are beginning an entry level job and attending higher learning on the side, you will need to give good thought of your schooling schedules. You may choose to attend classes at a physical school in your region or you may opt to take online courses. Either way, make sure that your choice of studying coincides with your lifestyle and daily schedule. You will need to consider a shift in your daily routine to figure in time in order to get your accountancy courses completed. Study options these days have given many students of different mastery and courses the luxury of flexibility in terms of schedule.

If you are looking to advance your career by getting a PhD upon completion of a master's program, expect to put in a lot of hard work and gather an extensive work experience. Doing so will help open many doors of opportunities. CPA exams are comprehensive and you will need to pass each and every one of the four required examinations in order to get licensed.

Fortunately, there are many online accounting programs that are available for all the different degree levels from associate degrees, bachelor's degrees programs, as well as MBA and Mace degrees. In addition, distance learning programs prepare and equip an individual to get ready for the Certified Public Accountant Exam. An accounting student's coursework will largely depend on the degree level they are enrolled. Subjects could include:

- General or advanced studies of financial management and accounting

- Auditing
- Taxation
- Cost accounting and management
- Economics and information systems
- Classes in systems technology may be part of the curriculum, as well as
- Business law and ethics

Your Efforts

The effective use of your study time will be vital to your gaining knowledge on and about accounting. You will be studying systems, modern and ancient, you shall be working on fine tuning skills in computation, manually and with the use of various computers, you shall learn how to work with others, specifically in the area of research and investigation in relation to finances. One will have to expect that there will be long hours of work seasonally once they have successfully gained proper clients and employment.

Aside from numbers, and collaborative work, expect to work with a lot of papers, be ready to challenge your filing skills. An accountant is tasked to work in a company balancing its books, or they could be employed independently by clients who need their expertise and know-how. There is an honest truth about numbers that brings clarity to any economic situation of a business or an individual. You will need to bring your honed skills, not many possess, to the table each time.

Depending on how dedicated one is to completing their studies, it could take a person anywhere between 2 to 6 years to complete their education.

There are those who complete their studies all the way up to acquiring an MBA and then there are others who enroll in 2 year associate degree programs allowing them entry level positions in companies. Some of these individuals would gain experience by learning through working and may take up additional courses to get their bachelors degree. Bachelor degrees typically take 4 years to complete. Master's degree program typically take one to two years to complete. Make sure that you get credit that could shave off time on your studies.

Cost of Education

The monetary cost of getting a bachelor's degree, associate degree, and an MBA will fluctuate depending on the institution one chooses to attend. Here are some important facts you need to know regarding paying for an accounting course:

- An average cost of studying a four year course at a non-profit private school is around $34,740 annually.

- Attending a private for-profit learning institution can set one back over $16,000 each year for a four year course.

- The College Board's Trends in College Pricing forecast an average annual tuition fee of about $9,900 for a Masters Degree Program when attending an in state institution.

- Out-of-state tuition may cost well around $25,620 in the years 2017-2018.

- The College Pricing for 2017-2018 also forecast that a Master's degree program taken at an in-state public institution entail an annual cost of $8, 670 dollars.

- A doctorate program at in-state public institution costs $10,830 annually.

One who intends to carve a career in accounting has to make sure that they get solid preparation while in high school. This is where you can start building a strong foundation for a promising career ahead.

Take up courses in English, communications and speech. Pay mind to accounting and math whilst in high school and make sure you get classes that offer learning on computer technology. College admissions officers look out for applicants who display strong leadership qualities. All these skills are important to hone as these are features that will desirable and key to getting accepted.

Quick Look of Accounting Stats You Need to Know

It has been forecasted that the industry of finance, in the realm of tax preparation, payroll services and accounting will generate about 160 billion US dollars by the year 2018. In 2014, accounting services accounted for 94 billion US dollars, giving the image of a pie that is just getting bigger. A person with the dedication and determination, coupled with discipline for effective study can most certainly realize a dream of having a stable career that pays handsomely.

The stability and sustainability of career is promising one, whether one looks for employment in the business sector or if they decide to go into business on their own. Here are some important stats that could serve as your reference particularly in United States:

- 2016 saw four of the biggest employers of accounting and auditing companies around the world employing 887 thousand individuals. Also known as the "Big Four" accounting powerhouses, PricewaterhouseCoopers, KPMG, Ernst & Young, and Deloitte reported combined revenue of 128 billion dollars that year.

- The USA alone, in 2016, saw 1.57 million accounting clerks, auditing clerks and bookkeeping clerks employed in the financial sector. 1.25 million people account for the number of employed as auditors and accountants that year.

- There is an expected rise of 3.44 million job posts waiting for auditors and accountants as well as administrative accounting staff by 2022.

- The state of California reported the highest number of employed auditors and accountants in the USA, but the District of Columbia reported paying higher wages for auditors and accountants employed in that US state.

- The current forerunner of accounting firms in the US, Deloitte had 78, 642 employed staff by the close of the year of May 2016. Deloitte's revenue in the USA, as of March 2017 totaled 17.52 billion US dollars.

Accountants and auditors are primarily tasked to gather, prepare and scrutinize the financial records and cash flow documentation of their clients. One who has keen interest in working with numbers, a nose for investigative work and an attentive eye for details can be employed by a company for a variety of entry level positions within the finance department of a firm which can later on progress toward a much higher position equating to a higher take home pay.

An individual can also get into accounting by way of consultancy or through their own private practice. Whichever route one decides to take, they can be assured that the realm of accounting has a host of job positions available and in demand in many industries.

Making sure that the accountant's clients financial records are on the up and up, accurate and up to date, submitted and filed in a timely fashion are just some of the tasks an accountant assures. They are the ones who assess a company or individual's financial flow whilst making certain that all these are in order and that the organization runs smoothly as it is efficient. They are the ones who know and comply with laws and rules, they are skilled individuals who compute for taxes needed to be paid, they prepare returns and make sure that taxes are paid timely. They not only inspect accounting system, but they also are able to scrutinize accounting ledgers by way of employing widely accepted accounting methods. They study the financial position of their clients. They organize and maintain their client's financial records and able to make recommendations to senior managers of the firm they are employed.

Accountants are able to empower a company to improve profits, enhance its earnings and reduce cost by giving suggestions. Therefore accountants and auditors are also tasked with meeting their customers face-to-face in order to explain their findings through the written reports they create for their individual clients.

We have come up with a comprehensive list of accounting and auditing jobs from entry level to higher positions, which you will have the joy of discovering later. The US Labor of Statistics detected about 1.4 million jobs in accountancy and auditing in 2016:

- o Seven percent of the 1.4 million employed that year were self-employed individuals who could be working as part-time consultants as well.

- o Another seven percent of this number is accountants and auditors who held managerial positions in companies and private firms.

- o Eight percent of this worked in government and another eight percent was employed by financial and insurance entities, with a whopping 25% of them employed by companies doing accounting work, bookkeeping, payroll services and tax preparation.

- o Many auditors and accountant are employed in offices, with a small number who work independently from home. Many of these number crunchers are full time workers.

- o 2016 saw 1 out of 5 accountants and auditors worked beyond 40 hours a week. It is not unusual for auditors and accountants to work longer hours during specific periods of the year, like tax season or the end of the budget year.

Here is a quick statistical look of the results of 2016 in terms of salary and compensation for accountants and auditors.

- • May 2016 saw auditors and accountants take home a median annual salary of $68,150. The median income is the amount that separates the distribution of income into two equal groups, where one-half earn income above that amount, and the other half that earns income below that amount.

- The bottom 10% of the population of accountants and auditors earned wages lower than $42,140.

- On the other hand, $120, 910 was the annual wage earned by the top 10%.

- In 2016, financial analysts earned a median annual wage of $68,780.

- Auditors and accountants, in 2016 earned a median annual wage of $68,150.

- All other individuals who worked in finance in 2016, earned a median annual salary of $37,040

The employability of auditors and accountants has been projected to leap and grow by 10% between the years of 2016 to 2026. That is a faster than average growth in all areas of occupation globally. This expected increase for the demand of accountants and auditors is largely owed and due to globalization and the growing economies of many countries. And because of the complex tax and regulatory implementations, the demand for both accountants and auditors is expected to be a strong contender in the job market worldwide. Tied in closely to the employment spike of auditors and accountants is the overall wellness of the economy.

As economies flourish, the need for workers as such, will be continually required because more and more financial records will need to be prepared and examined by experts. Public accounts, which are skilled and certified to handle legal financial documentation, will be needed as more companies go public. There may also be a greater demand for the expertise of accountants, and related accounting services as international trade increases, as well as when mergers and acquisitions are closed.

Chapter Two: Accounting Throughout the Ages

Many of us shy away from numbers because it can be a daunting affair that can confound and leave us scratching our heads. But this is the beauty of math, the truth in numbers doesn't lie and this is something we can count on to be true. Knowing how to balance the books of finances gives one the power to adjust to the given economic situation. It is able to measure the financial results of a company's earnings, expenditures, and profits. Accounting can give an overview and a "prediction" of sorts in relation to whether an entity is in the position to gain profit or lose money. Accounting is a vital tool of business that requires the skill, mastery and dedication of accountants.

The Advancement of Accountancy

The use of accounting was developed back in the days of the ancient Mesopotamia. Accountancy was developed close to the time when formal writing came about. It was developed at the time when counting and money became a needful task. There has been evidence of the keeping of financial records in ancient Iran/ The Babylonians and the Egyptians also had a system of auditing during their heyday. The Roman Empire, by the time of the reign of the emperor Augustus already had a systematic form of detailed information on the kingdom's finances.

It was in medieval Europe when double-entry bookkeeping records were developed by an Italian teacher and philosopher. This was also when accounting was divided into two classifications along with the development of joint-stock entities. Financial accounting and management accounting were the two divisions of accounting employed by joint-stock companies of those times.

It was during this period that Luca Pacioli published his initial book on his work on the double-entry bookkeeping system. Much later on, in the nineteenth century, accounting started to become a more organized skill-set form. This was when it started to become an actual career and profession. It was in Scotland when the job of chartered accountants began cropping up. The accountants then would typically be part of the same firm as lawyers who would offer accounting work to their clientele.

In those days, there were no receipts to be given in place of monies paid or received, so the accounting techniques and methods then resembled and had similar aspects to today's modern day forensic accounting. Initial accounts of the early methods of accounting can be traced back to ancient Mesopotamia where vast records of accounting were found. Other evidence of accounting records was discovered in the ancient ruins of Sumeria, Assyria and Babylon where the populace of those days used what looks to be primitive methods of accounting but what effectively worked, to keep track of the growth of their herds and crops.

Physical evidence in the form of cylindrical bookkeeping clay tokens which kept tabs of property and monitored surplus became a great advancement for mankind between the 4th millennium BC and the 3rd millennium BC.

During this span of time the Babylonians and Egyptians of ancient times developed systems for auditing the movement of commodities in and out of their storehouses. One of the methods of auditing included oral "audit reports" which brought about the word "auditor". When taxation came about the process called for a method of recording payments and this was pretty much how accounting had developed in earlier times. An immense cache of clay tablets show the extent of record keeping in Mesopotamia.

The methodic documentation of administration affairs was found throughout the Middle East. It is estimated that there are about 50,000 Akkadian cuneiform tablets documenting administrative and legal affairs and about 150,000 in Sumerian. These cuneiforms reveal a talented and well-organized society who created not only a method of filing clay tablets containing mathematical texts but also tablets which showed bookkeeping systems listing salaries paid out, and account of an earlier dynasty, and a contract of land that was in the market.

There were also tablets which illustrated what we would call these days' receipts of sale or trade. The tablets found at Derham revealed names, dates, itemized commodities and transaction types, it did not show price or origin of product sale, unlike those of Sumerian texts, where price was part of the tablets.

The lack of information on these tablets is things that we now see to be vital bits of information when doing business. All these highlight the early systematic recording of business during ancient Mesopotamia, and Egypt.

By the time of the Roman Emperor Augustus, in 63 BC - AD 14, the Roman government already possessed information about finances in the "Deeds of the Divine Augustus". The inscription was an account provided to the Roman people which documented and listed the Emperor's public expenses. These included the funds given to veterans of the Roman army, the distributions of land grants.

It also included the finances spent on building temples, subsidies the government had put toward the treasury, expenses put toward gladiator games, theatrical shows and religious offerings. This documentation evidencing the monies that flowed in and out of the Roman purse covered 40 years. Not only does it show the planning and decision-making of the ruling governance, it also displays the scope of what was available at the emperor's disposal.

Chapter Three: Branches of Accountancy

There are a few accounting task types ranging from the preparation of tax returns to auditing. Aside from general bookkeeping tasks, accountants, at least most of them, are skilled to carry out intricate tasks like payroll reporting, fraud auditing. They are also able to give an accurate report on detailed, financial information to shareholders as well as the government. Accountants give individuals and businesses the ability to comprehend and study profitability and outgoing cash flow.

These financial aspects of an individual or a business make the need for accountants a constant. The work of an accountant is one that is engaging and dynamic. It calls for the keen attention to detail of the individual. It calls for the investigative work of a diligent accountant to keep business thriving.

The area of financial accounting deals with the collection of financial information and creating external reports, requiring the knowledge of the accounting framework used by the company's financial statement reader like the International Financial Reporting Standards (IRFS) or Generally Accepted Accounting Principles (GAAP). They also have to be knowledgeable of the specific standards imposed by the governing entity that handles public company reportage within a specific country. In the case of the United States, that would be the Security and Exchange Commission.

Public Accounting

The field of Public Accounting deals with studying financial statements. A public accountant supports a company's accounting system, giving assurance that the financial statements gathered and collected by clients are representative of the client's financial position as well as their financial results. A public accountant will have to possess exceptional skill and knowledge of the accounting framework relevant to the company, business or individual person. They have to have the inclination to investigate deeper into the client's systems as required of them. A potential public accountant can transition from auditing positions to advance to an audit partner.

Government Accounting

The area of Government Accounting utilizes an accounting framework that is unique from others. The framework of government accounting creates and manages funds where cash is handed out to cover expenses associated with the service provided by any government entity. Government accounting requires a specific skill set from an individual that most of the accountants who are in these positions specialize within this area of accounting for most of their careers. Government accountant earn an annual wage of $59,000.

Government accountants are responsible for managing the funds given to a specific unit or money is used for a specific person Government accountants are responsible for managing the funds given to a specific unit or monies used for a specific purpose in accordance to specific regulations and standards. They are focused on government organizations and their financial affairs by using a fund accounting syste. Government accounting focuses on the measurement of the influx and outflow of the finances of a government rather than measuring the economic activity.

Forensic Accounting

Forensic accounting is much like what it sounds. Forensic accounting was one of the first accounting models in medieval days. Today, this specialty is sought out when accounting involves the reconstruction of financial information when records are absent, missing or no longer available. A forensic accountant will be responsible for reconstructing financial documentation of a wrecked business. They are tasked to rebuild records which are fraudulent. They convert cash-basis accounting documentation. Because few businesses require the services of a full time forensic accountant, they are usually employed on a temporal basis as consultants. The average salary of a forensic accountant is $73,000 annually.

- The forensic accountant has the responsibility of analyzing and investigating all financial records for any irregularities which may be a sign for possible embezzlement or fraud.

- They are tasked to give recommendations to avoid fraud within the company.

- In the event of fraud they reconstructed scenarios that may have been involved in any economic and financial wrongdoing.

- Friends of accountant based on what they discover may be needed to testify and provide information in a court of law
- A forensic accountant specializes in the field where they are required to gather evidence and collect pertinent information using investigative techniques for litigation steps.

An accountant working for the FBI is an agent who specializes in the tracking down of criminal behavior. **Forensic accountants** are experts at investigating business crimes and the investigation of corporate criminality like embezzlement and fraud. Provided with the proper training and if in possession of the critical skills of financial analysis needed in accounting and auditing businesses an accountant can get hired and be given priority by the FBI. Forensic Accountants are agents who work for the FBI during any criminal investigation

Tax Accounting

The field of **tax accounting** focuses on the rightful tax regulations compliance, filings of tax, and tax plotting aimed at reducing the tax burden of a company later on.

Chapter Four: Common Types of Accounting Positions

Knowing the fundamentals of accounting will allow you to prepare for a vast range of possibilities in the accounting sector. One is not only employable but they will also be able to go into business for themselves with a private practice. Several career paths involved in financial accounting like in external reporting will entail an intricate knowledge of accounting standards. Another path for an accountant to consider is the controller path, requiring a good combination of management and financial accounting. There are different career paths that an accountant can specialize in which we have listed in this chapter.

Types of Accounting Positions

Internal auditors work on the area focused on the study and examination of all categories of risk, a company's transactions, systems, waste, fraud, mismanagement as well as the reportage of all of these inclusive of the outcome to the company's management. Internal auditors go on to become information systems auditors whilst others opt to move on to be environmental auditors. Some of their main responsibilities are listed below.

- They provide an objective perspective which is unbiased.
- They work independently from the operations of the firm and give evaluated reports to the utmost level of the firm's governors and managers comprised of the board of trustees, the board of directors, the audit committee or the accounting officer.
- Internal auditors must be qualified and experienced individuals who comply with accordance of the International Standards as well as the Code of Ethics.

Environmental Accountants

Calculating the costs of a business activity is a task relegated to an environmental accountant. Many environmental accountants work solely for the company costs of which they are employed, whilst others may delve into the actions of society in terms of environmental costs. This subject matter of environmental costs singles out specific environmental costs, whilst keeping tabs of the cost origins, allowing for better cost reduction schemes. Environmental accountants, aside from the tasks mentioned above, are also expected to:

- Help reduce environmental costs to the company.

- Making calculations and looking for alternative sources of processes, products designs, mixture, ingredients and chemicals needed in production, and give recommendations of alternative sources of these.

- They aid companies in identifying environmental costs which would allow their companies to create cleaner products whilst making the proper use of available resources.

In order to qualify for a position as an environmental accountant in some states of the US, one must have at least a bachelor's degree with a good solid background in the accounting profession. However, most companies require a person with a master's degree along with a rich background in the financial work arena. An environmental accountant's average salary $67,000.; starting salaries for environmental accountants may begin at $40,000 whereas, environmental accountants in Washington DC are said to be able to garner an annual wage of $100,000.

A **bookkeeping clerk** is responsible for the upkeep, gathering and compilation of the company's accounts.

- They maintain the company's financial ledgers by making countless computations in order to update the company's accounting records.

- They are the ones who verify and input data of the company's transactions into a ledger.

- They gather information from cashiers so they can prepare bank deposits.

- Aside from handling different payroll duties, they also prepare financial reports and summaries.

- A bookkeeping clerk prepares the invoices for billing purposes; these include summing up the numbers, inputting dates and making sure that the financial data provided is accurate.

- They keep tabs on and oversee accounts that are overdue and refer those that are overdue to the collections department of the firm.

- They are the verifiers of balancing receipts.

- Bookkeeping clerks are those who are tasked to make sure that balanced receipts are on the up and up.

- They are tasked to send out cheques, cash and other payment forms to specific banks.

- They post credits and debits of the firm.

- They post total accounts, details of transactions and compute interest charges.

- They are expected to keep up and stay familiar with tax and accounting regulations.

- They are tasked to handle expenditures.

- They prepare monthly invoice statements.

- They prepare tax reports.

- They are savvy in the use of computers and input data.

A **budget analyst** is an accountant who is involved in the efficient distribution of funds throughout an organization. The average take home pay of a budget analyst is about $68,200 a year. The top 10 percent of budget analysts earn over $100,000 a year.

- The budget analyst approves any new plans of the company but not after comparing it with the businesses financial goals.

- The budget analysts also keep an eye out of the spending of any department the whole year round.

- They provide the guidelines by which a firm makes its annual budget.

- They meet with supervisors and managers to find out the monetary needs of each unit and department of the firm for the coming fiscal year.

Accounting Clerks are tasked and responsible for giving accounting support to managers and supervisors within a department of the firm. They are tasked with the upkeep and maintenance of the general ledger system. They ensure that all company files are complete and collated to the very current transactions of the firm. They handle accounts payable tasks and help the accounting personnel with the aim of maintaining the proper running balance of the company.

The 10% of the best paid accounting clerks receive $55,170 yearly whilst those on the bottom 10 percentile take home $22, 020. Accounting clerks are required to perform clerical and accounting functions that complement and support supervisors.

- They handle the research and tracking as well as the resolution to accounting issues and problems.

- They are tasked to sort and compile cheques and invoices.

- They are able to issue cheques for accounts payable. They are the ones who insert the payments in envelopes and mail out to the proper recipients.

- Accounting clerks are those who document business transactions and input the daily worksheets to the company's general ledger system.

- They document refunds and changes as they support personnel in the accounting department of the firm.

- Provide front desk customer service the input invoices bell church account statements reports checks and other records regarding finances.

- They are tasked to tally and file deposits.

- They are skilled workers able to understand the functionality of calculators, adding machines, bank accounts and databases.

- They prepare invoices of work orders and process bill payments.

- Inclusive of their tasks, they are the ones responsible for opening mail, pairing invoices with payment.

- Among others they are tasked to arrange for cash to be delivered to banks.

- They are skilled in using computer systems to run databases to pay bills and to order supplies.

- They're the ones who make sure that a customer receives payment refunds.

- They're the ones responsible for contacting individuals with delinquent accounts.

Anti-money Laundering Specialist Accountants are also called **Bank Secrecy Act and Anti-money Laundering Officers.** They are those who are tasked to understand the rules and preceptors in association to the bank secrecy act. With the knowledge of regulations of the Act this officer implements regulations and rules within the bank including the identification of parameters to make sure that the bank is in compliance with the BSA/AML regulations and the patriot act.

- Anti-money laundering specialists are to be self motivated they must be able to monitor adjust and explain the banks operational procedures within this framework.

- They are tasked to make sure that operation of the bank and within the context of regulations.
- They must be very keen on catching all pertinent details by staying on top of regulatory changes.

- They must correctly analyze the implications for the daily functioning of the bank.

- These bank officers need to be able to work accurately and efficiently by themselves with little room for mistakes.

- They provide the Board of Directors detailed reports a few times a year.

Auditing clerks maintain accounting records and verify those reported by other employees. They check the numbers as well as documents making sure that all are accurate and encoded correctly they make notations of any mistakes for future corrections, bookkeeping, accounting and auditing clerks take home a median wage of $35,730. The ones best-paid in the field earn an annual salary of about $55,170 whilst the one paid the lowest earn a median salary of $22,020 per year. Auditing clerks ensure that postings documents and figures written by accounting are correctly encoded and are accurate.

- They justify transactions and records and make corrections to errors or notations for other workers the correct.

- They type in information from receipts into company computers and perform payroll functions.

- They check out to make sure that records are accurate and used computer software to input and crunch numbers.

- Case studies investigate and supplies expense accounts lunch account payment inventory commission's interests, bank records and sales tickets.

- Skilled in computing results by use of calculators and adding machines.

- They accomplish tax returns and tax forms, pension contribution forms, and workers' compensation forms.

- They are tasked to encode documents correctly, write financial, auditing, statistical, and accounting reports.

- They prepare trial balances of the company's or individual's books.

An **auditor** provides services counter in hands to streamline the financial records company. I make sure that all financial information of the client is valid and legal and is ready and accordance with the client. They guarantee that the financial information provided is valid and legal. They review the accounts of the clients and give corresponding advice. In order to provide risk free decision making auditors usually examine and test the internal message on the business's accounting system.

Cost estimators are required to have a bachelor's degree associated with a specific field. Cost estimators are at an advantage with a faster than usual growth in employment by 26% between 2012 and 2022. The median wage for cost estimators annually is $56, 860.

- They should have a strong background in math.
- Cost estimators are professionals who estimate all of the necessary resources which are going to be needed to make particular products or to provide specific services.
- They should have a strong background in math.

An **accounts receivable clerk** holds the main role is ensuring that the firm or individual gets payment for services and goods.

- They properly record transactions of the firm.

- They need to have a keen attention to detail well-developed organizational skills and a good knack for numbers.

- The duties they perform are a variety of bookkeeping and accounting tasks according to standing procedures and policies.

- Accounts receivable clerks keep in contact with lawyers vendors clients and staff observing confidentiality of client as well as matters of the company.

- The average annual salary received by accounts receivable clerks generally range between $23,000 and $41,000. The average hourly rate for an accounts receivables clerk is approximately about $14.13.

Another entry level position is an **Accounting Assistant** post, whose job responsibilities cover the supervision and direction of cost accounting, general accounting and payroll. The ballpark figure of salaries paid to an accounting assistant in the United States is about $15.07 per hour; this makes a grand total of between $25,000 to $45,000 annually including cash earnings in forms of bonuses and profit sharing proceeds. Other tasks of an accounting assistant can be:

- The sorting out of documents of the account they handle.

- The verification of correctness of documents that had been completed by the accountant, you are employed under, for any mistakes.

- An accounting assistant is expected to make adjustments to various records and documents to input important, pertinent information that the chief accountant will need.

- They are tasked to make sure that the numbers are accurate. An accounting associate will have to make sure that the final ledger is error-free.
- The recording and inputting of numbers on the spreadsheet and accompanying documents of the client being served.

- Answers questions from the chief accountant as well as the different clients the firm is handling.

- Basic administrative and office work such as answering phones, typing, and sorting mail.

An **accounting assistant** has the job of overseeing and directing one or all of the following accounting functions of payroll, cost accounting as well as general accounting. Other tasks include making sure that the documents received are accurate, sorting out documents, and making necessary adjustments to different documents. They are tasked to verify the accuracy of the math and check the work of a previous worker. The enter information regarding a certain documents and input numbers into a spreadsheet. They answer inquiries from different customers and carry out clerical duties like sorting answering phones and typing.

Billing Clerks are primarily responsible for cash management, budget control as well as budget planning. They are responsible for treasury and handle tax related functions as well. Billing clerks earn 13.81 hourly with annual salary ranging between $22,472 and $41,160. Other jobs a billing clerk may do are listed below:

- A billing clerk's primary scope of responsibilities are keeping track of budget as well as budget planning and control, treasury, tax handling and management functions.

- They gather the sum of purchase orders, sales tickets, and charge slips

- They record transactions and prepare invoices they record while maintaining all records of payments.

- The charges slowly verify billing with the accounts receivable ledger and calculate sales tickets.

- They make necessary changes in the firm's information system supporting efficient and accurate billing processes.

- They prepare invoices and bills.
- They are responsible for calculating charge slips, sales tickets and verify bills against the ledger that records all accounts receivables.

- Carry about making adjustments in information system backing up an accurate and efficient billing process ensuring a correct financial close.

- Billing clerks are expected to be aware of standard, methods, practices and concepts within a specific area.

Accounts Payable Clerks are those who are tasked to gather the financial figures owed by a firm to their suppliers, vendors and other individuals or organizations.

- An accounts payable clerk collect charge slips, purchase orders, sales tickets, and others related to the company's finances and prepare the payments to be sent.

- Their task is to maintain all transaction records.

- They are tasked to collect sales tickets, charge slips, purchase orders and prepare the payments to be sent out.
- It is their job to maintain the transaction records of all payments and cash and credit transactions.

- This position usually calls for a high school diploma or a minimum period of exposure in the same or related field.

- Accounts payable clerks work under direct supervision, relying on guidance and instruction of a manager or supervisor.

Bookkeepers are essential for the good of any business, whether the business is small or big, starting up or established. They are the ones who pay company bills, handle incoming monies. They are also expected to keep track of the cash output of the company. As compared to non certified bookkeepers certified ones can charge a higher fee for their services. Other tasks they are responsible for are listed below.

- They work closely with the CPA in order to ensure the accuracy of accounts.

- They fill out tax forms.

- Commissions and payrolls are also other.
- They usually work with accounting clerks.

- They are expected to be good at math and enjoy working with numbers.

- They have to be able to work with people.

- They should have a good attention to detail.

- Most companies conduct background checks to ensure the absence of criminal activity associated with thievery so they must be of good moral character.

- Certified bookkeepers are able to charge higher fees than non-certified counterparts and organizations are willing to pay prime figures to those who possess higher credentials and better experience. Bookkeepers typically earn an annual salary of about $39,000.

A **management trainee** is an accountant in training who works with the senior manager, a senior controller or a senior accountant. Management trainees are paid anywhere between $52,000 and $56,000 every year.

- Accountant trainee's double check accuracy and make necessary corrections before filing documents as needed.

- They tasks include making expense or income entries into the firms accounting system.

- In smaller company's management trainees and accounting part has to pay bills create invoices for clients and enter vendor invoices and bigger companies these tasks are usually segregated by field.

- Accountants in training may have the opportunity to work on quarterly taxes cost accounting asset inventory or payroll with the accounting department.

Chapter Five: More Jobs in the Market

When we said that the list of possible jobs in the accounting and finance realm abounds, we weren't kidding. There are so many possibilities available to one who chooses to build a career in the accounting industry. With corporations going international and others going public, the need for skilled experts at sorting out the business of cash inflow and outflow, distribution of company finances, has a keen eye for details, has good investigative skills, one who employs good, unbiased judgment of the task and who is compliant with and up to date with financial tax rules and laws shall remain a standard demand in the job market.

A good place to begin a solid foundation for a career in finance and accounting is in high school where one can get the necessary start in the skill sets an accountant would need to develop and possess.

Additional Accounting Jobs

It is important that anyone considering a profession in this industry be aware of the many job opportunities available to them so that choices of specialty can be determined early on. Having a good idea of where you want to begin your accounting career will help you determine the number of years of studies before you can either become employed or when you can start preparing for licensure exams.

At any rate, the advantages of starting a career in finance and accounting is that an individual can get into the business by way of starting with an associate degree complemented by actual training and work experience. Many who start out this way aim to get certified later for specific specialties and to pass the CPA exams allowing them a wider range of job options based on their qualifications.

Below is the next set of jobs that is sought after by large companies and small private businesses and individuals. As with the previous chapter, these accounting jobs list not only the skill set required by the job, the following information also reveals the average annual wage that can be expected by a skilled candidate.

Make sure that you take advantage of resources that give information about specific employability requirements as required by specific states. There are also specific details on statistics on the data of median wages for each sub-specialty in accounting.

A Payroll clerk is given the responsibility of gathering and posting work hours in order to determine the amount of wages for an employee. A payroll clerk gathers the payroll data information. A person skilled at being a payroll clerk and who has experience and background in human resources has a higher chance of getting offered more money as annual wage compensation. The annual salary for a payroll clerk ranges between $24,000 and $44,000 annually, depending on experience and background.

- They are tasked with managing employee work time and hours clocked

- They create and disburse paychecks according to employee hours worked
- They compute the earnings of employees by looking to their annual earnings to figure out number of hours worked to determine the salary of the worker from the recorded timesheet
- They initiate payroll at specific, and given times of the month
- They correct paycheck errors before printing and disbursing pay cheques
- They post information onto individual and designated records that are comprised of attendance work hours and any pay adjustments
- When computing earnings they factor in vacation pay or sick pay to the salaries of employees
- Payroll clerks are those who check for exempt and nonexempt status of the workers in the company
- They get these checks approved by the managers and signed off by then
- Payroll clerks distribute paychecks to the workers
- They were put internal clients handling any questions about payments whilst answering any complaints about discrepancies
- They carry out calculations on the work tickets and worksheets

- They make sure that there are no electronic data errors
- They gather and compile employee work time production and payroll information from timesheets
- They include in their calculations any deductions like withholding income tax, payments for Social Security, union dues and insurance.
- They provide any wages of the employee due to child support or intervention of the IRS
- Payroll clerk's manage bonuses and commissions as well as handling 401K contributions
- They give out employee time cards

An **assistant controller** helps the corporate controller and maneuvering accounting functions of an organization. These accountants take home and annual salary of about $80,359.

- They are tasked to present their findings to top management
- They observe accounting procedures, practices and principles of the organization
- They are tasked to evaluate a company's operating budget and financial reports
- They oversee the preparation of financial operating reports and budgets

- They are responsible for giving recommendations to upper management
- They are the leaders who directs the tasks of others in the department
- An Assistant controller would usually report to the corporate controller

A **cost accounting manager** is responsible for preparing and direct in the use of cost accounting method. The Job requires that the individual have a bachelor's degree in a related area and that they have at least seven years of field experience. They need to be in the know and familiar with different practices and procedures as well as concepts of the field.

- They manage and interpret cost hundreds
- They oversee the cost control systems
- They prepare and present cost accounting reports to top management

A **corporate entertainment accountant is** a CPA who can work for a record company a production company or a studio. The starting salary reportedly earned by a corporate entertainment accountant is at $30,000. Other responsibilities of a corporate entertainment accountant would include:

- Evaluating the company's budget for touring and concerts
- They oversee production costs
- Making sure that any changes in the set can be afforded and is within the budget

Apparel industry accountants are those to manage the finances and file for taxes of company brands in the fashion industry. A good springboard position would be with a supply-chain as a finance manager handling the funds of the long term procurement of materials while coordinating the over all budget, headcount analysis, forecast and financial plans. Apparel industry accountants earn an annual salary of $40,000.

Cost accountants figure out the price of manufacturing services through the determination of variable and fixed expenses needed for production including equipment human resources marketing as well as research and development. All information collected by cost accountants are useful and needed for budgeting purposes as well as product pricing as these affect the future earnings of a business. Cost accountants typically work with the executive team creating and mapping out a financial plan for the firm.

Cost accountants get offered a starting salary ranging anywhere between $40,000 and $51,000 each year. The Bureau of Labor and Statistics report the median yearly salary of a cost accountant to be $60,340 a year. Gaining a three year experience doing the job can earn an average salary of $45,000 up to $70,000 a year for a cost accountant.

A **credit analysis manager** is an accountant who basically focuses on getting back money that is owed to their company for services rendered or as payment for a particular product. It is the credit analysis manager who initiates legal action when individuals neglect to pay what is owed to the company. The median annual salary for a credit analysis manager is $61,000. The pay range starts at $40,000 that goes as high up as $80,000.

- They also have a big role when it comes to payment options negotiations.
- These would include a restructure of payment plans making payments more manageable for the party in debt to the company.
- They track certain accounts and keep close tabs on companies who have not been making payments for a long period of time.

Treasury analysts are responsible for an organization's financial activity. They manage the cash flow of the company and they manage the credit levels, liability and income of a company. Treasury analyst is reported to take home an annual wage of about $52,000 at an entry level position. An individual with experience can earn over $90,000.

- They work with internal accounting account departments and internal finance ensuring proper money management.
- Treasury analyst may also be given jobs of analyzing financial patterns to make projections for an upcoming expenses and income.
- They also assist in developing investment strategies for the company
- Treasury analyst maintain the company's cash debits and interest schedules as well as the company's bank account
- They study and recommend cost saving measures to the firm
- They analyze bank fees, treasury accounts and processes
- They study and prepare foreign exchange transactions

Vice President for Finance gives coordination and leadership to the firm's financial planning budget management and debt financing. It is up to them to make sure that the procedures of the company's accounting reportage is in line with the general accounting principles accepted and that paperwork and documentation are reviewed and submitted on time. A vice president for finance can take home an annual wage pay of about $124,000 excluding the amount of yearly bonuses.

- Finance VPs give recommendations that sets the bar of the financial and operational performance of the company
- It is them who make sure that daily operation of the accounting department as well as the finance department runs smoothly
- They prepare financial forecasts and outlooks
- They're responsible for complying with local state and federal budgetary requirements when they give reports
- They gave help establish short and long term goals of department.
- The assist in setting departmental objectives, policies, and operating procedures
- They take part in planning and policy making committees of the company

- They coordinate financial audits
- They give recommendations for procedural improvements
- They keep tabs on the operating results against the budget and analyze this
- They prepare all financial reports of the company
- They prepare financial analysis in relation to contract negotiations
- They were closely with managers of specific departments in order to create five year business plans
- Finance vice president's make, establish and maintain the organizational structure so that each department meets their goals and objectives
- They are the government liaison in relation with financial issues

The **Chief Financial Officer** is responsible for overseeing and directing and organizations and its short and long-term financial budget and goals. They're accountable for timeliness, reporting accuracy, as well as regulatory and legal compliance of the company's overall financial reporting. But she financial officer or creates and implements accounting and financial systems and tools which are aligned with a businesses long-term goals.

The salary of a chief finance officer hinges primarily on the industry of the business. Salary also depends on location of the organization, extent of professional experience, company size as well as the level of education attained by the individual. Data collected put the average median annual salary of a chief financial officer at around $173, 000, but it is probably safe to assume that most CFO's of big companies earn more than that amount.

With many companies going worldwide and doing business internationally and because of an increasingly competitive global market, international accountants are needed more and more to carry about these tasks. International accountants are those who do the following:

- Handles the financial balance sheets
- They are the ones concerned with company cash expenses
- Their skills allow them to scrutinize and review financial company records and make projections
- They know the and comply with local and international taxing laws
- They are responsible for keeping abreast with international laws of trading and financing of which they are compliant

International accountants are able to analyze and determine exchange rates between collection dates and selling dates that may result in significant profit gains or losses which they record. International accountants are pivotal in international companies because they're able to understand and abide by different country tax laws and regulations. The median salary of an international accountant is about $54,000. Candidates who have gained ample experience and expertise in international accounting laws earn a much higher annual salary of $94,000 a year.

A **personal financial advisor** to the stars is an accountant who finds work in the traditional field of accounting but get to do it for people who are famous and known. A personal financial advisor would be involved from estate planning to analyzing best investments on which to put money, as well as every day expenses and random purchases of their clients.

Managerial accountants are those who prepare financial information for the internal customers of a company, such as executives and managers. They are tasked to hand in financial reports on a weekly, quarterly or yearly basis, depending on the clients requirements and needs. These forms and numbers are confidential and used to make decisions for the company. The aim of this area of specialty focuses on the examination of a company's financial data in order to make forecasts. The average annual salary a managerial accountant takes home ranges between $45,000 to about $70,000.

- They are the ones given the task to analyze the financial information of the organizations where they work.
- They are also tasked to record and organize these financial documents.
- All information about financial findings prepared by managerial accountants for the organization is only meant to be seen by the company's internal clients like business managers.
- Management accountants usually work on performance evaluations.
- They evaluate the organization's budget.
- They also aid the organization they work for in determining the budget of a business.
- They are also tasked with asset-management which concerns the planning and selection of possible investments.

Management accounting is a field that focuses on the affair of gathering accounting information for the purpose of internal operational reportage. This involves areas like target costing and cost accounting. A management accountant can typically lead up to a controller position. It can also meet up with a host of other specialty positions like billing clerk, cost accountant, payroll clerk and payables clerk.

Spectator Sport Accountant

An accountant employed in the spectator sport industry is another position which promises great perks and rewards should the candidate have the proper skills and education to back them up. The Bureau of Labor and Statistics reported that accountants employed in the sporting industry were paid and average salary of $68,070 in 2011. Out of a million accountants in the financial sphere, 820 of them were employed in the spectator sport industry. A big edge for an individual seeking employment as a spectator sport accountant possesses an MBA. Perks, like front-row center seats to your favorite team's matches are just one of the many for those who get their foot in the door.

A **Senior Financial Analyst** is usually employed by big, international companies who have a large enough population that would require a financial team. Accountants who hold positions as this in a company can earn an annual salary of $74,000. A senior financial analyst is the one who:

- Tasked to review the finances of the company
- Gives recommendations to management about the company and how they can lower operating costs without taking away from the quality of the service or product
- Makes recommendations on how the company can improve its financial stance
- These MBA accountants lead a group of financial analyst who work with company funds spent and made in all areas of the business.
- They are expected to be detail oriented, diligent in their work and accurate to a tee.
- Senior financial analysts also make financial forecasts for the company in order for the firm to get a clear idea of the direction it is headed in its present state.
- Accountants in this position prepare reports and review them as well.
- Senior financial analysts typically lead a team of lower - level financial analysts

- Accountants in this position report to the director of finances.
- Their tools to carry out the trade are computers, statistical and financial software, a phone and other usual office supplies

An **Accounting Software Developer** supports teams of developers and managers of a software firm; they are tasked to do the following:

- Assume time tracking and billing responsibilities
- They are concerned with license audits
- They may act as software production consultants developing accounting and finance software, assisting in user experience design.

An individual with a master's degree has a better edge on landing this job, but there are many who start with a PhD. or a bachelor's degree and work their way up or continue on with leveling - up themselves through further studies. Those who have a background in and are hired specifically to develop reportedly earn an annual salary of $89,000.

A **finance director** position requires the candidate to possess and advanced degree in academic studies and a minimum of at least 10 years working experience in the field. The candidate should be familiar with the concepts of the field and its diversities in practices and procedures. . They are ones who are given the burden and confidence of sound judgment towards accomplishing company goals. They lead and direct the tasks of others and are expected to have a good measure of creativity. A finance director is said to earn an annual salary average of $101,300 and usually reports to the company's top management.

Information Technology Accountants are specialists who are equally skilled in both computer and accounting systems of organizations they work for. They are tasked to assist the company in the selection and maintenance of the information systems utilized by the company's accounting department. There are many positions in this field and the education requirement, the job outlook, certification options and salary are diverse and variable. An Information technology accountant could earn an average yearly wage of $103, 910.

A **corporate controller** is an accountant with a bachelor's degree or and MBA, who keeps track of and maintains the many financial areas of a company and is generally given the responsibility of preparing the firm's taxes. The median wage for a corporate controller according to the Bureau of Labor and Statistics in the United States is $112,000.

- Corporate controllers are those who have a say on how company funds are spent
- They lead rank and file employees who work in the finance departments of the company.
- They are tasked to set financial targets for the company
- Corporate controllers are expected to have good interpersonal and communication skills as they shall work closely with a variety of internal and external clients.
- They are expected to be versed well with a host of computer applications in order to launch financial reports and review them.
- They are expected to keep abreast with changes to financial laws which concern the company.

In order to be a professor to teach accounting to those who want to build a career in the industry, they will have to earn a doctoral degree in accounting. An accounting professor is the individual who researches and imparts learning to students of accounting. They are also those individuals who teach fellow accounting professionals helping keep the professionals in the business abreast with local and international financial laws and taxing regulations.

They are tasked to carry out research on:

- Accounting information systems
- Financial accounting
- Managerial accounting
- Tax accounting and
- Auditing

Accounting professors are usually given an annual starting salary offer of $127,400 whilst an assistant professor takes home $113, 800 annually. A full time accounting professor earns about $137,800 each year whilst and associate accounting professor takes home $114,900 every year.

Chapter Six: Financial Services Regulation

Both federal and state regulates US banking laws. The sort of written grant a banking organization possesses as well as its structure is bound to a number of state and banking regulations. The US keeps separate commodities, securities and insurance agencies aside from the bank regulatory agencies, at a state and federal level in contrast to the system that the UK or Japan observes. To ensure entities are on the up and up and in proper compliance with these regulations, bank examiners are typically utilized to supervise banks.

The banking regulations in the United States are concerned with disclosure and privacy of individuals, corporations and organization. It is centered on anti-money laundering as it is with fraud. It addresses anti-terrorism, the lending f money bearing exorbitant interest rates. It is given the responsibility of lending to people of the lower income bracket. There are some cities around the United States who have their own laws on financial dictum.

The central banking system in the United States is known as the Federal Reserve. The Fed, as it is better known, was established after a succession of financial panics in the early 1900. The financial crisis of 1907 happened over a span of three weeks when the NYSE plummeted to almost 50% from its position the year before and was pretty much what led to the need for a way to centrally control the monetary system. The role of the Federal Reserve has expanded in terms of the responsibilities and roles it has played ever since the 1930 Great Depression to the new millennial's Great Recession.

There are twelve districts within the Federal Reserve and these revolve around 12 regional Federal Reserve Banks. Each of these regional Federal Banks has the regulatory responsibilities of the Federal Reserve Board and implements them in their designated districts. The National Credit Union regulates and supervises local credit unions, establishing across the board standards, principles and report forms for the other governing agencies is the Federal Financial Institutions Examination Council (FFIEC).

State-chartered banks as well as some non-banking entities affiliated with federally chartered banks are state and federally regulated. The rules of Federal Reserve as well as the rules of the state regulatory agency of which a state-chartered bank is located are what the bank or entity follows. The chief federal regulator of a bank can be delegated to any of the four regulators; the Federal Reserve Board, Office of the Comptroller of the Currency or The Federal Deposit Insurance Corporation.

- There is an organization that sees to the standards of accounting in the USA called the **American Institute of Certified Public Accountants**. It is a group of professional certified public accountants whose purposes are to find out and employ proper, upstanding accounting standards and principles.

- The **GAAP or Generally Accepted Accounting Principles** is a set of commonly adhered to standards and regulations applied to financial reportage. Its specifications are inclusive of principles and concepts, and it also deals with industry-specific regulations. GAAP was established to make sure that there is transparency in financial reporting and that there is a level of consistency met from one organization to the next. The specifics of the GAAP can be different from one location to another. It can also be different for every industry. The GAAP requirements are mandated by the SEC making sure that all financial reports adhere to the rules state. Overall, it is the Financial Governmental Accounting Board (FASB) which stipulates GAAP, whereas the Governmental Accounting Standards Board (or the GASB) stipulates GAAP for local and state government. Companies that are publicly traded have to follow and adhere to both the GAAP and SEC requirements.

- **The International Financial Reporting Standards** is created so as to give a global framework of how public companies set up and give out information about their financial statements. All around the world, countless countries have adopted this system of financial reporting. This set of world-wide standards makes the accounting process simpler for countries whilst providing its auditors and investors a clear view of an organization's finances.

- The AICPA created the **Committee on Accounting Procedure or the CAP** after the Great depression. It was the institute's initial attempt to address the accounting issues in these modern times. 51 Accounting Research Bulletins were issued between 1939 and 1959, which dealt with a plethora of accounting issues that were faced then. Setting aside all the successes of CAP, the work they put out still di not create the needful structured set of principles needed in proper accounting. It was then that it was realized something more had to be done; thus the formation of the Accounting Principles Board in 1959.

The U.S. Financial Report

The body that is governing the content and form of financial statements in the United States is the Securities and Exchange Commission. The SEC adds functions and needs as a mechanism for enforcing standards which is propagated by individuals in the private sector. Although, much of this burden is transferred to the Financial Accounting Standards Board, it does implement requirements directed to private individuals and entities.

Financial statements which have been audited along with supplementary data and footnotes related to such are submitted and filled with the SEC as well as presented in annual report forms which are given to stockholders. These documents contain vital details not presented in stockholder reports given to them on a yearly basis. There are also quarterly financial reports which contain abbreviated financial figures that may or may not need auditors to audit.

Chapter Seven: Qualifications for Aspiring Accountants

People aspire to become accountants come from all walks of life. Some may be fresh graduates, there are those who may already have had a long career and is pondering the idea of upgrading or changing careers. Then there are those who are already well into raising a family. Whichever time in life one finds them in, their interest toward accounting is what binds them together and the ultimate question about their qualifications crop up. What are the qualifications indeed to start a career in accountancy?

The beauty of accounting is the ability it gives to an accountant for them to be able to provide a visual and progressive report of scientifically kept, recorded transactions. Accounting allows the viewer to analyze an entity's stance and position at any given time without hitches. The sturdy and stringent rules of the system allow the person holding the books the possibility to provide the proper financial position as well as the profitable stance of an entity.

A person who is knowledgeable in math and economics is not necessarily in the position to talk about the proper position of a company. They will not be able to confidently tell you of a company's financial position; they won't have the proper skills and background to be able to tell if a company is weak or strong.

Career journeys, most but not all, need a bachelor's degree or a baccalaureate. Depending on the institutions discipline, a baccalaureate is an undergraduate degree which is given by colleges and universities to students who have successfully completed a course of study which could last anywhere between three to seven years.

A bachelor's degree is typically a four year course of full-time studies. One will have to complete a total of 120 credits each semester which equates to about 40 courses. A college using the quarter system would require a student to complete, at a minimum, 180 college credits per quarter for them to earn the accredited degree.

A bachelor's degree could be the minimum academic requirement one will need to have in order to get an entry-level post in the field of accounting, but not all the time. It is desirable but not necessarily a requirement. What you will need to ask yourself is; "do I have dexterity for numbers? Is this natural skill with numbers coupled with sound analytical abilities?" Degrees are advantageous because it would give you the background on the theoretical aspects of business. A degree in economics and mathematics, of course, would always work toward your advantage.

Theoretical knowhow is what one gets from completing a degree, but employers will still look for the practical skills one has gained to begin a career in accountancy. Depending on a person's ambitions toward their career, one will need a range of certified qualifications. In accountancy though, you will not be required to present one specific qualification. Although a bachelor's degree is the academic certification will work toward your advantage, it is not always necessary. An individual who has been able to accomplish a bachelor's degree will still have to undergo a vocational course to qualify.

A CEO, with all their knowhow of the ins and outs of managing the business, will not be able to give information about a company's financial position. The formal training and the skills of an accountant would be able to give a clear idea of a company's economic and financial position. But how does one become one? How does an individual get to become an accountant? What is required of the person and what sort of education should they get in order to get prepared for a career in accountancy? These are the details we shall be looking into so that you get a clear picture of what you need to do to start a promising, lucrative and stable career in accounting. Read on.

A variety of roles is needed in the finance sector. Jobs like being a bank clerk, internal auditor and even a stockbroker are other jobs, apart from accountancy one can go into. In any of these disciplines, one would need to have a solid business sense, sound organizational skills, and they will need to have dexterity for numbers.

The tasks of an accountant would include the following:

- The study and upkeep of records of the financial sort.

- As representatives of firms and individuals who hire them, they would be responsible for the preparation and submission of documents relating to an individual's or a company's tax.

- Aside from the daily management of funds, they are also the ones responsible for assessing financial operations.

- They are there to provide to concerned individuals, sound recommendations for fiscal efficiency.

- It is not unusual for an accountant to work longer hours, especially during tax season.

Qualifications You Need

Let's talk about getting qualified. Whether you are an experienced worker wanting to further their discipline or an incoming university student carving a career path, you will want to question your academic accomplishment will come crop up. Though having a degree is desirable, anyone who wants to build a career in accountancy doesn't necessarily need one. You neither need to take levels nor would one need to take up specific BTECs. We will, nonetheless go over the usual route different people from different walks of life take preparing for a career in accountancy.

As we discussed earlier, it takes at least a minimum of four years to complete a bachelor's degree, an equivalent of 120 semester credits or 40 college courses.

A degree program focuses on rounding out an individual to not only be employed but arms graduates with knowledge and skills focused on a particular field which would potentially carve for them a path toward professional and middle management job positions. In order to complete a bachelor's degree, one needs to take up and finish general courses in the liberal arts and specific courses centered on the major chosen.

Now, while a bachelor's degree takes that span of time to complete, an associate degree only takes two to complete and generally gets the student ready for entry-level positions in a specific field of work.

Associate degree students are given an opportunity to complete education requirements via a two-year course program to equipped and ready them for a four-year degree. This can be an affordable way to earn a bachelor's degree since many traditional colleges, as well as online ones, junior and community colleges, and universities offer 2 plus 2 programs, where a student, an associate degree graduate, upon completion of the two-year program can continue on with post-associate studies at a larger college or university.

Bachelor Degrees

The three typically chosen bachelor degree types are Bachelor of Arts or BA. A BA degree is typically concentrated on a exploring the liberal arts. BA Students are given a little more freedom in choosing and customizing their learning in order to accomplish their career aspirations and goals. The typically offered majors are Art, Theatre, English, Modern Languages, Communications, and Music.

A **Bachelor of Science or a B.S. degree** is targeted to a very particular concentration and less centered on exploration. BS students are more career - centered in their fields of major. They focus specifically on building a career centered on their particular career path choice. Some popular BS majors include degrees on Business, Nursing, Biology, Computer Science, Economics, and Chemical Engineering.

Bachelor of Fine Arts (BFA degree) is professional degree aiming for graduates of the four year program to become professionals in the world of creative arts. Individuals seeking career professions in the creative arts and entertainment fields are good candidates for a BFA degree. Singers, dancers, artists like sculptors, painters and actors are just a few of the career paths a BFA graduate can pursue.

A BFA is much like a BS degree being that they are tended toward focusing on building specific career skills in the individual, unlike the BS program which is centered on its major concentration.

The Road to Accountancy

As much as a career in accountancy doesn't entail completion of a 4-year bachelor's degree, it will in fact be a requirement for anyone who intends to gun on becoming a Certified Public Accountant. There are also states which require advanced coursework outside the scope of a normal BA degree. Some of these courses could be on:

- Taxes
- Auditing
- Financial reporting,
- Another non-accounting courses

One requirement would be the completion of 150 hours in accounting and associated works. If in pursuit in seeking a professional career as a certified public accountant, be sure to check with your city or state specific requirements within your desired jurisdiction of practice. CPA's usually continue on to obtaining a master's degree and go on to study post-secondary education.

In the next chapter we shall be looking at the types of accounting services in the field of accountancy. We shall be running down the details that entail a specific area of accountancy, for your information and guidance, in the following chapter.

Chapter Eight: The Road to Employability and Credibility

The world of accounting is a vast realm of opportunities and varied tasks that can be a lucrative and long lasting profession which pays well and a job that gives handsome compensation. Getting a feel of the path you want to take by reviewing the many, available jobs for accountants allow an individual a glimpse of what it is they want to achieve later. Positioning yourself at an advantage is one way of ensuring a career in accounting. In order to do that, one must map out their future at the earliest stage of education as much as possible. Doing so will put the individual at an advantage of having the proper network of people, which equates to better job opportunities.

Organizations for Accountants

Organizations for accountants are useful venues to research on best practices, information technology updates, legalities and tax rules that may have been modified or updated. **School organizations** for budding accountants are also great places to practice your people skills, enhance leadership qualities, hone accounting and investigative skills that will serve you well in the profession you desire.

Apprenticeship or Internship is also another avenue you may want to consider on your way to becoming a fully-fledged accountant. Apprenticeship has gained great popularity in the finance and insurance world, providing a path for the new talent as the talent brings their skills and knowhow to a company. A high demand in apprenticeship jobs are positions of bank tellers, insurance underwriters, claims adjuster and credit coordinators. Make sure that you look into any school organizations you can be a part of. Check out apprenticeship programs in in-state companies that may need to fill vacant apprenticeship positions.

These are just some of the ways you can proactively take control of your career path whilst giving value to your time and efforts. The following are some of the organizations locally and worldwide that one can check out for themselves. Make sure that you inquire with your local area for any organizations that may be present in the locality. Make it a point to get in touch with school or university administration and inquire about accounting organizations they may know of and can direct you toward.

The AICPA is short for the **American Institute for Certified Public Accountants** and it is a group that is concerned with creating and grading the Uniform CPA exams. Founded in 1887, the group represents CPAs in terms of setting standards and creating rules within the profession. The organization acts as advocate in front of legislative bodies, representing public interest groups as well as other organizations.

The AICPA provides their members study materials that give guidance and structure to members. The AICPA are the ones who enforce compliance of CPA members of the organization to the technical and ethical standards they have set for themselves. The AICPA is present in 128 countries across the world and is 386,000 strong in worldwide membership.

This is the organization which defined the profession of accountancy giving it the character it is today, setting the standard of education one must complete, setting the standards of the profession, coming up with a code of ethics observed by the member-professionals and streamlined with the interest of serving the public.

The **American Accounting Association** is an organization for accountants that were founded in 1916. It is rich in history and is of upstanding repute in the community of financial workers, leading in the research and publication of studies they conduct. It is an organization that is rich and diverse in the members they keep, allowing for a thriving environment of creativity and innovation as well as collaboration.

The American Accounting Association fashion the path of future accounting via way of lectures and teachings, they widen their scope of knowledge through research and have founded a vast and powerful network which ensures that the stance in the job market and positioning their members as thought leaders of accounting in the country. Publications on studies and research can be obtained for study allowing members to keep abreast with systematic operations, whilst upholding a high standard on work ethics.

The AAA concerns itself with being the forerunners for Thought Leadership, accomplishing their objectives through the constant research, imparting education and their contribution to accounting policies as well as setting accounting standards.

The NABA or **The National Association for Black Accountants** is an organization that was established in 1969 with the vision for unlimited opportunities for growth and leadership for black Americans in the accounting and finance field.

The national associations for black accountants are dedicated to help bridge the employment gap and make available job opportunities to African-American professionals by giving their members the edge through leadership and technical skills trainings. The organization allows its members to also have a good network of contacts and career opportunities which would otherwise prove to be difficult to get without the support of an organization to back the individual up.

Accountant organizations provide the support and services that give the individual a leg up in the profession by way of networking, exposure to the discipline, and makes available to up and coming, as well as seasoned, accountants the documentation and research materials that provide them with the knowledge of set-standards, laws and regulations of their localities as well as those observed internationally. Students studying to become an accountant are also given the opportunity to network with their counterparts through student organizations in the college or universities they attend. It is but wise to get to know the different organizations a student can join to further their student career as they carve a path toward becoming an accountant.

The IPPF or the **International Professional Practices Framework** is a concept that sorts the guidance of the Institute of Internal Auditors in the UK. The mission of the IPPF is to enhance organizational value as it protects it by giving objective and risk-based assurance to their members. The IIA or Institute for Internal Auditors was founded in 1941 in Altamonte Springs, Florida and is a recognized authority in the profession with a global reach. The organization is known to be a leader in the field, advocating ethical work methods, good governance as it practices internal control and security.

The **Nevada Society of Certified Public Accountants** is an organization of accountants in Nevada and has been around for more than 60 years. The NVCPA continues to work on improving the accounting methods in Nevada by way of member support, advocacy and services.

The **ISACA** is a global association for professionals working in the field of information technology and information systems. This organization is made up of a diverse, international membership committed to providing their member professionals with the tools needed in their jobs to achieve success whether on the organizational level or individually. The organizations globally accepted research make for greater trust and value in their mission.

The **Institute of Management Accountants** is another organization of accounting professionals who are committed to widening the network plain of their members, giving them useful knowledge on how to better manage their business and improve careers in finance and accounting. Joining one or more club and/or organization will allow the individual to get a better scope of the industry, keep up-to-date with principles of the business or changes in standards and rules. Organizations allow for a place where a person can learn from others whilst usually having access to important and relevant materials that concern the profession and ultimately their individual careers.

Another accounting organization is the ALPFA or the **Association of Latino Professionals for America** which is the oldest operating organization for Latinos. Most of these organizations are established to protect the interests of their members by way of expanding job opportunities, providing a venue to share best practices, whilst aiding in the development of leadership compliant with local, state and international tax laws and financial regulations.

The world's leading and largest organization on anti-fraud is the ACFE or the **Association of Certified Fraud Examiners**. It is a 75,000 member strong group aimed at lessening the instance of fraud worldwide. It is aimed at inspiring confidence in the profession and what their members can bring to the table as it targets to reduce the instances of fraud, whilst providing its members with the tools they need to carry out their trade.

Beta Alpha Psi is aimed at improving educational experiences of university students of finance and accounting by providing useful interaction of its members. They conduct personal development programs as well as technical development courses through regional and campus meetings. Beta Alpha Psi has founded a set of programs and activities which if fulfilled through the provided guidelines provides excellent value for students and their members alike.

Chapter Nine: What It Takes to Become a Certified Public Accountant

An honest assessment of one's goals and a strong dedication to putting in the needful work and time will be needed from any individual who intends to go further into the field of accounting to become a licensed Certified Public Accountant. There will be a good chunk of time one will need to put in to studies and preparing for exams. On top of that, one has to invest energy for them to gain a vast amount of experience in the financial industry. A lot of time will be spent burning the midnight oil, gaining this experience through trainings and actual apprenticeship.

Time spent pondering on your discipline and ultimate career goal would be time spent wisely. Yes, the career of a CPA is one indeed that has been proven to have lasting power and stability in the job force market. This has been seen time and again in recorded documents of antiquity dating back to the Rome, Egypt and Mesopotamia.

It is apparent that individuals, working in the finance sector, whether starting from an entry level position all the way to being licensed certified public accountant, get paid quite handsomely.

There are descriptive differences between an accountant and a CPA. Accountants, also known as a public accountant, are typically those employed to do accounting tasks in the accounting departments of companies and businesses. However, not having state certification and licensure limits their scope of reach because are not certified to do tasks of Certified Public Accountants.

Accountants carry out limited tasks, one being the preparation of financial statements. They are also, once they have received their Preparer Tax Identification Number after passing the required IRS exam, are tasked to gather and ready the tax returns of the company or business. Accountants, however, may not review financial statements or carry out audits.

On the other hand, a Certified Public Account can perform all the tasks of a public accountant, but has a wider scope of tasks they are able to carry out. A CPA has to be qualified college degree holder and has to meet specific requirements in order to eventually earn their license. For one to become a CPA they would have to pass all the parts of the CPA exam.

They would also need to work under the close supervision of an actively licensed CPA for a set number of hours, usually set at 1800 hours. CPA's are licensed to review statements, represent clients before the IRS and conduct audits. In order for one to file with the Securities and Exchange Commission, one has to be an actively licensed CPA.

Certified Public Accountant (CPA) exam

All states require Certified Public Accountant candidates to pass all four parts of a CPA exam which include Audit and Attestation, Regulation, Business Environment and Concepts and Financial Accounting and Reporting. The exam to be a CPA is offered to aspiring hopefuls during the first 2 months of every quarter of the year. The exam takes a course of a few days to accomplish.

Candidates have the option of choosing which part of the CPA exam they wish to take first. Once a candidate commences with and completes one of the exams, they will need to take the remaining three exams within a period of 18 months of the first exam. Many CPA test candidates opt to sign up with private test preparation courses because of the vast subject matter and the level of exam difficulties.

Tips in Preparing For Your CPA Licensure Examination

Efficiency is the name of the game when it comes to prepping up for your CPA Licensure Exam. In this section, we've listed the ultimate tips you need to know before and during the examination. Read on.

Ultimate Tip No.1: Know Your 'Enemy'

This is the classic tactic that most students tend to forget when taking a 'make or break' examination. You have to understand that taking exams and passing them is not always about studying everything, it's a combination of studying the most important concepts and being strategic about it. If you want to pass, you should know what you'll be tested on, what kinds of questions you'll face, and what your limitations are (your strengths, weaknesses, time limit etc.). In short, you have to know "the game" and "the player." Examiners will not just test your memorization or analytical abilities; you'll be tested on how you will apply the concepts in real business circumstances. The usual format of the exam is this:

o   Multiple Choice
o   Task – Based Simulation Questions (FAR, AUD, REG exams)
o   Written Communication Tests/ Business Application Tests (BEC exams)

Ultimate Tip No.2: Maximize your time in Review Centers

Now that you have an idea on how to approach the test and have formed a strategy on how to face this challenge, the next thing you need is to sharpen your knowledge and skills through learning everything you can in review centers (if you are enrolled in one). Some students don't enroll in review centers for their CPA exams, but this is highly recommended because it'll give you a more in – depth knowhow when taking the exam. They'll also teach you on how to navigate the interface online since most CPA exams are now being given online. Review centers will serve as your training ground before the exam.

Ultimate Tip No.3: Test Yourself and Learn from Your Mistakes

There are now lots of online resources available that can help you prepare for this big test. You never know exactly what kind of questions, style, and exam format you're going to be facing or whether or not it will be subjective, objective, computational or theoretical. The best way is to study each type through the help of test prep software or other similar study tools. The more exposed you are, the better your chances of passing the exam. You need to take each question seriously as if it's already the real exam. Pay attention to the question types, the format, the pattern, and the right answers to the questions you got wrong. This is the most critical part of your review, it's better that you fail in the practice tests (and learn from it) than failing in the real one. This is also an advantage for you because you'll be able to plan and strategize how you're going to maximize your time when answering, and how you can score more points despite of your mistakes.

Ultimate Tip No.4: Make Time Your Ally

It doesn't matter how much you know or how well you've study or strategize, if you don't know how to use the allotted time wisely for each exam type, you're doom to fail.

Time management is perhaps the most important key if you want to pass the exam. Your strategy and your knowledge about the format of the exam should all play out within the allotted time frame. This is where pressure also comes in, so make sure that you know how to handle it, and handle it with grace and with precision. Know how to allocate your time; know how to make time your ally because this is your key in passing. Here's my suggested time allocation for each exam type:

- o **FAR Exam (4 hour exam):** This is one of the hardest tests in the CPA Exam. Allocate only 45 minutes for the 3 testlets and the 2 simulation tests giving you a 15 minute spare time to review your answers (adjust accordingly).
- o **AUD Exam (4 hour exam):** This is a relatively easier test than the FAR exam and most don't need to consume the 4 hours to finish the test. Nevertheless, stick to your schedule and have enough time to spare for a review.
- o **BEC Exam (3 hour exam):** Most takers find the time given to be just right. Again, stick to your time allotment for each test and have enough time to spare. This is where the written communication part and practical questions come in.

o **REG Exam (3 hour exam):** Most takers don't complete the REG part so make sure to allot enough time for each testlet. You can allocate 30 minutes for each simulation test so that you can have 15 minutes to spare.

Ultimate Tip No.5: Keep Calm and Become a CPA

Learn to relax! Learn to have time for study and for other things that will help you absorb what you've learned. Don't stress yourself too much. Don't be too invested in becoming a CPA, don't be obsessed with it. Sure, you have to take it seriously, prepare as much as you can, and work hard to pass the exam, but at the end of the day you just have to put your best foot forward, and trust that if it's meant to be, it's meant to be. After all if you don't make it the first time, you can still retake the exam, you'll be better and wiser this time. And if by any chance you really don't make it (just in case), you're going to be fine! Consider it a learning opportunity. There's liberty in just doing things because you simply want to do them, and not because you have to. If you have that kind of mindset, you'll be fully prepared to crush the exams!

CPA Frequently Asked Questions

What's the difference between a CPA and an Accountant?

All CPAs are accountants but not all accountants are Certified or Official Public Accountants. The main difference between the two practically is the additional education and examinations that needs to be taken. Another main difference between the two when they enter a workforce is that CPAs have better opportunities, higher salaries, and are generally more trusted than ordinary accountants. CPAs have a guaranteed reputation so to speak since they are certified.

What opportunities are available for women and minorities who are CPAs?

Women and minorities in general receive equal opportunities once they enter the workforce. There are a lot of accounting graduates that are from minorities, and there are also a lot of accounting positions for women. As long as you have the right qualifications, and you're hard – working you'll surely achieve your dream position in accountancy.

What are the advantages of getting a CPA License?

Aside from the title itself, you'll get a credential that will give you an edge when applying to companies. A CPA license is a symbol of credibility, trust, recognition, and professionalism. Certified Public Accountants are one of the most trusted financial advisors in the world of business. Acquiring a CPA license also means that you adhere to the highest standards of the profession. You have maintained not just the quality that the profession demands but also the commitment and honesty that is needed.

What's the process of becoming a CPA?

Three E's: Education, Exam, and Experience.

For you to become a CPA you need to be able to render at least 150 hours of college coursework. Once you've received your Bachelor's degree, the next step is to take and pass the standard CPA Licensure Exam. For you to become eligible to take an exam there'll be certain regulations and requirements that you need to follow depending on where you live. After passing the exam, you'll then receive a CPA certificate but this is not yet considered as a license to practice. In order to get your formal CPA License you need to either get additional education or professional working experience. The requirements will vary from one state to another. And in order to retain your license, you should continuously take educational courses or trainings to ensure that you maintain the CPA standards, and that you stay updated for any changes.

Do I need to have a Master's degree?

No, not necessarily. The reason why most people do so is for personal purposes. Most CPAs wanted to have better career opportunities and/or increase their salaries that are why they take Master's degrees. Some find it useful in their current line of work. But you don't need to have a Master's degree to become a licensed CPA.

What skills do I need if I wanted to become a CPA?

Generally you'll need to have strong personal skills, analytical skills, communication skills, and technological skills (you are updated with the emerging business technologies). In addition you also need to maintain high ethics, have an eye for business perspective, be strategic and also project management/ leadership abilities. Don't worry about acquiring all of this, skill is something you study and not something you're born with, it'll take time and different professional experiences but this is what should be striving for if you want to be a competent and dynamic CPA.

Chapter Ten: Landing Your First Job

After all the education, tuition and time you have put in to establish yourself as a competent accountancy academic, you will want to become a useful tool that oils the machinery of business in the corporate world while earning a decent living doing a noble job that has lasting power in terms of employability. A career in accountancy looks promising because the employment of auditors and accountants is primed and projected to grow in the next decade. It is said to be a career which has a higher than average employability rate amongst all occupations.

Getting a Career in Accountancy

The growing need for globalization entailed by a more intricate structure of international financial laws, there is an expected demand for both auditors and accountants alike. Along with the prevalence of globalization, the increase in seeking out skilled individuals in math, strategic abilities and accounting skills will be talents that will only be more in demand for employment to handle accounts and all the legalities and regulatory aspects of the financial side of a business.

As long as you have the proper educational background that has given you to the necessary skills and tools to be employed as an accountant or an entry level associate, the possibilities of leveling - up along the way and promotion can be evident.

Keep in mind that if you wish and target for more prestigious positions in accounting, you will need to put in the proper time not only in terms of education but also in gaining the right experience for the position you are ultimately gunning for.

This is why it is important to know how far up the corporate ladder you intend to go in the long run, as there are certain subjects that are particular to a specialization, so it is important that you consider these details in your journey to becoming an accountant.

Do remember that the best job prospects are reserved for those who have gained professional status most especially those who have passed board exams and have managed to complete their CPA exams. So goes for those who have a master's degree in business administration or a master's degree in accounting. The US Labor Statistics projected a total average of about 1.4 million accountants and auditors employed in 2016. This is projected to hit the 1.5 million mark by year 2026.

You can widen your network by joining accounting associations and organizations, allowing one to broaden their prospects and further their employability. The rewards of having a career in accounting can be a difficult journey for many and one will need a leg up once in a while. The rewards of becoming can be great, as long as those who pursue it keep their sights set on their goals. Joining these clubs, and organizations meant for accountants also gives one the opportunities of knowing first hand about review in preparation for the exams for a CPA.

One will be able to get to know and learn and be exposed to the different and varied careers in accounting by way of joining student and professional organizations. Joining accounting and auditors clubs and organizations allows the individual to build a professional network which opens up the possibilities of better job opportunities.

Becoming a member of these accounting and auditing organizations allows ne to keep up to date with current processes, systems and any changes and updates on policies and regulations. They are given an opportunity, if grouped with the right organization, to be part of standard-setting in the realm of finance and accounting.

Top 5 Job Interview Questions for CPA and Accountants

Your resume or Curriculum Vitae may get your foot in the door but it's the interview that will bring you to the desk. This section will cover the top 5 job interview questions being asked by the HR for CPAs and Accountant candidates:

Why do you want to be an accountant?

Best Answer: The best answer in this very general but important question is something that will give the HR the chance to know YOU. Not your education or your awards or whatever is written in your resume (though you can also include a bit of it). This is more of a personal question, though not too personal (to the point that you'll bore the interviewer). Give a concise answer that will give the HR a 'teaser' of who you really are and your big 'why' in pursuing this profession. But don't also make it about you, give hints on how your 'why' can help the company you're applying to.

Do you have knowledge about the accounting standards or the company (you're applying in)?

Best Answer: This kind of question is how the HR will spot if you did your 'homework.' Even if you've never had any experience in the field, you should ensure that you have an idea about the International Accounting Standards (IAS) and the company you're applying in. You don't have to know everything, just study up on the most recent updates or changes to the standards/company and give a brief overview if you can. Brush up on how you can help improve the system or some details about the company. Don't explain too much though as there could be follow up questions that you may not be able to answer. If you can't answer it, don't pretend. Be respectfully honest that your knowledge is limited (especially if you haven't had any job experience yet). Interviewers know if a candidate is just pretending that they know the answer or not.

How can you minimize errors in your work?

Best Answer: Accountants are held to high standards which is why accuracy and excellence is a must, otherwise errors could lead to a serious financial issue, you can't avoid the fact that you're human though, and you are at risk for committing mistakes, so make sure that when answering this kind of question, you want to showcase how deliberate you are when checking your work. Give examples of your own method on how you ensure that your work is always accurate. You might also want to brush up on what you'll do to fix any problems or errors you may encounter, or how you'll provide solutions to your mistakes (if ever).

Describe to me that time when you've helped reduce costs

Best Answer: This is a tricky one especially for those who've never had working experience before. What you can do is share a story about that time (if you did experience one), emphasized the steps you took, and the recommendations you gave that resulted in something positive. If you don't have any experience, then perhaps describe a scenario during your internship, and show the interviewer how you'd be willing to go beyond your job to help the company.

Where do you see yourself 5 or 10 years from now?

Best Answer: Your answer should be something that will highlight what you want to learn during your stay in the company you're applying for and also sharing your short – term plan in what you want to do in your career as an accountant, perhaps getting additional training or pursuing further studies to help the company is one best way to put it.

Top Accounting Careers in the Workforce

Accountants in the workforce are not lone wolves working on their own as we are often led to believe. Accountants not only develop skills for understanding financial statements, making reports and balancing financial sheets. They are also individuals who work hand in hand with other accountants, corporate clients, upper management teams, rank and file personnel as well as law enforcement and government officials. In other words, accountants are faced with opportunities and situations which call for them to collaborate and work with others.

Management Accountants

Management accountants are the ones who analyze financial information of the organizations for which they are employed. They are also tasked to record and file these financial documents. All information about finances of the organization which management accountants prepare is only used for internal clients like business managers. These records are not meant for the public.

Management accountants are those who typically work on performance evaluations and evaluated the organization's budget. They can also help organizations in determining the budget of a business. Others may work on asset management and work side-by-side with financial managers. Tasks carried out on asset-management involve the planning and selection of potential investments like bonds, real estate or stocks.

Public Accountants

Public accountants have clients that may be comprised of private individuals, governments, and corporations. Their tasks include consultancy, auditing accounting, tax reportage. Public accountants are those who work on documents that are required to be disclosed.

These are financial statements that need to be scrutinized including tax forms balance and Balance sheet statements which are provided by corporations to possible investors. Public accountants usually are also certified public accountants who run their own business or maybe employed by public accounting companies. Public accountants can specialize in a number of fields in accounting such as friend sick accounting concentrated on the investigation of crimes of the financial support which could include fraudulent monetary exchanges or company cash embezzlement.

Certified public accountants and public accountants are very well-versed with tax laws and are compelled to keep themselves up to date with ay changes in the rules of accounting. They are adept at working with the most up to date accounting systems and give recommendations to improve the financial standing of their clients.

Budget Analysts

Budget analysts are accountants who assist private and public institutions by helping them organize and sort their finances. Budget analysts are the accountants who prepare the institutions budget reports. They are also the ones who monitor the movement of the outflow of the institutions' finances.

Accounting Clerks, Auditing Clerks and Bookkeeping Clerks

Producing the financial records for the organizations they work for are accounting clerks, auditing clerks and bookkeeping clerks. These individuals are responsible for documenting financial transactions. They are tasked with the updating and maintenance of financial statements and records. They are the ones who check the financial ledgers and statements for accuracy making sure there are no mistakes in the records.

Financial Managers, Financial Analysts, Financial Advisors

Financial managers are those who are responsible for maintaining the financial health of the organization they serve. An important part of their task is to create financial reports. They are the ones who direct the monies of the organization and produce direct investment plans. Financial managers are those who make long term plans and build financial goals of the organization they are part. They develop strategies on how to improve business and profitability.

Financial Analysts are the individuals who give guidance to business people and corporate businesses. They are the individuals who are responsible for making decisions on investments to make. They are the assessors of the performance of socks, bonds and other various sorts of investments.

Personal financial advisors are accountants who aim to give advice on insurance, investments, estate planning, college savings, retirement and taxes so that their clients are able to manage their assets and finances better. They are tasked to find the best advice for their clients depending on the client requirement at any given time.

Tax Collectors, Tax Agents and Revenue Agents

Tax collectors, tax agents and revenue agents are the accountants who are tasked with figuring out the amount of taxes owed by an individual or a business. They are agents working on behalf of local, state or federal governments and collect taxes due to the respective areas of governance. They are tasked to study tax returns of individuals and businesses. They conduct audits. They determine the amount of taxes owed and collect what is overdue.

Chief Financial Officer, Management Consultants, Top Accounting Executives

Top executives are those who are given the job of devising plans, policies and strategies that set an organization in its path to meet the company's financial goals. They are those who work on the direction and coordination of operational processes of organizations and companies they work for.

Management consultants or management analysts are those who suggest how to make better the efficiency of an organization. They provide recommendations to the organizations management team on how to gain better profit by way of reducing company costs which results to increased revenues for the company.

For a more in depth look and a detailed listing of tasks and responsibilities related to a specific job description in the financial and accounting world, refer back to our comprehensive list of accounting jobs at the beginning of this book.

The Rewards of Being an Accountant

Most people have come to realize that jobs are not just sources of wages but have come to understand that jobs can also be sources of inspiration and creativity on a personal level. Jobs are not tedious and boring if you enjoy what you do. This is true for any career or profession across the board and needs no translation. Career satisfaction makes up for job productivity and advancement.

No one wants to be stuck in a job that brings them no sense of fulfillment, or purpose. Understanding what you bring to the table, how you contribute to the bigger picture and how your work makes a difference in the bigger scheme of things provides satisfaction and inspiration to do a job well and do it properly.

The long history of the practice and discipline of the accounting profession is evidence to a discipline that is not going to disappear any time soon or ever, as long as there are big companies and corporations needing the skills of people who will be able to manage assets, finances, funds and monies, accountants will always be a staple skill required by the job sector. Knowing how to position yourself in this in demand and competitive realm of jobs in finance will be a vital measure you want to consider in order to position yourself in the best possible light.

Your initial investments of time spent studying will pave the way for a disciplined structure of learning and absorbing what is required to get closer to your goals. Identifying where you are weak also identifies the areas of your strengths, Make sure that you not only get objective feedback from lecturers, professors and leaders, but make it a point to self-assess periodically. Doing this gives you a better chance of adjusting to improve areas that you need to enhance.

Upstanding work ethics and unbiased judgment are just some of the featured qualities accountants need to have in order to build a good reputation for themselves. Compliance to standards and regulations are other expectations of an upstanding accountant.

It is a profession that finds out the truth of a financial situation, giving an entity the power to determine their financial standing and seeking solutions to improve the profitability of the business whilst seeking out methods that reduces the cost for companies.

It is indeed a noble profession that gives way and oils the wheels of commerce and industry. Historically, the face of accounting has changed with better understanding, improved financial accounting systems and techniques. Presently, accounting allows the world to continue to expand and reach out to each other in terms of trade, business and commerce.

Photo Credits

References

"5 Common Accounting Interview Questions" - LiveCareer.com
https://www.livecareer.com/interview-tips/industry/accounting

"40 TOP-PAYING ACCOUNTING JOBS" - Accounting - degree.org
https://www.accounting-degree.org/top-paying-accounting-jobs/

"AICPA (American Institute of Certified Public Accountants) Definition" - Techtarget.com
http://searchcompliance.techtarget.com/definition/AICPA-American-Institute-of-Certified-Public-Accountants

"Accountancy Resources" - The American Accounting Association
http://aaahq.org

"Accountants and Auditors" - Bureau of Labor Statistics
https://www.bls.gov/ooh/business-and-financial/accountants-and-auditors.htm

"Accounting" - Wikipedia.org
https://en.wikipedia.org/wiki/Accounting

"Accounting industry in the U.S. - Statistics & Facts" - Statista.com https://www.statista.com/topics/2121/accounting-industry-in-the-us/

"Apprenticeship: The Workforce Solution for the Financial Services Industry" - United States Department of Labor https://www.dol.gov/apprenticeship/industry/finance-business.htm

"Forensic Accounting" - Wikipedia.org https://en.wikipedia.org/wiki/Forensic_accounting

"Frequently Asked Questions FAQs: Become a CPA" - AICPA.org https://www.aicpa.org/becomeacpa/gettingstarted/frequentlyaskedquestions.html

"History of Accounting" - Wikipedia.org https://en.wikipedia.org/wiki/History_of_accounting

"How to Become an Accountant: Education and Career Roadmap" - Study.com https://study.com/articles/How_to_Become_an_Accountant_Education_and_Career_Roadmap.html

"Professional Accounting Body" - Wikipedia.org https://en.wikipedia.org/wiki/Professional_accounting_body

"Professional Association" - Wikipedia.org https://en.wikipedia.org/wiki/Professional_association

"The Significance of Ancient Mesopotamia in Accounting History" - Accountingin.com http://www.accountingin.com/accounting-historians-journal/volume-11-number-1/the-significance-of-ancient-mesopotamia-in-accounting-history/

"Ultimate CPA Exam Prep Strategies and Last-Minute Tips on Exam Day" - IPassTheCPAExam.com
http://ipassthecpaexam.com/cpa-exam-tips/

"What is a Bachelor's Degree?" - GetEducated.com
https://www.geteducated.com/career-center/detail/what-is-a-bachelors-degree

"What Qualifications Do I Need to Become an Accountant?" - Babington.co.uk
https://babington.co.uk/blog/accounting/what-qualifications-do-i-need-to-become-an-accountant/

Feeding Baby
Cynthia Cherry
978-1941070000

Axolotl
Lolly Brown
978-0989658430

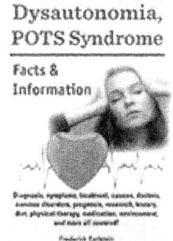

Dysautonomia, POTS
Syndrome
Frederick Earlstein
978-0989658485

Degenerative Disc
Disease Explained
Frederick Earlstein
978-0989658485

Sinusitis, Hay Fever,
Allergic Rhinitis Explained
Frederick Earlstein
978-1941070024

Wicca
Riley Star
978-1941070130

Zombie Apocalypse
Rex Cutty
978-1941070154

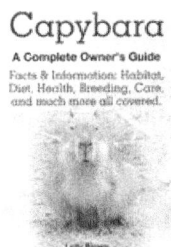

Capybara
Lolly Brown
978-1941070062

Eels As Pets
Lolly Brown
978-1941070167

Scabies and Lice Explained
Frederick Earlstein
978-1941070017

Saltwater Fish As Pets
Lolly Brown
978-0989658461

Torticollis Explained
Frederick Earlstein
978-1941070055

Kennel Cough
Lolly Brown
978-0989658409

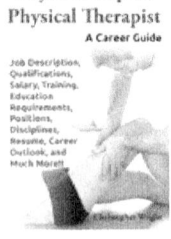

Physiotherapist, Physical
Therapist
Christopher Wright
978-0989658492

Rats, Mice, and Dormice
As Pets
Lolly Brown
978-1941070079

Wallaby and Wallaroo Care
Lolly Brown
978-1941070031

Bodybuilding Supplements
Explained
Jon Shelton
978-1941070239

Demonology
Riley Star
978-19401070314

Pigeon Racing
Lolly Brown
978-1941070307

Dwarf Hamster
Lolly Brown
978-1941070390

Cryptozoology
Rex Cutty
978-1941070406

Eye Strain
Frederick Earlstein
978-1941070369

Inez The Miniature Elephant
Asher Ray
978-1941070353

Vampire Apocalypse
Rex Cutty
978-1941070321

Printed in Great Britain
by Amazon

18280415R00081

Contents

John Ford at Work

To Kristin and in memory of David

John Ford at Work
Production Histories
1927–1939

Lea Jacobs

British Library Cataloguing in Publication Data

Ford at Work: Production Histories 1927–1939

A catalogue entry for this book is available from the British Library

ISBN: 9780 86196 757 5 (Paperback)
ISBN: 9780 86196 995 1 (ebook-EPUB)
ISBN: 9780 86196 996 8 (ebook-EPDF)

Cover photo: John Ford, Bert Glennon and a Mitchell BNC S/N: 1 camera in use at the United Artists Studio.

This volume is published with the support of Le Giornate del Cinema Muto, Pordenone.

Published by
John Libbey Publishing, 205 Crescent Road, East Barnet, Herts EN4 8SB, United Kingdom
e-mail: johnlibbeypublishing@gmail.com; web site: www.johnlibbey.com

Distributed worldwide by **Indiana University Press**,
Herman B Wells Library – 350, 1320 E. 10th St., Bloomington, IN 47405, USA.
www.iupress.indiana.edu

Printed and bound in the United Kingdom by Short Run Press, Exeter

Acknowledgments

I am grateful for a professorship from the Wisconsin Alumni Research Foundation, University of Wisconsin-Madison, which enabled me to undertake this research. An earlier version of my discussion of *Arrowsmith* in chapter two was published as "Dialogue Scenes in the Period of Multiple-Camera Shooting: the Example of *Arrowsmith*", in Daniel Wiegand, ed., *Aesthetics of Early Sound Film: Media Change around 1930* (Amsterdam: University of Amsterdam Press, 2023).

My research would not have been possible without the expert staff in special collections at the following libraries and archives:

- Lilly Library, Indiana University;

- Manuscripts Division, Charles E. Young Research Library, University of California Los Angeles;

- Margaret Herrick Library, Academy of Motion Pictures Arts and Sciences;

- Cinematic Arts Library, Doheny Library, University of Southern California;

- L. Tom Perry Special Collections, Harold B. Lee Library, Brigham Young University;

- Moving Image Research Collections, University Libraries, University of South Carolina;

- Wisconsin Center for Film and Theatre Research, University of Wisconsin-Madison.

Additionally, in 2015 the former staff members of the Twentieth-Century Fox Legal Department, Los Angeles, went out of their way to provide access to archival materials.

Many thanks to Mike Pogorzelski, formerly of the Academy Film Archive and Schawn Belston, formerly of Twentieth Century-Fox, who have meticulously preserved several of John Ford's films, and made beautiful 35mm prints of many more available to me and my students over the years. Thanks to Janet Bergstrom, Matthew Bernstein, Kaitlin Fyfe, Kathryn Kalinak, Dave Kehr, Patrick Keating and Barry Salt for pictures, clarifications and corrections. Vance Kepley and John Belton kindly took time from their schedules to read and comment on the manuscript. John Libbey was the most gracious publisher an author could wish for. Ben Brewster improved this book in every possible way except for his patriotic adherence to British conventions for punctuating quotations. My dear friend David Bordwell did not live to see this book completed but his scholarship remains an inspiration.

Introduction

I love making pictures, but I don't like talking about them.
    John Ford[1]

Like all who met him, I sat down with his filmography in hand and asked him myriad questions, telling myself that all those people who had tried the same tack didn't know his films well and hadn't known how to speak to him about them. Well, it was a total flop ... .
"Why have you made so many Westerns?"
"For health reasons. Westerns are a chance to get away from Hollywood and the smog. You live in the open, sleep under a tent, eat from a chuck wagon, barbecue your meat. It's great fun. At night, you get together and sing songs."
"Why did you become a film director?"
"I was hungry."
"What do you think is most characteristic of Hollywood?"
"The incredible number of churches. There are more than in any other town in the world."
    Bertrand Tavernier interviewing John Ford[2]

John Ford's well-known reluctance to discuss his films was partly the result of a career spent in the Hollywood studio system covering his tracks. Seeking to protect his autonomy and creative control, he routinely tried to intimidate and dismiss any studio underlings who dared to come on set during production to check on his progress.[3] He avoided watching rushes in the company of studio executives, preferring to watch them privately with one or two selected members of his crew, sometimes going so far as to maintain that he never watched rushes.[4] When queried about drawings of settings from *They Were Expendable* in the Ford papers, Dan Ford explained that they did not originate with the director, since his grandfather never gave away his intentions by storyboarding shots.[5] Ford's reluctance to explain himself also extended to his actors. His well-documented habit of picking on and humiliating at least one cast member over the course of a production was only partly out of a sadistic pleasure in asserting his authority; it also reduced questions and unsolicited advice from all members of the cast.[6] Even his practice of cutting in the camera, drastically reducing the number of camera setups and takes so as to limit

1   Peter Bogdanovich, "The Autumn of John Ford", in Gerald Peary, ed., *John Ford Interviews* (Jackson: University Press of Mississippi, 2001), 58, originally published in *Esquire* (Apr 1964): 106–107.
2   Bertrand Tavernier, "Notes of a Press Attaché: John Ford in Paris", trans. Jean-Pierre Coursodon, in Peary, ed., 105–106, originally published in *Positif*, 82 (Mar 1967).
3   Peter Bogdanovich, *John Ford* (Berkeley: University of California Press, 1978), quotes anecdotes by cinematographer Joseph LaShelle, 8, and editor Robert Parrish, 14.
4   Robert Parrish, *Growing Up in Hollywood* (New York: Harcourt Brace Jovanovich, 1976), 130; Joseph McBride, *Searching for John Ford: A Life* (New York: St. Martin's Griffin, 2003), 250.
5   There are eleven items labeled "storyboards" for *They Were Expendable* in Ford, J. mss, 1906–1976, Scripts and Production Materials, Oversize, Box 2, Lilly Library, Indiana University, Bloomington, Indiana. The drawings do not match any shot in the film.
6   The stories about his rude and abusive treatment of actors are legion see, for example, Parrish, 132, on Ford's treatment of Margot Grahame in *The Informer*; Robert Montgomery on Ford's treatment of John Wayne and Donna Reed on *They Were Expendable* in Lindsay Anderson, *About John Ford* (London: Plexus, 1981), 226–228.

the cutter's options, can be seen as a tactic for controlling editing without having to explain or justify his plans to anyone.[7]

Ford's particular animus towards interviewers became pronounced in the latter part of his career, after the commercial failure of *The Fugitive* in 1947, when he became ever more suspicious of educated elites and what he called "the traps of aestheticism and, above all, intellectualism".[8] Confronted by the first wave of admiring auterist critics in the 1950s and 1960s, he employed multiple tactics to stonewall any serious discussion of his films. A common gambit was to claim that he had never seen them fully assembled or did not remember them or was not very interested in cinema. Another, more subtle, strategy was to deny any artifice on his own part – his Westerns were realistic, he was simply representing how the West had been.[9] He would also frequently assert that his job was purely intuitive, defying verbal explanation. When Axel Madsen asked him how he made decisions about camera placement, he asserted: "I say, this is the best shot here, let's put the camera here. You don't do that ahead of time, you do it the day you're shooting … . You do it by instinct. I mean, here's a river and a tree and in the background mountains and over there flats, so you shoot the prettiest. You shoot what would look best on screen."[10] Peter Bogdanovich usefully summarized the problem of interviewing him: "He will go out of his way to discourage the conception that he is a man who consciously tries to create something of value … . If Ford can convince you that he's a 'hard-nosed director' who just takes a script and does it, he is content."[11] In this context the young Steven Spielberg's encoun-

ter with Ford, as represented in Spielberg's film *The Fabelmans*, takes on a certain poignancy. Gruff and surly, Ford rapidly dismisses the aspiring director, but at least he mentions the word "art" with reference to two Western paintings hanging in his office and, referring to their respective placements of the horizon line, slyly brings up what, in the cinema, is a problem of camera placement.

There is little doubt that Mr. Ford would have hated the study proposed here. It seeks to illuminate how he developed as a director within the studio system as the system itself changed over time. It has entailed detailed investigations of the collaborations with the producers, screenwriters, actors and cinematographers that had the most impact on his production practices. It has traced his major sources and models – the literary, cinematic and musical sources from which he drew. It has taken into consideration relevant changes in film technology and sought to explain how they were incorporated into his style. It is not concerned with the life except insofar as Ford's life was governed by his obsession with filmmaking. The nature of this project may thus be explained with reference to a noted Beethoven biographer who qualified the scope of his essays as "biographical contributions, in the sense that the word 'biographical' is meant to refer to the working artist, and 'contributions' refers almost exclusively to studies of Beethoven's working papers and sketch leaves".[12]

The study picks up in 1927, in the middle of Ford's twenty-year tenure at Fox, at the moment of William Fox's expansion of his studio and consequent recruitment of the esteemed

7   Dan Ford, *Pappy: The Life of John Ford* (Englewood Cliffs, New Jersey: Prentice-Hall, 1979), 108, quoting Ford's assistant director Wingate Smith. The editor Dorothy Spencer, in "The Company Remembers *Stagecoach*", *Action: Directors Guild of America* 6/5 (Sep–Oct 1971): 28, recalled: "Ford was right; he cut in the camera. He got what he wanted on film, then left it to the cutter to put it together". The editor Barbara McLean, in Thomas Stempel, "An Oral History Interview with Barbara McLean", Darryl F. Zanuck Research Project (Los Angeles: American Film Institute, 1970–1971), 43, mentions Ford's *Arrowsmith* which she edited for Goldwyn: "He never did bother too much about the cutting on it. But, it's on the film. You couldn't hurt a Ford picture, you know."
8   Éric Leguèbe, "John Ford", trans. Jenny Lefcourt, in Peary, ed., 73, originally published in Leguèbe, *Confessions 2: un siècle de cinéma américain par ceux qui l'ont fait* (Paris: Ifrane, éd., 1995).
9   Jean-Louis Rieupeyrout, "A Meeting with John Ford", trans. Jenny Lefcourt, in Peary, ed., 45, originally published in *Cinema 61*, 53 (Feb 1961).
10 Axel Madsen, "Ford on Ford 1", Interview of 14 March 1966, in Peary, ed., 87, originally published in Per Calum, ed., *John Ford: En Dokumentation* (Copenhagen: Det Danske Filmmuseum, 1968).
11 Bogdanovich, *John Ford*, 32–33.
12 Gustav Nottebohm, *Zweite Beethoveniana* (1887), translated and cited in Lewis Lockwood, *Beethoven's Lives: The Biographical Tradition* (Woodbridge, Suffolk: The Boydell Press, 2020), 48.

German director F. W. Murnau, who would have a decisive influence on Ford and his colleagues. It concludes with the *annus mirabilis* of 1939, in which Ford directed *Stagecoach* for United Artists and *Young Mr. Lincoln* and *Drums Along the Mohawk* for Twentieth Century-Fox. The decision to focus principally on this stretch of a fifty-year career that began with the director's apprenticeship at Universal in 1914 and closed with the production of *7 Women* for MGM in 1965, requires comment. Ford's œuvre is so vast and varied that comprehensive accounts, while invaluable, must necessarily limit the discussion of individual films and many other facets of his career.[13] In contrast, this study has focused intensively on a smaller portion of his œuvre so as to be able to examine the films closely and to uncover as much as possible about their production. One justification for examining the 1930s in particular is that this is easily the best documented period of Ford's career. The surviving studio records for the silent period are scanty at best. After World War II, the director most frequently worked for independent production companies in which record keeping was rather haphazard. For the 1930s, however, extensive paper records survive for those studios where Ford made most of his films – not only Fox (later Twentieth Century-Fox), but Samuel Goldwyn and RKO. The same level of coverage is not available for each studio. For example, the RKO files reveal much more about budgeting than the Fox files, while the Fox files show more about script development; the Goldwyn files contain many more, and more detailed, Daily Production Reports than either Fox or RKO. Nonetheless, when taken in concert, these document collections provide a much clearer sense of the institutional context within which Ford operated than it is possible to reconstruct for any other period of his career.

The 1930s are also of interest because one can observe the director negotiating quite different work environments. Within the confines of his home studio, he dealt with three distinct managerial regimes: William Fox for the expansionary period of the late 1920s, Winfield Sheehan and Sol Wurtzel during the early 1930s, and Darryl F. Zanuck after the merger with 20th Century in 1935. In addition, the director sought to create an alternative production base, first at RKO between 1933 and 1936, and later at United Artists where he made two films with producer Walter Wanger.

The 1930s encompassed two important sets of technological innovations which had a lasting influence on Ford's style: the transition to sound and the development of much more sensitive black-and-white negative. In interviews, Ford maintained that the transition to sound was not noteworthy: "We just made them with sound."[14] In fact, the director seems to have been quite enthused by the possibilities of the new sound medium, and the transition was transformative for him in several respects. In contrast with the silent period, where the choice, placement and timing of the musical accompaniment was done live by the musicians in performance, recorded sound offered the director the opportunity of directly co-ordinating music with the timing and mood of his scenes. Ford, who had cited folk songs even in his silent films, immediately seized on this opportunity, a facet of his work explored here through analyses of the directly recorded song-based score of *The Black Watch*, and Ford's later collaborations with composers Max Steiner and Alfred Newman.

Ford is often thought of as a director who sought to reduce dialogue: "I too am a silent picture man. Pictures, not words, should tell the story."[15] However, he also paid a lot of attention to line readings. Bogdanovich reports Ford's exacting directions for pronunciation and pitch, and his corrections of his actors' speech, during the shooting of *Cheyenne Autumn*.[16] From the very

---

13   The best comprehensive account of the life is McBride, *Searching for John Ford*; the best comprehensive account of the films is Tag Gallagher, *John Ford: Himself and His Films*, digital edition (Apple Books, 2020); all references to the latter are to the more recent ebook edition as opposed to the print edition entitled *John Ford: The Man and His Films* (Berkeley: University of California Press, 1986).

14   Ford, quoted in Axel Madsen, "Ford on Ford 1", in Peary, ed., 84: see, also, Walter Wagner, in Peary, ed., 155, originally published in Wagner, *You Must Remember This* (New York: Putnam, 1975).

15   George J. Mitchell, "Ford on Ford", in Peary, ed., 64, originally published in *Films in Review*, 15/6 (Jun Jul 1964).

earliest years of recorded dialogue, Ford seems to have been preoccupied with the challenges of writing and delivering plain-spoken language. *Men Without Women* (1930), Dudley Nichols's first script for the director, was praised in the period for its idiomatic, and often funny, dialogue. The most successful films of the middle 1930s were made with dialect comedians Will Rogers and Stepin Fetchit (Lincoln Theodore Monroe Andrew Perry). They were adapted from novels by Irvin S. Cobb and Ben Lucien Burman, which, following Mark Twain, deliberately sought to recreate the dialects of the South. This general trend reached a high point in the rhythmic, overlapping line delivery and the mixture of accented and vernacular speech found in the late 1930s films, especially *Young Mr. Lincoln*.

Ford does not seem to have been putting on an act in the 1936 interview in which he stated: "Lighting, as a matter of fact, is my strong point. I can take a thoroughly mediocre bit of acting, and build points of shadow around a ray of strong light centered on the principals, and finish with something plausible – anyway that's my one boast."[17] Over the course of the 1930s, Ford worked closely with his cinematographers in a series of films that exploited improvements in the light-sensitivity of negative stock. One can see his exuberant experiments with high-contrast, low-key lighting in the films that immediately follow each of Kodak's successive releases of new emulsions. Super Sensitive Panchromatic Stock, released in June 1931, was employed for *Arrowsmith* (Director of Photography Ray June) and *Air Mail* (DP Karl Freund); Panchro Super X made possible the very dark prison escape in *The Prisoner of Shark Island* (DP Bert Glennon); Panchro Super XX made possible the dark, deep-focus shots in *Stagecoach* (DP Bert Glennon). This study will not only explore the way in which Ford's lighting schemes developed across the 1930s, but also the impact of these innovations on other aspects of

his style, particularly his use of the long take, and the way in which the predilection for deep space compositions, evident from his very first silent films, becomes one of the defining features of his style in the late 1930s films.

Ford was undoubtedly an auteur. As Bogdanovich has pointed out, the continuities in his œuvre are unmistakeable, multiple and deep, running from the very first films to the very last. Nonetheless, this study must inevitably confront one of the hoary conundrums of authorship criticism: reconciling the emphasis on an individual director's talents and proclivities with the obvious fact that, at least in the case of the Hollywood studio system, filmmaking was a group effort. Although Ford often described his relationship with the studios as a battle against producers, he was in fact a consummate coalition builder who drew upon a deep and rich network of industry connections in order to make his films. His status as "author" is as much a function of the alliances he formed as of anything he did on set. He maintained a good relationship with producer Sol Wurtzel at Fox as well as Merian Cooper at RKO and, eventually, an uneasy one with Zanuck at Twentieth Century-Fox. There is no doubt that he preferred to pick his own stories and to develop them himself, and he struggled assiduously across the course of the decade to create situations where this was possible. During the 1930s he frequently accomplished this through his close association with screenwriter Dudley Nichols; the two were viewed, and indeed promoted themselves, as a semi-independent creative team.[18] But Ford also took the scripts he was assigned seriously, near the end of his life telling an interviewer: "A director can either make a film or can break it. He must be conversant with the subject. He must hypnotize himself to be sympathetic toward the subject matter. Sometimes we are not. Being under contract you make pictures that you don't want to make, but you try to steel yourself, to get

---

16   Bogdanovich, *John Ford*, 10–11.
17   Howard Sharpe, "The Star Creators of Hollywood", in Peary, ed., 19, originally published in *Photoplay*, 50/41 (1936).
18   See the advertisement publicizing the Ford-Nichols collaborations in the *Hollywood Reporter* (17 Dec 1934): 5; "Ford-Nichols, H'wood's Hecht and MacArthur", *Variety* (26 Jun 1935): 2; and the joint Ford-Nichols interview promoting *Stagecoach*, Michel Mok, "The Rebels, If They Stay Up This Time, Won't Be Sorry for Hollywood's Trouble", in Peary, ed., 21–23, originally published in the *New York Post* (24 Jan 1939).

enthused over them. You get on the set, and you forget everything else."[19] It seems clear that, despite his tenacious efforts to maintain control of the production process, Ford saw his job as one of imaginatively engaging with the scripts he was assigned, and doing his best to improve and enrich them. At this level, he was not concerned about asserting himself as an author.

A related authorial conundrum concerns the contributions of cast and crew. Obviously Ford's career may be charted through the stars he worked with and sometimes helped to create. Henry Fonda and John Wayne are the most famous examples, but Victor McLaglen and Will Rogers are much more important for the first half of the 1930s, and their influence on Ford's œuvre and career remains to be fully explored. On a par with the famous actors, Ford's crews were built around the directors of photography. He identified so closely with this aspect of filmmaking that he sometimes claimed the distinction of being a cameraman himself.[20] After making *The Grapes of Wrath*, *The Long Voyage Home*, and the documentary *December 7th* with Gregg Toland, the director went so far as to propose sharing his closely guarded supremacy on set: in September 1944, he solicited the cinematographer to be co-director for *They Were Expendable*, although, in the event, Goldwyn would not release him.[21] But the example indicates the closeness of the collaborations that Ford often developed with his directors of photography.

Ford seems to have moved through the studio system, a highly divided and extremely hierarchical organization of labor, with a clear awareness of the importance of less visible members of the profession. This is most obvious in the case of the well known "Ford stock company", the group of actors that the director repeatedly cast in secondary roles. He was partial to stuntmen, having been one himself in Francis Ford's

films, and valued the friendship of property men, including, in the 1930s, Duke Morrison. With only slight exaggeration, Nichols describes the social scene at the Fords' home in the late 1930s: "No movie star or executive may ever be found visiting it. Electricians, property men, and cameramen are the people invariably hanging around … ."[22] Technicians were also valued. In an interview in the early 1960s, he sang the praises of a good camera crew: "You have to have people who know how to pick it up and put it down where you want it. These gaffers and grips are good – they have to be."[23] Thus, before cameras ever started rolling on a John Ford production, there were numerous professionals at every level of the labor hierarchy on call, most of them familiar with his prior films and methods, and banking on his strengths, fearing his wrath, and soliciting his advice. And, despite the fact that he was jealous of his own prerogatives on set, he trusted his cast and crew to do the jobs for which they had been hired. While making *Stagecoach*, cinematographer Bert Glennon noted: "Ford knows what he wants and when he has it, so I had better be right the first time because he will not take a scene more than once if he gets it the first time."[24] Henry Fonda recalled that he and Jane Darwell were left on their own to figure out how to perform the scene near the end of *The Grapes of Wrath* in which Tom Joad says goodbye to his mother:

> Yes, he hated to rehearse. As a matter of fact, he just wouldn't … he wanted to get it on the first take, partly because he liked the things that could happen the first time through … . He wouldn't say, "Now look, this is an emotional scene, I don't want you to blow it and leave it in the locker room" – but if you knew him, as I did by this time, you were aware that this was what he was up to … . Jane and I never got to do [rehearse] the scene. We didn't even run it together sitting on the floor. But I knew her well enough, we both knew that we

---

19   Wagner, in Peary, ed., 158.
20   Axel Madsen, "Ford on Ford 2", Interview of 4 Apri 1967, in Peary, ed., 116, originally published in Per Calum, ed.; and Mitchell, in Peary, ed., 66.
21   Ford, Letter to Toland, 6 Sep 1944, and Ford, Letter to Toland, 16 Sep 1944, both in Ford, J., mss., 1906–1976, correspondence, Lilly Library, Indiana University, Bloomington, Indiana (hereafter Ford correspondence, Lilly Library, IU).
22   Cited by Eisenberg, "John Ford: Fighting Irish", in Peary, ed., 14, originally published in *New Theatre* (Apr 1936).
23   Mitchell, in Peary, ed., 66.
24   John Castle, "Bert Glennon Introducing New Method of Interior Photography", *American Cinematographer* (Feb 1939): 83.

knew the lines, we were aware we had a good scene to play, we wanted to say "Hey fellas, let's do it". Now I feel, and I've felt ever since, that Ford knew this was building up in us … . And both Jane and I were so charged with the scene we knew we had – I've never talked to Jane about it, before or since, but I'm sure she felt the same way – that when we did get into it, the emotions all came up so that we had to hold them *back*.[25]

One finds Ford at work, then, partly through the study of his preferred casts and crews, tracing the strands of mutual invention from film to film and studio to studio.

This study focuses on the most consequential films for the director's career and stylistic development in the 1930s, a selection process that has inevitably created regrettable gaps. For example, given its prestige in the period and the number of doors it opened for the director professionally, it seemed important to analyze *The Informer* in detail at the expense of *The Plough and the Stars*, a film that Ford lost control over and that did not have much of an impact on his subsequent career path. The decision to end in 1939 with *Young Mr. Lincoln* was made partly for considerations of length, and partly because I have treated the production process for *How Green Was My Valley* elsewhere.[26] Moreover, as will be argued, *Stagecoach* and *Young Mr. Lincoln* represent high water marks of Ford's style in the 1930s

and are key to understanding the transition to independent production which culminates after World War II.

Ford's reputation has been in decline since the turn of the century. Some recent commentary, often justifiable but sometimes ungenerous, has been focused on his personal failings, racial biases and militarist leanings. Aside from the Westerns, critical work has been thin in comparison with directors of comparable stature such as Hitchcock or Welles. In this context, I would like to emphasize how much I have learned in a decade spent dwelling on Ford's films and puzzling over how they were made. His reach was impressive: I have had to consult sources in American and Irish history, Anglo-American and Gaelic folk traditions, major and minor twentieth-century American regional writers and comedians, and, for the films shot on location, the landscape and geography of California and the West. I have come to understand new aspects of the Hollywood studio system when viewed through the lens of his career. Most importantly, my appreciation of films and filmmaking has expanded immeasurably by attending to his decision-making processes, the carefully wrought storytelling and ceaseless experimentation with sound and image that he was at such pains to conceal during his lifetime.

---

25   Interview with Henry Fonda in Anderson, 218–219.
26   Lea Jacobs, "Making John Ford's *How Green Was My Valley*", *Film History*, 28/2 (2016): 32–80.

Part I
Ford's Transition
to Sound,
1927–1932

Chapter 1

Ford and Murnau at Fox

A *Variety* headline of 1928, "Fox's 4 B'way $2 Houses", trumpeted the fact that the Fox studio had four nearly simultaneous roadshows on Broadway.[1] F. W. Murnau's *Sunrise* was playing at Times Square, John Ford's *4 Sons* was at the Gaiety, Frank Borzage's *Street Angel* was about to open at the Globe as was Ford's *Mother Machree* at a theater yet to be named. This triumphant lineup was the capstone of an extraordinarily rapid corporate expansion between 1925 and 1929. In this period, Fox grew from a mid-sized company with a steady business making modest genre films for smaller theaters to a major company with a production slate that played with great success in the best first-run theaters, some of which it owned. Ford's career in the late 1920s and early 1930s is intertwined with this dramatic expansion, and the subsequent even more dramatic contraction, of his home studio. As the company grew, a coterie of A-list directors were hired – Borzage, Raoul Walsh and Victor Schertzinger were later joined by Murnau. Along with this group, Ford briefly enjoyed higher budgets and longer production schedules, as well as having access to newly built studio facilities. With the onset of the Depression, however, the debt that had funded the studio expansion became a severe liability. A power struggle ensued among the corporate directors, one which would lead to William Fox's ouster in 1930.

Amidst this highly volatile work environment, Ford assimilated two powerful and distinct creative inputs: exposure to Murnau's aesthetic program and production methods, the subject of chapter one and the conversion to sound, the subject of chapter two.

Studio Expansion

When Ford signed on at Fox in 1921 it was decidedly a second-tier studio in a field that was dominated by Famous Players-Lasky/Paramount, MGM/Loew's and First National. It did not have the substantial theater holdings that Paramount and the rapidly growing consortium of exhibitors, First National, were already competing to acquire.[2] Nor did it have the roster of big-name stars that were proving essential to first-run film sales and marketing at the big three.[3] Fox tended to book its films at lower prices than the majors and in what Derek Long describes as "exhibitors running daily or thrice-weekly changes and looking for a feature program to fill their bills for one or two days a week".[4] Nonetheless, it is clear that William Fox aspired to grow his company, releasing several "specials" each season. In 1920, *Over the Hill to the Poorhouse* was one of the highest grossing films of the year.[5] In 1923, Ford was allowed to make his first big-budget production – the Western *The Iron Horse*, shot on location and made to rival James Cruze's epic Western for

---

1   *Variety* (15 Feb 1928): 47; see also for a slightly different line-up of specials but including both *Sunrise* and *4 Sons*, "Fox's 4 Film Runs at Carthay Circle", *Variety* (21 Dec 1927): 9. The studio seems to have contemplated a similarly grand opening for the 1928–1929 season: "6 B'way Houses Contemplated for Fox Film", *Variety* (18 Apr 1928): 3.
2   Derek Long, "Reprogramming the Movies: Distribution Strategy and Production Planning in the Early Studio System, 1915–1924" (PhD diss., University of Wisconsin-Madison, 2017), 106: "Fox simply did not keep up in the 'race for theaters' that so dominates the received historiography of this period; the distributor's small circuit barely grew between 1917 and 1925."
3   Long, 111–112; Richard Koszarski, *An Evening's Entertainment: The Age of the Silent Feature Picture, 1915-1928* (New York: Charles Scribner's Sons, 1990), 83–84.
4   Long, 110.
5   Long, 112.

9

Paramount, *The Covered Wagon*. Given a road-show release in 1924, Ford's film was highly successful and moved the actor George O'Brien to star status, helping to augment the studio's line-up of male stars.[6]

But the pronounced expansion of the studio did not really begin until 1925, when Fox stock was offered publicly for the first time with the aim of raising capital to underwrite theater acquisition.[7] In November 1925 *Film Daily* reported: "With the bankers' announcement that the Fox theater stock issue will appear at an early date comes information of a definite nature that William Fox has set plans to either have representation, or have a big 4,000 or 5,000 seat theater in the key cities of the country."[8] By the 1926–1927 season Fox had large theaters under construction in Boston, Brooklyn, Detroit, Kansas City, Los Angeles, Newark, Philadelphia and San Francisco.[9] The company also purchased theaters in the Midwest, particularly Illinois and Wisconsin, as well as stock in Wesco Holding Company (West Coast Theaters), which dominated exhibition in California, Oregon and Washington state.[10] In March of 1927 Fox acquired the recently built Roxy theater on Broadway, designed under the auspices of manager and showman Samuel L. (Roxy) Rothafel. This move gave Fox a flagship theater on Broadway that rivaled Paramount's Paramount, and Loew's Capitol and State theaters. In 1928, Fox made even more substantial acquisitions of theater circuits, with the purchase of a controlling interest in Wesco, the acquisition of the Moss-Sapiro New York circuit and the Fox-Poli circuit of twenty-two theaters in New England.[11] Early in 1929, he expanded to Great Britain, securing a controlling interest in the Gaumont-British Picture Corpo-ration, which owned a chain of three-hundred major theaters in England.[12] In the same year, he attempted to acquire the vertically integrated Loew's/MGM, drastically increasing his company's level of debt just prior to the onset of the Great Depression. Douglas Gomery characterizes this period as one in which William Fox "aggressively reinvested all profits and borrowed the maximum available during the economic distension of the 'Roaring Twenties'".[13]

While most of Fox's investments were aimed at enlarging the exhibition sector, substantial investments were also made in production, including studio facilities, new technologies and staff. In the early 1920s, the company had a studio on Western Avenue and Sunset Boulevard in Los Angeles.[14] In 1924, Fox bought 100 acres west of Beverley Hills between Santa Monica and Pico Boulevards.[15] This parcel, initially known as the Fox Hills lot, was conceived as a place to build standing sets. With the conversion to sound, however, it became the company's central facility for A-film production. In 1928, larger, state-of-the-art sound stages and numerous other structures were built on the lot at a cost of $12,000,000 and it was renamed "Movietone City" in honor of the studio's proprietary sound system.[16] The spacious exterior sets found in the films of the late 1920s were made possible by the studio's investments in the Fox Hills lot. Examples include the French village streets first used in *What Price Glory* (1926) as well as Rochus Gliese's famous modern city set built for *Sunrise*.[17]

In addition to physical plant, in the late 1920s the studio invested in new technologies: the Grandeur widescreen system and, more important, the innovation of sound.[18] As Gomery has argued, the successful expansion of both the Fox and

6   McBride, 144–153; Aubrey Solomon, *The Fox Film Corporation, 1915–1935: A History and Filmography* (Jefferson, North Carolina: McFarland & Company, 2011), 64–65.
7   Solomon, 69–70, 75–76.
8   Solomon, 76, citing *Film Daily* (8 Nov 1925): 1.
9   Solomon, 91, 93, citing *Film Daily* (16 Jun 1927): 3.
10   Solomon, 70, citing *Film Daily* (12 Jan 1926): 1.
11   Solomon, 116–117, 123.
12   Solomon, 123.
13   Douglas Gomery, *The Hollywood Studio System* (London: MacMillan, 1986), 81.
14   There were also facilities at 55th Street and 10th Avenue in New York City, Solomon, 38, 61.
15   Solomon, 79, 105–106; Century City Chamber of Commerce website, https://centurycitycc.com/fox-studios-historical-timeline/.
16   Solomon, 84, 94, 105–106, 114–115.
17   Solomon, 80.

Warner Brothers studios in the middle 1920s was due to their early investment in sound technology as well as their acquisitions of theaters and theater chains.[19] In contrast to Warner Brothers, which adopted the sound-on-disk system it dubbed Vitaphone for the production of sync-sound vaudeville shorts, Fox first used its Movietone technology to produce sound newsreels. The first Movietone newsreel was screened at the Roxy on April 30, 1927, to great success, and Fox had about a dozen shorts available for rental by January 28, 1928.[20] The Movietone newsreel division expanded rapidly. By September 1929, Movietone had forty-four sound trucks in the field and had ramped up production to two reels a week.[21] Gomery notes: "Movietone was able to sign hundreds of theaters to five-year exclusive agreements for Fox newsreels – at rates double those for silent newsreel competitors".[22]

In the latter half of the 1920s the studio also geared up to produce films at higher budget levels. Fox began competing for well-known literary properties for its "specials" as well as hiring new directors for the proposed adaptations. Aubrey Solomon notes that, beginning in 1925, the proportion of relatively inexpensive original screenplays in the studio's output went down in favor of well-known novels and plays, pointing to an increase in expenditures for literary properties.[23] When Fox made a package deal to acquire the rights to plays produced by theatrical impresario John Golden late in 1924, two were given to John Ford: the long-running Broadway hit *Lightnin'* and *Thank You*.[24] Victor Schertzinger, recently

recruited to the studio, was given the Golden property *The Wheel* for his first production.[25] Borzage, hired away from MGM in April 1925, produced a series of specials from the Golden package: *Lazybones* (1925), *Wages for Wives* (1925, from the Golden hit *Chicken Feed*), *The First Year* (1926) and *7ᵗʰ Heaven* (1927).[26]

Walsh, a Fox director in the 1910s, had departed from the studio in 1920 to direct a series of high-budget films released through various studios: First National, United Artists (where he directed *The Thief of Bagdad* for Douglas Fairbanks) and Paramount. He returned to Fox in 1925 as what *Variety* called "a super feature director".[27] *What Price Glory*, his first "super feature", had purpose-built street sets and spectacular battle scenes staged at the Fox Hills lot. It was an adaptation of the long-running Broadway success *What Price Glory* by Maxwell Anderson and Laurence Stallings, for which Fox was reported to have paid over $75,000.[28] The film lived up to the play's enormous success, making stars of Victor McLaglen, Edmund Lowe and Dolores del Rio.

Along with the recruitment of directing veterans such as Borzage and Walsh, Fox hired the studio's first art and technical director, William S. Darling. The designer, originally Wilmos Bela Sandorhaji, recalls working on *The Iron Horse*, although this credit has not been confirmed. The earliest Darling credit for Fox indicated in the *American Film Institute Catalog* is *What Price Glory* (1926) and the elaborate standing sets built for that film are likely to have necessitated a dedicated

18   Solomon, 123–124.
19   Douglas Gomery, *The Coming of Sound: A History* (New York: Routledge, 2005), 23–54.
20   Solomon, 101.
21   Solomon, 101–102; Gomery, *Hollywood Studio System*, 79–81.
22   Gomery, *Hollywood Studio System*, 81.
23   Solomon, 70; see also trade press references to Fox competing with the other studios for theatrical properties: "Authors' League Criticizing Shuberts on Film Rights Sales", *Variety* (2 Dec 1925): 1; "Only 13 Out of 151 New Plays Sold to Pictures This Season", *Variety* (19 May 1926): 5.
24   The earliest references to Fox's deal with Golden that I have found in *Variety* are: "Not *First Year* Title", *Variety* (5 Nov 1924): 31; "Coast Studios", *Variety* (19 Nov 1924): 27; "Fox on Coast Feb. 1", *Variety* (14 Jan 1925): 21.
25   "Los Angeles", *Variety* (25 Mar 1925): 58.
26   Hervé Dumont, *Frank Borzage: Sarastro à Hollywood* (Paris: Cahiers du cinéma/Milan: Edizioni Gabriele Mazzotti, 1993), 107–108; Borzage seems to have been recruited to direct Golden material, see "Two More Directors Leave M-G – Stroheim-Borzage", *Variety* (22 Apr 1925): 26.
27   "Raoul Walsh with Fox", *Variety* (9 Dec 1925): 34.
28   "Inside Stuff", *Variety* (16 Dec 1925): 37; see also "Conferring on *Glory*", *Variety* (30 Dec 1925): 21; "Fox Gets *Glory*", *Variety* (19 Aug 1925): 31.

designer.[29] Darling went on to design many sets for Ford at Fox including *Hangman's House, The Black Watch, Men Without Women, Pilgrimage, Doctor Bull, The World Moves On, Judge Priest, Steamboat Round the Bend, The Prisoner of Shark Island, Wee Willie Winkie* and *Submarine Patrol*.[30]

The purchase of expensive literary properties, the recruitment of directors of the caliber of Borzage and Walsh, and the creation of the position of art director for William Darling all suggest a deliberate corporate strategy to make films of greater ambition, scope and cost beginning 1924–1925. The capstone of this effort was the recruitment of Murnau, who signed his first contract with the studio on January 24, 1925, for the film that would become *Sunrise*.[31] As Janet Bergstrom has documented, the unprecedented level of control that Murnau was promised and able to exercise over the production of *Sunrise* was not entirely sustained in the director's subsequent two Fox films, *4 Devils* and *City Girl*. But before Murnau left the studio early in 1929 he had given a new direction to William Fox's aspirations for technical innovation and artistic prestige through the example he provided to Fox technicians and directors of his working methods and the visual effects he achieved.

Solomon evokes the creative ferment at the studio during the time that Murnau worked there:

> Eleven companies were using every inch of studio space in the last quarter of 1926. The West Coast production schedule was so crammed that Raoul Walsh was working on two pictures at the same time, completing principal photography on *The Monkey Talks* and sitting with editors and titlers on *What Price Glory*, John

Ford was directing *Mother Machree*, and Howard Hawks was directing *Gaby* (released as *Paid to Love*) starring George O'Brien and Virginia Valli. Frank Borzage was preparing to start on *7th Heaven* and F. W. Murnau had begun his first production for Fox, *Sunrise*.[32]

Of the group of A-list directors at Fox, Hervé Dumont has suggested that Borzage was the one most influenced by Murnau's aesthetic. The two directors were certainly close, drawing on the same group of stars – Janet Gaynor, Charles Farrell and Mary Duncan. In addition, cinematographer Ernest Palmer and set designer Harry Oliver, who worked frequently with Borzage in the late 1920s and early 1930s, also worked on the two films Murnau made for Fox after *Sunrise*. In contrast, by the late 1920s Ford had become increasingly interested in working with Victor McLaglen, who starred in both *Hangman's House* (1928) and *The Black Watch* (1929). Moreover, his technical team remained distinct from Murnau's. He continued to work with George Schneiderman, cinematographer for most of his Fox silents, and Joe August, who would shoot most of his early sound films. Nonetheless, in describing the "brilliant amalgams of German and American style" that were produced at Fox in this period, Richard Koszarski classes Ford's *Hangman's House* as well as Walsh's *The Red Dance* with Borzage's *7th Heaven* and *Street Angel*.[33] All of these films contain elaborate sets, camerawork and special effects, suggesting that Murnau's presence on the lot inspired the A-list directors to try the virtuosic filmmaking techniques associated with him in this period.

Dumont quotes Fox cameraman Paul Ivano

29   See the entry in *The American Film Institute Catalog of Feature Films*, https://aficatalog.afi.com. The Internet Movie Database, http://www.imdb.com, lists Darling as the "uncredited" art-department supervisor for *The Iron Horse*. The entry for Darling on the Art Directors Guild Hall of Fame website also contains *The Iron Horse* credit, https://adg.org/awards/hall-of-fame/william-s-darling/. The first references to Darling working at Fox in *Variety* are: "Fox's Annual Picnic with 2,500 Present", *Variety* (28 Jul 1926): 4; and "Hollywood Studios Hold only 677 Staff People Under Term Contracts", *Variety* (9 May 1928): 12. "Coast Notes", *Variety* (11 Jul 1928): 21, describes the expansion of the technical department at Fox Hills: "Owing to the rapid expansion of the technical department and the library on the Fox lot, the entire upper floor of the administration building has been turned over to them. William Darling, technical director, has been given the north wing." It seems likely that Darling was hired in 1924 or 1925.

30   Darling was nominated for numerous Academy Awards for set design and won for *Cavalcade* (1933), *The Song of Bernadette* (1943) and *Anna and the King of Siam* (1946). He worked at Fox until the middle 1940s, although after Darryl F. Zanuck took over in 1935 he was replaced as Supervising Art Director, see Michael L. Stephens, *Art Directors in Cinema: A Worldwide Biographical Dictionary* (Jefferson, North Carolina: McFarland, 1998), 70–71.

31   Janet Bergstrom, "Murnau in America: Chronicle of Lost Films", *Film History*, 14/3–4 (2002): 432–433, explains that the contract signed on July 8, 1926, upon Murnau's arrival in New York was actually his second, covering four additional films of which two were made. See also the announcement of Murnau's arrangement with Fox in the *New York Times* (22 Mar 1925): 131.

32   Solomon, 83.

33   Koszarski, 85–86.

to suggest the spirit of experimentation that reigned at the studio at this time:

> In a general way, the presence of the German filmmaker also encouraged more experimentation; technical staff were fascinated by his ingenious special effects (miniatures, false perspectives), aimed at enriching the visual aspect by new investigations and an increased mobility of the camera. Paul Ivano amusingly recalled: "See I come from the William Fox school of photography, where we had a man by the name of Wurtzel who was running the thing, and he had glasses as big as beer bottles, and he sat two feet away from the screen. So Ernie Palmer and I, we used to play with filters, diffusion, as long as we like it, it was fine. After all 7ᵗʰ Heaven got an Academy Award. Street Angel got an Academy Award in '28 or '29. So I guess the pictures were good, but we were experimenting on Mister Fox's money." The use of practicable sets, elevators, and the first cranes to move the cameras (the "unleashed camera") also changed customary modes of scripting and editing.[34]

But, far from putting one over on Fox and his producers, as Paul Ivano apparently imagined, studio administrators such as Sol Wurtzel seem to have encouraged their A-list directors to "experiment on Mr. Fox's money". One indication of this is that both Borzage and Ford were given much longer periods to prepare their films after Murnau's arrival, partly in order to allow them to interact with him. Borzage, who had previously directed six features for Fox between the time he was hired in April 1925 and the completion of

"Marriage License?" in 1926,[35] spent almost six months on 7ᵗʰ Heaven, his only film of 1927. Preparation began in October 1926, when he was sent to France, his cameraman Ernest Palmer having already preceded him, to scout possible locations and soak up atmosphere (eventually the director decided to recreate the Paris locale in the studio, perhaps inspired by the example of Murnau's set designs). Production began in January of 1927 and wound up in mid-March.[36]

Ford's situation was similar to Borzage's. He had directed nine features for Fox from the commencement of Lightnin' in March 1925 to the completion of Upstream sometime in January 1927.[37] In February 1927, Ford was sent to Europe for three months.[38] He scouted possible locations for 4 Sons and consulted with Murnau, who had returned to Berlin in March after completing production on Sunrise. Ford then traveled to Britain, and to Ireland where he shot location footage for the horse-race sequence in Hangman's House.[39] In addition to the three months abroad, he seems to have spent at least five months from June to October 1927 working on 4 Sons, a relatively leisurely pace for a director who had been averaging a film every three months.[40] Thus, it seems clear that in the 1927–1928 season, the Fox directors were given the time and support to emulate Murnau's production techniques and to make the best films they could.[41] Fox's investment would have a lasting effect on Ford's filmmaking methods.

---

34 Dumont, 119: I have taken the Ivano quote from the original English source, *Paul Ivano: an American Film Institute Seminar on his Work*, held 20 Apr 1974, The American Film Institute Seminars, Part 1, no. 91, *New York Times* oral history program (Glen Rock, New Jersey: Microfilming Corporation of American, 1977), T1B/P40.

35 The films were *Lazybones* and *Wages for Wives* in 1925 and *The First Year*, *The Dixie Merchant*, *Early to Wed*, and "Marriage License?" in 1926, the last title completed in the early fall of that year.

36 Dumont, 118–119, and "Winnie Sheehan Has Made Fox Stand Up and Others Sit Up", *Variety* (29 Sep 1926): 4.

37 Ford directed the following films in this two-year period: *Lightnin'*, *Kentucky Pride*, *The Fighting Heart* and *Thank You* in 1925; *Shamrock Handicap*, *3 Bad Men*, *The Blue Eagle* and *Mother Machree* in 1926. Although *Mother Machree* was not released until 1928, it was in production between late August and October 1926, see "Fox Active", *Film Daily* (31 Aug 1926): 3, and "Malcolm Boylan Active", *Film Daily* (24 Oct 1926): 6. Production on *Upstream*, released in February 1927, does not seem to have begun until after the new year, see "Coast Studios", *Variety* (22 Dec 1926): 48, and "Ambitious Fox Features", *Kinematograph Weekly* (6 Jan 1927): 93.

38 "Fox's German Cast", *Variety* (2 Feb 1927): 10; F. W. Murnau, Radio-Telegram to Jack Ford on the SS *Hamburg*, 20 Feb 1927, and Winfield Sheehan, Memo to Jack Ford, 29 Jan 1927, referring to Ford's upcoming trip to Europe and ordering him to shoot *Grandmother Bernle Learns Her Letters* (later retitled *4 Sons*) before *Hangman's House*, both in Ford correspondence, Lilly Library, IU.

39 McBride, 160–161.

40 For the start of work see "Ford and *Grandma*", *Variety* (1 Jun 1927): 9; the document notes in the entry for the film in the *American Film Institute Catalog* suggest that it was still in production in early October.

41 This is in stark contrast to the early 1920s when William Fox's overriding concern was to drive down production costs, as indicated in the Fox/Wurtzel correspondence in Lillian Wurtzel Semenov and Carla Winter, *William Fox, Sol M. Wurtzel and the Early Fox Film Corporation: Letters, 1917–1923* (Jefferson, North Carolina: McFarland & Company, 2001).

Ford and Murnau

The results of Ford's encounter with Murnau are usefully divided into short-term effects and more enduring veins of stylistic experimentation. One of the most evident immediate changes in Ford's style was the more pronounced use of camera movement and the long take, the so-called "unchained camera", which had begun influencing American directors in the late 1920s with the distribution of Ewald André Dupont's *Variety* (*Varieté*) and Murnau's *The Last Laugh* (*Der letzte Mann*).[42] The German films were striking not only for their technical skill but also, as Barry Salt points out, for the bold freedom with which the camera moved independently of the actors.[43] In Charles Rosher and Karl Struss's well-known swamp shot in *Sunrise*, for example, the camera begins by tracking with the Man, then turns off from his path and strikes out over the marshland, moving through foliage to reveal the Woman from the City waiting for him. He re-enters the frame and they embrace.[44] Ford's camera in *4 Sons* moves somewhat less independently, but no less spectacularly. Consider the scene in which Joseph (James Hall), fighting with the US Army in the trenches in France, goes behind enemy lines to locate a wounded German soldier heard off screen crying piteously for his mother (the spoken word "*Mütterchen*" is heard in the music-and-effects score). He eventually discovers the man, who turns out to be his brother Andreas. Thus, like the swamp shot in *Sunrise*, this fifty-second-long take builds up to an important meeting between two characters. Moreover, it seems to have been taken on the exterior set that was built for Murnau's swamp. While the camera does not completely depart from the main character's path as in the *Sunrise* example, it does follow its own independent route at an irregular pace while keeping the protagonist in view. The variations in speed and camera/object distance lead to striking alterations in the framing. The shot begins with a fairly distant framing of Joseph kneeling in the trenches (figure 1.1). The camera tracks right "over" a rock barrier as he climbs over it and into some foliage. Once he emerges, he slowly creeps rightward, the camera panning right and tracking forward at an even slower pace, creating an even more distant framing which emphasizes the low-lying terrain (figure 1.2). As he climbs a small hill, the camera moves closer and tilts up (figure 1.3). He runs quickly down the hill, coming to rest just behind the German trenches as the camera speeds up, gets ahead of him and moves in on his new position (figure 1.4). The camera then pulls back and tracks right as Joseph slowly advances, climbing over some abandoned German guns (figure 1.5). Pan right as he moves right and closer to camera searching through the bodies to locate the German soldier who is crying out. Unlike the *Sunrise* example, the actual meeting of the two characters occurs after a cut in, leading into a forty-second static take of the brothers' mutual recognition.

There are many other camera movements in *4 Sons* of comparable length and complexity to the track over the battlefield. Shot 4, a fifty-second traveling shot, follows the Postman down the main street on his rounds. In shot 66, twenty-four seconds, the camera tracks with the train bringing Von Stomm to the city. In shot 222, over twenty-one seconds, the camera moves with Joseph and his wife on a swing.[45] Shot 530, an eighteen-second shot, follows Joseph and his comrade-in-arms (Jack Pennick) seen through the plate-glass window of the new restaurant that has taken the place of his old delicatessen. It is followed by a thirty-eight-second track back with them as they enter through the front door and move progressively farther into the space. Later, in a nod to the elevator shot in Borzage's *7th Heaven*, the camera tracks back with Joseph and his wife as they move through the lobby of their apartment building, then up – a movement visible through the open grillwork of the elevator – and then forward with them down the hall to their front door.[46]

42   Patrick Keating, *The Dynamic Frame: Camera Movement in Classical Hollywood* (New York: Columbia University Press, 2019), 24–36; Katharina Loew, *Special Effects and German Silent Film* (Amsterdam: Amsterdam University Press, 2021), 227–266.
43   Barry Salt, *Film Style and Technology: History and Analysis*, 3rd edition (London: Starword, 2009), 174.
44   Loew, 250–251, provides a nuanced description and interpretation of this shot.
45   Keating, *Dynamic Frame*, 26, discusses moving shots produced by attaching the camera to swings or circulating platforms in *The Last Laugh* and *Variety*.

1.1

1.2

1.3

1.4

1.5

Despite Tag Gallagher's description of *4 Sons* as an "almost self-effacing imitation" of Murnau,[47] the film is important not only for the inventiveness of the camerawork and the intrinsic beauty of the mise-en-scène, but also, considered historically, as

the first of a series of Ford's early sound experiments with the long take. Ford began making films at a point in the 1910s when the American film industry was in transition from a long-take or tableau style of filmmaking to a shot-based mode of scene construction.[48] Unlike a previous generation of directors such as his mentors D. W. Griffith and his brother Francis Ford, the younger man readily embraced the new conventions of cutting around within a scene. Even his earliest feature, *Straight Shooting* (1917), while employing some longer takes as was typical of the period, displays both fast Griffith-style cross-cutting during last-minute rescues and, more unusually for 1917, a real facility with scene dissection. Consider the conversation scene after the climactic race to the rescue. Sweetwater Sims (George Berrell), who has lost his son, asks Cheyenne Harry

---

46   Loew, 253–254, discusses Murnau's use of elevator shots.
47   Gallagher, 50.
48   Salt, 99–109, 149–154; Kristin Thompson, "The Formulation of the Classical Style, 1909–1928", in David Bordwell, Janet Staiger and Kristin Thompson, *The Classical Hollywood Cinema: Film Style and Mode of Production to 1960* (London: Routledge & Kegan Paul, 1985), 155–230.

1.6

1.7

1.8

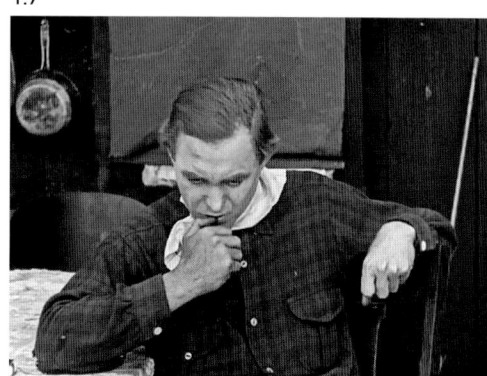

1.9

(Harry Carey), to settle down on his homestead in his son's place. Sweetwater's daughter Joan (Molly Malone) does not speak but conveys her wish for him to remain through a series of pleading looks emphasized in close ups. Figure 1.6 shows the initial establishing shot with Sims in the rocking chair front right and his daughter leaning on the chair back, both looking at Harry, seated front left. Cut in to Sims, who invites Harry to stay (figure 1.7). After the title, cut in to his daughter (figure 1.8). Cut to Harry, torn between his attraction to the girl and his impulse to continue life as a saddle tramp (figure 1.9). Cut back to the establishing shot as Sims continues to make his case, resting his right hand on Harry's chair back. As the men talk, Joan moves behind them. Pausing in center frame, she turns to Harry who looks away from Sweetwater in her direction (figure 1.10). At the end of the shot she proceeds to the doorway and leans against the jamb so that

she is framed in silhouette just behind Harry's head (figure 1.11). Cut in for a closer view of the girl (figure 1.12). Cut back to the long shot with Harry still undecided and Joan now turned towards him (figure 1.13). Ford's elegant staging is already in evidence in this scene, given the use of the doorway to frame Joan while the men talk in front of her, as well as the clever exchange of looks in figure 1.10. But what is particularly impressive for a first feature made in 1917 is the break-up of the scene into an alternation between long shots and closer framings, a pattern that is used to bring out the girl's unspoken wish juxtaposed with her grieving father's verbal plea.

While Ford was always interested in staging in depth, in the silent period he was not by any means a long-take director. His 1920s films were cut with average shot lengths of between 5 and 6 seconds, a rate in accord with industry norms for this decade.[49] For example, *The Iron Horse*

---

49   David Bordwell, "The Introduction of Sound", in Bordwell, Staiger and Thompson, 304, and Salt, 192–193.

1.10

1.11

1.12

1.13

(1924) has an average shot length (ASL) of 5.5 seconds and *3 Bad Men* (1926) is even faster at 5 seconds.[50] His use of consistently longer shot lengths seems to have been initiated with *4 Sons* and then solidified with his early sync-sound films. *4 Sons* has an ASL of 7.6 seconds, an increase of about forty per cent over the silent films cited above. This increase is pretty clearly a result of his experimentation with camera movement. In contrast, *Hangman's House*, made after *4 Sons*, has an ASL of 5.3. The return to faster cutting rates is partly due to the very-fast-cut horse race in the second act[51] and partly to the reduction in the number and extent of camera movements. While *Hangman's House* is still heavily indebted to Murnau in respect to other stylistic parameters,

only four per cent of the total number of shots have camera movement, and those tend to be briefer tracks that run parallel to character movement or reframings, not virtuoso movements of the sort described in *4 Sons*.[52] Experimentation with the "unchained camera" thus seems to have inspired Ford to alter his cutting rate in *4 Sons*, and as he backed away from this device in *Hangman's House*, his cutting rate picked back up.

As many commentators have noted, Ford was not influenced by the late 1920s vogue for camera movement for very long. Joseph McBride quotes Renoir who, after seeing *The Informer*, is reported to have said: "I learned how not to move my camera".[53] But camera movement is by no means the extent of Murnau's influence on Ford.

50   In calculating the ASLs for the late 1920s films, I have worked with DVDs at 23.97 frames per second, which seem to me "correct" on the basis of natural movements such as wind, smoke and water.
51   My references to act structures in Ford's films are based upon my own segmentations unless otherwise noted; my methodology for segmentation relies on Raymond Bellour, "To Segment/To Analyse (on *Gigi*)", in *The Analysis of Film*, ed. Constance Penley (Bloomington, Indiana: Indiana University Press, 2000), 193–215, originally published as "Segmenter/Analyser", in Bellour, *L'Analyse du film* (Paris: Éditions Albatros, 1979), 247–270.
52   Two exceptions are discussed below.
53   McBride, 162; Keating, *Dynamic Frame*, 172, 188, 191,

17

To understand the long-term impact of their encounter, it is helpful to examine how Murnau's tenure at Fox changed the broad spectrum of production practices of the A-list directors there. Janet Bergstrom emphasizes that one of the hallmarks of the German films as well as *Sunrise* was lengthy preproduction planning sessions between director, set designer and cameraman.[54] *Sunrise* was designed by Rochus Gliese, who accompanied the director from Germany and was responsible for both set design and matte painting. The director of photography, Rosher, had spent considerable time in Germany observing Murnau and cinematographer Carl Hoffman's methods on *Faust*. The production in Hollywood resembled Murnau's late German films in that it involved large numbers of extras and utilized monumental sets built in false perspective, as well as special effects including split-screen techniques, matte painting, and intricate combinations of studio and location shooting. The close co-ordination between cinematographer, set designer and director facilitated complicated camera movements since sets could be designed to accommodate tracks, and the framing at each stage of the movement could be anticipated and controlled. But Murnau's team carefully planned *every* shot, moving or still, in this way.

Murnau's methods of production pre-planning and control ran counter to Ford's *modus operandi* during his first decade of filmmaking. From the very beginning of his career Ford was, in Henry Fonda words, a "location director".[55] As McBride has demonstrated, Ford's earliest Westerns, made with Harry Carey at Universal, involved extensive location shooting: "Most of the filming was in the Placerita Canyon, near the Vasquez Rocks. Ford sometimes ventured farther afield, as in three films released in 1919. He used the spectacular San Bernardino Mountains around Big Bear as the setting of *A Fight for Love*, filmed scenes for *The Outcasts of Poker Flat* along Northern California's Sacramento River, and went to Arizona for *The Ace of the Saddle*."[56] Typically, Ford shot in and around Newhall, California, about twenty miles north of Universal City. McBride also cites his interview with Olive Carey, which reveals that Ford, Carey and their crew actually lived near Newhall for a time on a homestead that the Careys acquired in 1916.[57] Ford's later films for Fox, and especially his highest-budget films of the middle 1920s, also often involved extensive location shooting. For *The Iron Horse*, the company spent six weeks in wintry conditions in and around Dodge Flat near the town of Wadsworth, Nevada. Parts of *3 Bad Men* were shot in Jackson Hole, Wyoming, while the land rush was filmed in California's Mojave Desert.[58]

The films made between 1917 and 1926 display richly detailed and active backgrounds. Depth effects are created by the natural contours of the locations, heightened by aperture framings – shooting through a natural or manmade opening – or gradations of light and shadow.[59] Ford and his crew exercised control over mise-en-scène and composition by scouting locations and carefully staging actors and animals in the frame. The films bear witness to Ford's talent for mobilizing the natural topography, making good use of hills and valleys, bodies of water, rock formations, and trees and foliage. Consider some characteristic shot compositions from the last-minute race to the rescue in *Straight Shooting*. The sequence works by cross-cutting between the homesteaders inside the Sims's cabin, the attacking ranchers outside it, and Cheyenne Harry and his allies riding to protect the homesteaders. The striking shot compositions almost interrupt the effect of the quick-cut montage – shots stand out as

54   Janet Bergstrom, "Murnau's *Sunrise;* In-Camera Effects and Effects Specialists", in Martin Lefebvre and Mark Furstenau, eds, *Special Effects on the Screen: Faking the View from Méliès to Motion Capture* (Amsterdam: Amsterdam University Press: 2022), 347–351.
55   Interview with Henry Fonda, in Anderson, 221.
56   McBride, 106–107.
57   McBride, 109. A description and pictures of the Careys' ranch may be found at the Santa Clarita Valley history website, https://scvhistory.com/scvhistory/lw2142c.htm.
58   McBride, 144–153, 156.
59   The term "aperture framing" derives from David Bordwell, *Figures Traced in Light: On Cinematic Staging* (Berkeley: University of California Press, 2005), 104–105.

1.14

1.15

1.16

1.17

isolated pictorial units. Figure 1.14 uses aperture framings through foliage, as Joan hails Harry and tells him that an attack threatens. The dark foreground and soft, bright background behind the girl and horse are made more dramatic by the low angle, effected by situating her on a hill. Sometime later, Harry sees the ranchers massed for attack in a deep-space composition taken from a higher vantage point looking down at the line of horses (figure 1.15). As he rides to ask for help from the outlaw Black-Eyed Pete, Harry encounters the gang's look-outs guarding their lair (figure 1.16).[60] In figure 1.17, the ranchers encircle the Sims's cabin, while others watch the fray from above. They are silhouetted against the light in another example of a dark foreground.

Made at Fox on a much higher budget, *The Iron Horse* has more elaborate sets than the simple open-air ones found in *Straight Shooting* (the set for the 1917 film is illustrated in figures 1.6–1.13).

Nonetheless, the big scenes and most striking pictorial effects are taken on location – compositions of men and animals grouped in and around the train, with the Pah Rah mountains that abut Dodge Flat, Nevada, in the background. Figure 1.18 comes from the sequence in which the railroad construction crews shift their center of operations from North Platte, Nebraska, to Cheyenne, Wyoming (both towns were represented in the film by the street set built in Nevada). Judge Haller's "bar of liquor and justice", moving along with the railroad, remains in operation on the flat car in the foreground. Note how the composition in depth is organized along the train itself, emphasized by the size of the men standing on top of a distant car. Other vehicles and an array of tents are spaced out in a line perpendicular to the lens axis far in the background, echoing the still farther horizontal line of the mountains. Figure 1.19 is another composition in depth,

60   This shot was taken near Newhall at the Fremont Pass, also known as Beale's Cut, a favorite location of Ford's that also appears in *The Iron Horse* and *Stagecoach*.

1.18

1.19

1.20

of Gliese's city streets. One also finds extremely impressive newly constructed exteriors. Figure 1.21, the eponymous mansion from *Hangman's House*, was built with a studio tank for the middle ground and a practicable road in the foreground (note that the top floor and projecting turrets on the left and right of the mansion were done by matte painting as is evident in figure 1.22 when the set is burned for the last act). In figure 1.23 from *The Black Watch*, the faithful pray in the main square in Peshawar with the crowd extending into depth through two arched gates.

The interior spaces in *4 Sons* are not only better furnished than those associated with the rough western towns portrayed in the silent Westerns, they are also clearly designed with greater forethought, to permit shifts of camera position and re-arrangements of the actors in space. This becomes obvious if we compare one of the biggest and most ambitious of the interiors from *The Iron Horse*, Judge Haller's bar in Cheyenne, with the tavern set in *4 Sons*. Judge Haller's bar is the setting for the first violent confrontation between Davy (George O'Brien) and the traitorous railroad employee Jesson. Davy has publicly called out Jesson and everyone in the camp is expecting a fight. An establishing shot of the bar set is shown in figure 1.24. There are three clearly delineated planes of action: the foreground, including the men seated at the bar and the accoutrements in front of it, the middle ground, where Jesson and his ally Deroux stand, and a background area delineated by a railing with a crowd behind it. Most of the action leading to the bar fight will take place in the area between the bar and the

organized around the track rather than the train. Figure 1.20 is an unusual variant of an aperture framing. Slattery, Schmidt and a confederate have taken shelter under the crew's railroad car which is stuck at the end of the track and encircled by mounted Cheyenne braves. The movement of the Cheyenne is visible in the interstices between the heads of the foreground figures.

The example of Murnau's films and working methods, and the new resources that became available to Ford as a result of Fox's expansion, opened the way to much more studio-based production for the director. Of the three films that were most immediately influenced by Murnau's work – *4 Sons*, *Hangman's House* and *The Black Watch* – only the horse race in *Hangman's House* has many shots taken on location. Some of the studio-built exteriors found in Ford's films of this period were originally constructed for *Sunrise*. Not only was the battlefield in *4 Sons* derived from Gliese's swamp set, but the New York street adjacent to Joseph's deli in the same film is adapted from one

20

1.21

1.22

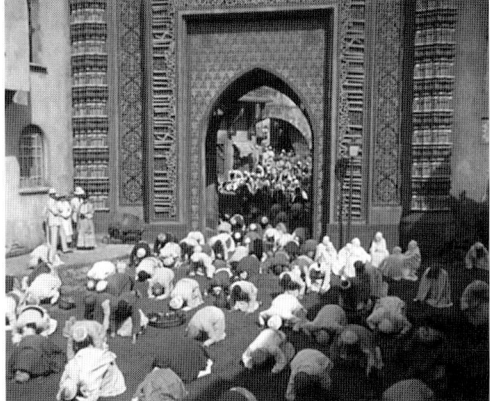

1.23

railing, indeed one of the problems with the set is that so little of the space is activated in the confrontation that follows. As figure 1.25 illustrates, the resolute frontality of the bar set with its stacked lateral planes of action and more or less inert background crowd pushes the action into the midground plane.

In contrast, the tavern set in *4 Sons* uses all the space in depth, and allows for much greater variation in staging. It has been designed to be filmed from two distinct setups, allowing for three different configurations of the mise-en-scène. Figure 1.26 is from the shot which introduces us to the space and the Innkeeper, an important character in the town. A wide corridor on the left stretches from the foreground to the rear wall as the Innkeeper and his staff trot from foreground to background carrying beer to the tables. The lateral movement of extras on the street outside is just visible through the large windows. In figure 1.27, from later in the same scene, the table in the midground has been moved further back and the placement of another table much closer to camera blocks our view of the corridor but dramatically increases the sense of depth beyond (it functions in part as a *repoussoir*). This staging also provides a better view of the comic byplay between the Innkeeper and his chess-playing guests that is

1.24

1.25

1.26

1.27

1.28

about to ensue. The space is transformed again in a later scene in which the camera has been moved forward and angled to emphasize the front door (figure 1.28). Note the internal archway on the left that further articulates the entrance way. This architecture helps to set off the moment of Von Stomm's appearance in the formerly cheerful public space of the tavern. A table has been placed within what was formerly the open corridor so that it is visible as Von Stomm and his fellow officers enter, about to displace the Schoolmaster from his favorite seat. At this angle, the space outside the front door is now clearly visible, showing off the detail and solidity of the set. The depth and substance of the glassed-in alcove to the right has a similar effect.

In addition to the careful construction of interior and exterior sets, there is more frequent recourse to devices that are more easily deployed in a studio setting than on location. Ford begins to make greater use of backdrops and scrims, artificial lighting and low-key lighting effects, and manufactured mist and fog.[61] Superimpositions, lengthy dissolves and other special effects also become more frequent and prominent with the move to studio-based production.

Murnau and his production team made extensive use of miniatures, matte paintings and painted backdrops. In addition to matte paintings such as the one noted above in *Hangman's House*, Ford employed painted backdrops to augment the sense of scale and the depth of his sets. As opposed to the vista of the Nevada mountains which serve as background for the train in *The Iron Horse* (figure 1.18), the shot of the train carrying soldiers to the front in *4 Sons* deploys a painted backdrop framed through the arch of a studio-constructed railroad bridge (figure 1.29). Note, however, that in both cases Ford places men on top of the train to emphasize the recession into depth, an effect doubled in the case of *4 Sons* by the double ranks of helmeted soldiers lined up along the train. From the same film, near the end of act three, a thirty-six-second shot of veterans entering the Burgendorf church on Armistice day begins with the rear center doors closed. About nine seconds into the shot the doors open, reveal-

---

61   Of course, Ford had previously worked with artificial light. For example, early in his career he and cinematographer Ben Reynolds experimented with artificial light in *Hell Bent* (1918) in a style reminiscent of Cecil B. DeMille and Alvin Wyckoff in the same period: fill light is minimized, and arcs are placed close to the subject, generating deep, hard shadows. Similarly in *3 Bad Men*, there is pronounced edge- and backlighting during the night-time scenes in the camp, which were selectively illuminated with arc lights. The point is simply that artificial lighting schemes become more prominent in Ford's work as a result of the control of light provided by increased studio-based filmmaking, as well as the example of Murnau's calculated use of light and shadow.

1.29

1.30

1.31

ing a practicable interior with a backdrop of a cathedral-like space illuminated by painted light. About 28 seconds into the shot, our attention is drawn back to the foreground as the silhouetted Postman walks from left to right (figure 1.30). The Cave of Echoes sets in *The Black Watch* were also augmented with backdrops, as in this frame from the shot representing the Khyber Pass (figure 1.31). The actors on the winding practicable path stretching from foreground center to midground right have been lit to match the painted silhouettes in the distance.

In addition to the use of painted backdrops, Ford's team followed the model of *The Last Laugh* and other films of the Weimar cinema in using cinematic devices such as superimpositions and prolonged dissolves to enhance the image and, frequently, to bring out the characters' subjective states.

In *Hangman's House*, images of condemned men appear over the fireplace as the judge recalls

those he has sent to the gallows. In *4 Sons*, praise of the German army voiced to Joseph Bernle in America gives rise to a superimposition of an arm which slaps him, as he remembers his previous treatment by Von Stomm (figure 1.32). The last act of *4 Sons* begins with the mother having dinner alone at the table where we saw her dining with all the boys in act one. Margaret Mann reacts with pleasure as superimposed images of the boys appear seated at the table.

As well as these psychologically motivated superimpositions, Ford uses a superimposed ray-of-light marked as painterly, frequently in tandem with actual lighting effects. There is a prominent light ray in *Sunrise* when the Man and his Wife look on as another couple wed, although this seems to have been done by effects lighting on mist, not through superimposition. A similar effect appears in *7th Heaven* when, near the end of the film, the atheist Chico returns from the war, blind, having undergone a religious conversion. As he embraces Diane, a heavenly ray appears, done through what seems to be a glass shot. Ford experimented extensively with the painterly ray effect in *4 Sons*. The scene of Mother Bernle serving her sons dinner in act one includes a superimposition of a painted lamp and light rays which are distinct from the actual lighting of the figures around the table (figure 1.33). During the military parade in act two, the passing soldiers are glimpsed through an archway at the rear of a graveyard. The graves marked by crosses in the foreground are lit from the top right augmented by a superimposed painted lighting effect. After the learning of the death of her first two boys at

1.32

1.33

1.34

the front, Mother Bernle goes to her bedroom, where light streams through the window on the left wall (figure 1.34). In this case, given the cast shadows on Mann's face, it is clear that the painted light effect was augmented by an effects light outside the window.[62]

The foregrounded light effects found in Murnau's work are indicative of his more general interest in manipulating light as a graphic element and also referencing painterly traditions of rendering light and shadow.[63] Even a cursory familiarity with Ford's films of the 1910s and early 1920s reveals his skill in using natural light to create highlights, shadows and silhouettes (see figures 1.14, 1.17). But it seems clear that his exposure to Murnau's methods, and the opportunity to work extensively with set designers in tandem with his own cinematographers, gave rise to ex-

tensive and prolonged experimentation with artificial lighting, a practice that would continue throughout his career.

4 Sons shifts decisively into low-key lighting at the beginning of act three, and it provides a virtual catalog of lighting effects made possible by shooting under the controlled conditions of the studio and calibrating set design with gradations of light. Figure 1.35 is from the scene of Mother Bernle's birthday at the beginning of the act when bread and soup is being distributed to the townsfolk outside the church. Effects lights rim the dark set, while rain diffuses the main arc lights. The foreground is extremely dark with a right side light catching the side of the Schoolmaster's face and the Innkeeper's shoulder. In the midground, Mother Bernle's face is illuminated from the top right as she approaches her friends while behind her another woman's face is haloed by an effects light and illuminated from the lower right. Later, as Von Stomm approaches the house to berate the mother for Joseph's enlistment in the American armed forces, he strides through a ray of light coming from an arc light at the back diffused by artificial rain as well as possibly filters (figure 1.36). The departure of the troop train that Andreas leaves in has been designed to contrast with that of the train that carried his brothers (compare figure 1.29 with figure 1.37). The crowded platform of the first departure contrasts with the deserted one of the second. Lighting for the second

62 The simplest way to create the effects described here is to do a second exposure after shooting the scene (without developing the negative) of a painted ray of light on a black ground. Thanks to Janet Bergstrom, Patrick Keating and Barry Salt for technical clarifications.

63 See Lotte Eisner, *The Haunted Screen* (London: Thames and Hudson, 1969), 285–293; on Murnau and painting also Éric Rohmer, *L'organisation de l'espace dans le Faust de Murnau* (Paris: Union générale d'éditions, 1977).

1.35

1.36

1.37

1.38

1.39

1.40

departure is restricted to selected areas along the platform so that the left side of the frame and the space at the rear are almost completely obscured.

Act three culminates in the scene on the battlefield. The low light levels and fog effects visible in the tracking shot across the German lines (figures 1.1 to 1.5) are similar to the effects employed in Murnau's swamp shot, although with stronger contrast and silhouette effects. In the static long take that follows this track, the moment of the recognition between Joseph and Andreas, the low-key lighting that has dominated the treatment of sets throughout the act is applied to spectacular facial modeling. Figure 1.38, from the beginning of the shot just after Joseph has turned over the dying man, shows a shaft of light picking out his features. A scrim behind them

25

softens the background, and slight head movements allow James Hall as Joseph to move in and out of shadow as he reacts to his brother's death.

Murnau was certainly not alone among directors in his explorations of the graphic dimensions of selective or directional lighting. It seems likely that Ford would have been aware of American directors and cinematographers who were also experimenting in this vein. At Goldwyn, George Barnes's soft, low-key cinematography in films such as *The Eagle* (Clarence Brown, 1925) and *The Rescue* (Herbert Brenon, 1929) may have been an influence. At Paramount, Josef von Sternberg's films, especially *Underworld* (1927), shot by Bert Glennon (who would later work with Ford), and *The Docks of New York* (1928), shot by Harold Rossen, utilized low-key lighting with heavy diffusion and deep shadows.[64] For example, compare figure 1.36, the low-key shot of Von Stomm in the rain, with figure 1.39 from *The Docks of New York*, a film produced one year later. In both these shots light is diffused by mist and the strongest light is behind the characters, leaving them in shadow. Similarly, Joe August's shot of Myrna Loy as Yasmini in *The Black Watch* (figure 1.40) plays up the effect of light rays coming through the window grid in the background leaving her face in shadow. Ford's preference for these sorts of dramatic high-contrast lighting schemes remains pronounced throughout his œuvre.

It seems clear that Ford's opportunity to follow up on the selective lighting of directors and cinematographers such as Brenon and Barnes or Sternberg, Glennon and Rossen, was due to the way that William Fox's expansion of his company and Murnau's ensuing presence on the lot helped to transform working conditions at the studio. Ford took advantage of the increase in production time and budgets, as well as Murnau's example of preproduction planning and extensive manipulation of the technical parameters of the shot, to begin seriously to craft artificial lighting schemes in tandem with studio-built interiors and exteriors. Of course, Ford never entirely relinquished

the preference for location shooting evident in his films of the 1910s and early 1920s. But even his approach to shooting outdoors began to show the effects of the stylization of lighting and composition association with his studio-based productions of the late 1920s.

Hangman's House provides a useful example of this interpenetration of production practices. According to contemporary reviewer Welford Beaton, the film was a program picture, unlike *Mother Machree* and *4 Sons*, which were receiving special Broadway runs.[65] Only seventy minutes and released without a music-and-effects score, the film nonetheless received critical encomia that frequently referenced Murnau. The *Variety* reviewer commented that "the photographic quality of the whole production is one of its outstanding merits … . George Schneiderman has caught some of the most striking touches of composition on the screen since those swamp land shots in *Sunrise* which they often resemble."[66] Beaton invoked not only Murnau, but Fox's whole investment in filmmaking technique and facilities:

> The Fox organization unquestionably is giving us the finest photography that is reaching the screen. *Hangman's House* almost outdoes for sheer beauty the amazing shots in *Street Angel* and *Sunrise*. The fog effects are marvelous, and all the out-door scenes are rich in pictorial value, but the cameraman was as compelling in the lighting and photography of the interiors … . The whole picture emphasizes the important part in story-telling that is played by the scenic investiture of a motion picture. Rob *Hangman's House* of the quality lent by its sets and locations, and we would have nothing left but rather conventional movie material.

The sequence in which McDermot (Larry Kent) and Connaught (June Collyer) take a boat-ride to the inn that hides Hogan (Victor McLaglen) contains the shots most overtly indebted to Rosher and Struss's swamp shots. The sequence builds up to a thirty-second tracking shot that follows the stately progress of their vessel through a misty, constructed landscape as reeds, trees and the occasional water fowl move past the

---

64 I am grateful to Patrick Keating for the example from *Docks of New York*.
65 Welford Beaton, *Film Spectator* (12 May 1928): 5–7, cited in Gallagher, 58. The Fox ledgers indicate that the negative cost for *4 Sons* was $495,661, for *Hangman's House* $277,188, and for *The Black Watch* $489,553.
66 *Hangman's House* review, *Variety* (16 May 1928): 13.

1.41

1.42

1.43

1.44

1.45

1.46

camera in the foreground (figure 1.41). Earlier in the film, as the outlaw Hogan walks through the countryside disguised as a monk, he gets information from the gatekeeper of the McDermot estate (figure 1.42). His robed figure stands in the left background, in an aperture formed by the gate and a tree branch top left. He is silhouetted by a sidelight off left which also illuminates the side of the gatekeeper and bounces off the mist

that comes through the gate. Balancing the leftward weight of the composition, a small effects light twinkles midground right on the wall beside the arched doorway.

The scenes at the race grounds were staged outdoors, likely on the Fox Hills lot. The use of scrims and soft focus in these shots taken in natural surroundings helps to integrate them with the studio-built exteriors. In figure 1.43, the line of

1.47

1.48

spectators approaching the race grounds is framed through an aperture formed by arched tree trunks and leafless branches. Hogan, in disguise as a blind beggar, sits back to camera in the foreground just at the end of a drystone wall (the film will later cut around to reveal his face). Schneiderman's soft focus blends the farthest reaches of the oncoming crowd into the background haze. In figure 1.44, composition and costume sharply distinguish the elegantly attired gentry, who are arranged in a wedding-cake composition. The lowest layer is a threesome standing in the right foreground corner of the frame. The next layer is defined by people on horseback in the midground (including Connaught on the most prominent horse). At the highest layer are the three seated figures on top of a carriage and one man standing near the top of the frame midground center. Top hats and bowlers decorate heads at all three levels; they are even part of the women's riding dress. This highly stylized composition also has a very efficient dramatic function, preparing for the upcoming confrontation between Connaught's corrupt upper-class husband D'Arcy (Earle Foxe) and Hogan, dressed as a poor beggar and actually a rebel outlaw, beloved by the populace. Figures 1.45 and 1.46 illustrate the confrontation between the two men – note the connotations of their respective hats. Note, too, how scrims are used to downplay the background activity and bring out the foreground figures in this shot-reverse-shot pair. *Hangman's House* is a good example of how Ford blended work inside and outside the

studio, melding constructed and real landscapes. The hallmarks of his style remain remarkably consistent, displaying a penchant for aperture framings, strong graphic contrasts between foreground and background, aerial perspective, diffusion of light via rain, fog, or dust, and composition and movement in depth.

The stylistic experimentation that Ford began with *4 Sons* and *Hangman's House* resurfaces repeatedly throughout the early 1930s. For example, the generally high-key prison comedy *Up the River* begins with a prison-break shot with very strong chiaroscuro and swirling mist. In *Arrowsmith* (Goldwyn, 1931) mist effects in combination with low-key lighting are strongly in evidence in the studio-built interiors and exteriors in the last third of the film. The bubonic plague has visited the West Indies and Martin Arrowsmith, a research physician, has been sent to the islands to trial a new serum for its treatment. On the plague-invested island of Caribe, the sick and dying are transported to a makeshift hospital (figure 1.47). On a neighboring island, Arrowsmith's wife reacts to a funeral procession outside her window (figure 1.48). An article in the *New York Herald Tribune* headlined "Producers Return to Cinematography of Silent Pictures" praised Ford and Ray June's *Arrowsmith*, which the reviewer considered a renaissance of silent cinematography in the sound era. He writes: "Fogs and steam mists that once marked the work of F. W. Murnau return again to drench the characters of the film in an unearthly atmosphere".[67]

---

67   *New York Herald Tribune* (24 Jan 1932): F12.

Chapter 2

Transformed by Sound

The conversion to sound was transformative for Ford's career in multiple ways. It brought drastic change to his home studio as well as to the personnel of his production team and their methods of work. Moreover, during this time, the director essayed bold experiments with the sonic capacities of the new medium. Perhaps because he had a strong musical orientation as well as a visual one, his earliest sync-sound efforts extended well beyond dialogue. For example, the railroad station scene in *The Black Watch* – singled out by contemporary critics[1] – presents an astonishingly dense mix of music, dialogue, continuous underscore such as tramping feet or the hissing of the steam engines, and punctual sounds such as whistles and bells. It is particularly impressive when one takes into consideration that there were substantial technical constraints on re-recording in this period, so that the mix would have been done on set, live, in real time. The challenge of orchestrating the multiple sound inputs and getting them mixed appropriately during shooting must have been formidable. It suggests the director's enthusiastic interest in exploiting the entire sonic palette that sync-sound filmmaking brought under his control. One of the paradoxes of Ford criticism is that while the films are widely praised for their visual beauty – Ford as "a painter with a camera" – the films usually regarded as his best and most distinctive were made after the innovation of sound. This chapter delineates how Ford's production methods altered with the move to "talkies", a period in which he established a virtual production unit with his preferred crew, and the new paths that sound opened up for him stylistically.

Making the Early Sound Films

Ford's early sync-sound films were made at a time of extreme volatility and uncertainty for the Fox studio. When *The Black Watch*, his first all-talking feature, went into production in February 1929, William Fox was at the acme of his corporate expansion. A little over a year later, after the completion of the director's *Born Reckless* in April 1930, William Fox no longer actively managed the studio that bore his name. Fox's ouster is usually attributed to two principal factors: the stock market crash in October 1929 that weakened his financial position; and the U.S. Justice Department's suit against his purchase of a controlling interest in Loew's stock that was filed in November 1929.[2] More fundamentally, the Fox companies became vulnerable to takeover due to the founder's speculative business practice of mortgaging assets for expansion and then borrowing more against other assets to meet the interest payments on the debt. Although a common practice in the 1920s, such speculations left him in an exposed position when his stock holdings lost value as a result of the crash and banks started

---

1 Mordaunt Hall, "The Screen", *New York Times* (23 May 1929): 34, writes: "Those who witnessed the trains carrying soldiers to the front during the black nights of London town, will be affected by these sequences, for they are without a doubt the most realistic thing of their kind that has come to the screen, and the fact that these scenes are presented with a variety of sounds such as singing, the tramping of fighters' feet, the officers' commands, the chug-chug of the locomotives, render them particularly vivid."

2 Good general accounts of the complicated concatenation of events that undermined Fox's position may be found in Solomon, 122–134, and Vanda Krefft, *The Man Who Made the Movies The Meteoric Rise and Tragic Fall of William Fox* (New York: Harper Collins, 2017), 550–635; on the Justice Department suit see "Fox and Warners are Sued as Trusts", *New York Times* (28 Nov 1929): 1.

calling in their loans. While other film companies also experienced financial difficulties at this time, and several went into receivership, the extent of Fox's debt meant that it was severely crippled. Gomery judged that Fox "staggered into the Great Depression in the worst shape of any of the Big Five".[3]

In December 1929, with substantial short-term loans coming due, Fox authorized the creation of a three-person trust to raise capital. In addition to Fox himself, the trustees were the representatives of major creditors – John Otterson of ATT and Harry Stuart of Halsey, Stuart and Company. These firms had issued Fox bonds for the purchase of the British Gaumont theaters and Loew's stock among other investments. Otterson and Stuart almost immediately attempted to assert control of Fox Film, Fox Theaters and the Loew's stock. They found allies in a number of important Fox executives, most notably head of production Winfield Sheehan and James Grainger, head of sales and theaters. William Fox tried to hold out against them but as additional loans became due Otterson and Stuart employed legal and financial maneuvers that hampered his ability to raise the necessary money to service his debt. In April 1930 he was forced to sell off his stock in Fox Film and Fox Theaters or see his companies go into receivership. Financier Harley L. Clarke, a former Fox ally who also collaborated with Otterson and Stuart, replaced Fox as president.[4]

Given the disarray of the company and dissension among Fox executives, it seems clear that the early sound films were made under a much more decentralized form of administrative control than had been the case under William Fox's leadership. Winfield Sheehan, ostensibly in charge of production, was in Europe from October to December 1929. Upon his return, he remained in New York through late May engaged in the political and legal battles for control of the company.[5] During this time producer Sol Wurtzel remained on the ground in Hollywood but in a somewhat tenuous position due to his continued loyalty to William Fox.[6] In 1930 *Film Daily* announced that Sheehan had appointed seven associate producers to manage the films in production.[7] Although Sheehan returned to the West coast as General Manager and Vice-President in May 1930, in practice the production sector would remain divided into discrete units for years due to the infighting for control. Sheehan and Wurtzel, the most powerful studio executives, remained at odds.[8]

The last Ford film Sheehan supervised was *The Black Watch* (in production February–May 1929).[9] James Kevin McGuinness effectively supervised *Salute* (in production May–July 1929) in tandem with H. Keith Weeks.[10] McGuinness was the credited associate producer on *Men Without Women* (in production November–December 1929) and *Born Reckless* (in production February–April 1930), at which point he left the morass of Fox politics to work at RKO and MGM.[11] The correspondence indicates that Sol Wurtzel acted as producer for *Up the River* (in production May–September 1930) and presumably for *Seas Beneath* (in production October–December 1930).[12]

During the time he remained at Fox, McGuinness, who would become a life-long friend and ally of Ford's, helped to constitute what was effectively a small production unit in which the director was able to exercise more con-

---

3   Gomery, *Hollywood Studio System*, 84.

4   Solomon, 128–132.

5   "Sheehan's Sailing", *Variety* (9 Oct 1929): 6; "Sailings", *Variety* (27 Nov 1929): 3; "Sheehan's Unique Record", *Variety* (16 Apr 1930): 5; "Sheehan's Own Term Contract", *Variety* (14 May 1930): 2.

6   "The Fox Mess", *Variety* (26 Mar 1930): 3.

7   "7 Associate Producers for 1930–1931 Program", *Film Daily*, 27 May 1930: 76.

8   Solomon, 154, 156–169.

9   Peter Bogdanovich, *John Ford*, 50, the director recalled that Sheehan added scenes to *The Black Watch* after he had left the production.

10 H. Keith Weeks, Memo to John Ford, 4 Jun 1929, Ford correspondence, Lilly Library, IU. Weeks asked for retakes of certain scenes, which suggests that he was supervising the production, but McGuinness clearly had the primary role in formulating the script and writing dialogue.

11 "James K. McGuinness leaves Fox Studios", *Film Daily* (15 Sep 1930): 2; "McGuinness' Radio Trio", *Variety* (2 Feb 1932): 6.

12 Sol Wurtzel, Memo to John Ford, 8 Sep 1930, Ford correspondence, Lilly Library, IU. Wurtzel asked for an additional shot and two short scenes in *Up the River*.

trol over the choice and development of projects than he had under Sheehan. McGuinness had started at Fox in 1927 writing titles and supplying story ideas (for most of his career he worked as a story editor and script doctor). Among other Fox films, he contributed to two Victor McLaglen vehicles – Howard Hawks's *A Girl in Every Port* (1928) and John Blystone's *Captain Lash* (1929). He first worked with Ford when the director stepped in to replace James Tinling on *Strong Boy* (1929), a part-talkie in which McLaglen starred as a rough-and-ready baggage handler. Ford and McGuinness played around with the script, writing in a part for comedian Slim Summerville after shooting had started.[13] McGuinness also wrote the dialogue for *The Black Watch* (scenario by John Stone) and the screenplay for *Salute* (from a story by John Stone and Tristram Tupper).

Two other staff members contributed to the screenwriting process within the loosely constituted unit: Dudley Nichols and William Collier. Nichols, a newspaperman who joined Fox in 1929, began his film career working with Ford and McGuinness on *Men Without Women* and *Born Reckless* and would become the director's preferred screenwriter in the 1930s.[14] He seems to have been hired after Ford's former script writer, John Stone, had been elevated to a producer's role at the studio. Dialogue director Collier, a true vaudevillian, was a stage performer, director and playwright[15] who had sold story material to Hollywood and worked intermittently as a film actor in the silent period. He was credited for "staging" in *Up the River* as well as playing the role of Pop. On *Seas Beneath* he was credited for "staging", and as "writer of gags, bits of business and dialogue", as well as playing the role of

Mugs O'Flaherty. He would continue to work with Ford on *The Brat* (as dialogue director and in the role of Judge O'Flaherty) and *Pilgrimage* (as dialogue director).

Up the River is an interesting example of how actively Ford worked with his team to transform scripts in the early sound period. Maurine Watkins contracted to write the script based upon her story synopsis of 1930.[16] After production finished in September, she suggested somewhat rancorously that the story credit be split since she had "acted as compiler of material for story rather than creator, and since the plot was based so largely on suggestions from others".[17] Moreover, Ford and Collier each subsequently signed contracts for "ideas, stage business and incidents" that they contributed to the story. A comparison of the treatment and the completed film reveals that the filmmakers completely altered the male characters while retaining the female characters etched by Watkins. In addition, the film has a different opening, dramatic climax and resolution than the treatment.[18]

Another important addition to Ford's unit at the time of the transition to sound was cameraman Joe August. George Schneiderman had shot most of Ford's silent films of the 1920s whereas August had shot only two: *Lightnin'* and *The Fighting Heart*. In contrast, August shot all of Ford's sound films from *The Black Watch* to *The Brat* with the sole exception of *Born Reckless* for which the director returned to Schneiderman. A sterling cinematographer skilled at shooting low-key interiors, August was praised in *International Photographer* for his ability to retain the use of arc lights while shooting sync sound on *The Black Watch*.[19] He left Fox for Columbia in 1932,

13 There does not seem to be a surviving print of *Strong Boy*. Tingling's assignment refers to the film under its original title, "The Baggage Smasher", *Exhibitors Herald-World* (2 Jun 1928): 102. McGuinness recalls rewriting this script in McGuinness to Ford, 24 Mar 1943, Ford correspondence, Lilly Library, IU.

14 Bogdanovich, *John Ford*, 52.

15 See the Internet Broadway Database website (https://www.ibdb.com) for a listing of Collier's stage credits, which include both revues such as *George White's Scandals* (1920) and *Earl Carroll's Vanities* (1923) and comedies such as *A Little Water on the Side* (1914).

16 "Characters and Synopsis of *Up the River*", Maurine Watkins, 20 May 1930, *Up the River* Story File; Assignment to Maurine Watkins, 20 May 1930, *Up the River* Legal File, both in Twentieth Century-Fox Legal Department. Twentieth Century-Fox Legal, Contract and Story files were viewed at 10201 West Pico Blvd, Los Angeles, California in March and June 2018.

17 Maurine Watkins to V. G. Hart, 22 Sep 1930, *Up the River* Legal File, Twentieth Century-Fox Legal Department.

18 This is based upon a comparison of the completed film with Watkins's "Characters and Synopsis of *Up the River*", 20 May 1930 and the Final Shooting script, 7 Aug 1930, both in *Up the River* Story File, Twentieth Century-Fox Legal Department. As indicated in note 12, producer Sol Wurtzel intervened only minimally, after shooting was near completion.

19 "A 100 Per Cent Arc Light Picture with Sound", *International Photographer* (Jun 1929): 6.

but would work intermittently with Ford throughout the decade and serve in Ford's Field Photographic Branch of the Office of Strategic Services during World War II.

The films of this period contain many appearances by actors who already were or would become staples of the Ford stock company. J. Farrell MacDonald (*Strong Boy*, *Men Without Women*) and Francis Ford (*The Black Watch*, *Seas Beneath*) had been working for Ford for almost a decade. George O'Brien (*Salute*, *Seas Beneath*) had first been starred in *The Iron Horse* (1925). Harry Tenbrook (*Men Without Women*, *Seas Beneath*) had his first role for Ford in *Thieves' Gold* (1918). Taking the first of multiple subsequent roles for Ford were Slim Summerville (*Strong Boy*), John Loder (*Seas Beneath*) and Lincoln Theodore Perry, stage name Stepin Fetchit (*Salute*). John Wayne (*Hangman's House*, *Salute*, *Men without Women*) and Ward Bond (*Salute*) had their first walk-on parts. Victor McLaglen, who starred in *Strong Boy*, *Hangman's House* and *The Black Watch*, became a vital and prominent member of the stock company, making his final film for the director, *The Quiet Man*, in 1952.

One of the most important changes that the transition to sync-sound filmmaking instituted in the working methods of Ford's unit was a return to location shooting. *The Black Watch* had represented a continuation of the studio-based production methods utilized in all of the Murnau-influenced Fox specials. However, the exteriors for the next film by the unit, *Salute*, were primarily shot on location at the U.S. Naval Academy in Annapolis, Maryland.[20] The move to location shooting seems to have been encouraged by the studio to showcase the distinct capabilities of Fox's sound system. The competing Warners sound-on-disk system, in use through 1930, locked that studio into production on the Vitaphone sound stages. Warners' system of recording

onto wax disks, while producing relatively higher-quality sound than Fox's early sound-on-film system, was not readily mobile. In contrast, Movietone cameramen were recording sound and capturing speech in the field from the very first newsreels.[21] As Sol Wurtzel explained in a newspaper interview: "Our mobile Fox Movietone apparatus finds us ideally equipped to make the most of outdoor opportunities. Any place man can go Fox Movietone can go."[22] This aspect of the Movietone system was highlighted in Fox's first all-talking feature, Walsh's *In Old Arizona*, which was produced in the fall of 1928 and widely praised for the many scenes shot outdoors.[23] Production on *Salute* commenced the following spring.

Salute deals with the rivalry between two brothers. George O'Brien plays the older brother, in his last year at West Point, confident with women and an accomplished football player. William Janney, a lesser-known Fox contract player, had the primary role of the shy younger brother who has difficulties fitting in during his first year at Annapolis and barely makes the team. The plot culminates at the Army-Navy game where the younger boy, jealous of his older brother's attentions to his girlfriend, is allowed to play and helps his team to a tie.

One of the striking aspects of *Salute* was the integration of disparate sources of footage in post-production. Location footage used in the completed film included actual or staged drills and parades on the Academy grounds as well as some interior shots and sounds taken in the dining hall. In order to stage the football practices and game, Ford recruited around ten members of the USC football team in addition to former team member and prop man John Wayne to go on location.[24] This group enacted the practices with William Janey as well as close shots of the huddles and plays on game day with George O'Brien. Ford

---

20 Ford and his company left for Annapolis around May 1, 1929, where they spent approximately five weeks, "Fox at Annapolis", *Variety* (1 May 1929): 4; "Exteriors for *Salute* Shot", *Film Daily* (18 Jun 1929): 5.

21 Solomon, 101.

22 "Fox Forming Outdoor Sound Picture Units", *Exhibitors Daily Review* (6 Feb 1930): 6; "Outdoor Films", *New York Times* (23 Feb 1930): X5.

23 "Fox's first 100%", *Variety* (26 Sep 1928): 19; review of *In Old Arizona*, *Variety* (23 Jan 1929): 18; Solomon, 109.

24 "May Bar USC Grid Boys Over Film Work", *Variety* (22 May 1929): 5; see also Randy Roberts and James S. Olson, *John Wayne, American* (New York: Simon & Schuster, 1995), 65–66, 75–77.

and McGuinness intercut their staged game footage with Movietone coverage of the Army-Navy game of 1927 (which in reality the Army won).[25] The Movietone footage also included long shots of the marching bands, cheerleaders and the crowd at the game. Crowd sounds and other ambient noise from the game were intercut with the dialogue and interjections of the actors during the staged scenes, although mixing the two sound sources was not possible with the recording technology then available.[26]

Salute has often been praised for its documentary qualities. Even at the time of its release Variety noted: "There is more intrinsic kick to some of the pictures of the navy cadets in drill on their parade ground, the pictorial splendors of real settings taken in the grounds of the Naval Academy and in the breathless atmosphere of the great American football classic itself, than in any fictitious literary maneuvering of hero and heroine."[27] But it is important to note the use of constructive editing in the film, with sound inventively used to weave disparate sources of footage together during its "great American football classic". Ford's reputation for naturalism and for filming in uncontrolled settings has tended to obscure the extent to which his sound films integrated shots taken on location with staged footage, in this case augmented by the newsreel footage to which he had access.

Ford's unit shot parts of two other features on location on the open sea in this period, projects made possible in part by the loan of Navy vessels and personnel. In Men Without Women, two Navy destroyers and their personnel contributed to filming the rescue of the crew of the fictional S–13, an incapacitated submarine. After having been confined to a studio set of the submarine interior for most of the second act, the film opens

up rather spectacularly to a shot of the destroyers, backlit and moving at high speed in open water. The technology and technique of the rescue are carefully delineated, showing the preparations aboard the ships, and divers suiting up and then submerging. A studio tank seems to have been used to photograph the divers under water encountering the wrecked submarine. Later, the actors or their stunt doubles are shown surfacing one by one and swimming to the safety of the smaller boats which float in the destroyers' wake.

Seas Beneath represented Ford's most extensive and ambitious sound recording outside the studio to date. The Navy loaned Fox two submarines and a minesweeper with personnel for the film.[28] In addition, the studio owned or rented a three-masted schooner, the Metha Nelson, on which much of the action takes place.[29] Ford and the camera and sound crew embarked upon tests on the schooner in early October.[30] According to Dan Ford, once shooting started the actors and film crew were housed on location on Santa Catalina Island while the ships' crews were aboard ships moored nearby. Trade press reports indicate that star George O'Brien, and therefore probably the company as a whole, were on location from October 29 through December 4.[31] While it is possible that a number of shots were taken on a studio-built set of the schooner's main deck, or on the schooner while it was safely docked, nonetheless there were clearly scenes taken on open water that encompassed simultaneous views of both the schooner and a submarine, or the schooner flanked by smaller craft. Close listening with modern headphones suggests that dialogue, effects and ambient sound were directly and simultaneously recorded on location. For example, when the dinghy carrying Anna Marie (Marion Lessing) and the shipwrecked sailors is seen approaching

25 See "Army versus Navy – outtakes", created 26 November 1927, Fox Movietone News, Moving Image Research Collections, University Libraries, University of South Carolina, Columbia.
26 On the difficulty of sound mixing in the early period, see Lea Jacobs, "The Innovation of Re-recording in the Hollywood Studios", Film History, 24/1 (2012): 5–35.
27 Salute, first review, Variety (21 Aug 1929): 18; Salute, second review, Variety (9 Oct 1929): 38, 41.
28 Dan Ford, 56. Claims about the extent of the loan in the trade press go as high as a "flotilla of ships", but Film Weekly (27 Jun 1931): 28, suggests it was two submarines. It took concerted negotiations with the USN to get permission to outfit the exterior of one of their subs as a German U-boat, Schuler, Telegram to Ford, 6 September 1930, Ford correspondence, Lilly Library, IU.
29 The schooner also appeared in The Sea Wolf (Alfred Santell, 1930) and The Painted Woman (Blystone, 1932), see the American Film Institute Catalog entry on The Painted Woman.
30 Exhibitors Daily Review (9 Oct 1930): 6.
31 Film Daily (29 Oct 1930): 8; Film Daily (4 Dec 1930): 5.

the schooner, O'Brien and another crew member (Harry Tenbrook) must shout to be heard over the sound of sails and rigging flapping in a high wind. As the dinghy nears the ship, the voices of the Spanish-speaking sailors on the dinghy and the English-speaking crew on the schooner interfere with one another and both are underscored by the sound of waves lapping against the hulls of the ships. Again, O'Brien can be heard shouting at the top of his voice to make himself heard over sea and sailors. Here, Ford seems to be actively pushing the limits of the recording technology with much more concern to situate speech within a range of environmental sounds than to secure a pristine rendering of the dialogue. The film's sound, as well as August's terrific cinematography, which often frames the *Metha Nelson* from a position on the moving U-boat or vice versa, forcefully places the spectator amid sea and ships.

While Ford's working conditions changed radically with the one-two punch of the onset of the Depression and the initiation of sync-sound filmmaking, the period proved fruitful for the director nonetheless. Despite the restricted shooting schedules and lower budgets necessitated by the deterioration of the studio's financial position, the director was able to take greater control over script development thanks to his collaborations with McGuinness, Nichols and Collier. Further, the relationships he established with Nichols, August and McLaglen at this time would have major ramifications for his filmmaking technique and style throughout the 1930s. Moreover, in the context of the studio's efforts to showcase the mobility of their proprietary method of sound capture, Ford's preference for location shooting reasserted itself. Thus, the films made after *The Black Watch* diverged from the studio-production methods employed in the late 1920s silents, even as Ford and August continued to integrate low-key atmospheric lighting for certain shots and scenes. Finally, the combination of greater control over scripts and location shooting enabled Ford to confront the technological problems posed by

sound with relative autonomy and increasing daring.

The Influence of *What Price Glory*

Five of the six films Ford made during the early sound period have military plots, subplots or episodes. *The Black Watch* may be divided into a main story taken from Talbot Mundy's novel *King of the Khyber Rifles* about Captain King, an agent for the British Raj, and a frame story added by Ford and his screenwriters in which King, a member of the titular Scottish regiment, is sent on a secret mission to India. Not only do *Salute* and *Seas Beneath* deal thematically with the Navy, they could not have been made as they were without the cooperation of Naval authorities. For *Born Reckless*, adapted from Donald Henderson Clarke's 1929 gangster novel *Louis Beretti*, Ford and his screenwriters built up an incident in the novel in which Beretti serves in the AEF in France during World War I. Ford recalled that the largely comic section concerning the enlisted men was what interested him most about the project.[32]

It is often assumed that Ford's interest in the military sprang from Mary Ford's family connections with the Navy and the couple's frequent fraternization with Navy officers and their wives.[33] However it seems likely that the play *What Price Glory* and its many film adaptations provided an additional impetus and important context for this emphasis in his films. The play, by Maxwell Anderson and Laurence Stallings, opened on Broadway in 1924. Kenneth Macgowan succinctly described it as "unromantic about war and women … neither patriotic nor respectable".[34] It was widely admired for its funny and cynical depiction of the sexual rivalry between two hard-boiled Marines amidst the chaos of trench warfare on the front lines in France during World War I. The play would be important for Ford, who directed a stage version in 1949 and a film adaptation in 1952.[35] His correspondence indicates that he be-

32   Bogdanovich, *John Ford*, 52.
33   Dan Ford, 56–57; McBride, 122–123, 126.
34   Kenneth Macgowan, "Introduction", *Famous American Plays of the 1920s* (New York: Dell, 1959), 19.
35   Gallagher, 410.

came friends with Stallings, who was also the screenwriter on the 1952 remake of *What Price Glory*, as well as on *3 Godfathers* (1949), *She Wore a Yellow Ribbon* (1949) and *The Sun Shines Bright* (1953).[36]

In the late 1920s, Ford was clearly influenced by the two major silent films drawing on *What Price Glory* – Walsh's 1926 film and King Vidor's *The Big Parade* (MGM, 1925), loosely adapted from a story of the same name by Stallings.[37] Ford reportedly helped direct some of the battle scenes in Walsh's film.[38] He also took up two of its actors for his own stock company: not only Victor McLaglen, but Jack Pennick, who first appeared as an extra in *What Price Glory* before taking a small part as Joseph's army buddy in *4 Sons*, the first of many such appearances in Ford's films. Echoes of major scenes from *The Big Parade* appear in both *4 Sons* and *The Black Watch*. In *The Big Parade,* Jim (John Gilbert), sheltering in a shell-hole from enemy fire, crawls out in response to the cries of a wounded comrade. Finding his buddy dead, Jim takes shelter in another shell-hole where he exchanges fire with a German soldier. As the German boy lies dying, they share a cigarette. In *4 Sons*, Ford reworked this incident into the recognition scene between Joseph and his dying brother. In *The Black Watch*, the terrific sequences set in France during World War I in which the regiment traverses difficult, wooded terrain under enemy fire recall the Belleau Woods sequence in *The Big Parade*.

The transition to sound inaugurated many Fox sequels to Walsh's 1926 adaptation of *What Price Glory*, with Victor McLaglen and Edmund Lowe reprising their roles as Flagg and Quirt. The most successful of these, Walsh's *The Cock-Eyed World* (1929), blocked the scheduled openings of other Fox releases when it was held over for a

record five weeks at the Roxy.[39] It was followed by two other Flagg and Quirt comedies: *Women of All Nations* (Walsh, 1931) and *Hot Pepper* (Blystone, 1933). Although Flagg and Quirt remained Marines in these films, there was little or no emphasis on the rigors of war. The men strategized for advantage with a succession of women, quarreled and fought, but were nonetheless bound by their underlying friendship and unquenchable thirst for alcohol. In other films derivative of *What Price Glory*, McLaglen played a rough sailor or stoker fond of liquor and women. In *Captain Lash* (Blystone, 1929) he was paired with a comic sidekick played by Clyde Cook and in *Hot for Paris* (Walsh, 1929) with El Brendel.[40] This group of films cemented McLaglen's comic ugly-mug persona. The *Variety* review of *Captain Lash* noted that McLaglen had "a roughneck part that fits him to the life", and additionally noted: "Fighting or wooing McLaglen is a joy. This player is runner up to Wolheim for capitalizing a homely pan. The radiant smile that can break through that ugly map is a drama in itself."[41]

Many aspects of the *What Price Glory* films were congenial to Ford. Most obviously, the comic treatment of drinking and bar fights was evident in his films from the very beginning of his career – as in *Straight Shooting* – and continued to the end – as in *Donovan's Reef*. It should be noted however that in McLaglen's two starring roles for Ford in this period, *Hangman's House* and *The Black Watch*, he played straight dramatic parts. Moreover, the negative reviews of his performance in *The Black Watch* implicitly compared it to the Flagg roles. Critics considered the actor incapable of carrying the love scenes with Myrna Loy in the role of Yasmini. The *New York Times* suggested that "it was perhaps embarrassing for McLaglen to have to speak some of the romantic

36 Ford to Zach [?], Mar? 1943 [archivist date], refers to previous Ford birthday celebrations with Stallings, John Thomason and Merian C. Cooper; Ford to Mary Ford, 19 Jul 1943 [archivist date], indicates that he socialized with Stallings and Frank Wead when all three were in the services during World War II, Ford correspondence, Lilly Library, IU.

37 For a discussion of the variants see Lea Jacobs, "Men without Women: The Avatars of *What Price Glory*", *Film History*, 17/2–3 (2005): 307–333.

38 Gallagher, 658; McBride, 154.

39 "Fox's Bookings Jammed by Hold-Over *World*", *Variety* (28 Aug 1929): 12. According to Solomon, 137, it was Fox's second highest earner of the year.

40 These may have also been partly inspired by Josef von Sternberg's *The Docks of New York* (1928) in which George Bancroft plays a tough stoker with Clyde Cook in the supporting role.

41 *Variety* (6 Feb 1929): 18. Stage and screen actor Louis Wolheim played Flagg in the original stage version of *What Price Glory*.

lines", while the *Variety* review concluded: "It will probably take much cajoling to induce McLaglen to play another love scene (house giggled at it), and they'd better give this boy some virile conversation if he's going to retain his popularity."[42] Ford attributed the problems with *The Black Watch* to a love scene requested by Sheehan and directed by Lumsden Hare, the film's dialogue director, after Ford had left the production and gone to Annapolis to shoot *Salute*.[43] However in retrospect it seems likely that the film's problems were the product of clumsy dialogue throughout, problems partly generated by the pseudo-archaic English that McGuinness took over from the novel.[44] In any case, McLaglen did not appear in any of the early sound films made by Ford's unit after *The Black Watch*. (The two did not work together again until Ford procured his services for *The Lost Patrol* and *The Informer* at RKO.) His absence may have been an advantage in some respects: the director was able to draw selectively from the *What Price Glory* films for his early sound films without being condemned to the repetition of the formula. In this way, Ford made the plot his own.

Ford made a couple of uncharacteristic experiments with the ribald sexual humor associated with Flagg and Quirt. The opening of *Men Without Women* is punctuated by a variety of comic interchanges between the sailors of the *S–13* and the prostitutes who work in and around a Shanghai Bar.[45] Chief Petty Officer Cobb, the "swordsman of the *S–13*" (Walter McGrail) succeeds with two women in an incident reminiscent of *What Price Glory* and *The Cock-Eyed World*.[46] A funny scene in *Born Reckless* appropriates the situation and style of mixed French and English dialogue found in Anderson and Stallings's play as Beretti (Edmund Lowe), stationed in France with the AEF, bargains with the innkeeper's daughter (Yola d'Avril), trading Army sugar for kisses.

The experiments with sexual humor did not, however, have a lasting impact on Ford's style. The director seems eventually to have abjured the amoral comic treatment of promiscuity. Even Cobb, the "swordsman of the *S–13*", repents of his many affairs and thinks of his wife and children when he faces death near the close of *Men Without Women*. More important for Ford's career was the typical sidelining of the romance plot in the *What Price Glory* films in favor of an emphasis on male rivalry and friendship. Following Warren Hymer's endearing performance as a tough, dim-witted sailor in *Men Without Women*, Ford began pairing him with better-looking and more suave companions for a Flagg/Quirt-style contrast. In *Born Reckless*, Beretti's attempts to go straight following his military service are threatened by his continuing loyalty to his old gang, especially his pal Big Shot (Hymer), who he has known since they were kids in the New York tenements. In a simultaneously suspenseful and comic sequence he helps Big Shot confront an informer within the gang. Beretti is mildly disapproving after Big Shot murders the rat but nonetheless helps him establish an alibi. Their relationship cannot be sustained after Big Shot and the gang kidnap a little girl, however, leading to their final, deadly, confrontation.

Up the River, often discussed today as a film with Spencer Tracy and Humphrey Bogart, was seen by contemporary audiences as a comedy that featured Tracy, in the role of St. Louis, and Hymer, in the role of Dannemora Dan (Bogart was simply there for the romance plot). *Motion Picture News* described the film's opening:

> The story has St. Louis and Dannemora Dan break jail and then fall out when the former

---

42 Mordaunt Hall, "Past Week's Pictures", *New York Times* (26 May 1929): X7; *Variety* (15 May 1929): 20.
43 Bogdanovich, *John Ford*, 50. Ford was likely the source of a complaint about these additions just after the film's release, see "Hot Love Scene Causes Big Laugh and Dialogue is Cut", *Motion Picture News* (18 May 1929): 1713, and the review in *Variety* (15 May 1929): 20.
44 For example: "*Yasmini*: Thou couldst find riches and glory in my service. *King*: In *your* service even *death* .... *Harrim Bey*: But it is not wise to lead an infidel among the faithful. *Yasmini*: Infidel or not, mine eyes hath marked him for my service. *Harrim Bey*: Thine eyes rove more than becomes a goddess."
45 The surviving print, preserved by the Museum of Modern Art, New York, is an "international version" with minimal dialogue but full effects and score, produced for distribution abroad. In what follows, I have tried to quote lines of dialogue that can be heard or were cited in contemporary reviews. Thanks to Dave Kehr for clarifying the status of the print.
46 Edwin Schallert, "Sub-Sea Tragedy", *Los Angeles Times* (16 Feb 1930): D3, compared Ford's film to Walsh's.

doublecrosses Danny and makes his getaway, leaving Danny to shift for himself. Dannemora gets religion and joins the Brotherhood of Man. The religious fervor burns until Danny spots St. Louis riding around town in a benzine buggy with two swell-looking gals on the leash. Then he bursts into flame, socks St. Louis and both are sent back to prison.[47]

Variety noted that "Spencer Tracy and Warren Hymer, as the laugh team, take the picture all of the time".[48] Edwin Schallert of the *Los Angeles Times* wrote: "The picture relies on the dumb deadpan comedy of Hymer, who is undoubtedly its funniest actor. Tracy is the polished purveyor of humor, and Hymer is his foil, all but stealing most of the scenes in which he appears."[49]

In addition to providing a narrative model for Ford's early sound films, *What Price Glory* also served as a reference for handling dialogue. The play was notorious for its use of curse words. Kenneth Macgowan told a story current in the period of a dowager who, "as the curtain fell on *What Price Glory*, muttered to her companion: 'Where the hell are my goddam overshoes?'".[50] But the dialogue of the play was not simply scabrous, it was deliberately low and rough, succinct and funny. Note, for example, this amusing antagonistic exchange, somewhere between pure vaudeville and an anticipation of *Waiting for Godot*, that initiates the final duel between Flagg and Quirt:

> *Quirt*: Flagg, you're out of this here detail. Your hands off my business after that dirty trick you put over on me. If I kill you there isn't a court can touch me for it in this man's army.
> *Flagg*: Quirt, you're drunk.
> *Quirt*: Both of us.
> *Flagg*: Yeah, both of us.
> *Quirt*: Well, then, Flagg, you're drunk. What are you going to do about it?
> *Flagg*: I'm gonna have a drink. [*Turns to bar and takes bottle; pours two drinks.*]

Quirt: Both of us.

Flagg: Yeah, both of us.[51]

A similarly clipped exchange, a combination of comedy and menace, leads up to the final confrontation between Beretti and Big Shot in *Born Reckless*. They stand face to face at the bar, never taking their eyes off each other, their hands in their coat pockets where their guns are hidden. The dialogue is spoken very slowly and pitched low with long pauses between the sentences. Hymer's thick New York accent is faintly echoed in Lowe's pronounciation.

Big Shot: Out kinda early, ain't ya?

Beretti: Yeah. You too.

Big Shot: Yeah.

Beretti: What's on your mind, Big?

Big Shot: I guess you know.

Beretti: Yeah.

Big Shot: How's your old lady, Louey? It's been a long time since I seen her. Too long, I guess.

Beretti: She's OK.

Big Shot: She always did a guy good.

Beretti: Yeah.

Big Shot: She's been just like a mother to me. The only one I ever knew.

Beretti: Sure. I remember when we was together. The time I got that slug in the shoulder.

Big Shot: All the other kids run away.

Beretti: Yeah. It was you who took me to the hospital.

Big Shot: You used to be a good guy Louey.

Beretti: Yeah. It's tough.

Big Shot: Too bad you couldn't keep your nose clean.

Beretti: Yeah. Too bad.

Shortly after the conclusion of this interchange, Big drops his drinking glass and both open fire through their coats.

The structure of the dialogue in *Men Without Women*, like that of *Born Reckless*, was indebted

---

47   *Up the River* review, *Motion Picture News* (11 Oct 1930): 53.
48   *Up the River* review, *Variety* (15 Oct 1930): 29.
49   "Prison Comedy Fantastic Burlesque Idea Pervades *Up the River*", *Los Angeles Times* (12 Oct 1930): 13.
50   Macgowan, 13.
51   *What Price Glory*, in Maxwell Anderson and Laurence Stallings, *Three American Plays* (New York: Harcourt, Brace and Company, 1926), 80–81.

to the *What Price Glory* films and the play, as contemporary reviewers noted:

> *What Price Glory* inaugurated the style on the stage, and the motion-picture production of the war story brought to the screen the jargon of men of adventure and action. *The Front Page* introduced realistic talk of reporters and associates in the newspaper world; *The Cock-Eyed World* presented the lively talk of marines in various parts of the world, and *Men Without Women* brings the terms and expletives of those who go down to sea in the submarine service.[52]

A prime example of Ford and Nichol's dialogue in *Men Without Women* occurs after a collision that sinks the incapacitated *S–13*. The men find themselves trapped, unable to make contact with any ships on the surface, and with a limited amount of oxygen. Some of them quarrel with Chief Torpedoman Burke (Kenneth McKenna) and each other about how quickly to release the canned air. Curly (George LeGuere), an inexperienced young sailor, goes berserk, ranting about going to hell and threatening to blow up the sub with explosives. But the old sea dogs stoically quip. An unnamed sailor breathes and exclaims: "Gee, I'd sure like to shake hands with the guy who discovered oxygen!" To which Radioman Jenkins (Stuart Erwin) replies: "He should have discovered more of it." After finding a canister of alcohol, Costello (J. Farrell MacDonald) adds: "You boys can have the oxygen … I'll take the gin." In an attempt to rally the men, Ensign Price (Frank Albertson) makes a noble speech: "Fellows, if we've got to go, let's die like men! Nobody will ever know how we met the end … but let's prove to ourselves that we can meet it like heroes!" This brings forth a gently mocking response from the men:

> *Jenkins*: Don't laugh at the kid, Costello … he's serious!"
>
> *Costello*: Well, he ain't gonna make no hero out of me!

Variety's analysis of such passages is apt:

> The punch of the acting is the surprise comedy bits of a number of minor characters. It is these

touches and the grim comedy of the lines that lift the picture out of melodrama to an illusion of reality that doubles its effect. Dialog is remarkable for its unlabored force, as a writer invited to slip a punch gag into a tragic scene like this might easily overstep. Not so here. The lines come with a naturalness that is innocent of preparation – with a patness and plausibility that point their grim unexpectedness. Dialog handling is a really high class bit of unassuming craftsmanship.[53]

In his interview with Peter Bogdanovich, Ford praised Dudley Nichols's script for *Men Without Women*: "He had never written a script before, but he was very good, and he had the same idea I had about paucity of dialogue".[54] But the dialogue is not just reduced. The talk of the ordinary sailors is rendered understated and tough in contrast with Curly's prolonged outbursts. Its stoicism stands out in contrast with the Ensign's heroics. Thus, taking *What Price Glory* as a model, Ford and Nichols began to showcase the diction, speaking rhythms and humor of tough but ordinary working men.

Scoring with Songs in *The Black Watch*

Ford's predilection for songs, marches and dances is evident from his best-known films, not to mention film titles such as *My Darling Clementine*, *She Wore a Yellow Ribbon* and *When Willie Comes Marching Home*. The preference for folk songs is apparent as early as *The Iron Horse*. Corporal Casey leads his construction crew, initially made up of Irish laborers but eventually incorporating Chinese, in "Drill, Ye Tarriers, Drill", a work song first performed in the U.S. in the late 1880s by the Irish comic singer Thomas Casey.[55] In *Hangman's House*, when Hogan returns to Ireland in disguise, he is recognized by a confederate who hears him singing "The Shan Van Voght", a traditional Irish song from the rebellion of 1798 that gained currency within the late-nineteenth-century Fenian movement. The transition to sound

---

52   "Film Features Realism", *Los Angeles Times* (4 Mar 1930): A9.
53   *Men without Women* review, *Variety* (5 Feb 1930): 24.
54   Bogdanovich, *John Ford*, 52.
55   Thomas Casey and Charles Connolly, "Drill, Ye Tarriers, Drill", see the entry on the song in Robert B. Waltz and David G. Engle, eds., *The Traditional Ballad Index*, http://balladindex.org/.

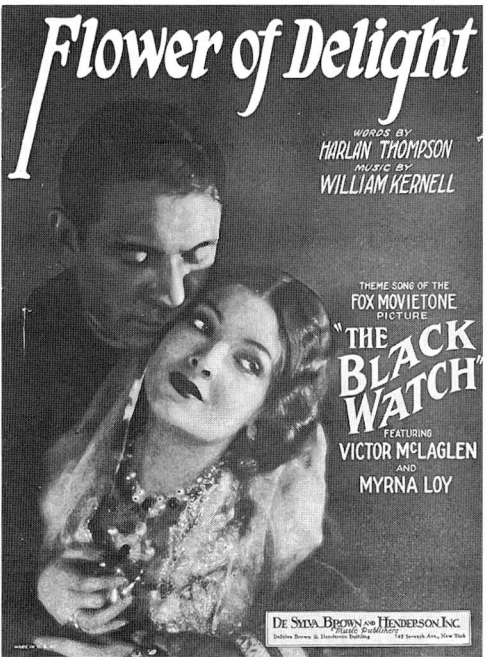

2.1

gave much greater latitude to the director's enthusiasm for song. Reporting on the production of *Men Without Women*, the *New York Times* noted that when Ford decided that some "sailor chanteys were needed to add authenticity", he called on four extras to make up a quartet and added his baritone to the mix.[56]

The main plot of *The Black Watch*, set in India and encompassing the love story, is dominated by a theme song written for the production – "Flower of Delight", with lyrics by Harlan Thompson and music by William Kernell (figure 2.1).[57] But the music for the frame story, concerning the titular regiment, is comprised of pipe-and-drum marches and Scottish folk tunes, as well as a drunken Cockney rendition of "Home, Sweet Home". The frame story seems oddly overdeveloped in relation to the main plot, at least partly as a result of Ford's experimentation with the panoply of music in these sections of the film.

It occupies the whole of the first act, twenty-three minutes of the film's ninety-minute running time. Additional scenes of the regiment in action are interpolated at the beginning of acts three and four, and King's inevitable reconciliation with his fellow officers after Yasmini's death provides the epilogue. All of these scenes rely heavily on music for their dramatic effects. The action advances in and through song.

All of the scenes with the regiment include performances by a pipe-and-drum band (figure 2.2), which plays two marches traditionally associated with the actual Black Watch regiment.[58] The title of the opening march, "All the Blue Bonnets are over the Border",[59] refers to the traditionally blue-hatted Scots who fought against the English in the border wars of the middle ages. Sir Walter Scott's lyrics for the tune include the following:

> Trumpets are sounding, war-steeds are bounding
> Stand to your arms and march in good order
> England shall many a day tell of the bloody fray
> When the blue bonnets come over the Border.[60]

This reference may not seem particularly apropos given that the film concerns a royal regiment about to march off to fight for King and country. But its relevance has to do with the idea of travel – the blue bonnets are again preparing to cross the border. The march recurs several times in the film in this connection: when the Colonel announces that the regiment has been posted to France, at the train station when the men depart for the continent, and later as the men are scrambling through the French countryside under fire.

The second march, "Wha Saw the Forty Twa", seems to be the actual anthem of the regiment, which in the mid-eighteenth century was known as the 42nd (Highland) Regiment of Foot and colloquially as the Black Watch.[61] The song about the 42nd Regiment refers to the troop marching along the Broomielaw beside the River

56 "In the Studios", *New York Times* (1 Dec 1929): 143.
57 William Kernell and Harlan Thompson, "Flower of Delight" (New York: De Sylva, Brown and Henderson, 1929).
58 I have not been able to identify the band, but the group seems professional.
59 See "Blue Bonnets Over the Border (1): Annotations", *Traditional Tune Archive*, https://tunearch.org/. The march is also heard in Ford's *Mary of Scotland*.
60 Scott's lyric, sung to "the ancient air of 'Blue Bonnets over the Border'", appears in chapter 25 of his novel *The Monastery* (1820).
61 Now the Black Watch, 3rd Battalion, Royal Regiment of Scotland.

2.2

2.3

Clyde in Glasgow (the traditional point of embarcation for Scottish troops shipping abroad). Perhaps they are going to war, although the song also teasingly refers to how they are dressed.[62]

> Wha saw the Forty Twa?
> Wha saw them gang awa?
> Wha saw the Forty Twa,
> Marchin' doon the Broomielaw?
> Some o' them had kilts and bunnets
> Some o' them had nane ava',
> Some o' them had tartan troosers
> Marchin' tae the Broomielaw!

The song also has an older Jacobite lyric, reported by the Scottish poet James Hogg:[63]

> Wha wad'na fecht for Charlie,
> Wha wad'na draw the sword,
> Wha wad'na up and rally
> At the Royal Prince's word?

Ford used this rousing march to evoke the regiment's martial traditions. The band plays it in the opening scene during a toast to the King, as the regiment marches in formation into the train station at the end of act one, and later during a dark moment of the war as, with the Colonel wounded, the men of the regiment gather to penetrate the wood held by the enemy.

The marches alternate with Scottish folk songs: "Annie Laurie", "Auld Lang Syne" and "Loch Lomond". These folk songs were not simply relevant to the shared national history of the regiment, they were also selected, and the film staged and cut, to make the words uniquely rele-

vant to specific dramatic situations. For example, in the opening scene in the officers' mess, the Colonel calls for a song, and four officers commence "Annie Laurie". The quartet sings the first four lines of the song as a messenger arrives summoning King to the Field Marshall's office. Cut briefly to the soloist (David Percy) who sings "Gave me her promise true/Which ne'er forgot will be … ". Cut to King who takes leave of his commander as the song continues. Cut to a spectacular new framing behind the rear door of the room (figure 2.3) as the verse concludes "I'd lay me doon an' dee". The last four lines are repeated as McLaglen extends the duration of his exit to allow for it. An extra helps McLaglen put on an overcoat. He takes out his pipe, lights it, listens. On "And for bonnie Annie Laurie/I'd lay me doon an' dee", King puts on his hat, looks back at the group, and exits right. Through repetition and emphasis, the song's original somewhat brooding pledge of love until death is transformed into a soldier's oath. The men of the regiment sing the refrain again while marching through the mud after their arrival on the Continent.

In addition to enhancing drama, the song score of *The Black Watch* provided Ford with multiple opportunities to experiment with timing his scenes to music. The director may well have employed music in this way during the silent period, when musicians were often present on set, and could help the actors synchronize their move-

---

62 See the entry: "Wha Saw the Forty Twa: Annotations", *Traditional Tune Archive*.
63 See the entry: "Wha Wad'na Fecht for Charlie: Annotations", *Traditional Tune Archive*.

ments in, for example, fights or love scenes. One also finds several hints of such efforts in his later work. An often cited example is the director's collaboration with Max Steiner to synchronize the initial shots of McLaglen walking with the performance of the composer's cue for the character of Gypo in *The Informer*.[64] Later in his career, the director retained Danny Borzage to play accordion on set in many of his productions, sometimes for mood music, but also to enable the pre-synchronization of certain scenes.[65] Danny Borzage can be seen performing on camera for the dance that turns into a brawl in *The Long Voyage Home*.

While "Flower of Delight" is not the most musically satisfying part of the score for *The Black Watch*, it organizes the action in several scenes. The song breaks into eight-bar units, an ABCCAB structure, with a four-bar introduction and coda. It is first heard without lyrics over the credits. It returns in the second act, following, and in direct contrast to, a haunting Islamic prayer sung as men kneel in the public square in Peshawar. Yasmini is asleep in her bedroom. A maid lifts the veil that covers her face and awakens her gently with the news that the "Strong One" is on the street below. As she rises, an instrumental version of the A section of "Flower of Delight" begins. One can see the actress waiting, timing her actions to the song's extension as she rearranges her veil, stands and slowly walks to the window over the duration of the eight bars. After the cut to a closer view of her at the window the B section begins. A nondiegetic male voice sings the lyrics as she opens the shutter: "Flower of delight, Come to my burning arms ...." This section of the song underscores a shot-reverse-shot segment of Yasmini exchanging glances with King on the street below. Ford cuts back to a long shot of Yasmini turning gracefully away from the window for the coda. The song is thus clearly identified with Yasmini's attraction to King, despite the fact that it is sung by a male voice and the lyrics are seemingly addressed to a woman (as-

2.4

suming that Victor McLaglen is no flower of delight).

The shots and scenes which mixed spoken dialogue and music in *The Black Watch* were almost certainly recorded on set with musicians off-camera. Re-recording to combine music, speech and effects in post-production did not become the norm until after 1934 due to the fact that early sound-on-film systems generated a great deal of noise that was exacerbated by re-recording or what was then called "dubbing". As Barry Salt has noted, the earliest sync-sound films usually had "either dialogue or music on the sound track, but hardly ever both together, unless they had been recorded simultaneously".[66] Figure 2.4 shows a sound engineer in the booth on a film set. Such technicians would adjust volume levels in real time during performance, a typical arrangement both for recording film sound and broadcasting radio sound in the late 1920s and early 1930s.

Consider the integration of theme song and

64   Kathryn Kalinak, "Max Steiner and the Classical Hollywood Film Score: An Analysis of *The Informer*", in Clifford McCarty, ed., *Film Music 1* (New York: Garland, 1989), 124–125.
65   McBride, 150.
66   Salt, 234; Jacobs, "The Innovation of Re-recording", 9–11.

dialogue in the four-way conversation between Yasmini, her general Harim Bey, her aide-de-camp Rewa Chunga and King at the point when the spy asks to join her army. "Flower of Delight" runs under the entire course of the scene and it seems that the actors react to changes in its speed and dynamics. Tempi have been mutually adjusted so that the B section ("Come to my arms...") registers at appropriate points in the conversation. The first iteration occurs just after King, pretending to be an outlaw to gain acceptance, confirms that he is "a fugitive and a murderer". The refrain unfolds as Myrna Loy silently motions for him to take a seat beside her. The conversation becomes denser and moves more quickly over the C section, as Yasmini overrides Harim Bey's objections. The reprise of the B section coincides with Loy's line: "Thou hast the build of a man, Captain King." After she exits, Rewa Chunga begins to taunt King, the supposed murderer, his words extending through the coda. At the close of his last sentence, and the final cadence of the song, he strokes a stringed instrument that he carries as if to stress the coincidence of words and music. This conversation was evidently designed to let the theme song carry the force of Yasmini's excitement at seeing King over the verbal objections of her political allies. But this does not quite work: the actors speak absurdly slowly, pausing between words and between phrases to allow the lyrics to be heard. Later repetitions of the theme song have the same dramatic function, but since the music is performed without the lyrics they are less intrusive.

The director's interest in the close interpenetration of song and action appears to much better effect in the scene at the train station. At this point in the story King has been assigned the mission of preventing Yasmini and her army from invading India through the Khyber Pass. Thus, he cannot accompany the regiment to France. And, because the mission is secret, he has been instructed to explain to his fellow officers that he has requested this posting and even to allow them to think him a coward in consequence. Nevertheless, King goes to the station to see off his younger brother, Malcolm, who is leaving with the regiment.

In shot 46 we briefly see a woman in a Salvation Army uniform step out of the crowd of onlookers and initiate a song for the soldiers standing in formation nearby. She sings "Loch Lomond" unaccompanied in an extremely slow tempo with long-held vowels that readily permits the layering of other sounds. Once the song has started, the film cuts away from the singer, and the music floats free of the initial source (as noted above it was likely sung on set if off camera). Cut to King standing among the crowd on the platform looking off right as he waits for the regiment to arrive. Over the words "O ye'll tak' the high road, and I'll tak' the low road/And I'll be in Scotland afore ye", the Colonel and some other senior officers approach from the left and King snaps to attention when he notices them. The Colonel speaks: "Sorry you are not going with us, King." An off-screen voice calls out orders to C Company and the Colonel immediately turns his back on King and walks away. As the singer begins the next phrase, two of the other senior officers of the regiment chime in, echoing their commander: "Well, cheerio, King", and "India, eh?" The officers' words of leave-taking, with the implication that King's assignment to India is less than honorable, thus match the distinction made in the song lyrics between high and low roads. This implication is augmented by the fact that King himself has already complained to the Field Marshall that his mission – to destroy Yasmini, by seducing her if necessary – is a "dirty job".

The staging and accompanying sound effects change radically with the last two lines of the refrain: "But me and my true love will never meet again,/On the bonnie, bonnie banks o' Loch Lomond." For these lines, the impending separation of the men and their families is brought to the fore. Under the line "But me and my true love … ." a drumbeat begins. The troops march on frame over the words "... never meet again", heard without any sonic interference. Two off-screen voices from the crowd are then layered over the subsequent phrase. "On the bonnie, bonnie banks …." overlaps with an off-screen male voice shouting "Aay, Chuck, I'll see ya in Aberdeen", followed by an off-screen female voice that calls indistinctly and breaks into a sob. Over the last words of the

42

last phrase " … o' Loch Lomond", the off-screen sergeant calls "C Company halt", so that the musical cadence coincides with the cessation of drums and marching feet.

As Malcolm runs on, a bit late and out of step with his men, his entrance is synchronized with the reprise of the refrain, the female voice now augmented by a male choir. Cut in closer on King and Malcolm as they clasp hands over "… the high road and I'll tak' the low road". An off-screen voice calls "Daddy, daddy" and a little girl with a Union Jack appears at the barrier separating the onlookers from the soldiers. King lifts her over the barrier and she runs down the platform.

Over "But me and my true love …" the men return to the pose of clasped hands. Over " … will never meet again" King adjusts the lapels of Malcolm's uniform as the puffing of the steam train is temporarily added to the mix. Over the beginning of the last phrase, "On the bonnie, bonnie banks … ", King turns the young man around to rejoin the line and adjusts the buckles on his pack. Cut to a medium-long shot of a train car with a group of soldiers at the window, singing the final phrase " … o' Loch Lomond". The song thus concludes, as it began, anchored in an on-screen source.

Ford's preference for folk music provided significant advantages over original movie theme songs such as "Flower of Delight". Folk music carried a history of associations, and served as a convenient shorthand for evoking ethnic and national contexts. Because familiarity with folk songs, dance tunes, hymns and marches could be assumed, repetition could be used judiciously, and reserved for emphasis. This alleviated the need for the incessant repetition of a tune to ensure it would be recognized – a feature of theme songs that ultimately turned film producers and critics against them.[67] And, because they were already known, folk song lyrics were immediately available for word play. Like taking a verse from Shake-speare or the King James Bible out of context, Ford could bend familiar lyrics to new purposes.[68]

But despite the differences between folk songs and theme songs, it is important to recognize that Ford's use of music also shared deep affinities with theme-song scoring practices and the older traditions of silent-film accompaniment on which they drew. They all required time – four bars, eight bars, twelve bars – for the tune to play out. During the silent era, the delicate process of fitting songs and song fragments to the time of the depicted action was in the hands of musicians playing live accompaniment in far-flung theaters, far removed from the director's control. The transition to sound made it possible for Ford and McGuinness and August, stopwatches in hand,[69] to stage action and dialogue to music and to capture them together on film. At the same time, however, the presence of spoken dialogue made it more difficult to let the music sing. Ford had to figure out plausible ways to reduce dialogue and effects or devise strategies for blending them with music for the necessary duration of a tune. The slow pace of the frame story in *The Black Watch* is partly a result of his efforts to accomplish this.

The industry practice of placing songs at the center of early sound-film accompaniment formed the basis for Ford's idiosyncratic, and eventually anachronistic, approach to film music. His early sound films are filled with songs and singable tunes. In *Salute*, repetitions of "Anchors Aweigh" unite the disparate sources of footage as it is performed by the actors on location, by a marching band on the Naval Academy parade grounds and by the band that was present on the football field in the Movietone footage. In *Born Reckless*, the sequence in France is a veritable operetta. It begins with a quartet of soldiers in a bar singing a chorus of "On the Banks of the Wabash, Far Away" (with a pronounced baritone that one likes to think was Ford's). As Beretti walks off into the kitchen with the pretty French girl, all

---

67 Katherine Spring, *Saying It with Songs: Popular Music and the Coming of Sound to Hollywood Cinema* (New York: Oxford University Press, 2013), 122–126.

68 As our familiarity with traditional song has waned, teaching Ford's films increasingly requires group sing-a-longs.

69 "Victor McLaglen's Film", *New York Times* (19 May 1929): X4, on the changes sound wrought on Ford's production methods, reported that for *The Black Watch* he kept to the script much more than he had in the past, that he and McGuinness timed the lines with a stopwatch and that cameraman Joe August was also equipped with a stopwatch for rehearsals.

the soldiers in the bar break into a chorus of "Mademoiselle from Armentières". They improvise new lyrics to tease the recently demoted sergeant who interrupts their song. Further repetitions of the chorus continue, heard faintly under Beretti's negotiations with the girl in the kitchen. The bugle calling all of the men to the front is followed by a non-diegetic rendition of "The Caissons Go Rolling Along". In *Up the River*, the great moment when Dannemora Dan, now marching with the Brotherhood of Man, runs into St. Louis and slugs him is scored with an amazingly ironic use of the hymn "Brighten the Corner Where You Are". Long after Hollywood had moved in the direction of through-composed orchestral background scoring, Ford would continue to seek out and utilize recognizable, singable tunes for his music tracks as a prime means of creating dramatic effects and developing thematic ideas.

Multiple-Camera Shooting and the Long Take in *Arrowsmith*

Interviewed by Mel Gussow in the 1970s, Zanuck recalled Ford's well known proclivity for static long takes. "He was an artist. He painted a picture – in movement, in action, in still shots. He would never move a camera setup – move in or zoom in. You would look at the set and think, maybe you need a closeup, but you didn't."[70] As already discussed, however, Ford's first systematic experiments with long takes in *4 Sons* often involved the elaborate camera movements initiated by his exposure to Murnau's use of the "unchained camera". Although there are some interesting static long takes in *4 Sons*, it was not until Ford confronted the technical limitations of early sync-sound cinematography and the consequent industry practice of multiple-camera shooting that he consistently began to exploit the advantages of static long takes for staging and performance. *Arrowsmith* is not part of the set of early sound films made by Ford's unit at Fox. It was produced by

Samuel Goldwyn with Ford on loan from Fox in the early fall of 1931. It merits discussion here, however, because unlike the Fox films, the daily production reports and engineer's sound logs for *Arrowsmith* have been preserved and are available for research.[71] These provide rare insight into how sync-sound technology affected the director's shooting and staging techniques.

Multiple-camera shooting was the primary method of filming with synchronized sound from the earliest Vitaphone shorts to the end of 1931. Several technical problems contributed to the practice. In order to avoid recording camera noise, the camera was initially sequestered in a booth or "ice box" (figure 2.5) and somewhat later, encased in a heavy blimp.[72] Moving the camera around the set to create new setups thus became difficult and time-consuming. Another motivation for the

2.5

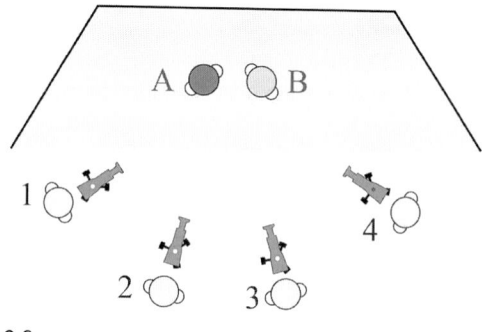

2.6

70   Mel Gussow, *Don't Say Yes Until I Finish Talking: A Biography of Darryl F. Zanuck* (New York: Doubleday and Company, 1971), 164.
71   *Arrowsmith* Production Reports, Samuel Goldwyn Papers, Box 4, Folder 26, Special Collections, Margaret Herrick Library, Academy of Motion Picture Arts and Sciences, Beverly Hills, California (hereafter Herrick Library, AMPAS).
72   David Bordwell, "The Introduction of Sound", in Bordwell, Staiger and Thompson, 298–308.

2.7

2.8

2.9

2.10

practice was the pronounced preference for un-interrupted sound takes in the early sound cinema. Editing sound was difficult prior to the invention of edge numbering and other devices for maintaining synchronization.[73] Figure 2.6 shows a present-day multiple-camera setup used for streaming or shooting a live television broadcast. In the early sound period, the cameras would have been enclosed in some way and one camera would have filmed the sound (in those studios that recorded sound on film rather than on disc) while others would have simultaneously photographed the action with different framings and slight variations in the angle of view. The editor would then have cut the picture track, matching it to the uninterrupted sound record. During multiple-camera shooting, the cameras tended to be stationary, although footage shot wild (without sound) was frequently inserted to introduce camera and figure movement before, after or during

a pause in a sync-sound conversation. It was also possible to record sync-sound dialogue with camera movement by panning or tilting cameras within a booth or, somewhat later, by placing a silenced or "blimped" camera on a dolly. But most commonly, the cameras were fixed in position, thereby restricting the movements of the actors during conversation scenes since they had to remain in view of all cameras simultaneously.

Multiple-camera shooting also diminished the sense of depth that could be achieved in the shot-reverse-shot configuration. It was hard for the cameramen to get in close to the actors for singles or over-the-shoulder shots since it was necessary to keep each camera out of the angle of view of the others. This meant editors did not have a nice variation of angle as they cut between interlocutors. David Bordwell has demonstrated the effects of multiple-camera shooting in a scene from the Warner Brothers film *The Lights of New*

73   Salt, 234–235.

2.11

2.12

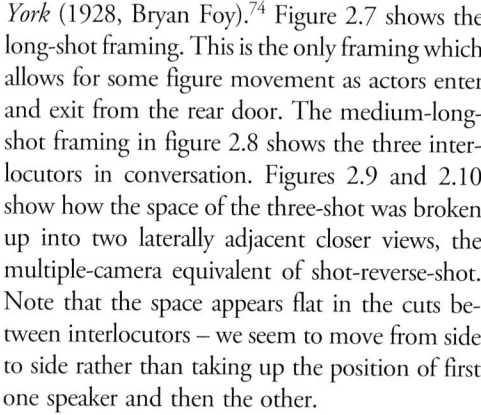

York (1928, Bryan Foy).[74] Figure 2.7 shows the long-shot framing. This is the only framing which allows for some figure movement as actors enter and exit from the rear door. The medium-long-shot framing in figure 2.8 shows the three interlocutors in conversation. Figures 2.9 and 2.10 show how the space of the three-shot was broken up into two laterally adjacent closer views, the multiple-camera equivalent of shot-reverse-shot. Note that the space appears flat in the cuts between interlocutors – we seem to move from side to side rather than taking up the position of first one speaker and then the other.

During the conversion to sound Ford, along with other directors such as William Wyler, Edmund Goulding, John Stahl and Howard Hawks, experimented with filming dialogue scenes in long takes. By this means they avoided the awkward framings and side-by-side cutting between adjacent views that we see in *Lights of New York*. Ford and Stahl in particular experimented extensively with long takes from fixed camera positions. Consider, for example, a shot of almost three minutes from *Seed* (1931, John Stahl). Lois Wilson, playing Peggy Carter, a mother of five, stands in back of her stove making soup while she confronts a rival for her husband's affections. The rival, Mildred (Genevieve Tobin), paces from foreground to background, hypocritically lauding Peggy's housekeeping skills and singing the praises of Peggy's husband (figures 2.11 and 2.12). Long

takes such as Stahl employed here offered an attractive alternative to the stylistic infelicities of staging and framing for multiple cameras. The actor could move with greater freedom and shots could be composed in greater depth. Moreover, the single, fixed take elevated the importance of small gestures by the actors. As she speaks or listens, Carter lifts the pot lid and stirs the soup, affirming her wifely and maternal role (figure 2.13). Mildred responds by lowering her veil and showing off her fur purse (figure 2.14).

It is important to recognize the novelty of this general approach to shooting conversation scenes for directors and actors used to the conventions of silent cinema. In the late 1920s dialogue scenes without intertitles, though possible, and of course championed by Carl Mayer, F. W. Murnau and others, were rare. For most filmmakers most of the time staging and shooting dialogue scenes involved anticipating the placement of intertitles by editors and title writers. Ford told Peter Bogdanovich: "In silent pictures we always had the actors speak the lines they were supposed to say anyway because there were too many lip readers in the audience."[75] Writing in 1919, the Danish director Urban Gad explained the way dialogue titles were inserted into scenes:

> Of course, the dialogue [title] must be so conceived as to match precisely with the acting … it must also be introduced precisely when it appears from the actors' expressions or move-

74 Bordwell, "Introduction of Sound", 305–306, discusses this example.
75 Bogdanovich, *John Ford*, 50.

46

2.13

2.14

ments that they are speaking just those words. Before a dialogue title is introduced, the actors have to be examined carefully over quite a long stretch of the film so as to locate the point at which glances and movements of the mouth and hands are appropriate. This point also has the advantage that the listener in the film will also have the right facial expression, since the director will have envisaged similar dialogue during shooting.[76]

That is, the editor sought to place the intertitles so that they "matched" the lines spoken by the actors. By the same token, the director and actors had to anticipate such a cut. Conversation scenes unfolded with the actors heightening and playing to the lines likely to be titled.

A scene from *4 Sons* illustrates Ford working around the alternation of picture and title that was at the core of dialogue scenes in the American silent cinema. In the scene, Colonel Von Stomm (Earle Fox) confronts Mother Bernle (Margaret Mann) and her youngest son Andreas (George Meeker) about the fact that her emigrant son Joseph is fighting on the American side in World War I. The scene contains a relatively long take of twenty-four seconds near the beginning and a very long take of fifty seconds at the end, but most of the scene is staged and acted in short takes, piecemeal fashion, in relation to the most important lines of dialogue. Following his entrance, Earle Fox as the commander takes a leisurely twenty-four seconds to build up to the accusation addressed to Mother Bernle in long shot: "You have a son in America. Give me his letters!" After the title, cut to a one-second reprise of the long shot. Cut to the mother's reply: "I have not heard from him in many months." Cut to a six-second closer view of the officer, his swagger stick reaching out to the mother in front of him, followed by the title: "The better for you! He is a traitor!" and return to the closer framing of Von Stomm for one second. Cut to a close up of the mother's reaction for ten seconds.

As the Colonel continues to insult Mother Bernle, cut away to Andreas who gestures to two framed government tributes on the wall and speaks to a sympathetic younger officer, an eight-second shot. Cut to the title: "He forgets my brothers Franz and Johann. They died fighting for the Fatherland." Cut back to Andreas and his interlocutor for four seconds.

In the scene's last shot, the fast-cut middle section gives way to the mother's prolonged reaction to the Colonel's plan to draft Andreas as recompense for Joseph's enlistment in the U.S. army. At the end of the second-to-last shot the Colonel gestures at Andreas with his swagger stick, followed by the title: "Report at the barracks tonight! You will take your brother's place!" Cut back to a longer framing of the same gesture (figure 2.15). As the Colonel snaps down the swagger stick, the mother comes from off screen to stand between him and her son. She comes

76   Urban Gad, *Der Film: seine Mittel seine Ziele,* trans. Julia Koppel (Berlin: Schuster & Loeffler, 1921), 245–246, originally published as *Filmen, dens midler og maal* (Copenhagen: Gyldendalske Boghandel/Nordisk Forlag, 1919).

2.15

2.16

2.17

2.18

forward and gestures to the government tributes previously indicated (figure 2.16). She then gives way to expressions of grief as the men prepare to depart (figure 2.17). After the Colonel's departure, the sympathetic officer kisses Mother Bernle's hand on his way out, and salutes her in the doorway (figure 2.18). The dialogue titles which are crucial to our comprehension of this scene are thus packed into its central portion but the editing builds to a long-take finish which focuses on the mother's responses to the Colonel enacted without interruption – no intertitles, no close ups.

The introduction of sync sound obviated the need for the manipulation of title placement of the sort the director resorted to in *4 Sons. Arrowsmith* contains inventive and varied stagings of dialogue scenes. Although Ford did employ multiple-camera shooting in many instances, he also experimented extensively with staging and timing dialogue in single static takes. His long-take strategy led to an average shot length of 12.5

seconds for the film as a whole, significantly slower than the 7.6 ASL of *4 Sons* although *Arrowsmith* contains many fewer shots with camera movement.

Consider the scene in which Martin Arrowsmith (Ronald Colman), a country doctor, is inspired to return to his early interest in medical research by an outbreak of blackleg which is killing off the cattle of local farmers. His attempt to improve on the ineffectual serum being administered by the state veterinarian will ultimately be successful and garner him national recognition and an appointment at a major research facility. Colman is first shown in close up at the microscope. He looks up and calls for his wife Leora (Helen Hayes). A cut to long shot reveals that the kitchen has become a makeshift laboratory (figure 2.19). The tubing that stretches from the stove in the foreground to the table in the background helps to transform the domestic space and establish that the pots are being used for scientific purposes. Leora enters from off screen left, and

48

2.19

2.20

2.21

2.22

their conversation unfolds in a long take of just over one minute. The shot may be divided into two parts: the first is the scientist's monologue punctuated by Leora's repeated phrase of assent, "Yes, Martin". The second part is Leora's attempt to engage Martin in conversation on the subject of dinner.

After Hayes's entrance, Colman comes forward on the line "Now *I'm* ready to go. We'll try mine [my serum] in the morning", dropping a slide into the boiling kettle in the front left corner for sterilization (figure 2.20). He then moves to the background, fetches a towel from behind a half-opened door, then comes forward again, using the towel to take hold of the hot flask in which he cooks his serum (figures 2.21 and 2.22).

Colman returns to the background once again, dodging around the tubing, to set the serum on the table. He moves farther back into the area in front of the microscope, leans forward, and taps a cigarette on the table, creating an aperture framing within the tubing (figure 2.23). In this

position, he begins to explain his plan for administering different dosages to the cows. Then he comes forward, stopping to light a match just prior to the most important phrase: "And then we can see which gets well quickest and which dies quickest" (figure 2.24). This establishes the necessity of a control group in medical trials, an important point for the subsequent development of the plot. Then, exhaling a cloud of smoke, he returns to the table in the background.

Thus, in the first half of the shot Coleman synchronizes his words and his gestures as he moves around the set. From the point of view of the actor, one of the great advantages of having a set designed for a single as opposed to multiple cameras is the deep playing space. Colman moves from the table to the stove and back again three times, each time coming forward to deliver an emphatic line or phrase, all the while manipulating props – the slide, the flask, the cigarette – and dodging the tubing. Thus he demonstrates his control over the kitchen, previously Leora's

49

2.23

2.24

2.25

2.26

2.27

face of her husband's abstracted indifference. Standing in the foreground with back to camera (figure 2.25), she speaks: "Darling, are you hungry?" Two-second pause. Repeated with more emphasis: "Darling *are you hungry?*" There is a four-second pause as Colman takes his time responding. He works head down, then hems and haws before finally looking up from his work, pencil in hand (figure 2.26). The sound of the pencil dropping on the table emphasizes his response: "Hungry. Yes, by gosh, I am famished." He resumes his pencil and his work. "Let's have some dinner." Hayes turns to camera revealing her face (figure 2.27). Exasperated, she asks: "How can I cook dinner when you are using the whole stove to cook your old cow medicine?" His slow and distracted responses eventually drive her out of the kitchen. She exits left, followed by the sound of a door slamming off.

Hayes questions, waits, questions. Colman hesitates, lifts his head, hesitates with pencil in hand, until he finally confesses to being hungry.

domain, and his practiced use of the instruments of his trade. While his movements may seem ordinary, incidental, they are in fact carefully timed in relation to his lines, and serve important dramatic functions.

In the second part of the shot, Martin finally stops talking and settles down to work at the table. The timing reaches comic proportions as Hayes attempts to bring up the topic of dinner in the

These subtle calculations of the actor's craft lend a sense of spontaneity and freshness to their interactions. In the highly edited form which was the norm in silent cinema, the timing of the conversation, the pauses, the subtle interplay of gestures, would have been largely controlled by the editor and the director in post-production. This is not to say that silent film acting was not skilled, but rather that it occurred piecemeal, and that the timing across the arc of a conversation was not under the actor's control as it would have been on the stage. The long-take style of the early sound period restored some of that control over timing.

In a later scene from *Arrowsmith*, Ford used a modified form of the multiple-camera technique in much the same way as the long take in the kitchen scene – to allow the performance to unfold in continuity. The scene involves Arrowsmith and his colleague Sondelius (Richard Bennett) who have traveled to the West Indies where there is an outbreak of bubonic plague. Arrowsmith has been charged with conducting a trial of a new plague serum, inoculating only half of the population of the island and administering a placebo to the other half as a control.[77] Sondelius has refused to take the serum. This decision is not motivated in the film, but in the Sinclair Lewis novel on which it is based Sondelius opposes the use of a control group and will not take the serum himself until everyone can get it. Sondelius contracts the plague and dies in the makeshift hospital that he has constructed, tended by Arrowsmith and surrounded by patients and assistants who mourn his passing.

The conventional way to treat a tender death scene like this would be to use shot-reverse-shot. Even if Arrowsmith does not say very much, you would expect to see his face in close up and see him react to his dying friend's words. And as it was typically used in this period, multiple-camera shooting was designed precisely to preserve the possibility of this kind of editing. But although this scene employs the multiple-camera technique, there is no shot-reverse-shot and no close up of Colman.

The death of Sondelius was shot simultaneously from two basic camera positions both centered on Bennett: a frontal long shot (figure 2.28, setup 1) and a medium shot taken with a long lens from the right (figure 2.29, setup 2).[78] An additional close up (setup 3) was taken singly. This angle of view could not have been shot simultaneously with the first and second setups because the third camera would have been visible in their angle of view. Editing the footage from the three camera positions created seven total shots with three long takes as follows (long takes indicated in italics):

Shot 1	Long shot	Setup 1	10.23 seconds
Shot 2	*Medium shot*	*Setup 2*	*52.29 seconds*
Shot 3	Long shot	Setup 1	11.75 seconds
Shot 4	Medium shot	Setup 2	13.54 seconds
Shot 5	*Close Up*	*Setup 3*	*29.75 seconds*
Shot 6	Medium Shot	Setup 2	4.79 seconds
Shot 7	*Long shot*	*Setup 1*	*41.33 sconds*

77 In both the film and Sinclair Lewis's original novel the situation in the West Indies is explicitly racialized, although the film seems more aware of the potentially offensive aspects of this. In both film and novel, the white governor of the island refuses to allow the experiment to proceed on the largely white population. In the novel, a white plantation owner then invites the scientists to conduct their experiment on the Black workers on his plantation. In the film, Dr. Marchand (Clarence Brooks), a Black physician, approaches Arrowsmith and Sondelius and suggests that they conduct the experiment on "his people", the largely Black population of the island of Caribe. In both novel and film, Arrowsmith finally breaks down and administers the serum to all who want it, abandoning experimental protocol.

78 *Arrowsmith* Production Reports, Samuel Goldwyn Papers, Box 4, Folder 26, Special Collections, Herrick Library, AMPAS. I consulted the Daily Production Report and the Stage Log for September 24, 1931, which indicate that scene number 177 was shot with two cameras, one long shot and one medium.

2.28

2.29

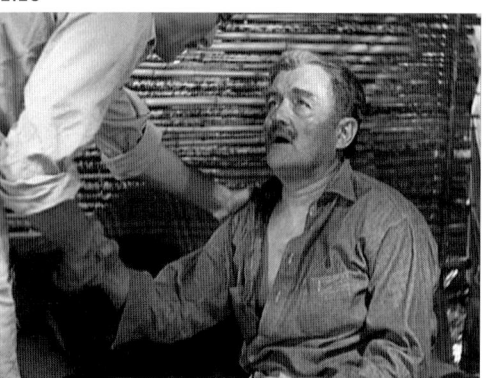
2.30

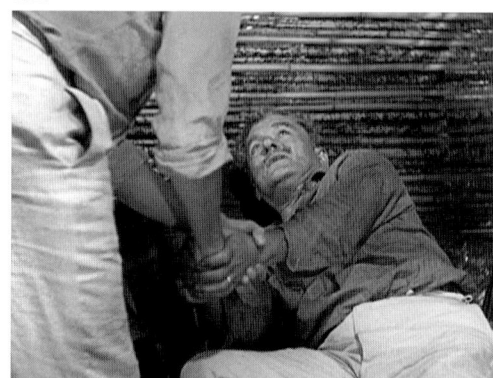
2.31

Shot 7, the long-shot framing held for over forty-one seconds at the end of the scene, shows Arrowsmith's actions after the death as he covers the body and allows himself a brief expression of grief before returning to his labors (figure 2.33). Shots 2 and 5, the other two long takes, concentrate on Bennett. In the shooting script Bennett's lines were shorter and less colloquial than in the film. I surmise that Ford or Bennett (an experienced stage actor) expanded the length of Sondelius's speeches in performance, making them more vivid and colloquial. Shot 2 (figure 2.29), the longest shot in the sequence, is largely comprised of the dying man's reminiscence of his homeland:

> Martin, you ever think of the jokes God plays? The best one is on the tropics. He made them so beautiful and so rich and then he give them the plague … . Oh I … . I am quite peaceful. Martin did you ever see Stockholm? I would like yust once more to see the Strandvägen at dawn with the young snow, falling, white … .

And stagger home through it with one more last good drunk. Yeah, eh … .

In shot 4 (the same medium framing as shot 2), Colman bends into the top left corner of the shot as Bennett moves away from camera, resting his head back on the pillow, while reaching out to retain his friend's hand (figures 2.30 and 2.31). It is followed by the unique closer view in which he speaks his final lines (figure 2.32). In this shot, Bennett pleads with his friend to abandon the controlled experiment and give all the occupants of Caribe a chance of being cured: "You try to save all these poor devils [*Rain sound diminishes over speech.*] Save all of them! Let science … let experiments go. Huh, I never know before people could hurt me so much. [*Thunder. Rain sound increases.*] I think I sleep, yust a little." For shot 5 alone Ford took advantage of the spatial and temporal ubiquity typical of single-camera shooting to move his camera in on the actor creating a dramatically and pictorially arresting shot. Nonetheless he shot and staged the rest of the

2.32

2.33

scene with two cameras running simultaneously, holding onto the early sound practice that was on the verge of becoming obsolete. What advantages did this system ultimately provide?

By abjuring shot-reverse-shot and concentrating Bennett's lines in the relatively close framings of shots 2 and 5, Ford allowed the actor the same opportunities that Colman had enjoyed in the kitchen scene but on a smaller shot scale. He could extemporize, pause as necessary, repeat himself, make interjections, and vary the volume, tempo and phrasing of his lines. In addition to multiple-camera shooting, the practice of mixing the sound live gave Ford and Bennett the added resource of the simultaneous recording of sound effects. The shooting script had called for silence in the last two shots, with images of the rain falling through the hospital roof and wetting Sondelius's face and body at the moment of death. In filming, Ford kept to the basic idea of no dialogue, but utilized sound rather than the image track to emphasize the rain. The film marks Sondelius's passing in shot 7 by the cessation of his energetic voice, and the continuation of the weather noise at high volume augmented by a fainter sound of weeping. In general, the rain sounds are quite pronounced in this scene and in the short scene outside the hospital which precedes it. The sound engineer's log complains of several takes "ruined by rain noise", suggesting the scenes were technically difficult to shoot and mix. It seems likely that the director was pushing against the limits of the technology in making the rain sounds as loud as possible, trying to keep them in the sonic

foreground even as the actor spoke. Despite the difficulties, it was advantageous for the actor to be able to hear and react to the sound effects on set. Bennett could drop his voice when he was not very concerned to be heard, as he did in shot 4, and raise it when the words really mattered, as in shot 5. He could hear when the thunder started in shot 5 and pause to allow the crash to register before continuing his speech. The temporal integrity of the long take, and the simultaneous recording of voice, sound effect and picture gave Bennett a chance to control and modulate his performance across the arc of the long takes.

Multiple-camera shooting has usually been considered a clumsy but necessary stop-gap measure – a way of maintaining high cutting rates in a period when the camera was imprisoned in its booth or blimp. But the example of *Arrowsmith* suggests another approach to the technical constraints and opportunities of the conversion. Ford, along with several of his colleagues, responded positively to the elimination of dialogue titles and the consequent demise of relatively fast-cut silent conversation scenes organized around intertitles. They took advantage of the conditions of early sound recording to go in the opposite direction: experimenting with long takes. Indeed, the technical restrictions which favored the continuous recording of sound may also have helped to inspire a similarly continuous visual record of the performance.

As with *Arrowsmith*, the early sound films Ford made at Fox took great inspiration from direct and spontaneous sound capture utilizing both multiple-camera shooting and the long take. In *The Black Watch*, for example, the dense weave of dialogue, pipe-and-drum marches, folk songs, and effects is achieved by multiple-camera shooting in the opening scene in the officers' mess and by static long takes in alternation with shots taken wild in the scene at the railroad station. The sequence referred to above in *Seas Beneath*, in which Marion Lessing as Anna Marie comes aboard the *Metha Nelson* from a small dinghy, includes a forty-eight-second segment shot with two cameras, one for the long shot and one for a closer view of George O'Brien, used for two brief cutaways. The sound in the segment is continuous, and since it includes instructions shouted to the men in the boat below and their responses in Spanish, it is hard to distinguish what is scripted from pragmatic, spontaneously-generated speech. The most exciting uses of location sound in *Seas Beneath* tend to be shot in this way, with direct sound and either single takes or multiple cameras. Although both *Born Reckless* and *Up the River* frequently resorted to multiple-camera shooting, they tended to employ long takes in moments of high drama or carefully timed comedy. Typical examples from *Born Reckless* include Beretti's first meeting with his sister's boyfriend (seventy-three seconds), Beretti trading sugar for kisses (forty-eight seconds), and the final confrontation between Beretti and Big Shot (over two minutes). Similar examples from *Up the River* include Steve's proposal to Judy through the prison gate (sixty seconds), St. Louis and the boys reading Judy's message to Steve (seventy-two seconds), and St. Louis's effort to stop Steve from going after Frosby (over four minutes, with some camera movement). Ford's adoption of relatively longer shot lengths in the films of this period is thus best understood in the context of experiments with dialogue given the new-found freedom from intertitles. The use of the long take allowed for ease of movement and precise timing by the performers and also let them interact with their sonic environment in real time. In this sense, the beginnings of his long-take style are best understood as a product of the transition to sound rather than as an effort to display camera movement or reduce editing as such.

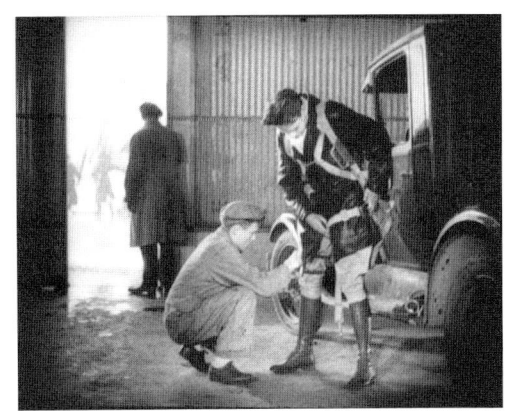

Part 2
Between Fox and RKO
1931–1935

Chapter 3

Forced to Freelance

Between 1920 when he made *Just Pals* and 1930 when he completed *Seas Beneath* Ford directed thirty-one features for Fox in addition to a sound short and additional footage for films directed by others. He was a company man who worked almost exclusively with stars, cinematographers and scriptwriters who were also under contract to the studio. Between 1931 and 1937, however, Ford made nine features outside the studio and only eight for Fox or 20th Century, as indicated in the following list of the features directed by Ford from 1931 to 1937 (dates of production are given, not release dates).

The Brat (Fox, May–July 1931)
Arrowsmith (Goldwyn through United Artists, August–October 1931)
Air Mail (Universal, June–Sept 1932)
Flesh (MGM, September–November 1932)
Pilgrimage (Fox, February–April 1933)
Doctor Bull (Fox, June–July 1933)
The Lost Patrol (RKO, August–September 1933)
The World Moves On (Fox, February–April 1934)
Judge Priest (Fox, June–July 1934)
The Whole Town's Talking (Columbia, October–December 1934)
The Informer (RKO, February–March 1935)
Steamboat Round the Bend (Fox, May–21 June 1935)
The Prisoner of Shark Island (20th Century, November–January 1936)
Mary of Scotland (RKO, February–April 1936)
The Plough and the Stars (RKO, July–August 1936, retakes October 1936)
Wee Willie Winkie (Twentieth Century-Fox, January–March 1937)
The Hurricane (Goldwyn, through UA, May–September 1937)

Even after 1937, when he was more closely bound to Twentieth Century-Fox by contract, Ford continued to finesse his working arrangements so as to retain the ability to make some films independently. This chapter is concerned with the initiation of Ford's pattern of alternating films for Fox with films made for other studios. It will consider the industrial circumstances that led Fox to fire the director in the fall of 1931 during the tumultuous period of the studio's near bankruptcy. *Air Mail*, made for Universal in the summer of 1932, will be examined as a prime example of the way in which the director was able to turn his expulsion from Fox to his advantage.

The management of Fox during the five years between the exodus of William Fox and the merger with 20th Century that put Darryl Zanuck in charge of the studio is not very well understood.[1] It should be divided into two regimes. First, from 1930 to 1932, after President Harley Clarke put together a new group of creditors to take over the debt, the Chase National

---

1   An exception is Aubrey Solomon's *Fox Film Corporation*, which contains an informative account of the five years prior to the merger.

Bank became increasingly active in the management of the company.[2] The *New York Times* commented on the situation in June 1931:

> For the first time in the history of the motion picture industry, banking interests have come into control of the directorship of a major motion picture-distributing company. Through the action of stockholders of the Fox Film Corporation at the annual meeting last week a board of directors was elected that included only two active executives of the company of a membership of twelve. The ten others are representatives of large banks, banking houses or industries classed as "big business".[3]

While Clarke was reportedly elated following the election of this board, nine months later he was replaced by Fox board member Edward Tinker, president of Interstate Equities Corporation, who himself lasted but four months in the post.[4]

The second management regime began in April 1932 when Chase finally convinced an experienced film executive, Sidney Kent, to take over from Tinker.[5] Kent had been Paramount's vice-president and general manager working in the area of distribution and sales. He abruptly left his position at Paramount when the business interests taking control of that company seemed primed to undermine his control of distribution.[6]

He worked successfully with Chase to keep Fox Film from bankruptcy, although the company's two major theater subsidiaries, Fox-West Coast and Fox Metropolitan Theatres, did go into receivership.[7] By March 1933, however, W. W. Aldrich, president of the Chase bank, had relinquished his post as chairman of the finance committee of the Fox board of directors and he and representatives of other financial interests withdrew from the Fox board in favor of film executives.[8]

The financial difficulties that Fox experienced in retiring its debt in the period between 1930 and 1934 severely taxed the production sector as the cost-cutting measures that most companies experienced during the Depression were exacerbated by political infighting within the studio. In late 1931, *Variety* described salary cuts across the industry in an attempt to limit average film budgets to $200,000 or $225,000 per picture.[9] Similarly, as the Depression worsened in 1932 and 1933 deeper salary cuts as well as the elimination of positions and temporary layoffs were instituted.[10] Against the backdrop of the industry-wide effort to cut costs, Fox executives struggled for personal advantage and blamed each other for the company's downturn. Moreover,

---

2   Solomon, 150; "Morgan Behind Fox", *Hollywood Reporter* (30 Mar 1931): 1, 6; "New Finance Com. in Fox Film Corp.", *Hollywood Reporter* (16 Sep 1931): 1; "Those of you who are wondering 'what is going to happen to Fox' …", *Hollywood Reporter* (22 Dec 1931): 1.

3   "Fox Film Case Seen as Bankers' Tryout", *New York Times* (14 Jun 1931): N9.

4   "New Clarke-Sheehan Understanding Born?", *Hollywood Reporter* (11 May 1931): 3; "E. G. Tinker Succeeding H. L. Clarke as Fox Film Pres.", *Variety* (17 Nov 1931): 5; "Edward R. Tinker Is New President of Fox Films", *Hollywood Reporter* (18 Nov 1931): 1, 9.

5   "Kent at Fox as V-P April 1", *Variety* (15 Mar 1932): 5; overtures had been made to both Kent and Nicholas Schenck of MGM at least six months before Kent took the job, see "Kent-Schenck Finally Say No for Fox", *Variety* (1 Sep 1931): 5.

6   "Sid Kent Stirs Up Trade", *Variety* (26 Jan 1932): 3, 25. Founder Adoph Zukor was not expelled from Paramount as William Fox had been from Fox. However, according to Gomery, *Hollywood Studio System*, 31–33, John Hertz of Lehman Brothers became chair of the finance committee of Paramount's board of directors in November 1931 and banking interests controlled Paramount as losses mounted in the period 1931 to 1933.

7   *Variety* discusses the impending receivership: "Fox Wesco May Go to Wringer", *Variety* (31 Jan 1933): 6; "41 Houses in Fox-W.C. $25,000,000 Bkptcy", *Variety* (7 Mar 1933): 6; "Fox Theatres Reorg. Means Some Go Back", *Variety* (28 Feb 1933): 6; "F-WC Receivers Ask Houses Be Kept Open Despite $7,051 Loss", *Variety* (28 Mar 1933): 23. The debt on the Fox theatre holdings was retired in 1934: "Sid Kent to Head Reorganized Fox-W.C.", *Variety* (24 Apr 1934): 5; "Fox-West Coast Bankruptcy Washed Up", *Variety* (20 Nov 1934): 4; see also "Fox Film Board Gives Sid Kent New 3-Year Contract", Variety (6 Nov 1934): 5.

8   "Chase Out of Fox Regime", *Variety* (7 Mar 1933): 5; "Fox Film Elects 5 New Directors", *Hollywood Reporter* (9 Mar 1933): 1.

9   "$200,000 Top Film Cost", *Variety* (6 Oct 1931): 3; "Fox Salary Slash", *Variety* (27 Oct 1931): 4; "Studios Await Onslaught", *Variety* (27 Oct 1931): 5; "Coast Secret Meetings, No Salary Rise, Less Production", *Variety* (1 Dec 1931): 3, 42; "First WB Slash Drops Average Cost Per Picture to $225,000", *Variety* (8 Dec 1931): 4; "Columbia Has Lowest Production Cost for Feature at $175,000 with Metro Tops at $450,000 – Others Too", *Variety* (3 Jan 1933): 4; Fred Stanley, "Production Costs Not Chopped", *Variety* (3 Jan 1933): 4.

10   "Fox, Universal Further % Cuts", *Variety* (19 Apr 1932): 4; "H'wood Will Become Acquainted with Depresh When a 25% 'Must' Cut Goes into Effect this Summer", *Variety* (7 Jun 1932): 5; "Warner's Shorter Film Schedule to Trim Costs to Within $200,000", *Variety* (20 Dec 1932): 4; "Wholesale Closings, If –", *Variety* (21 Mar 1933): 5; "WB Studio will be Kept Closed to June 1", *Variety* (4 Apr 1933): 4; "Fox Walk-Outs on Salary Slices", *Variety* (21 Feb 1933): 4.

throughout the period from 1930 to 1935 reporters for the trade press had questions about who was actually running Fox studio operations on the west coast. While Winfield Sheehan had a contract as vice-president and general manager and was nominally head of production, both the Clarke-Chase regime and the Kent-Chase regime found reasons to undermine him. Trade press coverage was rife with rumors about Sheehan and/or Sheehan's subordinate and sometime antagonist Sol Wurtzel being replaced. But in fact no administration was in a position to dispense with these highly experienced executives, given the extreme pressure to cut costs during a period of declining box office. When Sidney Kent, addressing a stockholders' meeting in 1935, recalled the condition of the company in 1932, he commented that if he had known about Fox's "internal troubles" he would not have taken the job.[11]

Out of Fox

Upon the completion of *Seas Beneath*, Ford took a three-month leave, embarking upon a South Seas voyage with George O'Brien. When he and O'Brien returned to the Fox payroll in April 1931, the director was assigned to *The Brat*.[12] Unlike the films Ford made in 1929–1930, which had been planned and budgeted under the William Fox regime and made within his own unit, *The Brat* had been developed under Sheehan's administration, and its sixty-seven minute running time as well as the choice of Sally O'Neil as its leading player were indicative of severe budget constraints. The project seems to have been selected by the studio, ever on the lookout to increase its roster of stars, as a "comeback" role for O'Neil.[13] Dudley Nichols did not work on the

script, which was adapted from Maude Fulton's play by S. N. Behrman and Sonya Levien. Ford worked with two other preferred crew members, however: dialogue director William Collier and cinematographer Joe August. *Variety* deemed *The Brat* a programmer, a light romantic comedy in which Ford was out of his element and in which the fancy "angles", e.g., the camera movement which follows O'Neil on a swing, evoking a similar shot in *4 Sons*, were out of place.[14] Similarly, Mordaunt Hall, in the *New York Times*, thought the film did "not deserve the talented direction and photography which John Ford has brought to it".[15]

One of the problems that Fox faced in the period of declining budgets was how to employ the expensive A-list directors under contract. The studio either had to gamble on high-risk, high-budget projects that it could ill-afford to have misfire – as was disastrously the case, for example, with Walsh's 70mm super-feature *The Big Trail* (1930) – or it had to place high-priced directorial talent in charge of modest or even low-budget projects without big-name stars. *The Brat* is only one instance of the latter strategy, and one can find similar assignments made with the other A-list directors. For example, Dumont notes that in the case of Borzage's programmer *Young America* (1932), the director's $37,000 salary represented a third of the film's entire budget.[16] Fox's decision to loan Ford out to independent producer Samuel Goldwyn seems to have been an attempt to avoid this kind of situation. It relieved Fox of the obligation to cover the director's $3,000 per week salary for up to fifteen weeks and the terms of the contract also guaranteed the studio a small profit on the deal.[17]

11 "Kent Details the Advantages of 20th Century-Fox Film Merger", *Variety* (21 Aug 1935): 4.
12 In Bogdanovich, *John Ford*, 54, Ford described the film as "just one of those damn things they handed you".
13 "Noonan Sisters Set After Long Layoff", *Variety* (7 Jul 1931): 3. O'Neil (real name Virginia Noonan) had played prominent roles in several MGM silents, including Edmund Goulding's *Sally, Irene and Mary,* but had moved to the Poverty Row studio Tiffany-Stahl in 1928.
14 *Variety* (25 Aug 1931): 20.
15 "The Screen", *New York Times* (24 Aug 1931): 19.
16 Dumont, 184. Borzage was said to be earning about $5,000 a week in this period; see "Fox Studio Cools Off Over Raoul Walsh", *Variety* (21 Jul 1931): 2, for a discussion of Borzage's position at the studio at this time.
17 As per his two-year contract, Ford was guaranteed $3,000 per week for the first year and $3,250 per week for the second year, Renewal Letter signed by W. R. Sheehan and John Ford, 27 May 1930; Goldwyn was to pay $50,000 for Ford's services at a rate of $3,000 per week with the balance due after the work was completed, Contract, Samuel Goldwyn Inc., Ltd. and Fox Film Corporation, 28 Apr 1931; the studio calculated that their profit, after accounting for his rise in wages in October, 1931, would be slightly less than $5,000, Sol Wurtzel, Memo to John Tracy, 24 Apr 1931 and JHT [John Tracy], Memo to Sheehan, 28 Apr 1931, all in John Ford Contract File, Twentieth Century-Fox Legal Department.

From Ford's perspective the loan-out was also advantageous. The Goldwyn company, which released no more than five or six films a year through United Artists, was in a much better financial position than Fox. An article in the *Los Angeles Times* discussed Goldwyn's generous budgets, citing *Arrowsmith* specifically as a rare example of near million-dollar production at a time when most studios were cutting back.[18] Moreover, the project boasted top-flight talent: a script by Pulitzer-Prize winning dramatist Sidney Howard from Nobel-Prize winner Sinclair Lewis's novel, and Ronald Colman, a major star. The director had not had an opportunity like this since *4 Sons* and *The Black Watch*. Indeed, the film was eventually released as a two-dollar special on Broadway and nominated for Academy Awards for Best Picture (then "Outstanding Production"), Art Direction (designer Richard Day), and Cinematography (Ray June, perhaps with a little help from Ford himself).

For his part, it is likely that Samuel Goldwyn decided to adapt *Arrowsmith* in order to provide a change of pace for Colman, whom he had under contract. In the 1920s, Colman regularly had leading roles in period romances and romantic comedies. With the coming of sound, Goldwyn had played up Colman's Englishness in light, comic vehicles such as *Bulldog Drummond* (1929) and *Raffles* (1930). Lewis's novel, with its resolutely mid-Western setting ("Wheatsylvania") and its weighty theme – the institutional trappings of and limitations on medical research – must have seemed the antithesis of these stories. Critics were eventually divided on the question of whether or not Colman was up to the switch; nonetheless the attempt at off-casting is clear, and Goldwyn's choice of Ford seems to have been part and parcel of this change of pace for the actor.[19]

Ford went on Goldwyn's payroll on July 17, 1931.[20] He began screen tests, and, after the first draft of Sidney Howard's script was completed on August 3, conducted readings and participated in budget meetings.[21] A second version of the script, dated August 19, was completed after shooting began on August 14.[22] It is likely that Ford had a hand in the preparation of the August 19 shooting script, especially in the division of the script into what were called "scene numbers", the major camera setups used for budgeting and keeping track of the company's progress. Ford continued to consult with Sidney Howard about changes to the script throughout the production process.[23] Thus, the director was much more than a hired hand: he helped plan and budget the production and was consulted about story, casting and costuming.

Goldwyn faced a problem with the schedule of Colman's co-star Helen Hayes, who was due back in New York on September 15 for rehearsals for a stage production.[24] Ford did not shoot her final scenes until September 14 to 16 and her *Arrowsmith* retakes were not completed until September 20. The need to wrap up Hayes's involvement as quickly as possible must have contributed to the pace of work. The company had only three days off during the month of September. They typically worked from approximately 9:00am to 6:00pm with one long day each week when they stayed on set as late as midnight. After principal photography wrapped on September 29, Ford continued at the studio for several days, making inserts and process shots and traveling to Big Bear with a small company for shots on location. After

---

18   Mollie Merrick, "Million-Dollar Films Shelved", *Los Angeles Times* (23 Aug 1931): 20.
19   "Goldwyn Buys Lewis' *Arrowsmith*", *Hollywood Reporter* (1 May 1931): 2; "John Ford to Direct *Arrowsmith* at UA", *Hollywood Reporter* (4 May 1931): 3; "Ford on *Arrowsmith* with Colman for Goldwyn", *Variety* (6 May 1931): 3.
20   JHT [John Tracy], Memo to Sheehan, 29 Sep 1931, John Ford Contract file, Twentieth Century-Fox Legal Department.
21   Daily Production Reports for *Arrowsmith*, which commence with screen tests on 21 July 1931 and conclude with retakes on 29 October 1931, Samuel Goldwyn Papers, Box 4, Folder 26, Special Collections, Herrick Library, AMPAS.
22   Sidney Howard, *Arrowsmith*, full script, 3 Aug 1931, Box 3, Folder 18; Sidney Howard, *Arrowsmith*, revised script, 19 Aug 1931, Box 3, Folder 20, both in Samuel Goldwyn Papers, Special Collections, Herrick Library, AMPAS.
23   The *Arrowsmith* Daily Production Reports for 28 August, 5 September, 8 September, 9 September and 25 September 1931 indicate that shooting halted for story conferences between Ford and Howard.
24   James F. Reilly, telegram to Sam Goldwyn, 17 Sep 1931, Samuel Goldwyn Papers, Box 4, Folder 25, Special Collections, Herrick Library, AMPAS. Hayes was engaged for Gilbert Miller's production of *The Good Fairy*, which eventually opened three weeks later than scheduled, "*Good Fairy* Deferred", *Variety* (8 Sep 1931): 110.

October 4, the director effectively stopped working, appearing only intermittently at the studio and in an inebriated state. These events were carefully documented by Fox assistant counsel John Tracy, who collected statements from Goldwyn staff members: assistant director Herbert Sutch, producer Arthur Hornblow, production manager R. B. McIntyre, and their various assistants.[25] Goldwyn expected Ford at the studio from Monday October 5 through Wednesday October 7 to work with the editor Hugh Bennett, but the director failed to report. He attended a screening of the rough cut with Goldwyn, Hornblow and others on Thursday, October 8, when he was instructed to reduce the length of the film (which assistant director Sutch estimated at 11,500 feet or about 126.5 minutes). He was also told to make retakes for two scenes. Ford did not report again until Wednesday October 14, when Hornblow reported he was under the influence and "not at all himself". Eventually Hornblow supervised editing the film down to its running time of 108 minutes as well as the retakes, which consisted of two shots of Richard Bennett speaking revised lines for the lecture scene and eight shots of a child actor playing Arrowsmith as a boy for the opening.

McBride explains Ford's behavior at this juncture as an effect of the director's chronic alcoholism, exacerbated by marital problems. He describes Ford's abrupt abandonment of his wife in favor of George O'Brien as a traveling companion for the 1930 South Seas trip, a trip during which Ford was frequently inebriated.[26] However, it seems likely that the drinking bout following the completion of *Arrowsmith* in the fall of 1931 was motivated not so much by the stress of his personal life as by the demands of carrying a major

film to completion in a new studio.[27] Not only was the *Arrowsmith* production under a very tight deadline due to Helen Hayes's theatrical commitments, but Ford was working without his loyal assistant directors – his brother-in-law Wingate Smith and his brother Edward O'Fearna – and without a friendly producer such as McGuinness at his back. An incident documented in the Daily Production Reports suggests how carefully his actions on set were monitored. Herbert Sutch, the assistant director Goldwyn provided, carefully tabulated and explained time lost by the company in his report each day (the production eventually closed eight days "behind"). On August 19, while shooting on the exterior set of the Arrowsmith home in Wheatsylvania, the company fell a half day behind. Sutch noted that the delay was due to "some scenes taken by Mr. Ford which have good cutting and picture value". These are likely to have been the beautiful long shot of Arrowsmith hanging up his shingle as viewed by his wife through a window, as well as the shots of Arrowsmith being watched by locals seated in front of the country store across the street from the house. One imagines how Ford enjoyed the request to justify his shots.

From the point of view of the film companies involved, there was not very much at stake in Ford's delinquency after the production had closed. They both agreed that Ford had worked for twelve and one-third weeks. Goldwyn thus had a more or less complete film and had saved two and two-thirds weeks of Ford's salary. Fox was out less than $1,000 in profit, since Goldwyn paid them $4,111.11 above Ford's salary, the appropriate proportion of the $5,000 profit they expected had the director worked for the full fifteen weeks.[28] Why, then, did Fox terminate

25 JHT [John Tracy], Fox Legal Department, Letter to Abraham Lehr, Samuel Goldwyn Inc., 6 November 1931, and accompanying statements (typescript versions dated by hand 30 October 1931). Scott Eyman, *Print the Legend: The Life and Times of John Ford* (New York: Simon & Schuster, 1999), 132, assumes these affidavits were compiled by Goldwyn, but they were collected by John Tracy, a Fox lawyer, after Fox fired Ford, presumably in order to protect the studio in the event that the director sued them for breach of contract. H. Bruce Humberstone, an assistant director at Goldwyn during the production, provides a different, self-aggrandizing account of Ford's dismissal, see the interview in Jon Tuska, *Encounters with Filmmakers* (New York: Greenwood Press, 1991), 16–17.

26 McBride, 182–184.

27 As discussed in chapter 6, Ford would later object to Zanuck's practice of taking charge of editing on all major films at Twentieth Century-Fox, but the practice also provided him with a much needed release from the strain of production.

28 John Tracey, Memo to McIntire [sic], Wurtzel, Bagnell, 28 Dec 1931, John Ford Contract File, Twentieth Century-Fox Legal Department.

Ford's contract? In a letter to W. C. Michel of Fox Film Corporation, John Tracy discussed the termination in legal terms:

> Of course, under the agreement we are not responsible for Ford's failure to render his services in accordance with the terms thereof, but since Goldwyn notified us in time for us to take Ford off the payroll as of the 10th, which was the only step we could take since we could not compel Ford to render the services, we believe that the legal rights of both parties are fairly and clearly stated.[29]

But even if legally justified, it is not clear that the termination made sense from a business point of view. The fact that Goldwyn executives pursued Ford even after he was taken off the Fox payroll on October 10, as late as October 20 according to the statement by production manager McIntyre, suggests that they valued the director's talents and simply wanted him to sober up and come back to work, though of course they did not want to pay for his services if he could not. But if Goldwyn's actions seem sensible, Fox's seem out of proportion. Given the director's long record of distinguished service to the company one would expect Ford to have been reprimanded and docked several weeks pay or sent on unpaid leave. Instead, the company took advantage of Ford's lapse to sever their contractual commitment to him. The logic of this decision needs to be understood in the larger context of the political situation on the Fox lot.

By August 1931, Clarke was reputedly dissatisfied with the box-office performance of Fox films during the 1930–1931 season as well as the high cost of Sheehan's salary.[30] He appointed Richard Rowland as head of a new Fox story department in New York. In a matter of months Rowland was countermanding Sheehan's decisions about scripts, stories and casting, and was rumored to be the new production chief.[31] Even William Wilkerson of the *Hollywood Reporter*, an avowed enemy of Sheehan, thought the Chase-Clarke management had made a poor choice in elevating Rowland:

> The Chase heads could and would save a lot of money and a lot of annoyance if they would permit the making of their pictures in Hollywood instead of over a desk in a New York office, and if they would decide either that W. R. Sheehan is the right man for the production job, or that he is a dud and should be replaced. Their present procedure of embarrassing their studio head in taking away most of his authority is costing them more money than it should and reducing the morale of their company to zero.[32]

As Rowland's star rose, the Clarke-Chase management instituted much stricter budget controls. In early November, *Variety* reported that the Chase bank would place a liaison in the Fox studio to supervise budgets and production costs, a position *Variety* initially thought would belong to Rowland but was ultimately assigned to D. A. McIntyre. The trade journal also noted: "Fox directors have been advised to trim everything and keep production costs down. *Bad Girl*, with its under-$200,000 budget, was cited as a good example of smash b.o. strength at minimum investment."[33] McIntyre apparently took control of studio operations for a short period in December 1931 and January 1932.[34]

Budget-cutting efforts were accompanied by more or less open salary cuts and by letting go of staff. Unionized workers faced intermittent layoffs, with the studio closing once seasonal production quotas had been met or even laying off

29 John Tracy, Letter to W. C. Michel, 8 Dec 1931, John Ford Contract file, Twentieth Century-Fox Legal Department.
30 *Variety* reported Sheehan's salary as $4,500 a week even after a twenty-five per cent cut, see "Sheehan Rumors on Coast Now Touch on 2nd Salary Cut", *Variety* (22 Dec 1931): 7; "New Clarke-Sheehan Understanding Born?", *Hollywood Reporter* (11 May 1931): 3; on the generally bad reputation of Fox's film program see "What About Fox Film Plans for 1931–1932?", *Hollywood Reporter* (13 May 1931): 1–2.
31 "Dick Rowland Made Story Chief", *Variety* (11 Aug 1931): 5; "Rowland is Fox Chief", *Hollywood Reporter* (8 Dec 1931): 1; "Efficiency in Fox Coast Studio Limits Sheehan to Producing Only", *Variety* (8 Dec 1931): 4. An example of Rowland countermanding Sheehan is his review of the script and casting for *Pilgrimage*, R. A. Rowland, Telegram to Sheehan, 27 November 1931, Ford correspondence, Lilly Library, IU.
32 "Those of you who are wondering...", *Hollywood Reporter* (22 Dec 1931): 1.
33 "Dick Rowland as Fox-Chase Liaison", *Variety* (3 Nov 1931): 5; Borzage directed *Bad Girl* (1931).
34 "The Lowdown", *Hollywood Reporter* (16 Dec 1931): 2; "Hollywood, McIntire [*sic*] Assures", *Variety* (29 Dec 1931): 163; "Fox Reorganizing Soon", *Hollywood Reporter* (8 Jan 1932): 1, 3; "McIntyre Recalled by the Chase Bank", *Hollywood Reporter* (2 Mar 1932): 1.

technicians between pictures.[35] In October 1931, salaries for contracted executives were cut twenty-five per cent.[36] In January 1932, Tinker, the new company president, tried to repudiate the contracts of ten high-salaried executives, including Sheehan and Wurtzel, and directors Walsh and Henry King. This ploy was challenged on legal grounds, however, and the studio eventually tried to buy out some of the contracts.[37] By March 1932, Fox had managed to drop thirty writers, actors and directors (including Ford) for a reported savings of $20,000 weekly.[38]

A comparison between the treatment of Walsh and Ford reveals telling similarities. By July 1931, Walsh had been reportedly "consigned to the dog house", partly as a result of the lackluster performance of *Women of All Nations* (1931), which had not been nearly as successful as *The Cock-Eyed World*. In retrospect it seems clear that the *What Price Glory* series had run its course, with *Variety* (unsuccessfully) suggesting that *Women of All Nations* "terminate the association of Walsh, McLaglen and Lowe as regards these military characters".[39] But Clarke apparently blamed the film's poor reception on Walsh's direction and fired several members of his production unit in consequence.[40] After Tinker repudiated Walsh's contract in January 1932, the director signed a one-picture deal with MGM.[41] While Walsh, unlike Ford, was not fired for cause, both directors were ultimately taken off the payroll in 1931–1932 due to the studio's reluctance to finance high-budget projects entailing costly salaries.[42]

The Fords left Los Angeles for Honolulu in early November 1931. Later that month, the director was contacted by the agent Harry Wurtzel, brother of Sol, who offered to represent him.[43] Wurtzel's follow-up letter is worth quoting at length for what it reveals about the situation at Fox at the time that Ford was fired:

> I was over to Sol's house the other day and during the course of conversation your name was brought up and I did not think it wrong to inquire from him as to the possibility of your returning to the Fox Studio. He said that he was also waiting for your return and did not know what would be done because of very unsettled conditions. There is a fellow here from New York by the name of Mr. McIntyre who has complete control and is making very drastic changes. All people under contract are being asked to take a cut in salary anywhere from ten to twenty-five percent. Some have accepted, others have not but will finally fall into line and at the present time they are not hiring any new directors.[44]

After leaving Hawaii, the Fords traveled in the South Pacific for over three months. During this time Harry Wurtzel explored possibilities for his client at a number of other studios, as described in the same letter:

> We were over to Paramount the other day and they asked us your status on the Fox lot and we told them what it was and they were very much interested in securing your services. This also applies to RKO. I know that Metro-Goldwyn- Mayer is interested as is Universal and First National.

35 This matter requires further research, but incidental references to the practice include "Paid Off Technicians", *Variety* (8 Apr 1931): 5; "Set Wurtzel Shutdown", *Hollywood Reporter* (10 November 1933): 1; "Wurtzel Decides Fox Studio Remains Open", *Variety* (14 Nov 1933): 5.

36 "Fox Salary Slash from 5% to 25% Covering All Depts. and Executives", *Variety* (27 Oct 1931): 4.

37 "Fox Spurns Contracts", *Hollywood Reporter* (16 Jan 1932): 1–2; "Fox Dodging Contracts", *Variety* (19 Jan 1932): 5; "Tradeviews", *Hollywood Reporter* (19 Jan 1932): 1–2; "Johnson, Suing on Fox Letout, Tells His Side", *Variety* (2 Feb 1932): 5.

38 "Fox Drops 30 from Talent List", *Variety* (15 Mar 1932): 2.

39 Review of *Women of All Nations*, *Variety* (2 Jun 1931): 15. Walsh directed one more with McLaglen and Lowe, *Under Pressure* (1935), as well as another with a very similar plot, *Sailor's Luck* (1933), with James Dunn, Sammy Cohen and Frank Moran as the sailors.

40 "Fox Studio Cools Off over Raoul Walsh", *Variety* (21 Jul 1931): 2.

41 "Raoul Walsh with Doug on South Seas Trip", *Hollywood Reporter* (4 Feb 1932): 1; "Fox Pays Off Walsh", *Hollywood Reporter* (4 Mar 1932): 1; "Raoul Walsh Now an MGM Director", *Hollywood Reporter* (9 Mar 1932): 6; "Another All-Starrer for M-G by Walsh", *Variety* (12 Apr 1932): 3.

42 *Variety* seems to have assumed that Fox fired Ford due to his salary and not his drinking problem, see "3 Directing Teams Replace John Ford at Fox – Drawing but Half His Salary", *Variety* (3 Nov 1931): 2.

43 "Fords to Honolulu", *Hollywood Reporter* (3 Nov 1931): 2; "Hollywood", *Variety* (8 Dec 1931): 6. It seems clear that Harry Wurtzel was not yet Ford's agent since he asks Ford's permission to represent him, H. Wurtzel, Telegram to Ford, 31 Nov 1931, Ford correspondence, Lilly Library, IU.

44 Harry Wurtzel, Letter to Ford, 10 December 1931, Ford correspondence, Lilly Library, IU.

Ford's business manager Fred Totman also reported "many calls from agents saying the studios are anxious to secure your services".[45] True to his word, Harry Wurtzel secured several one-picture deals for Ford following his return to California in early March 1932. The director first made *Air Mail* at Universal, the studio where he had begun as a director in 1917. This was followed by *Flesh* at MGM.[46] In May 1932, one month after Sidney Kent took over as president, Fox opened negotiations with Ford over a new contract that was essentially the same kind of deal he received at Universal and at MGM – a limited-term engagement at a fixed cost per picture.[47] His career as a freelance director had begun.

Air Mail

Faced with freelancing in 1930s Hollywood, where actors and technicians tended to be bound to studios by contract, Ford confronted the prospect of adjusting to new crew members and a new producer with each deal he made, as had occurred when he moved from Fox to Goldwyn for *Arrowsmith*. But the situation he encountered at Universal in March 1932 was unusually propitious, unlike that at Goldwyn, and it provides a compelling demonstration of the appeal of freelance work for the director. *Air Mail* was produced by Carl Laemmle, Jr., son of the studio's founder, who had taken over as general manager of the studio early in 1929 with the aim of increasing productivity and building an organization capable of turning out ten specials in a year.[48] The plan was over-ambitious, especially in the light of busi-

ness conditions following the stock market crash of October 1929, but in the event, the studio was able to sustain a small program of high-budget sound films of road-show calibre. In April of 1929 it released two musicals, *Show Boat* and *Broadway*, the latter produced by Laemmle at a cost of one million dollars.[49] In the following season Laemmle brought in Broadway impresario John Murray Anderson to direct *King of Jazz*, a high profile musical revue featuring Paul Whiteman and his Orchestra among other performers. He engaged Lewis Milestone for the critically esteemed and financially successful special *All Quiet on the Western Front*. Laemmle also expanded the studio's range of top directors. William Wyler was promoted out of the B Western unit with *The Shakedown* in 1928. Two years later, two other directors were hired who would become mainstays of the company – John Stahl in 1930, James Whale in 1931.[50]

In this context, Ford was welcomed back to Universal with open arms. The director was initially hired to direct two films as part of a group of prestige productions for the 1932–1933 season, a group which also included John Stahl's *Back Street* and Tay Garnett's *Okay America*.[51] But, by the time Ford settled on adapting the story *The Mail Goes Through* in early May, he had commitments pending at MGM and Fox and only had time to direct one feature for the Laemmles.[52] Laemmle paired Ford with the distinguished German cinematographer Karl Freund whose credits included, among many other films, Ewald Andre Dupont's *Variété* (1925), Fritz Lang's *Metropolis* (1927) and Murnau's *Der letzte Mann* (1924)

45   Fred [Totman], Letter to Ford, ? December 1931 [archivist's date], Ford correspondence, Lilly Library, IU.
46   "Beery a Wrestler in Next Picture", *Hollywood Reporter* (28 Jan 1932): 3; "Goulding with Beery", *Hollywood Reporter* (10 Feb 1932): 7; "Robert Leonard, Not Raoul Walsh On *Flesh*", *Hollywood Reporter* (11 Jun 1932): 3; Ford's participation is first reported in *Flesh*", *Hollywood Reporter* (31 Aug 1932): 4.
47   The first correspondence in the Fox Legal files on rehiring Ford is from producer Al Rockett, Memo to John H. Tracy, 4 May 1932, also George Bagnall, Memo to John H. Tracy, 9 May 1932, both in John Ford Contract File, Twentieth Century-Fox Legal Department. The contract was signed in late May, John H. Tracy, Letter to Mr. C. E. Richardson, 28 May 1932, Fox Legal Department. The contract was for $40,000 a picture paid in weekly installments until completion of production.
48   "Young Laemmle, Pop Away…", *Variety* (13 Feb 1929): 5; "Young Laemmle's Economy May Spread Over U", *Variety* (20 Feb 1929): 6; "U After High Calibre Execs", *Variety* (12 Feb 1930): 11.
49   On the cost of the production see Clive Hirschhorn, *The Universal Story* (New York: Crown Publishers, 1983), 63.
50   Axel Madsen, *William Wyler* (New York: Thomas Y. Crowell, 1973): 62–65; "Stahl Leaves Metro for U's *Sincerity*", *Variety* (12 Apr 1930): 1; "Whale with U", *Variety* (11 Mar 1931): 4.
51   "Universal Signs Up Ford and Garnett," *Hollywood Reporter* (11 Mar 1932): 1; "'U' Has 'Prestige' Group," *Hollywood Reporter* (9 Aug 1932): 1-2; "Figure 26 Strong Films," *Variety* (9 Aug 1932): 7, 10; "'Junior Laemmle' Sales Drive Set," *Hollywood Reporter* (18 Aug 1932): 2.
52   "Ayres in Mail Story", *Variety* (3 May 1932): 6; "Ford's Delays", *Variety* (24 May 1932): 6.

and *Herr Tartüff* (1926). His Universal credits included Tod Browning's *Dracula* (1931), Stahl's *Strictly Dishonorable* (1931) and *Back Street* (1932), and Robert Florey's *Murders in the Rue Morgue* (1932). Shortly after the completion of *Air Mail* (in production from early June to mid July 1932, with retakes in early September) Laemmle gave the cinematographer his first directing assignment, *The Mummy* (in production September to October 1932). At about the same time, the producer gave an interview to the *American Cinematographer* in which he opined that "the director is the most important single factor in the success of a motion picture", and explained that cinematographers were good candidates for promotion to this position by virtue of their highly developed sense of pictorial values and their close on-going collaborations with directors on set. He added that Universal had "developed" Freund's talents accordingly.[53] Given the proximity of the interview with the production dates of *Air Mail* and *The Mummy*, it seems likely that Laemmle viewed Freund's collaboration with Ford in this light. The Ford-Freund team was given considerable latitude to experiment with set design, lighting and camera movement, and the newly emerging technique of back-projection. Although the resulting film has been dismissed as a negligible low-budget programmer by critics, in terms of style and technique it should be classed alongside *Arrowsmith* as a high point in Ford's work in the early 1930s, and it had a significant impact on other directors, particularly Howard Hawks.[54]

Although Universal contract player Lew Ayres was announced as part of the cast of *Air Mail* in early May, the studio eventually opted to use him in Garnett's feature. Ford seems to have persuaded the studio to borrow young actors who were not yet fully-fledged stars, and therefore not too expensive to hire, but who already had a good track record. For the role of Mike, Universal borrowed Ralph Bellamy from Fox, where he had played major roles in films directed by Borzage, Walsh and Henry King. Pat O'Brien, a stage actor who had experienced a runaway success in his first film role as Hildy in Milestone's *The Front Page* (1931), was borrowed from Columbia for the role of Duke. The choice of O'Brien was an intelligent one, since the plot of *Air Mail* revolves around a tussle of wills between the principal male characters, as *The Front Page* does between Hildy and Walter Burns.

Air Mail was scripted by Dale Van Every, a Universal screenwriter and producer, and Frank Wead, a freelance writer in the early stages of his career. A Navy pilot who had served in World War I, Wead made many daring trials of planes in the period following the War until a freak domestic accident disabled him. No longer able to fly, he developed a career as a screenwriter, frequently writing about aviation and/or life in the military. He and Ford became friends following the production of *Air Mail* and during World War II they collaborated on *They Were Expendable* (1945). Following Wead's death, Ford directed a film based on his life, *Wings of Eagles* (1957).

Air Mail's reputation has suffered by comparison with two later films by Howard Hawks: *Ceiling Zero* (1936) and *Only Angels Have Wings* (1939). *Ceiling Zero* was adapted from Wead's play of the same name, which reworked the plot of *Air Mail*.[55] *Only Angels Have Wings* was from a story by Hawks with a screenplay by Jules Furthman. The following is a partial list of the striking similarities between the films.

> 1. *Air Mail* and *Ceiling Zero* both revolve around a conflict between the manager responsible for an emerging commercial airline and an "old school" daredevil pilot. Pat O'Brien plays the daredevil in *Air Mail* and the manager in *Ceiling Zero*. In *Only Angels Have Wings* the two types are merged in the character of Geoff Carter (Cary Grant, in one of his best performances).

---

53   Carl Laemmle, Jr., "Why I Choose Cinematographers as Directors", *American Cinematographer* (Nov 1932): 11, 35.

54   On the film's supposed low-budget status see Eyman, *Print the Legend*, 134; McBride, 179, quotes Gloria Stuart's characterization of it as a "*potchkeh*" low-budget picture; Gallagher, 130, who admires the film, writes that it "seems too much a depressed little commercial programmer to attract the critical attention it merits".

55   *Ceiling Zero*, produced by Brock Pemberton at the Music Box Theatre on Broadway, opening 10 Apr 1935. The production seems to have been financed by Warners, the studio that produced the film version, "'Save B'Way for H'Wood'", *Variety* (1 May 1935): 1, 51.

2. All of the versions have a pilot who is threatened with losing his license to fly: in *Air Mail* it is the manager, in *Ceiling Zero* the daredevil, and in *Only Angels Have Wings* the Kid, a long-time confederate of the manager, who must ground him.

3. All the films begin with a plane in trouble. In *Ceiling Zero*, a nervous pilot flying in a fog parachutes to safety when his instruments begin to malfunction (he is later fired for abandoning his craft unnecessarily). In both *Air Mail* and *Only Angels Have Wings*, the manager attempts to land down a competent pilot trying to land in a dense fog (and looking forward to hot java in one case and a girl and a steak in the other). The attempt fails and the pilot dies in the crash. The pilot is called "Joe" in both cases, and the incident in Hawks's film is clearly borrowed from the beginning of Ford's.

4. All the films have some version of a cowardly pilot, one who has parachuted out of a malfunctioning plane, as in the opening of *Ceiling Zero* described above. In *Air Mail*, the subplot concerns Tony, a pilot who in a former job had jumped and left his passengers to die in the ensuing crash. Tony has continued flying under an assumed name but when his identity is discovered the manager, although desperately short of pilots, refuses to let him fly, indeed refuses to speak to him. *Only Angels Have Wings* inverts the situation in *Air Mail*. When the manager discovers the cowardly pilot's true identity he decides to keep him on staff, since he wants someone he can send out in dangerous weather without worry (he has "too many friends" among his other pilots). This coward redeems himself by flying several dangerous missions, thereby winning acceptance among the professional group, a prototypical Hawksian situation.

These mutual borrowings and their accompanying inversions or condensations of plot elements should not necessarily be considered to the detriment of any particular version. Rather, the successive iterations of the plot may be considered par for the course in genre cinema, where stories are necessarily passed from hand to hand. Hawks may have improved on *Air Mail*, but he also liked it well enough to take it as a model.

There have also been objections to the triangle in *Air Mail* between the pilot Dizzy (Russell Hopton), his wife Irene (Lilian Bond) and Duke.[56] The film suggests that Irene has been unfaithful and that her husband enjoys punishing her for this, maliciously threatening violence to keep her under his control. Duke, an inveterate womanizer and fearless in the pursuit of his own interests, makes a volatile situation even worse. Mike and Ruth (Gloria Stewart), the normative romantic couple, are rendered rather pallid in contrast to this highly charged, if unpleasant, triangle of abusive husband, vituperative wife and self-absorbed lover. But despite the presence of two romance subplots, *Air Mail* is above all a movie about weather and the technology, careful planning and stoicism required for men to confront it in flight. Joe's horrific death might seem too dramatic for a film's opening, but it has the advantage of establishing these elements at the start. As they prepare for Joe's scheduled arrival, Mike and Pop (David Landau) receive weather reports by radio and ticker-tape machine, study the fog outside the window, and communicate with Joe by radio. Once the plane's engines are heard, all rush outside to the field, the ground crew lighting fires to illuminate the runway as Mike communicates with Joe via a handset and the other pilots study his successive landing attempts. The failure of these concerted efforts to effect a safe landing demonstrates the fragility of the technological systems meant to protect the men, and the bravery that is required every time they take off.

The weather, and the attempts to safeguard against it, become leitmotifs in what follows. The *Variety* review noted: "Picture ... is full of technical touches of an air mail depot routine. ... Radio exchanges are coming and going out all the time, couched in technical language such as 'Visibility zero, ceiling zero. Caution to all planes'. All this is delivered in a deadly monotone as a sort of obbligato to the action itself." The reviewer suggested that the emphasis on routine ultimately delayed the action, taking time away from the "human drama" that he assumed was at the heart of the story. But it could be argued that this routine comprises the most essential part of the

---

56   For example, the review of *Air Mail* in *Variety* (8 Nov 1932): 17.

action. Pilots land and take off in tandem – if one brings in the mail from the west coast, the next takes it east. Not even death disrupts this rhythm. After Joe's crash, the ground crew collects the charred mail and Mike, who always takes the next flight after "something happens", flies it to the west coast. As the film dwells on the successive pilots suiting up, their exits from the control room to the runway, their brief interactions with the ground crew, their reports by radio, it highlights the day-to-day handling of risk.

The fog gives way to a bright, clear day in act one, but act two begins with pouring rain which escalates to snow and ice at the beginning of act three. As the weather becomes more severe, action in the control room pauses every time a pilot radios in. To make matters worse, Mike learns that the pilot Tex is "deserting", quitting for a new job in Florida and thinning out the staff in the middle of the busy Christmas rush. Later, airport alarms go off as a passenger plane with ice accumulating on its wings initiates an emergency landing that comes off successfully. At the close of the act, Dizzy crashes and dies in a nearby canyon.

The relatively brief fourth act begins as Irene, Duke and Ruth wait in the control room for Mike to return from the crash site. From the control room windows, they see Mike unloading mail bags without Dizzy, and Irene and Duke realize that the way has been cleared for their affair. The crux of act four is the question of who is to fly the mail from Dizzy's flight east during the violent storm. Mike initially assumes responsibility given that "something has happened". Pop then reveals that Mike's doctor has diagnosed weakening eyesight and, with Ruth, prevails upon him to give the job to Duke, who was originally scheduled for it. Tony begs to be allowed to take the flight for his own "redemption" but Mike will not even consider it. Duke then refuses to take it, sneering at Mike for cowardice and revealing that he is running away with Irene. Mike thus has no choice but to take the flight under circumstances in which he is almost certain to come

to grief. In an ironic juxtaposition, Mike's plane takes off as three pilots – one coward, one shirker and one deserter – take the bus to the train station.

The last act redeems the nonetheless unrepentant Duke from his association with Tony and Tex, the other pilots who took the bus. After hearing on the radio that Mike has crashed in a supposedly inaccessible canyon, he brags to Irene that he could land there. Learning that Mike is likely to freeze during the night, he abruptly leaves her and somewhat improbably gets access to a plane. His landing in the canyon involves a series of risky maneuvers that severely damage the plane's wing and landing gear. Nonetheless he manages to take off with Mike on board and once they approach the field, to get the manager to jump. Duke, without a parachute, goes down with the plane, but in the ambulance at the film's close he claims to have "walked away from it".

Air Mail called for the close coordination of special effects, set design and cinematography and it appears that Ford and Freund worked closely with the art and special-effects departments, both relatively well-developed at Universal given their importance for the horror genre in which it specialized. Freund had already relied upon special-effects man John Fulton for matte painting and process work in *Dracula* and *Murders in the Rue Morgue*. These techniques were used in *Air Mail* along with miniatures constructed by Cleo E. Baker. John Brosnan has described the miniature that evoked the tiny figure of Mike trapped at the bottom of a snow-covered canyon viewed from the point of view of a pilot circling in a plane above.[57] Miniatures were important for many other scenes as well. For example, the model shot of Joe's plane hitting a radio tower and bursting into flames was matted into a live-action shot of the assembled pilots, who apparently run towards it. A beautiful miniature of the large plane hangar, lights shining in the snow, is shown from the mobile point of view of the pilots of the passenger plane coming in for a landing.

Air Mail may well have been the first time that Ford extensively employed back-projection.

---

57   John Brosnan, *Movie Magic* (London: Macdonald, 1974), 68–71, cited in Gallagher, 132; see also Donald A. Jahrous, A.S.C., "Making Miniatures", *American Cinematographer* (Nov 1931): 9–10, 42; J. Devereaux Jennings, A.S.C., "How Miniatures are Photographed", *American Cinematographer* (Jun 1934): 60, 66.

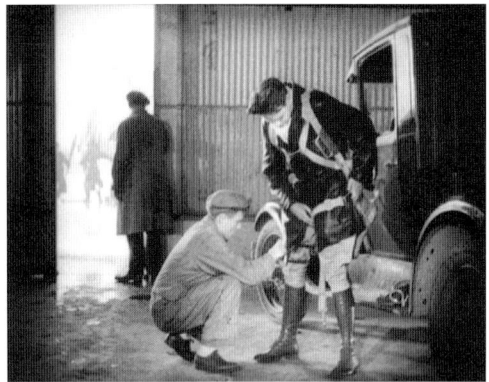

3.1

3.2

3.3

3.4

3.5

It was a relatively new process in the early 1930s, described by Farciot Edouart of the Paramount special-effects department as the projection of film on a "translucent screen of large dimensions as a background for action photographed in the studio". Farciot explained that the process was made

possible by the introduction of a "high-powered projection apparatus" developed for Fox's wide-screen Grandeur process in 1929–1930, and by the introduction of Super-Sensitive Panchromatic negative in 1931.[58] In *Air Mail*, actors seated in model planes "fly" against back-projected aerial footage of the mountainous landscape augmented with fog or snow effects. More importantly, several sets were designed to incorporate back-projection, which effectively provided a means of integrating action on interior sets with the air field outside. Figure 3.1 shows the hangar set with Dizzy suiting up in the right foreground while a back-projection visible through the door rear left suggests the ground crew preparing his plane in the pouring rain.

The main studio set of the control room prominently featured back-projected views of planes as well as dramatically conveying a sense

58   Farciot Edouart, "The Transparency Projection Process", *American Cinematographer* (Jul 1932): 15, 39; Ralph G. Fear, "Projected Background Anematography", *American Cinematographer* (Jan 1932): 11–12, 26. See notes 65 and 66 on the introduction of Super-Sensitive Panchromatic negative.

3.6

3.7

3.8

of weather conditions. Reminiscent of Rochus Gliese's design of the cafe in *Sunrise*, the set is dominated by large windows which take up most of the rear wall. Figure 3.2 illustrates the left side of the set with Mike at his desk in the foreground and Pop's unoccupied station behind it, his radio visible in the background. The rainstorm effect outside the window begins act two. Figure 3.3 shows the right side of the set with the door, background right, leading to the airfield. Pop is now visible at his station in the far left background. The snow-storm effect outside the window begins act three. In the shot illustrated in figure 3.3, the lateral movement of a plane outside is paralleled by Bellamy pacing back and forth in the midground. Cuts "outside" to the actors climbing into and out of planes make the illusion of back-projected images in the control room more vivid. In figure 3.4, the pilot Heinie (Hans Fuerberg) has previously exited through the doorway rear

right. In the film, he can be seen through the window, in the back-projected image, putting on his pack as he stands adjacent to a plane. Cut to figure 3.5 which shows Fuerberg in the studio-constructed exterior beside the plane.

The special effects deployed in the film were augmented by a creative blend of footage taken on location. Ford and his company traveled to Bridgeport, California (probably shooting in and around the airport at Bryant Field).[59] Elmer Dyer did the aerial photography along with two other stunt pilots, Jimmy James and Paul Manz. Figures 3.6 through 3.8 are from the scene of Duke's first landing at Desert Airport, in which he buzzes the control room, flies low enough to threaten pilots and ground crew on the field, and flies through an open hangar. If the first landing we see in *Air Mail*, Joe's, ends in disaster, and the second, Mike's at Pacific Airport, is well executed and routine, the third, Duke's, is pure pleasure. Although the sequence of Duke's approach involved actual planes and stunt flying, it also incorporated aspects of the studio-built set. A comparison of figure 3.6, the plane seen through the window of the control room, with the control room in figure 3.3 reveals the differences between the sets (compare the framings of the large windows and the configuration of the furnishings). The shot of Duke's fly-over thus seems to have been done by building an open-air mock-up of the studio set on location.

59   "*Air Mail* on Location", *Hollywood Reporter* (2 Jun 1932): 2; "A Little from 'Lots'", *Film Daily* (14 Jun 1932): 6; "U Sends out Caravan with Two Companies", *Hollywood Reporter* (22 Jun 1932): 3.

Due to Freund's participation and the film's generally low-key lighting schemes, critics have often referred to *Air Mail* as Expressionist, or in the style of Murnau.[60] But the film's distinctive style is highly dependent upon the highlights and delicate tracery of grays produced by Super-Sensitive Panchromatic negative, the new stock that enabled back-projection. It was introduced by Eastman Kodak in February, 1931, and tested by the American Society of Cinematographers and the studios over the next six months.[61] In daylight, the new stock was 100 per cent faster than the previous panchromatic stock, Panchromatic Type II, but it was 200 per cent more sensitive to the green portion of the spectrum and 400 to 500 per cent more sensitive to red, frequencies which were more pronounced in the incandescent lights often used to shoot interiors.[62] Cinematographers particularly praised the stock's capacity to render detail in shadows and its excellent color separation. Charles Lang, A.S.C., advised his colleagues: "If we can contrive to see to it that our sets are not monochromatic – that there is a pleasing visual color-contrast in them, the superior color rendition of the new emulsion, which closely approximates that of our eyes, will help us to get depth and brilliance into our sets".[63] That is, the stock excelled at rendering all the colors visible to the eye in tones of grey. Oliver Marsh, A.S.C., commented:

> You will find that the tonal quality, color-separation, and general gradation of your picture will be vastly improved, and with this improvement will come a surprising improvement in perspective. I have seen comparative tests, made with the same camera, lens, and set-up, but with Type Two Panchromatic and Super-Sensitive Panchromatic films, in which the difference in perspective was so marked as to make experienced cinematographers doubt that the same lens was used in both instances.[64]

Few problems with the stock were reported in the pages of *American Cinematographer*, save that the film was very soft, sometimes lacking in contrast, and brilliant light sources (e.g., men's white dress shirts) glowed to the point of losing definition, bleeding around the edges.[65]

Air Mail was probably the second film that Ford made with Super-Sensitive Panchromatic. It seems likely that he tried it first on *Arrowsmith*, given that Ray June was experimenting with the stock at Goldwyn as early as February 1931.[66] But the director would not have had additional opportunities to explore the actinic properties of the negative due to his dismissal and seven-month hiatus from filmmaking. Following Ford's return to Universal, he and Freund seemed to have made up for lost time very rapidly. For example, note the detail in figure 3.3, a soft image with a dark and complicated foreground that sets off the lighter, back-projected snowstorm visible through the window. The brightest lights are in the midground, top left, bouncing off Bellamy's right shoulder and Slim Summerville's back as he bends over the stove. The left top light also catches the shoes and the edge of the face of the figure lounging in the right foreground (Tom Carrigan as Sleepy). But the effects light emanating from the stove on the right and reflected off Summerville's face is quite distinct in tone and glows softly. Pop at the window in the background is seated back to camera and squeezed between Heinie foreground left and the left edge of the frame but

---

60 McBride, 180; Gallagher, 130.
61 "Eastman Issues Super Sensitive Panchromatic Negative Type Two at a Dinner Given by Brulatour Company", *International Photographer* (Mar 1931): 4; William Stull, A.S.C., "A.S.C. Conducts Fast Film Tests", *American Cinematographer* (1 Jun 1931): 19; "A.S.C. Recommends Fast Film", *American Cinematographer* (2 Jul 1931): 19. A panchromatic stock with similar actinic properties was available from DuPont, see Luci Marzola, "Better Pictures through Chemistry: DuPont and the Fight for the Hollywood Film Stock Market", *Velvet Light Trap*, 76 (Fall 2015): 3–18.
62 Emery Huse and Gordon A. Chambers, "Eastman Issues Super Sensitive Panchromatic Negative Type Two – Motion Picture Film", *International Photographer* (Mar 1931): 5–6.
63 Charles Lang, "Some Thoughts on Low-Key Lighting", *American Cinematographer* (Oct 1931): 15, 45.
64 Oliver Marsh, "Super-Sensitive Film in Production", *American Cinematographer* (May 1931): 11; for a visual comparison between the two stocks see Emmett Schoenbaum, "Super-Sensitive Film and the Still Man", *American Cinematographer* (Jun 1931): 8–9.
65 Charles G. Clarke, A.S.C., "Fast Improvement of Fast Film", *American Cinematographer* (Jul 1931): 10, 40; Dr. V. B. Sease, DuPont, "Halation", *American Cinematographer* (Jul 1931); 14; Virgil Miller, A.S.C., "A Standard Grey for Linens", *American Cinematographer* (Sep 1931): 16, 24.
66 Fred Westerberg, "New Negative to Improve Quality", *International Photographer* (May 1931): 29.

3.9

3.10

3.11

inherently subtle color gradations are augmented by the rain effect which diffuses the light coming through the window. It seems clear that Ford and Freund used the stock's softness to their advantage in these dazzling shots of faces.

No set designer is credited for *Air Mail*, but one imagines that Ford and Freund had substantial input in the design. Just as the sets were built to accommodate back-projection, which increased the apparent depth of the sets, they were also built to facilitate composition, and actual movement, in depth. In figure 3.3, the foreground figures, Heine and Sleepy, are largely still and carefully positioned to open up an aperture through which Slim and Mike can be seen in the midground. Pop, in the background, is the icing on the cake. Ford also created compositions in depth through arrangements of actors on narrow

remains nonetheless immediately recognizable and distinct.[67]

In figure 3.9, note the stripes and checks of Lillian Bond's costume, which pop due to the superior color rendition of the negative. Figures 3.10 and 3.11, from the same sequence, illustrate an exchange of looks between Mike, outside the window, unloading the mail bags from Dizzy's plane and Duke, inside, triumphant over the fact that Dizzy has not come back. The facial modeling on the left side of each actor's face is highly variegated, as is the network of shadows generated by Mike's hat and the folds of his coat. In both shots, the apparent frost which suggests the presence of a window has been thrown out of focus, exacerbating the halation of the multiple pin-points of reflected light. Figure 3.12, a close shot of Irene from an earlier scene, demonstrates the extreme softness of the negative. In this case, the stock's

3.12

67 The stills were taken from an older 35mm print which was softer and brighter than the contrasty video copies now available. Given that Universal, with the Library of Congress National Audio-Visual Conservation Center, Culpeper, Virginia, has completed a 4K restoration, it is high time that a good quality blu-ray of this beautiful film is made available.

3.13

3.14

3.15

slices of the wide expanse of the set. The framing in figure 3.13 sets up a contrast between Pop, seated in the center background, Mike at his station in the left midground and Duke, foreground right. Duke also stands out by virtue of his standing posture which places his head much higher than the other men's in the frame. The composition underlines the conflict between manager and pilot, and Duke's great exit line: "Don't fly that desk too fast".

In figure 3.14, a medium-long-shot framing of Mike, Slim and Tommy near the stove, the men examine the Santa Claus costume that Ruth expects Mike to wear. Figure 3.15 is from the same shot, after Pop enters to answer the phone for a report about Heinie. The men have moved out in a diagonal line extending toward the window, with the back of Tommy's head providing a low foreground object, a *repoussoir*, to heighten the sense of depth. The transformation of the space mirrors the sudden change in the focus of the men's attention, from office banter to a matter

of life and death, while simultaneously calling attention to the storm visible beyond the window.

The design of the interior of Dizzy and Irene's house similarly favored composition in depth. It was built as one continuous set as demonstrated by a shot of Dizzy having breakfast in the kitchen with the living room visible beyond (figure 3.16). Later, after Dizzy's exit, Duke enters uninvited and approaches Irene in the space outside the kitchen, with a corner of the bedroom suggestively visible behind them (figure 3.17). A passive-aggressive seduction scene that deserves Gallagher's adjective "Antonioni-like" is later conducted across the depth of the living room, the distance between the characters emphasized by Pat O'Brien's insouciant slouch in the foreground (figures 3.18 and 3.19).

Like the set of Dizzy and Irene's house, the control-room set also makes use of a contiguous room, a recreation area off the main part of the set. The recognition of Tony as Larry Thomas, the pilot of ill repute, occurs as characters move into and across this hitherto rarely used space. In figure 3.20 the doors to this room are opened to receive the passengers from the downed plane, revealing the control room beyond. In figure 3.21, a long take is initiated on a jolly passenger smoking a cigar. Pan right as the passenger approaches Mike and offers him one. Slim pops out from behind Mike and also helps himself (figure 3.22). Pan right with Slim who stops to speak to a woman passenger, a flying enthusiast, who asks about the captain (figure 3.23). Slim jokingly claims the captain, who is short, is a pilot named "Frenchy Bocquel".[68] Pan left as Slim walks

3.16

3.17

3.18

3.19

through the double doors leading to the control room and turns to point out the shorter of the two pilots, mouthing "Frenchy", with the taller co-pilot also visible in the background (figure 3.24). This elaborately staged joke establishes the presence of the pilots from the downed plane who will identify Tony from the same doorway a few shots later. Mike summons Tony to help with the passengers, opening a door to reveal another contiguous space where the pilot has sequestered himself on his bunk away from prying eyes. As Tony enters into the light of the recreation room he walks into direct contact with the co-pilot standing next to his boss in the doorway (figure

3.25). Ford and Freund then slowly track in to close up as the man says "Larry Thomas".

The compositions and movement in depth, and across contiguous spaces, are not simply a *tour de force* of camerawork and set design. They utilize graphic and/or kinetic means to distinguish narratively important gestures or actions – the re-introduction of the threat of the snow storm in the midst of the joke about Mike's costume, the passive-aggressive seduction scene, the recognition that upends Tony's life and further diminishes Mike's staff.

In addition to the experimentation with back-projection and set design, *Air Mail*

---

68   Joe Bocquel, a French-born aviator, died while performing a stunt at the Panama-California Exposition in San Diego in 1916, see "Four Aviators Meet Death While Flying", *The Billboard* (11 Nov 1916): 64, and Bocquel's entry in the Harold E. Morehouse Flying Pioneers Biographies collection, National Air and Space Museum Archives, Smithsonian Institution. The mysterious allusion to him may have been intended as a tribute by Summerville, Ford or Wead. Wead, in 1916 an ensign aboard the U.S.S. *San Diego*, which served as an attraction at the Exposition, would certainly have known about the crash. Summerville was acting for Keystone in 1916, when Bocquel is reported as flying stunts for a Keystone film, see "Keystone Activities'", *Moving Picture World* (4 Nov 1916): 683. "With the Workers at Universal City'", *Motion Picture News* (18 Nov 1916): 3141, has a composite picture which includes the aviator alongside Universal actress Priscilla Dean, placing Bocquel at the studio when Ford was working there (and incidentally confirming Bocquel's short stature).

3.20

3.21

3.22

3.23

3.24

3.25

represents an important consolidation of Ford's emerging sound style. This was the first sound film that Ford made after the industry's definitive abandonment of multiple-camera shooting. *Air Mail* is much more quickly cut than *Arrowsmith*, having an ASL of 7.5 seconds as opposed to the Goldwyn film's 12.5 seconds. The difference in cutting rate was largely due to *Air Mail*'s quick-cut action scenes. Such scenes frequently relied upon the integration of disparate sources of footage – shots taken in the studio, shots staged on location, footage taken by stunt pilots, and process shots with miniatures – into a coherent fictional space, a process which was facilitated by shorter shot lengths. For example, the scene in which Duke buzzes the air field has an ASL of 4.5 seconds, and the sequence of Duke flying in search of Mike and crash landing at his place in the canyon one of 3.6 seconds. Nonetheless the dialogue scenes in *Air Mail* follow the same basic strategy that Ford employed in *Arrowsmith*, downplaying shot-reverse-shot in favor of long takes to allow performances to unfold in real time. The sequence in which Mike reports to headquarters at Pacific airport contains three conversation scenes. While the first, a fast-paced conversation with his boss, employs shot-reverse-shot taken with a single camera and has an ASL of 5.8 seconds, the next two, which are dramatically much more important, are single static takes. The doctor's warning about the deterioration of Mike's eyesight has a duration of close to forty-six seconds. It is followed by a confrontation between Mike and Duke in which their shared past is indicated by the fact that they immediately begin trading insults, an amusing take of forty-eight seconds.

When considered in relation to Ford's earlier sound films, it is clear that *Air Mail* benefitted from new developments in recording and sound editing technology and technique. For example, the film includes several passages of overlapping dialogue, the actors stepping on each other's lines. In the earliest years of sound recording this standard theatrical technique of line reading risked inaudibility, but it became practicable once noise reduction was introduced in 1931.[69] Pat O'Brien and Adolph Menjou employed it in *The Front Page*, and it can be heard in *Air Mail* in several of O'Brien's altercations with Bellamy. David Landau and Bellamy also use it in the scene in which Pop argues with Mike over his decision to take Dizzy's flight during the snow storm.

Foley effects are more prevalent than music in the film and are frequently blended with dialogue. The introduction of noise-reduction technology had effectively increased the decibel range of optical sound, in particular making it possible to record at much lower levels. This made it more feasible to combine dialogue with sustained effects and also to create more dramatic contrasts between soft and loud sound. The seven-minute

sequence at the end of act four that culminates in Mike's taking off in the snow storm despite medical advice to the contrary unfolds against the intermittent drone of plane noise. The sequence begins with the plane that is to take on Dizzy's mail driving up the field accompanied by wind and engine sound. The engine is then often heard in the pauses between lines of dialogue as characters discuss who is to convey the mail. It is faintly audible as Ruth and Pop try to dissuade Mike from taking the flight. It becomes louder when Tony offers to take it and Mike refuses. The volume of the background sound increases again during the altercation between Mike and Duke, and this level is maintained as Mike suits up and bids goodbye to Ruth. As the door to the field opens for Mike to exit, the noise begins to dominate the track. During the shots in the studio-built exterior of Mike climbing onto the plane and bidding goodbye to Slim, the level of the background sound is elevated well above that of the dialogue. The noise of the take-off remains quite pronounced when the film cuts to the passengers and the rogue pilots boarding the bus. The control of relative sound levels is quite impressive for the period.

Another dramatic escalation of volume occurs earlier in the film, after the passenger plane radios in an SOS during the snow storm. A twenty-one-second shot of Mike and Pop at the radio builds swiftly in volume and sonic density. Mike immediately begins barking orders at the ground crew, off: "Hey Slim, Tommy, get some oil barrels out there and get a fire started, quick!" The density of the track begins to thicken as Tommy responds from off screen and slams the door on the way to the field while Mike leans over Pop, buttoning up his coat and picking up the pace of his speech: "Tell him to land here at Desert Airport. Tell him it's snowing here but it's just as bad further on and worse behind him. Tell him we are lighting a beacon to help him down." He turns and swiftly exits right on the last phrase. As Pop repeats Mike's words in a low voice into his microphone, a siren begins to blare at high

---

69   On the introduction of noise reduction, see Jacobs, "Innovation of Re-recording", 14–15; on the problem of recording overlapping dialogue, Lea Jacobs, *Film Rhythm after Sound: Technology, Music, and Performance* (Oakland, California, University of California Press, 2015), 201–202.

volume. The camera tracks in, the movement further emphasizing the crescendo. Cut to a high-angle long shot of the hangar, with men running towards camera and the siren at full blast. Cut to a medium shot of Mike barking orders as the siren continues. This is more than a simple scene transition, the siren noise becomes the functional equivalent of a rousing orchestral underscore.

The film makes extensive use of off-screen sound, flexibly concealing and revealing sound sources. In the scene which follows Joe's death, Mike stands in the control room, the double doors to the recreation room behind him, applying salve to his burns. Ruth sits grieving to his left. Sleepy, who had suited up to serve as co-pilot before the accident, waits discreetly behind Mike. A knocking is heard off, and Bellamy turns right, looking in the apparent direction of the sound. Pan right with him as he moves to reveal Slim outside the window, knocking on the glass. The plane is visible behind him, shrouded in fog. Cut around to a low-angle full-face view of Mike as Slim departs. He steps forward and slowly nods at Sleepy, off left. As Sleepy moves off towards the field, Mike stands impassive looking down at Ruth. Cut to a high-angle close up of Ruth in profile, eyes downcast. At the sound of a propeller starting up, she looks up right in alarm. The couple exchange glances as Mike begins to suit up. No dialogue has been exchanged to this point in the scene and it is cut with the fluidity of a silent film, based upon eye-line matches between Mike and Slim, Mike and Sleepy, Mike and Ruth. Nonetheless, off-screen sound is crucial to the scene as the knock and the propeller noise viscerally evoke Mike's impending departure and his girlfriend's response.

In the final analysis the sound in *Air Mail* is impressive not for its deployment of any single new technology or technique, but for its structuring role: the complex interplay of the dialogue with what *Variety* called the radio "obbligato",

the imaginative use of off-screen sound, the carefully articulated changes in the volume and density of the track considered as a whole. One has the sense that the possibilities opened up by sound recording have been as integral to the filmmakers' initial conception of the scenes as the lighting or the special effects.

There is little direct evidence of how Ford personally experienced the making of *Air Mail*, although in retrospect he liked the film.[70] Nonetheless the production seems to have been inspired in several ways. At the level of technological innovation, it benefitted from the end of multiple-camera shooting, the adoption of noise-reduction technology, and the new Super-Sensitive film that allowed for back-projection and favored composition in depth as well as the film's dazzlingly soft highlights. Moreover, the working conditions at Universal seem to have been particularly congenial. Many aspects of the film – the spontaneity of the location footage taken with the stunt pilots, the myriad and subtle staging and editing techniques devised to suggest continuity between back-projection and foreground action, the set designs which cleverly accommodated both the lateral movement favored by back-projection and movement in depth – testify to the close collaboration of a director and a cinematographer at the top of their form, mobilizing an excellent technical team, and given the latitude to solve problems without much interference from top studio brass. In contrast, it seems likely that the production of *Arrowsmith* ended so badly for the director because, hemmed in by time pressure, an unfamiliar crew, and a top-down studio hierarchy, he lacked this kind of elbow room. While not all of Ford's subsequent freelance assignments proved as supportive or fruitful as the one to make *Air Mail*, one can see why the director subsequently turned to this arrangement as a means of both escaping the infighting at Fox and controlling the production process at other, "foreign" studios.

---

70 Claudine Tavernier, "The Fourth Dimension of Old Age", translated Jenny Lefcourt, in Peary, ed., 101, originally published in *Cinéma*, 137 (Jun, 1969).

Chapter 4

Ford at RKO

I n 1933, upon the completion of *Flesh* at MGM, Ford returned to Fox under a two-picture contract the delimited terms of which left him free to take on projects at other studios. Fox had opted for this arrangement as a cost-saving measure so that they could employ him for only a limited number of high-budget projects. The policy had attendant risks, however, since Ford and Harry Wurtzel took advantage of it not only to make one-off deals, as at Columbia for *The Whole Town's Talking*, but also to develop a more sustained arrangement with RKO. Ford eventually managed to create an alternative production base at the studio which paradoxically allowed him to reunite key members of his old Fox unit: Victor McLaglen, Dudley Nichols and Joe August. In addition to building on working arrangements he had already established at Fox, Ford's tenure at RKO also gave rise to new collaborations: with Max Steiner, still making his way as a film composer, and Van Nest Polglase, who had just received the first of six Academy-Award nominations for art direction. Most importantly, he made a connection with Merian C. Cooper, head of production at RKO from 1933 to 1934 and later an independent producer associated with Pioneer Pictures. In 1937, Cooper would become involved in the initial negotiations over the production of *Stagecoach*, paving the way for the creation of Cooper and Ford's independent film production company Argosy.[1]

New Deals at RKO and Fox

The deal with RKO seems to have originated with James McGuinness, then associate producer to David O. Selznick during Selznick's tenure as head of production. Following Ford's dismissal from Fox, McGuinness cabled the director, who was in the South Seas, offering a one-picture deal with John Barrymore as star (the project was eventually produced as *State's Attorney*, directed by George Archainbaud).[2] After his return to the U.S., Ford pitched McGuinness a different film based on Donn Byrne's novel *Blind Raftery and his Wife, Hilaria*, about the Irish-language poet Antoine Ó Raifteirí. After Ford signed with Universal in mid-March, McGuinness rescinded his offer.[3] In February 1933, McGuinness and Selznick moved to MGM, victims of one of RKO's many management turn-overs. Cooper, who had just completed work on *King Kong* (1933), took over Selznick's job for little more than a year.[4] In a 1965 letter to Lindsay Anderson, Cooper recalled deciding to hire Ford after seeing *Air Mail*.[5] However, Richard Jewell has pointed out that Cooper followed through on several projects initiated under Selznick's administration

---

1   Matthew Bernstein, *Walter Wanger: Hollywood Independent* (Berkeley: University of California Press, 1994), 146–147; I discuss the negotiations in chapter eight.
2   "Joyce-Selznick Spot Nice Array at Radio", *Variety* (2 Feb 1932): 4; "McGuinness' Radio Trio", *Variety* (2 Feb 1932): 6. McGuinness, Telegram to Ford, 3 Feb 1932; McGuinness Telegram to Ford, 18 Feb 1932: Frank Joyce-Myron Selznick (talent agency), Telegram to Ford, 18 Feb 1932, all in Ford correspondence, Lilly Library, IU.
3   Harry Wilson, Letter to John Ford, 12 Mar 1932, and Harry Wilson, Letter to John Ford, 21 Mar 1932, both in Ford correspondence, Lilly Library, IU.
4   Richard B. Jewell, *RKO Radio Pictures: A Titan in Born* (Berkeley: University of California Press, 2012), 69, 85, writes that Cooper was hired as production head in February 1933 and that he resigned in May 1934.
5   Cooper, Letter to Lindsay Anderson, 25 August 1963, Merian C. Cooper Papers, Box 21, Folder 2, L. Tom Perry Special Collections, Harold B. Lee Library, Brigham Young University, Provo, Utah (hereafter Harold B. Lee Library, BYU).

and securing Ford's services seems to have been one of them.[6]

In early June 1933, Ford signed a one-picture deal with RKO to direct what was eventually entitled *The Lost Patrol*.[7] Pre-production on this film began in August after Ford had fulfilled his Fox contract. While *The Lost Patrol* was in production, Ford signed a new contract with Fox on essentially the same terms as the previous one: to direct two pictures in the course of a year starting in January 1934.[8] Close on the heels of this commitment, in early October, the director contracted with RKO to direct three pictures.[9] A rough draft of another contract from Fox for three pictures beginning in April 1934 was delivered to Ford at RKO in October of 1933.[10] Likely an effort to match the terms of RKO's offer, the draft suggests that Fox was beginning to sense the disadvantages of not having the director tied up.

Ford did not accept Fox's October offer but it became the basis of negotiations for a new agreement.[11] The final version, signed on September 21, 1934, was for four pictures to be completed over twenty-six months beginning in November 1934 at a salary of $45,000 per picture. While the studio retained the right to lend Ford out on its own terms, the contract specified that he was otherwise to render his services exclusively to Fox with the exception that the director could continue to honor his contractual obligations to RKO.

> The artist will not, during the term of the employment hereby created, engage with any

other producer of motion pictures or render any service or services of any kind or nature whatsoever, either for himself or for his own account or benefit, or to any person, firm or corporation, other than the producer either within or outside of business hours, excepting, however, that the artist shall have the right to complete the rendition of his services for RKO-Radio Pictures Corporation.[12]

The contract called for the studio to give Ford thirty days notice before the start of a production, and gave Ford the option of refusing the Fox project if he had commitments to fulfill at RKO. The period of his contract would then be extended for the length of time that he was employed elsewhere.

Despite the apparent legal insistence on exclusivity, in practice Fox would find it quite difficult to keep Ford down on the farm. For example, on September 5, about two weeks before the director finally signed the four-picture contract with Fox, he signed with Columbia to direct *The Whole Town's Talking* with Edward G. Robinson.[13] *Variety*'s report of Ford's new Fox contract acknowledged the many contingencies it entailed: Ford was currently employed at Columbia, due at RKO after that, and would then return to Fox to direct *Steamboat Round the Bend* while owing more films to RKO.[14] Fox may have pushed Ford into ad hoc freelancing arrangements, but the director clearly took to them as his new *modus operandi*.

In his relations with RKO Ford did not operate as a fully independent producer but he had

6   Jewell, *RKO Radio Pictures*, 75–76, 81.
7   "Ford and Radio Dicker", *Hollywood Reporter* (10 May 1933): 1; "*Patrol* for Ford", *Hollywood Reporter* (2 Jun 1933): 3; "Ford Will Do *Patrol*", *Hollywood Reporter* (21 Jun 1933): 4. Cooper, Letter to Anderson, 25 August 1963, Merian C. Cooper Papers, Box 21, Folder 2, Harold B. Lee Library, BYU, recalled making one deal for both *The Lost Patrol* and *The Informer*, but the trade press evidence indicates that the first contract was for one film, *Patrol*.
8   Ford's second two-picture contract is described in George Wasson, Letter to Sydney Towell, 7 September 1933, John Ford Contract File, Twentieth Century-Fox Legal Department: "I enclose herewith one copy of a contract between the Corporation and John Ford, director, employing him to direct two (2) motion pictures, commencing January 2, 1934, at a compensation of $45,000.00 per picture".
9   On the RKO contract see "Ford to Do Three Radio Productions", *Hollywood Reporter* (7 Oct 1933): 1; Jewell, *RKO Radio Pictures*, 71–72.
10 Mr. Wasson [handwritten], Letter to John Ford, c/o RKO Studios, 10 October 1933, John Ford Contract File, Twentieth Century-Fox Legal Department.
11 A later offer approved by the Fox Executive Committee in April 1934 but not by Ford was for four pictures over twenty-one months at $50,000 each.
12 Agreement between Fox Film Corporation, producer, and John Ford, artist, signed 21 September 1934 by John Ford and J. J. Gain, John Ford Contract File, Twentieth Century-Fox Legal Department: the relevant pages are 1 and 5–9.
13 Ford stepped in to direct *The Whole Town's Talking*, initially titled *Jail Breaker*, when Howard Hawks, who was originally slated to direct, had obligations elsewhere, see "Choice of Director Delays *Jail Breaker*", *Hollywood Reporter* (8 Aug 1934): 10, and "Columbia Signs John Ford to Direct *Jailbreaker* [*sic*]", *Hollywood Reporter* (5 Sep 1934): 1.
14 "Ford Will Direct 4 Films for Fox", *Variety* (25 Sep 1934): 4.

a great deal of autonomy. This was partly due to the nature of his contracts, described by Jewell as highly advantageous to the studio: "They differed on each picture, but basically Ford would earn a small salary and a percentage of the gross receipts after each production returned twice its negative cost. This was considered a fine deal for RKO, as other studios had paid Ford as much as $50,000 per picture to direct."[15] Based on his examination of Ford's tax returns, McBride suggests that Ford actually realized substantial sums from the profit-sharing arrangements on his first two Radio films.[16] This conclusion is supported by an anonymous item in *Variety*, likely derived from the director, which appeared after *The Lost Patrol* began its run on Broadway: "Picture has so far hit a gross where Ford has collected double his regular salary per picture, and director figures more is coming."[17] By deferring his salary and taking most of it as a percentage of the gross, Ford effectively assumed the risk for one of the most expensive elements of *The Lost Patrol*'s production cost. While he did not raise any other kind of capital, he was in this limited sense helping to finance the production.

The Lost Patrol

The Lost Patrol was originally a Cooper project. In 1932 the producer had hired Philip MacDonald, the British author of the source novel *Patrol*, as part of a plan to augment the RKO program with adventure films.[18] The novel, drawn from the author's experience in the British cavalry in Iraq during World War I, concerned a small army unit trapped under enemy fire in the Mesopotamian desert. Although MacDonald was not formally credited as one of the screenwriters, financial records indicate that he was paid to help prepare the first draft of the script, dated August 8, 1933, which was credited to screenwriter Garrett Fort.[19] This draft evinces MacDonald's influence in its extensive use of Hindustani-inspired Indian Army slang, a prominent feature of the novel.[20]

Changes made to the novel's conclusion in the August 8 draft may have been motivated by Cooper's interest in aviation. In the novel, the men of the patrol are picked off by unseen snipers until only the sergeant remains. He sets a trap for the enemy and manages to see and to shoot them before being shot and killed himself. In the screenplay drafts and the film version, the sergeant is rescued by British cavalry after having thwarted the final attack. This reversal is motivated by the introduction of an Army plane in the last act. While the aviator is immediately shot down after landing his craft, the sergeant is able to lift the machine gun off the grounded plane and use it to defend himself during the final attack. Moreover, the flames generated by his burning of the plane are seen by a British cavalry unit which eventually comes to his rescue. Cooper had himself been an aviator in World War I and he was heavily involved in the establishment of Pan Am as a commercial airline in the 1930s. Mark Cotta Vaz describes his involvement with a prior RKO film, *The Lost Squadron* (1932), about a trio of World War I aviators who resort to stunt flying to make a living after the war.[21]

Given that Ford had signed the contract for

---

15   Jewell, *RKO Radio Pictures*, 71–72.

16   McBride, 219 note. Reports on *The Lost Patrol*'s grosses in the key cities also suggest the film was successful; when it reached Broadway in late March it was held over for three weeks at the small Rialto theatre and brought in what *Variety* considered a surprising $32,788 on its first week and $20,000 on its second, see "B'way Film Trade Okay Despite Lent", *Variety* (3 Apr 1934): 9.

17   "Inside Stuff – Pictures", *Variety* (20 Mar 1934): 51.

18   "RKO May Boost Program with Adventure Films", *Film Daily* (12 Dec 1932): 1, 4; "26 Books and Plays Purchased", *Motion Picture Herald* (31 Dec 1932): 18; "Radio Holds MacDonald", *Hollywood Reporter* (24 Feb 1933): 7.

19   Budget of Production Cost, itemization of scenario costs, 1 September 1933, *The Lost Patrol* Production File, ser.P, Box 38, Section 1, RKO Radio Pictures records, UCLA Library Special Collections, Manuscripts Division, Charles E. Young Research Library, Los Angeles, California (hereafter RKO Radio records, UCLA Library Special Collections).

20   Philip MacDonald, *Patrol* (New York: A. L. Burt Company, 1928) includes a glossary of the slang; *Patrol*, Estimating Script, 8 Aug 1933, by Garrett Fort, ser.S, Box 294, RKO Radio records, UCLA Library Special Collections. Note that the film's title was not changed to *The Lost Patrol* until the end of August, "*Patrol* Title Changed", *Hollywood Reporter* (30 Aug 1933): 3.

21   Mark Cotta Vaz, *Living Dangerously: The Adventures of Merian C. Cooper, Creator of King Kong* (New York: Villard, 2005), 31–56, 179–182, 226, 251–252.

Patrol in June, it is likely that he was consulted on Fort's initial August 8 script draft but he was probably not actively involved in its composition. He was busy at Fox with retakes in late July and trade-press evidence does not place him at RKO until the week of August 7.[22] Screenwriter Fort was taken off the production on August 7, and the first references to Dudley Nichols's involvement with the project in the trade press date from the middle of August.[23] Nichols's draft, labeled final, is dated August 28, two days before Ford and the company left to go on location.[24]

Nichols retained the basic structure of the August 8 script. In act one the lieutenant of the patrol is killed before he has explained his orders to the sergeant (who is not named in the film). The men ride aimlessly through the desert until they find an oasis where they settle in for the night. Act two begins the next morning when the patrol discovers that the sentry Pearson has been killed, the corporal Bell wounded and their horses stolen. Two men are sent out to try to locate their brigade and bring back help. In act three most of the men are gradually picked off by snipers and the mutilated bodies of the two sent out for help are returned to the oasis by the enemy. At the beginning of act four only the sergeant and two others are left – Morelli and Sanders. Sanders, rendered completely mad by their circumstances marches off into the range of the snipers' guns and Morelli follows in an attempt to bring him back. Both are killed. While preserving this structure, Nichols rewrote the dialogue, removing most but not all of the slang. He also created a characteristic Fordian touch, adding a comic Irish horse soldier to the novel's two Scottish ones.

Nichols also considerably softened the conflicts among the men of the patrol. In MacDonald's novel and the first screenplay draft, the men respond to their increasingly dire circumstances by quarreling among themselves. Sanders, an evangelical zealot, harangues the men about blasphemous language and references to women and he objects to their sometimes bawdy songs. The men generally rag on Sanders in return except when he is bullied by Abelson, a former boxer and a Jew. The tensions within the group eventually develop into a fight between Abelson and the normally phlegmatic Cook. Described in great detail in over fifteen pages in the novel, the fight is far from the comic fisticuffs typically found in Ford's films. Rather, it is a vicious expression of prejudice exacerbated by the anger and fear inspired by the patrol's military situation.[25] It retains this character in Fort's draft. One wonders if Ford and Nichols had planned to change the tenor of the fist fight, but in the event it was cut out entirely, and the part of Abelson drastically reduced, due to a last-minute change in casting.

From the point of the view of the studio, and maybe even of Cooper himself, Richard Dix was the obvious choice to play the sergeant. One of the studio's few leading male stars, Dix had acted opposite Irene Dunne in *Cimarron* (1931), one of RKO's highest-budgeted early sound films and the only one to win an Oscar for Best Picture in the 1930s.[26] Among many other starring roles he had taken the major part in *The Lost Squadron* and thus presumably had a connection to Cooper. The *Hollywood Reporter* announced his participation in *Patrol* as early as August 9 and the first budget estimate prepared by the studio on the

22 George Wasson, Memo to George Bagnall and J. J. Gain, 31 Jul 1933, John Ford Contract File, Twentieth Century-Fox Legal Department; "Hollywood Productions", *Variety* (18 Jul 1933): 42; "Retakes Hold Sheehan", *Variety* (18 Jul 1933): 4; "Hollywood", *Variety* (8 Aug 1933): 6; "Radio Wants McLaglen", *Hollywood Reporter* (10 Aug 1933): 1.

23 Budget of Production Cost, itemization of scenario costs, 1 September 1933, *The Lost Patrol* Production File, ser.P, Box 38, Section 1, RKO Radio records, UCLA Library Special Collections, indicates that Fort was taken off the budget on August 7; the first references to Nichols's involvement are "Fox's No. 2 Rattler Yarn", *Variety* (15 Aug 1933): 6; "'Dud' Nichols to RKO", *Hollywood Reporter* (15 Aug 1933): 2.

24 *Patrol*, [in pencil *Lost Patrol*], Final Script, 28 August 1933, by Dudley Nichols, ser.S, Box 706, RKO Radio records, UCLA Library Special Collections.

25 In the novel, the sergeant allows the fight to proceed provided that the men observe the Marquess of Queensberry's rules. Although Ford's film version does not include this fight, the director seems to have picked up from MacDonald the idea of referencing these rules when a fight is in progress; they are mentioned in this context in *How Green Was My Valley* and *The Quiet Man*.

26 Richard Jewell with Vernon Harbin, *The RKO Story* (New York: Crown Books, 1982): 33; Jewell comments on RKO's dearth of leading males, *RKO Radio Pictures*, 71, 98.

same date listed Dix at the "star salary" of $40,000.[27] McLaglen was listed in the role of Abelson for less than half of Dix's salary and he was hired with the stipulation that he was to receive second featured-player billing, behind Boris Karloff who played Sanders.[28] A temporary downturn in Dix's protracted negotiations with RKO over his new contract upset this arrangement. On August 15, Dix publicly accused the studio of cheating on his prior contract. According to the trade press, their relationship was temporarily patched up, but then fell apart sometime after August 23, less than a week before Ford and his crew were due to depart.[29] By August 29 the studio and Dix had come to an agreement, but by that time McLaglen had been slated for the lead role in *Patrol* although at his original salary of $5,000 a week. Dix had also been given new assignments, including *Stingaree*, an RKO special in which he played opposite Irene Dunne. One wonders if the actor delayed signing his contract to avoid taking the role, or if Ford found some means to convince Dix that his best prospects lay elsewhere, or if the director managed to convince the studio that they could have a better film at lower cost without him. In any case, through some combination of luck and strategy, the star of *Hangman's House* and *The Black Watch* became the star of *The Lost Patrol*.

McLaglen was by no means as important an actor in 1933 as he had been in the late 1920s after the successes of *What Price Glory* and *The Cock-Eyed World*. His reputation had diminished due to Fox's persistent casting of him opposite Lowe in increasingly cheaply made iterations of the Flagg and Quirt formula. Reportedly unhappy with the roles he was being given at Fox, McLaglen had negotiated a freelance agreement which began in June 1932.[30] While he continued to make films

at the studio, such as Blystone's Flagg-and-Quirt comedy *Hot Pepper* (1933), he had taken roles in several independent films. He played a dashing gun-runner in *Laughing at Life* (1933), a low-budget film from Nat Levine productions. He sailed for London in May 1933 for the title role in *Dick Turpin* (Victor Hanbury, John Stafford, 1933).[31] The *Hollywood Reporter* announcement that Ford had been engaged to direct *Patrol* in June would have been particularly salient for McLaglen since his brother Cyril had played the lead role in a silent British adaptation of the novel, the first to be called *The Lost Patrol* (Walter Summers, 1929). It is possible that he or his agent contacted Ford directly to solicit the part, although there is no record of this in the director's correspondence.

McLaglen's role in *The Lost Patrol* offered him a decided alternative to Sergeant Flagg's swagger, a contrast invoked in Nichols's script. The August 28 draft introduces a rivalry between two men of the company, the Scottish McKay (Paul Hanson) and the Irish Quincannon (J. M. Kerrigan). Like Flagg and Quirt, McKay and Quincannon have a long history of riotous behavior in the service and have alternated holding the rank of sergeant and being busted back to private. Early in act one we learn of their shared past:

> McKay [*referring to new recruit Pearson*]: Sure, he'll learn. Take for an example yon Matlow. I remember the time when he first came to the regiment – twenty years ago. The time Quincannon and meself had makin' a soldier of him. Michael, do you mind the time we were at the depot at Poona together? I was troop Sergeant Major at the time.
>
> Quincannon: Excuse me, but *I* was Troop Sergeant Major at the time.
>
> McKay: Oh no, Michael. You *were* Troop

27 "Ruben Named for Dix", *Hollywood Reporter* (9 Aug 1933): 7; Pre-Budget Estimate, 9 August 1933, *The Lost Patrol* production file, ser.P, Box 38, Section 3, RKO Radio records, UCLA Library Special Collections; in the same file, a Pre-Budget Estimate dated 24 August 1933 shows Dix's name crossed out, McLaglen's inserted and a considerable cost savings.

28 Pre-Budget Estimate, 9 August 1933; and Memo to Mr. Schuessler, 18 August 1933, both in *The Lost Patrol* Production File, ser.P, Box 38, Section 3, RKO Radio records, UCLA Library Special Collections.

29 "Radio Losing Its Connie; Asks New Harding-Dix Deals", *Variety* (6 Jun 1933): 2; "Dix and Radio Dicker", *Hollywood Reporter* (30 Jun 1933): 1; "Dix Claims % Loss on His RKO Contract", *Variety* (15 Aug 1933): 2; "Dix Atty. Patches Up His RKO Film Pact", *Variety* (22 Aug 1933): 3; "Dix Set with RKO", *Variety* (29 Aug 1933): 1; "*Stingaree* First for Dix", *Hollywood Reporter* (30 Aug 1933): 1.

30 Review of *Women of All Nations*, *Variety* (2 Jun 1931): 15; "McLaglen-Fox Settle", *Variety* (1 Mar 1932): 2.

31 "Hollywood", *Variety* (9 May 1933): 6.

4.1

4.2

4.3

Sergeant Major. But you had been broken for being drunk and disorderly, settin' fire to your tent, and appearin' on the parade ground with nothin' on but your drawers and your topee.

Quincannon: That's a dirty lie! I did *not* set fire to me tent.

The demeanor of McLaglen's sergeant is quite different from these comic ones. McLaglen embodies the officer with a quiet and dignified professionalism until the end of act four, when he explodes with rage and grief at the killing of his men. He tends to speak softly, with the brisk, clipped enunciation of the British officer class. As the patrol makes its way through the desert, he shows remarkable gentleness as he reprimands Pearson, a new recruit, for not rationing his water. While at one point he harshly rebukes Abelson for being hard on his horse, later, when the soldier

becomes feverish, he attentively offers to stand his watch. When Sanders harangues the other men, the sergeant dispels this source of conflict by quietly packing him off to his assigned duty. Such a reserved performance of a steady, low-key commander is apt to be overlooked both in relation to the antics of the actors providing comic relief, and in relation to Boris Karloff's emotional displays as the crazed zealot. In fact, it makes the film.

One other aspect of the production process of *The Lost Patrol* requires comment: what seems to have been a joint decision between producer and director to shoot all principal photography on location in the Algodones Dunes, a sand-dune field extending from Glamis, California, south and east to Los Algodones, Mexico. During production the entire company camped in the dunes near Yuma, Arizona, from August 31 to September 19, enduring high winds and daytime temperatures as high as 119°F.[32] It seems likely that through his connection with MacDonald Cooper knew of the earlier English adaptation of *Patrol*, which was also filmed in difficult terrain on location in Tozeur, Tunisia.[33] In any case, Cooper would have been inclined to go outside the studio. He described himself to Lindsay Anderson as "an outdoor man's director".[34] Prior to making *King Kong* in the studio, the producer and his cameraman Ernest Schoedsack had shot all of their films in remote locations. *Grass: A Nation's Battle for*

32 Assistant Director Reports, daily from 31 August 1933 to 22 September 1933, *The Lost Patrol* Production File, ser.P, Box 38, Section 2, RKO Radio records, UCLA Library Special Collections.
33 The film is lost, but location shooting is discussed in "Those Amazing McLaglens", *Film Weekly* (11 Feb 1929): 5; review of *The Lost Patrol*, *Variety* (18 Dec 1929): 28.
34 Cooper, Letter to Anderson, 25 August 1963, Merian C. Cooper Papers, Box 21, Folder 2, Harold B. Lee Library, BYU.

4.4

4.5

4.6

4.7

4.8

4.9

Life (Paramount, 1925) was shot entirely in Iran with the filmmakers following the spring migration of a Bakhtiari tribe through difficult terrain. *Chang* (Paramount, 1927) was shot in Thailand using non-professional actors from the village of Nan and staged in the nearby jungle. The spectacular sequences in *Four Feathers* (Paramount, 1929) were shot in the Sudan over a period of months and were later integrated with dramatic scenes taken on studio-built exteriors in California.[35] For his part, Ford had had extensive production experience on location, as already noted, and he may have been aware of the phenomenally photogenic dunes, which had featured in the Fox film *Business and Pleasure* (1932).[36] Their mutual interest in utilizing real landscapes would, of

35 Vaz, 109–175.
36 See Elmer G. Dyer and Hatto Tappenback, "White Hell of Algadones [*sic*] Plenty Hot", *International Photographer* (Sep 1931): 20–23.

course, become an important part of their future collaborations for Argosy.

Much of *The Lost Patrol* was shot on an oasis set constructed in the dunes. It consisted of what the studio described as "an Arabian Mosque about the size of a five room bungalow" built of plaster and about forty artificial palm trees (figure 4.1 is an aerial view of the set from the film).[37] Part of the mosque was open to the sky (figure 4.2) but the dome was enclosed and apparently housed the interior set (figure 4.3). One of the strengths of the film is the way that Ford and cinematographer Harold Wenstrom utilized the contrast between the oasis and the actual landscape, framing shots of the desert through the tree trunks (figures 4.4 and 4.5). When the sergeant encounters the wounded Bell the film cuts to a flatter and more textured section of dunes (the cut is from the composition in figure 4.5 to 4.6). Ford and Wenstrom also made dramatic use of the desert's harsh light and deep shadows (figure 4.7). Figure 4.8 shows the crazed Quincannon vainly aiming his rifle in the direction of the unseen snipers after viewing the bodies of McKay and Cook. Figure 4.9, from the sergeant's point of view, shows Morelli, the last surviving man of the patrol, gunned down following his failed attempt to rescue Saunders. Ford and Wenstrom's visually inventive deployment of the landscape is all the more impressive given the logistical difficulties of working on the site – it obviously served as an inspiration as well as an obstacle.

Adapting O'Flaherty's *The Informer*

The Informer was a very important milestone in Ford's freelance career. In production from Feb-

ruary through March 1935, it swept the Academy Awards in 1936 when it was nominated for Best Picture and won for Best Director, Best Actor, Best Screenplay and Best Scoring, bringing Ford much prestige and greater international visibility.[38] It is clear from the director's 1932 proposal to McGuinness to make a film about Ó Raifteirí – a bard championed by W. B. Yeats, Lady Gregory and others associated with the Irish National Theatre Society – that he was already interested in making a film that dealt with Irish culture and national identity. His encounter with Liam O'Flaherty in the summer of 1934 gave new shape to this ambition.[39] It is worth carefully considering how the novel was altered during script development, however, as the many ways in which the film diverges from its source have often been minimized.

In the 1920s and early 1930s, critics frequently classed Liam O'Flaherty along with James Joyce and Sean O'Casey as part of a new Irish literary generation, a realist school understood to be a break with the work of established figures such as A. E., Lady Gregory and Yeats.[40] He was one of twenty-five younger writers invited by Yeats and George Bernard Shaw to join their newly constituted Irish Academy of Letters.[41] He had secured an international reputation and his novels of the 1920s and 1930s, including *The Informer*, had been published in American as well as British editions and respectfully received.[42] When O'Flaherty arrived in New York on May 1, 1934, he was en route to Hollywood to attempt to sell the film rights to *The Informer*.[43] An English adaptation, produced by British International Pictures and directed by Arthur Robison, had already been released in 1929 in both silent and part-talkie versions.[44]

---

37   Wallace Fox, Production Manager, RKO, Letter to J. H. Favorite, U.S. Custom House, 9 November 1933, *The Lost Patrol* Production File, ser.P, Box 38, Section 3, RKO Radio records, UCLA Library Special Collections.
38   Gallagher, 185, tabulates the many honors and awards the film received.
39   Ford claimed to have met O'Flaherty in Los Angeles in 1932, to have optioned *The Informer* as early as 1933 and to have shopped it around to several studios, see, for example, Dan Ford, 72, 82. While this account has permeated the secondary literature, I can find no evidence to support it. Judging from the letters published in A. A. Kelly, ed., *The Letters of Liam O'Flaherty* (Dublin: Wolfhound Press, 1996), O'Flaherty lived in England, France and Ireland during 1932 and did not travel to America during that year. Moreover, it is clear that he went to Hollywood in 1934 expressly to sell the rights to *The Informer*, and that RKO purchased the rights directly from the author in October, 1934, see notes 43 and 50.
40   Patrick F. Sheeran, *The Novels of Liam O'Flaherty* (Dublin: Wolfhound Press, 1976), 112–113.
41   "Irish Academy of Letters", *Irish Times* (19 Sep 1932): 7.
42   See, for example, William Troy, "The Position of Liam O'Flaherty", *The Bookman* (Mar 1929): 7–11, cited in Sheeran, *Novels of O'Flaherty*, 114–115.
43   "Ocean Travelers", *New York Times* (1 May 1934): 27; "O'Flaherty Off for Hollywood and 'Big Shots'", *New York Herald Tribune* (6 May 1934): 23; Kelly, ed., 272, editorial commentary.

One mark of O'Flaherty's reputation is that he rapidly he found work in Hollywood following his arrival there on May 8. Already represented by an agent, he first signed a contract with RKO but was soon released to Paramount where producer Budd Schulberg paired him with the German director G. W. Pabst to prepare a script from O'Flaherty's own original story.[45] In late June, O'Flaherty returned to RKO for about a week, then gave notice and traveled to San Francisco where the trade press described him as "investigating labor conditions".[46] He seems to have gotten caught up in the San Francisco General Strike that began in mid-July 1934, the result of a violent confrontation between striking members of the International Longshore and Warehouse Union, and police and National Guard troops.[47] The first mention of an O'Flaherty-Ford connection in the trade press appeared in early August, when *Variety* reported that they were cruising in Mexican waters in the *Araner*.[48] Some time after this cruise, Ford seems to have intervened to resurrect O'Flaherty's contract with RKO. In late September, Frank

O'Heron, a vice president at RKO, reported to B. B. Kahane that Ford had read O'Flaherty's treatment of his novel and was interested in directing *The Informer* as opposed to *The Three Musketeers* for which he had been tentatively scheduled.[49] About this time the *Hollywood Reporter* announced that the author was preparing a script of *The Informer* with Ford likely to direct.[50]

Three dated screenplay variants make it possible to trace the adaptation process. The draft of December 18, 1934, with a title page reading "Screenplay of *The Informer* by Liam O'Flaherty", does not bear Dudley Nichols's name and was probably prepared by O'Flaherty himself.[51] After he finished production on *The Whole Town's Talking* on December 11, 1934, Ford departed with Dudley Nichols for a planned three-week cruise to rewrite the script.[52] The next draft, labeled "Estimating Script", is dated January 14, 1935, and is thus likely the product of the *Araner* cruise. It contains the scene numbers necessary for budgeting, which indicates the director's

---

44   *The Informer* (British International Pictures, 1929), directed by Arthur Robison, with Lars Hansen and Lya De Putti. The British Film Institute restored the sound version of the film in 2005 and the silent version in 2016; both are available on a blu-ray disk issued by the BFI.

45   "Liam O'Flaherty Here", *Hollywood Reporter* (9 May 1934): 3; "Schulberg Closes with Pabst and O'Flaherty", *Hollywood Reporter* (22 May 1934): 3; "Studio Placements", *Variety* (29 May 1934): 28. A version of the script for Paramount was apparently completed although never filmed, see "Schulberg Readying Three for Cameras", *Hollywood Reporter* (27 Jun 1934): 2.

46   "O'Flaherty to Radio on Munitions Story", *Hollywood Reporter* (26 Jun 1934): 3; "O'Flaherty Out of Radio", *Hollywood Reporter* (6 Jul 1934): 3; "Liam O'Flaherty North", *Hollywood Reporter* (16 Jul 1934): 2.

47   On the strike, see Bruce Nelson, *Workers on the Waterfront: Seamen, Longshoremen, and Unionism in the 1930s* (Urbana and Chicago: University of Illinois Press, 1988), 127–155; David F. Selvin, *A Terrible Anger: The 1934 Waterfront and General Strikes in San Francisco* (Detroit: Wayne State University Press, 1996), 166–235; on O'Flaherty's disappearance, see "Mike Levee worried Over Liam O'Flaherty", *Hollywood Reporter* (20 Jul 1934): 2.

48   "Chatter – Hollywood", *Variety* (7 Aug 1934): 53; "Chatter – Hollywood", *Variety* (14 Aug 1934): 53, reports that O'Flaherty is ill from "sun bathing", which seems to be a code term for a hangover.

49   Frank O'Heron, Memo to B. B. Kahane, 26 September 1934, *Informer* file, RKO Radio Pictures research collection compiled by Richard Jewell, Herrick Library, AMPAS. On Ford's prior commitment to direct *The Three Musketeers* see "John Ford to Direct Informer at Radio", *Hollywood Reporter* (13 Oct 1934): 2; *The Three Musketeers* was eventually directed by Rowland V. Lee.

50   "Gael Scripts Own Yarn", *Hollywood Reporter* (26 Sep 1934): 1; RKO purchased the rights from O'Flaherty in early October, O'Heron, Memo to Daniel T. O'Shea, 11 Oct 1934, *Informer* file, RKO Radio Pictures research collection compiled by Richard Jewell, Herrick Library, AMPAS; the purchase is confirmed by O'Flaherty, Letter to Carol Hill, [end Oct, 1934, editor's date] in Kelly, ed., 273.

51   "Screen Play of *The Informer* by Liam O'Flaherty", 18 December 1934, ser.S, Box 3691, RKO Radio records, UCLA Library Special Collections. While several critics have assumed that this draft was prepared by Dudley Nichols, I find this unlikely. The wording on the title page is ambiguous, but Nichols usually put his name on his drafts, as was professional practice. The second draft, for example, is identified as follows: "*The Informer*, screenplay by Dudley Nichols, from the novel by Liam O'Flaherty". Similarly, the first draft of *Steamboat Round the Bend* is identified as "Screenplay by: Dudley Nichols and Lamar Trotti, From the Novel by: Ben Lucien Burman". Internal evidence also suggests that the first draft of *The Informer* was prepared by someone not concerned with standard Hollywood screenplay form: there are long prose descriptions of characters and settings, and paragraphs intermittently begin with awkward technical directions such as "Shot" or "Truck up to shot" which Nichols does not typically employ.

52   "*Passport* Delayed", *Variety* (18 Dec 1934): 6; this item, dated December 17, reports that the Columbia production was completed on the prior Tuesday, using an earlier title for *The Whole Town's Talking*; "Nichols and Ford to Do Script on Cruise", *Hollywood Reporter* (17 Dec 1934): 5; "Aquatic Scripting", *Variety* (25 Dec 1934): 2; Ford, Telegram to Cliff Reid, 31 December 1934, RKO Radio Pictures research collection compiled by Richard Jewell, Herrick Library, AMPAS, announces that he had finished the rough draft and would begin working on the shooting script.

4.10

4.11

4.12

input.[53] The script labeled "Final", dated January 30, 1935, is quite close to the January 14 version.[54]

O'Flaherty's novel is set during the Irish Civil War of 1922–1923, a period of conflict between Irish supporters of the Anglo-Irish Treaty and Irish opponents of the treaty (the latter supported, with dubious effectiveness, by the Irish Communist party, of which O'Flaherty himself had been a member). Patrick Sheeran points out that the novel thus deals with a time of "green against green" violence, a situation which undergirds O'Flaherty's pessimistic and highly ironic treatment of Irish revolutionary politics.[55] Having been expelled from a shadowy international revolutionary group, "the Organization", Gypo Nolan is desperately poor, without money to pay for a meal or rent a bed for the night. On impulse, he

informs on a comrade, Frank McPhillip, who is wanted by the police for murder and has a price on his head. When Frank is killed by the police during the arrest attempt, Gypo is summoned by his former boss, Dan Gallagher. Gallagher, a self-absorbed intellectual and power-hungry leader is amusingly introduced via a series of fictional assessments, one apparently a Comintern report:

> Comrade Gallagher rules the national Organization purely and simply as a dictator. There is a semblance of an Executive Committee but only in name. The tactics are guided by whatever whim is uppermost in Comrade Gallagher's mind at the moment. Contrary to the orders issued from Headquarters, the Organization is still purely military and has made hardly any attempt to come into the open as a legal political party. This is perhaps not entirely due to Comrade Gallagher's fault. There are local causes, arising out of the recent struggle for independence, which has left the working class in the grip of a romantic love of conspiracy, a strong religious and bourgeois-nationalist outlook on life and hatred of constitutional methods.[56]

Gallagher immediately springs into action to protect his organization, that is to say his own position and authority, from the potential threat posed by the presence of an informer. He enlists Gypo's aid in the search for the informer but also secretly has him watched. He begins to court Frank McPhillip's sister Mary, both because he is wildly attracted to her and hopes she will "join

53 *The Informer*, Estimating Script, 14 Jan 1935, screenplay by Dudley Nichols, from the novel by Liam O'Flaherty, John Ford papers, Scripts and Production Materials, Box 4, Folders 1–2, Lilly Library, IU.
54 *The Informer*, Final Script, 30 Jan 1935, screenplay by Dudley Nichols, from the novel by Liam O'Flaherty, ser.S, Box 3691, RKO Radio records, UCLA Library Special Collections.
55 Patrick F. Sheeran, *The Informer* (Cork: Cork University Press in association with the Film Institute of Ireland, 2002), 35.
56 Liam O'Flaherty, *The Informer* (London: Jonathan Cape, 1925, rpt. 1964), 79–80.

4.13

4.14

him" in the revolutionary movement, and because he needs her evidence to track down the informer. Mary co-operates, deluding herself that Gallagher will marry her and settle down.

Even before the December script was completed, the Production Code Administration informed producer Cliff Reid and associate producer Robert Sisk that O'Flaherty's novel was unacceptable for adaptation under the industry's Production Code.[57] The complaint did not center on the two prostitutes with whom Gypo is involved – Katie Madden and Connemara Maggie – although it did allude to the need to remove the novel's "brothel scenes". The main objection was to the representation of Irish politics. The reviewer complained that Gallagher was a Communist, a "wildly disintegrated nut", and that there was "not a single character in O'Flaherty's book capable of arousing any element of admiration or sympathy". The reviewer warned the RKO producers that any film adaptation of the book was likely to prove highly offensive both to the Irish and to Irish-Americans who "supported the Sinn Fein movement, leading to the establishment of the Irish Free State" (that is, supporters of the Anglo-Irish treaty). According to the PCA reviewer's report, associate producer Sisk assured him that Ford and Nichols already intended to eliminate the Communist element, and build up a love story around Gallagher and Mary McPhillip. Moreover, the story would be set in the period "before the Sinn Fein Government came out from

under cover through the Griffith-Collins Treaty", that is, during the Irish War of Independence, when Irish nationalists were more or less united behind the Irish Republican Army in opposition to the Royal Irish Constabulary, their Auxiliaries recruited in England (the so-called "Black and Tans"), the largely Ulster-protestant Special Constabulary and a British army of occupation. The reviewer concluded: "If Dudley Nichols and John Ford can reproduce the inspired exaltation of those days, expressed through a new Gallagher and a new girl, they may be able to tell on the screen a great story that has been crying for writing these dozen years." O'Flaherty's Communist rebel leader was a tremendous gift to Ford and Nichols. The character obviously could not be sustained as written given the state censor boards active in the U.S. and the fact that the Gallagher of the novel could not anchor a conventional romance plot. But, by promising the PCA that they would give him up the filmmakers gained considerable latitude in their representation of Katie Madden – in the film she is obviously a prostitute – and they even managed to retain the brothel scene set in Aunt Betty's shebeen.

O'Flaherty was clearly aware of Ford's intentions, since the first script draft of December 18, 1934, begins the transformation of Gallagher, who is there identified only as an officer in the Irish Republican Army (this script variant is actually more open about the IRA connection than later ones would be). Gallagher is not self-serving,

57   Mr. [John McHugh] Stuart, Memo to Mr. [Joseph] Breen, 20 November 1934, Production Code Administration file on *The Informer*, Motion Picture Association of America, Production Code Administration Records, Margaret Herrick Library Digital Collections https://digitalcollections.oscars.org/digital/collection/p15759coll30.

but trying honestly and fairly to protect his men and maintain army discipline. The scene from the novel in which Gallagher initiates a courtship with Mary McPhillip at the same time that he seeks information about Gypo is transformed into a love scene between a couple whose courtship is already well established. O'Flaherty even added an epilogue following Gypo's death in which Mary and Gallagher witness the signing of the Anglo-Irish treaty. This seems to have been overdoing it, at least as far as Ford was concerned. As the example of his proposed film on Ó Raifteirí suggests, Ford was interested in celebrating the richness and continuity of a specifically Irish tradition. When he turned to O'Flaherty's modern story it was not to take sides in the disputes associated with the Civil War but to project a much less complicated, perhaps sentimentalized, idea of Irish resistance to English rule, one that was shared by many Irish-Americans, including the industry censors under Joe Breen who eventually greenlighted his project.

In their January 14 script draft, Ford and Nichols abandon O'Flaherty's epilogue and end their story as the novel does with Gypo dying in the church where he is forgiven by Frankie McPhillip's mother (Nichols softened Frank's name with the diminutive suffix). But the filmmakers also introduced new material in the opening scenes of the film that establishes the enmity between the populace and the Black and Tans. Both of the January script variants begin with Gypo viewing the poster advertising the reward for information leading to the capture of McPhillip. The screenplay draft of January 30, 1934, adds the action of Gypo stopping on a street corner and listening briefly to a blind fiddler and street singer. In the film this incident has been expanded, perhaps as a result of Denis O'Dea, a member of a visiting company of Abbey Theatre players, being cast in the role of the singer.[58] As a Black and Tan patrol marches down the sidewalk, the onlookers melt away leaving only the musicians. One of the soldiers frisks the street singer, then gives him a coin. As the soldiers march off, the singer tosses it away with a contemptuous gesture, a small scale reversal of the action that Gypo is contemplating.

The January script variants introduce scenes of Frankie (the great Wallace Ford) sneaking into Dunboys under the threat of capture. Ford and Nichols also build up the scene of Frankie's death in a way that is very different from O'Flaherty's novel. The latter recounts Frank's death in a short two-paragraph chapter written in the past tense in stark, pared-down prose. While poignant by virtue of its brevity, O'Flaherty's depiction is of an anti-heroic death — Frank accidentally shoots himself while trying to escape. In contrast, both January script variants and the film include a long sequence that shows the reunion of Frankie with his mother and sister, immediately followed by one in which the Black and Tans break into the McPhillip house (figure 4.10). With his mother and sister looking on, Frankie engages in a gunfight on an interior stairway, the action photographed partly in dramatic high-angle framings from the fugitive's point of view (figure 4.11). Frankie is then shot dead by the Tans in the act of escaping through a rear second-floor window, another high-angle view showing the Black and Tans shooting from below (figure 4.12, likely a matte shot). Ford and Nichols emphasize the violence of Frankie's killing to bring out the value of Gallagher's and Mary's sober, pro-social commitment to the resistance and the terrible consequences that follow from Gypo's betrayal of the cause. Nevertheless, it is precisely because informing has such a horrific result that Gypo becomes an object of fascination and the emotional center of the film.

One of the primary ways that Ford and Nichols try to secure sympathy for Gypo despite his fall from grace is to make substantial changes to the subplot involving Katie. O'Flaherty's Katie is a drug addict and prostitute working out of Biddy Burke's lower-class shebeen. After sharing what little she had with Gypo during the time of his unemployment, she looks forward to enjoying herself when he comes into the reward money.

---

58   Adrian Frazier, *Hollywood Irish: John Ford, Abbey Actors and the Irish Revival in Hollywood* (Dublin: Lilliput Press, 2011), 3, 42, 53.

When Gypo abandons her for Aunt Betty's higher-priced shebeen and a younger, prettier girl, she publicly accuses him of taking "blood money". Later, when he seeks shelter with her after his escape from the Organization's prison, she alerts Gallagher, who finds and executes him. O'Flaherty's characterization of Katie was pretty much impossible given the constraints of the Hollywood Production Code. (It seems to have been impossible in England as well, since Robison's version backs off from any suggestion that Katie is a prostitute, instead making her independently employed as a milliner.) Ford, in contrast, retains the idea of Katie's profession but softens it through references to her saintly nature (as indicated, for example, by figures 4.13 and 4.14, from a single tracking shot). Although Ford's Katie resents Gypo's implicit condemnation of her profession when he does not even "have the price of a flop on him", she is not interested in the reward money. Indeed, she worries about what he did to procure his new-found wealth ("Did you rob a church?"). When he seeks shelter in her flat near the film's end, she goes to Gallagher to beg for mercy for her man, and only unwittingly reveals Gypo's whereabouts to Bartly, the IRA lieutenant in charge of the execution.

Another important addition that Ford and Nichols make to their characterization of the Gypo-Katie couple is the introduction of an emigration theme. Emigration is not even mentioned as a possibility in O'Flaherty's novel. In the 1929 film version, Frank McPhillip is about to emigrate to the U.S. before Gypo informs on him. The Organization has sent the money for his passage in order to avoid having him arrested for the killing of a policeman. But Frank is far from happy about the plan; for him it is exile, not escape. In Ford and Nichols's retelling emigration has an ambiguous status. The ultimate good, it is nonetheless out of the reach of the protagonists and even works to their detriment. Katie unknowingly aggravates Gypo's impulse to inform through her comments about a travel-agency shop window advertising passage to America for ten pounds

4.15

(figure 4.15): "Look at that thing giving us the ha-ha. Ten pounds to America! Twenty pounds and the world is ours!" However, the impossible dream of emigrating with Katie also exculpates Gypo to some extent, since he informs on Frankie in a misguided attempt to secure their passage and improve their lot. This point is emphasized through multiple returns to the travel-agency window. Just before he sets off for Aunt Betty's, he stares at a model steamship in the window and has a drunken vision of himself and Katie, in wedding attire, on its deck. Later, just before the IRA men drag him off to the court of inquiry, the inebriated and delusional Gypo assures Katie that he has the twenty pounds to take them to America, even though he has already spent all but five pounds of it.

Despite the romance that domesticates Gypo to some extent, Ford and Nichols remain fairly faithful to O'Flaherty's original conception of the character, what the author privately termed his "monster".[59] Sheeran describes O'Flaherty's protagonist as a specific Irish type, a "hardman". "Hardmen (the condition often ran in families) were local heroes whose whole endeavour was to keep their reputations for ferocious drinking, whoring and fierce fist-fighting alive in their areas. They had an instinctive recognition that one enters folklore, not be being quiet and decent, but by being wild and dangerous."[60] O'Flaherty's Gypo recklessly spends all the reward money on drinking and whoring without any reflection or

---

59 O'Flaherty, Letter to Edward Garnett, 7 Jul 1924, in Kelly, ed., 95.
60 Sheeran, *The Informer*, 38.

intention on the part of the character and without prolonged analysis or motivation on the part of the narrator. This is the nature of the beast. The novel even glories in Gypo's strength and heedlessness. In one incident, which Ford and Nichols included in the film, Gypo delights a crowd on the street when he insults and knocks out a passer-by, and then knocks out the cop who comes to investigate the disturbance. Several more cops then arrest the unconscious man for assaulting an officer.[61]

The Gypo of Robison's English version, in contrast, is a more conventional hero, strong certainly, and rough around the edges when compared with his better-educated comrades in the Organization, but decent and capable of understanding the moral consequences of his own actions. Robison's Gypo is motivated to inform because he mistakenly believes that Katie Madden is in love with Frank McPhillip. He is not interested in the reward money, gives it all away in a deliberate attempt to "make something good come of it", and ultimately accepts his execution as just. Lars Hansen's performance as Gypo is correspondingly restrained, almost elegant. It frequently depends on small movements of his facial muscles to convey the character's deepening sense of guilt, while his carriage and bearing consistently project a sense of dignity and self-respect as well as strength.

Ford's Gypo undoubtedly owes much to Victor McLaglen's Academy-Award-winning performance. There is a widely circulated story of Ford tricking McLaglen into giving a great performance by encouraging him to get hopelessly drunk the night before the trial scene was shot.[62] However that may be, anyone watching the film for its acting cannot help but appreciate McLaglen's nuanced performance of a role that could easily have been rendered a deadly one-note samba. In addition, he took considerable professional risks in embodying this unkempt, boorish and slow-witted character. For example, in Gypo's first confrontation with Gallagher, his rough clothes and uncouth demeanor are placed in contrast with Preston Foster's attractively trench-coated commander. During the course of a conversation in which Foster speaks calmly, smoking a pipe, McLaglen slurs his speech as if drunk, speaking at elevated volume. He consistently violates decorum in the course of the scene, slamming down his hat in frustration and spitting on his hand before shaking hands to seal the supposed reconciliation with his former boss. When Gypo pours drinks for Gallagher and his men, they put down their glasses, reluctant to drink with him. McLaglen has his character continue talking, oblivious, calmly taking up their glasses and consuming their whiskey as well as his own. Then, when Gallagher suddenly demands to know who informed on McPhillip, McLaglen spits out his drink in alarm. In the course of a long take (106 seconds), the actor first hesitates, as if trying to think up a lie. Then he falsely accuses Mulligan the tailor of informing and makes up a story about Mulligan's grudge against Frankie. The story is carefully articulated by repeated phatic gestures – pointing at Gallagher, touching Gallagher opposite or Tommy seated next to him in an appeal for their attention, snapping his fingers or hitting the table as he gets ideas, speaking with one hand to his mouth as if to whisper about the cause of the grudge – all intermingled with the continued business of drinking and pouring out whiskey. Five shots later he performs a memorable exit: picking his hat up off the floor, he slaps it on the table before setting it jauntily on his head, turns right to clap Bartly (Joseph Sauers) on the shoulder, then turns briskly back to Gallagher to come drunkenly to attention, kicking over a chair in the process, before executing a salute. Such felicitous bits of timing enliven many of the film's scenes.

Our sense of Ford's imaginative investment in *The Informer* shifts if we consider it in relation to the problem of casting and the director's multiple-picture contract with RKO. Ford's preferences for the part of Gypo were in place from

---

61   O'Flaherty, *The Informer*, 111–115.
62   Dan Ford, 86; Anderson, 81; Gallagher, 189–190; McBride, 223–224. In 1936 Ford specifically disclaimed this story, see Douglas Churchill's interview, "John Ford, the Man Behind *The Informer*", Peary, ed., 8–9, originally published *New York Times* (5 Jan 1936): X5. However, the persistent recurrence of the story in later sources suggests Ford at least acquiesced in its diffusion.

very early in the pre-production process. He wired Cliff Reid from Mexico in December 1934 that he was "still set on Victor McLaglen".[63] About a year earlier, in January 1934, prior to the release of *The Lost Patrol*, the *Hollywood Reporter* had published a rumor that Ford's next film for Radio would be a sequel starring McLaglen – a sensible idea given the strength of the actor's performance.[64] But, by August of 1934, RKO had scheduled him for *The Three Musketeers* with Walter Abel as the dashing young D'Artagnan. Ford's meeting with O'Flaherty in the summer of 1934 provided him with a much better alternative, and a step up from *The Lost Patrol* in terms of his collaboration with McLaglen. A radically new part for the actor, it nonetheless retained many components of his hard-fighting, hard-drinking Sergeant Flagg persona. The director deserves credit not for having tricked McLaglen into a good performance but for an extremely shrewd bit of casting – for realizing that Flagg could inhabit the heart of O'Flaherty's monster.

Stylistic Experimentation in *The Informer*

Writing in 1953, Dudley Nichols responds to Lindsay Anderson's question about stylization in *The Informer*:

> I believe honestly, though I may be mistaken, that it was I who pushed this idea of stylization the hardest. I never heard Ford mention *The Last Laugh* or *Dr. Caligari's Cabinet*, but it is very likely he had absorbed what they had to give in the way of new film ideas. He wanted some distortion in the sets from the beginning, and I don't think Van Polglase (or the rigid ideas of a major studio itself) gave him as much as he desired. But Joe August was a great cameraman, perhaps the most experimental and audacious I have ever known, and he could heighten desired effects with lighting. My idea was to use symbolism that would be felt but not analyzed by the audience; fog itself was the first symbol to get us into the region of Gypo's mind.[65]

The emphasis on character psychology and subjective states in *The Informer* stands in striking contrast to Fritz Lang's *M* (1931), also about a monster and also culminating in an informal trial. Focusing on the dual pursuit of the child murderer Hans Beckert by the police and by the organized underworld, *M* restricts our access to Beckert's activities and provides little sense of his emotions. He remains largely a cipher until the penultimate trial scene when he finally speaks passionately of his desire and his guilt. But from the very first scene in *The Informer*, Gypo's memories and desires are made explicit through the many subjective images. These superimpositions, initially described in Nichol's script, were clearly part of the director's design. For example, when Gypo looks at the wanted poster for the first time a superimposed shot shows Gypo drinking companionably with Frankie (figure 4.16). Similarly, during the conversation between Frankie and Gypo in Dunboy's, a phrase from the poster – £20 Reward – is briefly superimposed over a reverse angle of Frankie seated at the table. Even the dissolves used as scene transitions are given a subjective flavor. At the close of the scene in Dunboy's, as Gypo prepares to inform on Frankie, a dissolve connects Gypo with the travel agency window, the next space in which he will appear but also a realization of his thoughts and the motivation for his pending action (figure 4.17). Figure 4.18 is taken from a dissolve which highlights the match between two clocks in different locations, the one on the left observed by Gypo waiting in the police station, the one on the right situated in the McPhillip kitchen where Frankie will meet with his mother and sister. Later, as Gypo runs from the Blind Man after their first encounter, a dissolve creates the impression that the man is looking off into the new space in which Gypo will appear (figure 4.19).

The visual evocation of Gypo's powerful if inarticulate sense of guilt is reinforced by Max Steiner's assertive score.[66] The preponderance of

---

63 Ford, Telegram to Cliff Reid, 31 December 1934, *The Informer* file, RKO Radio Pictures research collection compiled by Richard Jewell, Herrick Library, AMPAS.
64 "Radio Plans Sequel to *Lost Patrol*", *Hollywood Reporter* (25 Jan 1934): 3.
65 Dudley Nichols, Letter to Lindsay Anderson, 22 Apr 1953, in Anderson, 239.
66 This analysis is indebted to the online documentation presented by Jeff Lyon and Brent Yorgason, Max Steiner's cues for *The Informer*, Max Steiner Digital Thematic Catalog, maintained by the Max Steiner Institute, https://maxsteinerinstitute.org/.

4.16

4.17

4.18

4.19

4.20

the film's music consists of a through-composed orchestral score built up of cues associated with characters or objects. The most frequently used cues revolve around Gypo's love for Katie and his betrayal of his comrade. "Katie's theme" occurs sixteen times over the course of the film, not only when she is present but also when Gypo thinks of her. For example, when he pauses in front of the travel-agency window on his way to the police station, we first hear a discordant fragment of

4.21

4.22

4.23

4.24

"Yankee Doodle" which segues into her synco-pated melody.[67] The "Informer" theme is first heard over the credits and occurs thirty-two times across the film, musically varied in relation to the narrative context. It comes to the fore in scenes which expose Gypo's guilt and/or punishment (as when he confronts Gallagher for the first time, and later when Gallagher forces him to confess). The "Blood Money" cue, first heard when he receives the reward in the police station, occurs twenty times. While these motifs are intrinsically interesting and combined in intelligent ways their cumulative insistence on the central character's emotions can become oppressive or irritating. Like the repeated use of superimpositions depicting Gypo's mental state, the score can seem over-emphatic.

These aspects of *The Informer*'s style have led to a decline in its critical reputation. Widely praised on its first release, later critics have tended to dismiss the film as a throwback to silent cinema or to German Expressionism. Andrew Sarris refers to the film's "calculated Expressionism and maud-lin sentimentality".[68] Tag Gallagher notes the ab-sence of "documentary-like detailing of social texture", finding *The Informer*'s Dublin "a sub-jective fantasy, a mood more than a place, an echo, like the sets of *Caligari*, of Gypo's gloom".[69] However, considered within the trajectory of Ford's career as a freelance director, the film, like *Air Mail*, provides an instance of a situation in which Ford was able to indulge in relatively un-bound experimentation. The effort to depict the protagonist's alcohol-fueled, angst-ridden night inspired filmmakers and composer to a high level of stylistic innovation. Steiner was led into won-derfully dissonant and irregular phrases in even the simplest passages in the score (consider, for

67 The "Yankee Doodle" cue is described as "distorted, octatonic" by Jeff Lyon and Brent Yorgason in the Max Steiner Digital Catalog.
68 Andrew Sarris, *The American Cinema* (New York: E. P. Dutton, 1968), 45.
69 Gallagher, 191.

4.25

4.26

4.27

4.28

example, the stop-and-go chromatic descending line which imitates the gesture of tearing down the poster at the beginning of the film). Working in concert, Ford, Polglase and August created a vibrant and eerie cityscape. It is important to account for the technical and technological means that were mobilized to create the film's distinctive look and sound.

By 1935 RKO's Culver City lot was overcrowded and *The Informer* was shot at the independently owned Prudential Studio at 5300 Melrose Avenue. The space had been rented by Merian Cooper, who was no longer head of production at RKO but acting in his capacity as unit producer for two big-budget films, *She* (1935) and *The Last Days of Pompeii* (1935). *The Informer* was the first to be made at Prudential, followed by *She*.[70] The *Hollywood Reporter* noted that Cooper had planned to combine two sound stages

into one large one for *She*, and it seems likely that Ford's production was moved because it also required a big sound stage.[71] Figure 4.20, of a visiting troupe of Abbey Players having lunch on the set of the street outside the Dunboy House, provides a sense of the size of the sound stage, which accommodated a street corner with multiple-story façades wide enough to seat close to thirty people. While Ford's subsequent accounts have emphasized the film's low production budget and negligible production values, Polglase and Julia Heron's sets, especially the studio-built exteriors, are quite impressive.[72] Figure 4.21 shows the main street that included the fish-and-chips shop and Ryan's pub on the corner, while figure 4.22 shows the view from in front of the pub looking further down the street. Figure 4.23 is the street corner where Katie is first introduced (the illuminated window is off to the right). Figure

70 "Radio Takes Prudential Lot for Increased Production", *Hollywood Reporter* (22 Jan 1935): 1, 3; "Radio's *She* Unit Moves to Prudential", *Hollywood Reporter* (29 Jan 1935): 2; "*Informer* at Prudential", *Hollywood Reporter* (18 Feb 1935): 4.
71 McBride, 219–220, offers a different account of the film's production history and set design.
72 John Ford's account may be found in Dan Ford, 84–85.

4.29

4.30

4.31

4.32

4.24 is the wonderfully foreshortened entrance to the underground armory where the trial takes place.

One reason the size and complexity of the sets has escaped comment is that they were partially obscured by fog effects and heavy shadows. As the above citation from Nichols suggests, the filmmakers envisioned an omnipresent fog during the night the action takes place. The fog effects in the film recall those employed by Murnau in *Sunrise* and taken up by Ford in the battle scene in *4 Sons* (figures 1.1 to 1.5) among other films. But unlike the studio-built exteriors in which fog appears in the late 1920s films, in supposedly natural environments, *The Informer* fog permeates city streets. Moreover, it does not accumulate in cloud-like drifts as in the swamp scenes but rather forms a still, translucent medium for diffusion. August strictly limited the number of lighting units used in exteriors and minimized general

illumination, likely employing the strong arc units recently devised for shooting Technicolor.[73] The *American Cinematographer* described August's illumination in these scenes as composed entirely of effects lighting.[74] Arcs positioned in the lamp posts were clearly a major light source and figure 4.20, the photograph of the set, shows the street lights illuminated while most of the lighting units high on the rails are turned off. However, it seems doubtful that the street lights were typically the only sources of illumination in street scenes. The highlights on the bike in figure 4.21, for example, suggest some degree of top light. The important point is that the reduction in the number of lighting units and general level of illumination give rise to a palpable sense of strong rays issuing from isolated sources such as the omnipresent street lights (figures 4.25 and 4.26) or spilling out from windows and doors (figures 4.27 and 4.28).

73 "The Return of the Arc", *International Photographer* (Jul 1934): 12; Walter Strohm, "One Hundred Percent Arc Lamps", *International Photographer* (Oct 1934): 14, 25; Peter Mole, "Arc Lights for Color", *International Photographer* (Oct 1935): 23; Hal Mohr, "Large Sets Call for Arc Lights", *American Cinematographer* (November 1935): 469, 478–479.
74 Harry Burdick, "Joe August Sets His Own Precedents", *American Cinematographer* (Jun 1936): 239, 246–7.

4.33

4.34

And, as the *American Cinematographer* reviewer noted, the light is "reflected by the particles of moisture in the misty atmosphere", giving rise to diffuse shimmering clouds and silhouetted bodies. The cinematography was highly praised at the time of the film's release, with members of the American Society of Cinematographers writing in votes for August for an Academy Award despite the fact that he had been overlooked by the larger nominating body.[75]

Given the low light levels on the street sets, the depth of field was necessarily shallow even for the middle 1930s. Ford and August nonetheless managed to create compelling deep space compositions by utilizing aerial perspective, showing background figures diffused as if by distance (figures 4.21 and 4.26). They shot through windows and doors into more strongly lit interior spaces to emphasize the difference between foreground and mid-ground planes (figures 4.29 and 4.30). Another strategy was to create receding arrays of street lamps and other lights (figures 4.31 and 4.32). Even in the relatively more highly-lit interior spaces, depth effects often depend upon a contrast between strong highlights and dark shadows (figures 4.33 and 4.34).

While complaints about Steiner's score for *The Informer* are legion, a fair analysis of the film needs to take account of how original his scoring techniques were in 1934–1935. As noted in chapter two, the majority of early sound scores, including the score for *The Black Watch*, were song-based. While *The Informer* includes two full song performances and several song fragments, these on-screen performances remain isolated from the score proper, which is composed of distinct modules that could be varied, combined, expanded or truncated as needed, a defining feature of the through-composed score. Moreover, the way that music and effects were synchronized with the filmed action was very different from the practices utilized in Ford's late 1920s films, as discussed in chapter two. In her study of *The Informer*, Kathryn Kalinak describes one illuminating throwback to the earlier scoring practice, in which Victor McLaglen synchronized his walk to a play-back of the "Informer" cue.[76] This method – having director and actors time the action to the music on the sound stage – was also used to integrate dialogue, effects and song in the scene at the railroad station in *The Black Watch*. But the technique that Steiner helped to pioneer at RKO in the early 1930s was based on the opposite approach – post-synchronization. This technique was made possible by improvements to RCA's and Radio's proprietary sound-on-film system, which by 1934 allowed for much more extensive re-recording than had been the case in the early 1930s. Once picture and dialogue were cut, the composer wrote the score so as to "catch" lines of dialogue or specific gestures. In segments which called for continuous and precise sync, the music was then recorded with the aid of a click track of Steiner's own devising that ensured that

---

75   "August Gets Write-Ins", *Hollywood Reporter* (21 Feb 1936): 4; see also "Rating the Cameramen", *Variety* (1 Jan 1936): 7.
76   Kalinak, *Max Steiner*, 124–125.

4.35

4.36

he could meet all of the preplanned sync points.[77] Then, in the final mix, the music track was combined with the dialogue and sound effects that Steiner had already written his music around. By the late 1930s, this was the normal procedure for scoring in Hollywood, but this was not necessarily the case in 1935. *The Informer* seems to foreground the new-found capacity to create a high density of sync points in post-production.

The scene where Gypo receives the twenty-pound reward illustrates the close integration of music and action that could be achieved. The previous scene, which culminates in the death of Frankie, is without music although the track is dense with the women screaming, Frankie yelling for them to get out of his way, and the sounds of gunfire. The density and volume diminish in the final shot – of Una O'Connor as Mrs. McPhillip quietly moaning in grief. Cut to the interior of the police station for a forty-second shot where the authorities pay off Gypo.

> *Shot 121.* LS. A police officer in uniform and two less formally attired Black and Tans stand motionless at the rear of a long table while Gypo, hat in hand, stands in the foreground (figure 4.35). After a noticeable pause without movement or sound, the phone rings. One of the Tans responds and reports to the officer that McPhillip was killed trying to escape. Without a word, the officer takes out his wallet, drops the money on the table and exits rear right (figure 4.36). The Foley effect of the paper hitting the table coincides with the commencement of the "Blood Money" cue, a broken descending dissonant chord played at a

very slow tempo. The fourth note of the motif is held as one of the Tans pushes the money across the table to Gypo with his cane. He speaks over the music.

> *Tan*: "Twenty pounds, you better count it." [*To his colleague.*] "Show him out the back way." [*He exits.*]

On the word "back", the motif extends lower, by two notes, the last of which is also held. Gypo's action of moving forward and abruptly grabbing the money is punctuated by a soft stinger chord followed by silence.

Note the close relationship between music and other sounds and gestures: the sound of the money hitting the table cues the commencement of the motif, the word "back" its extension, the end of McLaglen's emphatic grabbing gesture is matched by the stinger. Similarly, the next shot of McLaglen exiting the station begins in silence, a stinger chord resonates with the sound of the door slamming behind him and then segues into the "Blood Money" motif as he counts his money. The mournful "Blind Man" theme immediately follows "Blood Money", anticipating the introduction of this character at the close of the shot. Every second of each shot is accounted for, the silences as carefully tabulated as the musical modules, and the whole stitched together by a fine network of sync points, as well as by Steiner's sonorous harmonies.

Clearly, Ford's preference for scoring with recognizable songs carrying their own set of historical connotations was at odds with Steiner's scoring strategy to some degree. For example,

---

77 Jacobs, "Innovation of Re-recording", 5–34; Jacobs, *Film Rhythm after Sound*, 221–223.

narrative action seems to pause for Denis O'Dea's performance of the Irish ballad "The Rose of Tralee" and it is only the arrival of the patrol interrupting the moment of social communion that ties it back into the narrative thread. But other aspects of Steiner's style actively reinforced Ford's approach to film scoring. First, both Ford and Steiner liked the music relatively louder in the mix than the norm in Hollywood. Consider, for example, a particularly tense moment at the trial when Gypo sees the Blind Man and realizes that he has to accuse Mulligan (Donald Meek). This realization is first signaled without words, as McLaglen looks over the witnesses and sees the Blind Man, to the accompaniment of the "Informer" theme. As McLaglen stands and gives voice to the accusation and Meek raises his voice in response, the music remains prominent, echoing the actors' words and gestures, another "voice" in the dispute. Throughout *The Informer*, music remains in the sonic foreground if it is used at all. Sometimes it is brought to the fore by eliminating dialogue or reducing it to a minimum as in the scene in the police station and the film's wordless opening. At other moments, music is integrated into dialogue scenes at high volume, lending an almost operatic air to the proceedings, as at the trial.

Another shared preference implicit in Steiner's scoring strategy and Ford's directorial technique was for a strong rhythmic integration of gesture, sound and music. This rhythmic vocation is evident in Ford's work prior to his collaboration with Steiner. It is one of the compelling aspects of the scene at the railroad station in *The Black Watch* in which the performance of "The Bonnie Banks of Loch Lomond" is underscored by the rhythm of the soldiers' march and beautifully punctuated by interjections from the crowd and train noises. In *The Informer*, we find Steiner's score building upon the rhythm of Ford's scenes even in the absence of songs. The forty-second take in the police station is built upon the action of the Tan pushing the money toward Gypo in the foreground, an action underscored by the long-held descending notes of the "Blood Money" motif. The action is framed by two sharp distinct sounds. At the beginning of the shot, silence is broken by the loud ring of the telephone. At the end of the shot, the grab for the money, the stinger chord and silence. While the assertive score of *The Informer* may not appeal to present-day tastes, it can be seen as an important experiment with the new scoring techniques enabled by advances in sound re-recording in the middle 1930s. The experiment allowed both composer and director to refine their sense of rhythmic design.

At the time of its release, *The Informer* was considered a realistic film about an important political conflict – a depiction of the desperate conditions in the Dublin slums at the time of the rebellion. For example, Richard Watts's favorable review of the film in the *New York Herald Tribune* began with a plaint about films that represented Ireland in wistful romantic terms, in "the Kathleen Mavourneen manner", and opined that "the Irishman of Joyce, O'Casey and O'Flaherty is a more striking and admirable figure, even for the cinema, than the quaint and antic Gael of the Mother Machree tradition".[78] That is to say he understood the film in relation to O'Flaherty's novel and the author's reputation as a leftist and naturalistically-inclined writer. Moreover, as Watts pointed out, the tradition that O'Flaherty represented stood in stark contrast to the nostalgic and idyllic view of Ireland which predominated in American popular song and literature (and, it should be said, in films such as *Hangman's House*). *The Informer* stood out against this popular tradition, representing urban poverty, and the despair and violence entailed by the English occupation. In Ford's film, the IRA may have been romanticized in a manner quite contrary to the spirit of O'Flaherty's work, but the film was nonetheless daring for its depiction of the misery that gave rise to Gypo's heinous act. The Production Code Administration file for *The Informer* documents the large number of cuts required for its English release, suggesting that the film's politics were not entirely sentimental or negligible in the middle 1930s.[79]

---

78   Richard Watts, Jr. "*The Informer*: A Fine Tragedy of Irish Politics, Is Approaching", *New York Herald Tribune* (14 Apr 1935): D1.
79   There is an atypical three-and-a-half page list of deletions made for the territory of the United Kingdom, Production Code Administration file on *The Informer*, Margaret Herrick Library Digital Collections, AMPAS, https://digitalcollections.oscars.

As the memory of the political context that shaped both the novel and the film has faded in the U.S., the stylization of image and sound in *The Informer* has become more salient for present-day critics.[80] Indeed, stylistic experimentation shaped Ford's adaptation of O'Flaherty's grim novel in powerful ways. Gypo, abandoned by the IRA and suspected by the English, is barely surviving, his only friend a prostitute. Yet the city he inhabits is one of deep mystery and astonishing beauty. *Pace* Nichols, the fog is not simply an extension of Gypo's psyche. It is also, perhaps primarily, a vehicle for August's light. Similarly, Steiner's eerie harmonies are not simply imitations of actions but rather bring out their inner rhythm. These stylistic devices, which so strikingly call attention to themselves in their own right, provide the spectator with a sense of wonder, a bit of breathing space and a kind of compensation for Gypo's ineluctable fate.

When one considers all of the films that Ford directed on a freelance basis between 1931 and 1935 it seems clear that the control he exercised over his work varied considerably. Sometimes he took over projects that had been initially planned for a specific star and with other directors in mind. For example, *Flesh* was a Wallace Beery project from the start. It was based upon a story by Edmund Goulding, who was initially slated to direct. It seems likely that the project sprang from that director's work with Beery on *Grand Hotel*. The *Whole Town's Talking* was planned for Edward G. Robinson from the start, with Hawks as director. In both cases, when Ford took over, he worked with writers under contract to the respective studios, not with Dudley Nichols. This is not to claim that he exercised no control over these projects. In both cases he was hired four to five weeks prior to the start of production and therefore with time to work with the writers, to influence the casting of roles other than the star's and to participate in decisions about set design and costumes. Nonetheless, these projects seem quali-

tatively different from *The Lost Patrol*, in which he was able to hire Nichols to reshape the script, and to move McLaglen into a starring role. Location shooting and the decision to construct the set on site also contributed to his autonomy.

On *The Informer* Ford exercised even more initiative. He convinced RKO to buy the literary property. He employed a distinctive working method, effectively building the film's visual and aural design into the emerging script. Nichols recalled that he brought Steiner, Polglase and August together with the writer at an early stage of preproduction: "This, to my mind, is the proper way to approach film production – and it is, alas, the only time in 25 years I have known it to be done: a group discussion before a line of script is written."[81] One would like to know how Ford managed to secure the services of Joe August who was clearly crucial to the director's whole conception of the film's visual style and who had been under contract to Columbia since 1932. It is possible that Ford stepped in to direct Columbia's *The Whole Town's Talking*, which was also shot by August, in order to convince the studio to lend out the cinematographer and/or to convince him to request a leave. While it is not possible to ascertain exactly how the deal for Joe August was put over, it seems likely that Ford actively participated in recruiting him, effectively functioning as his own producer.

Following *The Informer*'s critical success, whether by luck or by strategy Ford was assured continued access to both August's and Nichols's services. August returned to Columbia for just two more features in 1935 and then joined the staff at RKO where he remained until his enlistment in World War II. Nichols scripted *The Arizonian* (1935) and *She* at RKO before returning to Fox to write *Steamboat Round the Bend* for Ford. He then worked consistently at RKO except for the films that Ford made with independent producers releasing through United Artists (*The Hurricane*, *Stagecoach*, *The Long Voyage Home*).[82]

org/digital/collection/p15759coll30.
80   Gallagher, 185–191, comments extensively on stylization in the film.
81   Nichols, Letter to Lindsay Anderson, 22 Apr 1953, published in Lindsay Anderson, 239.
82   Nichols worked on Cecil B. DeMille's *The Crusades* prior to joining Ford at RKO for *The Informer*, see "Irish War in Work", *Variety* (18 Dec 1934): 6. He returned to Twentieth Century-Fox to script Lang's *Man Hunt* and Renoir's *Swamp Water* in 1941 but he never worked with Ford at the studio after *Steamboat Round the Bend*.

These outcomes jive with two articles which appeared in the *Hollywood Reporter* on February 8, 1935, while *The Informer* was still in production. The first announced that Nichols was leaving Fox to work at RKO and the second that Ford was to split his time between Fox and RKO.[83] The director was building his own unit at the Culver City studio.

Despite his success in bringing together a crew, Ford was not able to continue exercising the control over choice of projects and script development that he had enjoyed on *The Informer*. This was partly due to the fact that Cooper, always a sympathetic ally, left the company in 1935 after completing *The Last Days of Pompeii*.[84] And, by the middle of 1936, B. B. Kahane, who had also been instrumental in bringing Ford to the studio, had departed for Columbia.[85] In addition to the turnover of executive staff, Ford had lost "his" star, making it harder to pitch his own projects. McLaglen stopped freelancing in July 1935 when Darryl Zanuck of the newly merged Twentieth Century-Fox signed him to a new contract on the basis of his performance in *The Informer*.[86]

For the second film on Ford's 1934 RKO contract, he collaborated with Nichols and August on *Mary of Scotland*, from a play by Maxwell Anderson. Producer Pandro Berman bought the play for Katharine Hepburn in an attempt to counter the star's declining popularity, which was considered a result of Cukor's *Sylvia Scarlett* (1936) among other films.[87] Jewell quotes from a letter written by executive producer B. B. Kahane to Ned Depinet: "Here we are about to spend around $800,000 to $900,000 on *Mary of Scotland* in the hope of bringing Hepburn back – giving her Frederick [*sic*] March to support her, John Ford to direct, and not stinting in any way on production. We certainly ought to be entitled

to her co-operation in combatting the ill effects of *Sylvia Scarlet*."[88] Ford is here discussed as an asset that the studio is throwing at the problem of Hepburn. Although Ford was given a large budget and he and Nichols were involved in pre-production from the start, it seems clear that in this situation he was following through on a project initiated by Berman in consultation with other top-ranked producers.[89] He was in many ways ill-suited to the genre and the project as the resulting film attests.

Ford had choice of story for the last production on his RKO contract, an adaptation of Sean O'Casey's *The Plough and the Stars*, but, as is well known, lost control of it. The director had hoped to bring a full cast of Abbey Theatre actors from Dublin for the production but the studio insisted on Hollywood stars Preston Foster and Barbara Stanwyck for the major roles.[90] And although the associate producers on the project, Cliff Reid and Robert Sisk, were the same as those on *The Informer* and generally well disposed toward him, Sam Briskin, newly hired in 1936 as executive producer, showed no sympathy for the project and ordered retakes over the director's objections.[91] Thus, freelancing did not automatically guarantee Ford the autonomy he so obviously enjoyed. Rather, each project presented a complex set of negotiations. The terms of Ford's engagement were determined by who could exercise the choices of story and star, who controlled script development, and the craft workers available to him. Moreover, these negotiations were themselves affected by more general studio policies and financial objectives. We can observe the same variables in operation at Fox where between 1933 and 1935 Ford managed to rebuild a unit at the same time that he was building one at RKO.

83   "Fox and Radio to Split Ford's Time", *Hollywood Reporter* (8 Feb 1935): 2; "Nichols Will Adapt Radio's *Musketeers*", *Hollywood Reporter* (8 Feb 1935): 3.
84   Jewell, *RKO Radio Pictures*, 103, 109.
85   Jewell, *RKO Radio Pictures*, 72, 115–116, 132.
86   "Zanuck Installing Own Producer System", *Variety* (24 Jul 1935): 4.
87   Jewell, *RKO Radio Pictures*, 84, 91, 116.
88   B.B. Kahane, Letter to Ned Depinet, 12 Feb 1936, cited in Jewell, *RKO Radio Pictures*, 120.
89   Ford and Nichols's participation was announced at the point that the play was purchased, see "*Mary of Scotland* Bought for Hepburn", *Hollywood Reporter* (25 Apr 1935): 1.
90   McBride, 242–243; Frazier, 81–82.
91   "Adding S.A. to *Plough-Stars*", *Variety* (21 Oct 1936): 3; Bogdanovich, *John Ford*, 64, 66.

Chapter 5

Fox Before Zanuck

It's a constant battle to do something fresh. First they want you to repeat your last picture. You talk 'em down. Then they want you to continue whatever vein you succeeded in with the last picture. You're a comedy director or a spectacle director or a melodrama director. You show 'em you've been each of these in turn, and effectively, too. So they grant you range. Another time they want you to knock out something another studio's gone and cleaned up with. Like a market. Got to fight it every time.

John Ford in a 1936 interview[1]

When Ford returned to Fox at the beginning of 1933 conditions within the production sector were still dire. Budgets remained low and the studio remained politically fraught and difficult to navigate. In addition, most of Ford's old Fox crew had dispersed. Although the director eventually managed to wrangle Joe August and Victor McLaglan together at RKO for *The Informer*, they were out of his reach at their original studio. Ford's career at Fox from 1933 to 1935 is of interest partly because it reveals him finding ways to exercise control over his work and stretch himself as a filmmaker even within the constraints of a financially-strapped and troubled studio. Unlike his colleagues Borzage – who left Fox to freelance in 1932 – and Walsh – who left Fox to freelance in 1933 – Ford stayed because he found a way to carve out a niche for himself at the studio. His success in this regard derived partly from the relationship he developed with Will Rogers, Fox's biggest star in the early 1930s, as well as a shrewd and fruitful alliance with Fox producer Sol Wurtzel.

Negotiating the Fox Production Sector After 1932

When Sidney Kent assumed control of Fox in 1932, he reinstated Winfield Sheehan and indicated that he was not interested in buying out the contracts of any Fox studio executives.

> S. R. Kent seeks no changes in present contracts of Fox personnel as regards the executive branches, [and] will strive for no settlement of present agreements (in the cause of economy) … those who make good will stay and those who fail must go, final verdict resting with Kent who seemingly is opposed to merely paying off on costly company commitments or contracts to individuals.[2]

But while Kent initially restored the executive status quo that had existed prior to the Chase-Rowland regime, over time he made changes, establishing a decentralized system of unit production that eventually brought general manager Sheehan's position into question. Indeed at the time of Sheehan's resignation in 1935 the *New York Times* described his last three years at Fox as a "three year fight" with Kent and the Chase banking interests.[3] In October 1932, only a few months after re-instating Sheehan, Kent hired Jesse Lasky, formerly head of production at Paramount, to make films independently through his company Jesse L. Lasky Productions. The two-year contract called for eight films a year with 100 per cent financing provided by Fox. Fox retained story approval but Lasky was otherwise guaranteed freedom from interference by east or west coast executives.[4]

Kent also elevated Sol Wurtzel from his previous role as studio manager to fully-fledged

---

1 Eisenberg in Peary, ed., 11.
2 "Fox Settlements Stopped", *Variety* (3 May 1932): 5.
3 "Sheehan Resigns as Fox Film Chief", *New York Times* (18 Jul 1935): 15.
4 "Former Para. Production Head Signs with Fox", *Hollywood Reporter* (18 October 1932): 1–2; "Fox will 100% Finance All Lasky Pix", *Variety* (25 Oct 1932): 5.

producer status, a role in which he experienced great success.[5] In 1933, while Fox Film posted a loss of fifteen million dollars and suffered salary cuts, production delays and the receivership of the Fox theater companies, Wurtzel quietly built up a successful low-budget filmmaking enterprise at the old Fox studio on Western Avenue. The unit included associate producer John Stone, several business managers, a script department of nine writers including Dudley Nichols and Lamar Trotti (who sometimes worked together), film editors, and support staff dedicated specifically to Spanish-language films.[6] While Sheehan and Lasky were producing films in the budget range of $250,000 to $300,000 (and sometimes more), Wurtzel's films were budgeted at $100,000 per picture.[7]

Like most B-units, the Western Avenue studio worked quickly. After ten weeks in operation, the unit had completed its first picture, had three in production, and six English-language and three Spanish-language films in preparation.[8] In the 1933–1934 season, while Lasky and Sheehan each produced seven features, Wurtzel and Stone produced eighteen English-language and six Spanish-language pictures.[9] The Western Avenue studio relied principally upon such directors as Lew Seiler, James Tinling, Louis King, George Marshall, and Eugene Forde. It turned out unpretentious and crowd-pleasing genre pictures such as the long-running Charlie Chan mystery

series starring Warner Oland. There were many Westerns. For *Smoky,* with lead actor Victor Jory, *Variety* was informed that the producer planned to take as much care in selecting the lead horse as was usually spent on human cast members.[10]

By September 1933, the *Hollywood Reporter* could plausibly assert that the Fox producers each had complete control of their production units, answering only to Kent, and that Sheehan was simply one among a group, in the same class as Lasky or Wurtzel.[11] Given that such an arrangement would have violated Sheehan's contract, the studio was led to assert publicly that Sheehan was in fact production head and all producers on all lots needed to submit their story ideas to him.[12] There is indirect evidence that Lasky and Sheehan faced off at this point.[13] For example, in March 1934 the *Hollywood Reporter* noted: "Battle front reports yesterday were that the Jesse Lasky-Winnie Sheehan situation was reaching the point of open warfare. Argument has grown up over new stories being considered, suggestions for casting, etc. The understanding is that the arrival of Sidney Kent before the end of this month is the only thing holding off the shooting."[14] One feels the force of Kent's reference to "internal difficulties" at Fox that worried him above and beyond the problems caused by falling box-office returns and the bankruptcy of the theater chains. However, there is no evidence that Sheehan actually meddled with production at the Western Avenue studio. More-

5 John (J. J.) Gain was appointed to the post of studio manager to handle all business details and operation of the plant so that Wurtzel could focus on production, "Sheehan Stays – Kent", *Hollywood Reporter* (12 Jan 1933): 1–2. There were several other producers at Fox: in 1933–1934 Al Rockett and Buddy De Sylva made a few films and in 1934–1935 Edward Butcher, Joe Engle, and Robert T. Kane were added to this roster. A detailed list of the Fox Film executive staff in 1933 may be found in "Studio Board Responsible for Fox Pix", *Variety* (18 Apr 1933): 4.

6 "Fox Foreigns Under New Wurtzel Setup", *Variety* (28 Feb 1933): 13; "Wurtzel Announces Production Set-up", *Hollywood Reporter* (10 Mar 1933): 2; "Hollywood: Writers Join Wurtzel", *Variety* (14 Mar 1932): 6, 28; "Wurtzel Travels for Program Huddle", *Hollywood Reporter* (3 Oct 1933): 11; "Wurtzel's Time Out", *Variety* (14 Nov 1933): 4; W. R. Wilkerson column, "We strolled on the Fox-Western Avenue lot yesterday … ", *Hollywood Reporter* (26 Apr 1935): 1. Prior to becoming a producer John Stone had prepared several scripts for Ford including *3 Bad Men, Salute* and *The Black Watch.*

7 "Sheehan-Lasky-Sol to Make 50 Fox Pix", *Hollywood Reporter* (10 Feb 1933): 1.

8 "Wurtzel in Fast Production Pace", *Variety* (16 May 1933): 25.

9 I culled each producer's titles from the *American Film Institute Catalog,* searching from August 1, 1933, to August 1, 1934, following the typical industry season, which opened in September.

10 "Wurtzel's Pet, Just a Horse Opera", *Variety* (30 May 1933): 25.

11 "Gain Will Run the Fox Plant", *Hollywood Reporter* (2 Sep 1933): 1; "W. R. Sheehan in Eclipse", *Hollywood Reporter* (26 Oct 1933): 1.

12 "Sheehan in Top Spot on All Fox Prod.; All A.P.'s Must Get His Okay", *Variety* (26 Dec 1933): 5; "'Winnie' Bluffs Chase", *Hollywood Reporter* (3 Jan 1934): 1, 4.

13 "Lasky May Follow Doran to Rival Lot if Both Leave Fox", *Variety* (9 Jan 1934): 5; "Jesse Lasky's Stand", *Hollywood Reporter* (13 Jan 1934): 1.

14 "Lasky-Sheehan Battle Ready to Break Open", *Hollywood Reporter* (1 Mar 1934): 1.

over, Wurtzel's unit was given Kent's go-ahead for a group of higher-budget films in 1934 in recognition of the good performance of its films at the box office. The producer was also cleared to work with Will Rogers, the studio's biggest star, at this juncture.[15]

Between 1933 and 1935, Ford worked with both Sheehan and Wurtzel and directed Will Rogers in films produced by both. When he renegotiated his contract with Fox in 1932, the director had requested the right to choose his own story material, a request which Sheehan apparently convinced him to waive.[16] Nonetheless, it is likely that the first picture Ford directed under his new contract was one that pleased him and that Sheehan had offered to him in the course of the negotiations. Sheehan already had an option on *Pilgrimage,* a mother-love story by I. A. R. Wylie, author of "Grandmother Bernle Learns Her Letters", on which *4 Sons* was based.[17] Ford undertook script development of the Wylie story in early December 1932, before the official December 20 start date of his contract with Fox. He departed on what the *Hollywood Reporter* dubbed a story-conference cruise with Barry Conners and Philip Klein, who had adapted "Grandmother Bernle".[18] Dudley Nichols and Henry Johnson subsequently revised the Ford-Conners-Klein draft.[19] The director continued working on the project past the thirteen weeks he was salaried, agreeing to continue without compensation during the month of April.[20]

Ford does not seem to have been as deeply committed to *Doctor Bull*, the second film he made on his 1932 Fox contract, as he had been to the first. In contrast with *Pilgrimage*, Ford did almost no script development for *Doctor Bull* and he worked his thirteen weeks exactly.[21] The script for the project, an adaptation of a novel by James Gould Cozzens,[22] was prepared by Paul Green and Jane Storm, not by Ford's preferred writers. Green had been co-author of Sheehan's previous Rogers vehicle, *State Fair*, making it likely that the screenwriters were the producer's choice. The first draft, dated April 23, 1933, was prepared prior to Ford's May 1 start on the production. The only other extant draft, dated May 24, 1933, is labeled "Final Shooting Script".[23] Ford likely had input on this draft, and it is divided into "scene numbers", the numeration of master setups used for budgeting and other kinds of preproduction planning.

15 "Orchids for Wurtzel on New Fox Line-Up", *Hollywood Reporter* (21 Dec 1933): 7; "Wurtzel to Handle Next Will Rogers", *Hollywood Reporter* (29 Dec 1933): 3.

16 Al Rocket (on behalf of Sidney Kent), Telegram to John Tracy, 23 May 1932, John Ford Contract File, Twentieth Century-Fox Legal Department, confirms that the contract could be finalized since Sheehan reported that Ford had waived his request for story approval; Assistant Counsel [unsigned], Letter to C. E. Richardson, Fox Film Corporation, 28 May 1932, reports that the Ford contract has been executed.

17 Contract between I. A. R. Wylie (agents Collier & Flinn Ltd) and Fox Film Corporation (W. Sheehan), 5 November 1931, *Pilgrimage* Legal File, Twentieth Century-Fox Legal Department. The date of the option suggests that Sheehan had not intended it as a property for Ford, since the latter had already been fired.

18 "Ford, Connors, Klein in Ocean Conference", *Hollywood Reporter* (2 Dec 1932): 4; Sol Wurtzel, Memo to George Wasson, 16 November 1932, John Ford Contract File, Twentieth-Century Fox Legal Department, requesting that the start date of Ford's contract be moved up to 20 December 1932. It seems likely that Ford took a "vacation" prior to the start of his contract to give himself time to work on the script with Conners and Klein.

19 There are two important script variants: *Pilgrimage*, 16 December 1932, screenplay and dialogue by Philip Klein and Barry Conners, Twentieth Century-Fox Collection, Cinematic Arts Library, Doheny Library, University of Southern California, Los Angeles, California (hereafter Doheny Library, USC); and "Pilgrimage", Final Shooting Script, 25 January 1933, screenplay by Philip Klein and Barry Conners, re-written by Dudley Nichols and Henry Johnson, *Pilgrimage* Story File, Twentieth Century-Fox Legal Department (two earlier revisions by Nichols and Johnson, dated 13 January and 21 January 1933, are held in the Cinematic Arts Library, Doheny Library, USC).

20 Per the 1932 contract, Ford was paid $40,000 per picture at the rate of $3,076.92 per week for thirteen weeks, see George Bagnall, Memo to John Tracey, 9 May 1932, John Ford Contract File, Twentieth Century-Fox Legal Department. Ford signed an amendment to his contract after the thirteen-week period ended in late March agreeing that he would continue to work on *Pilgrimage* without further renumeration, Letter of Agreement, John Ford and J. J. Gain, Fox studio, 31 Mar 1933, John Ford Contract File, Twentieth Century-Fox Legal Department.

21 J. J. Gain, Memo to Ford, 4 May 1933 confirming Ford's May 1, 1933, start date on *The Last Adam* (title later changed to *Doctor Bull*) and George Wasson, Memo to Sydney Towell, 18 August 1933, confirming that Ford's work was completed and his contract closed out on Jul 29, both in John Ford Contract File, Twentieth Century-Fox Legal Department.

22 James Gould Cozzens, *The Last Adam* (New York: Harcourt, Brace, 1933).

23 There are three items all bearing the film's original title, "The Last Adam": First Treatment, 1 Apr 1933, by Paul Green and Philip Klein; First Rough Draft, 23 Apr 1933, screenplay by Paul Green, continuity by Jane Storm; Final Shooting Script, 24 May 1933, screenplay by Paul Green, continuity by Jane Storm, all in *Doctor Bull* Story File, Twentieth Century-Fox Legal Department.

Ford's second two-picture contract specified an explicit *quid pro quo*. He was to direct *The World Moves On* for Sheehan beginning on January 2, 1934, but was guaranteed his choice of story for the second film.[24] He complained about the Sheehan project in a later interview: "I'd like to forget that. I fought like hell against doing it. 'What does this mean?' I'd say. 'Does it amount to anything?' I pleaded and quit and everything else, but I was under contract and finally I had to do it, and I did the best I could, but I hated the damn thing."[25] For his second film, Ford moved to Wurtzel's unit to make *Judge Priest*. This arrangement was made possible by the fact that Kent had cleared Wurtzel's unit for some higher-budget films and the use of Will Rogers late in 1933. Without permission to go over his $100,000 per picture budget, and without the services of a major star, Wurtzel could not have managed to cover the director's $40,000 per picture salary and returned a profit.

The Ford-Wurtzel alliance went back at least to the middle 1920s, when Wurtzel convinced William Fox to continue production on *The Iron Horse* despite the snow storms on location in Nevada that had put the company severely behind schedule.[26] Following an old Hollywood tradition, familial ties bound them as well. Not only had Ford hired Sol's brother Harry as his agent, but Wurtzel had hired two of Ford's brothers: Edward O'Fearna worked as assistant director for some of the other directors in Wurtzel's unit and Francis Ford was cast in many of the B unit's films, including Charlie Chan mysteries, Jane Withers comedies, and the aforementioned *Smoky*. *Variety's* announcement of the start of production on *Judge Priest* identifies the film with Wurtzel's unit considered as a "studio" apart from the main Fox Hills or "Westwood" lot:

> Fox Hollywood studio completed its current year's program Friday [May 25, 1934] with the closing of *She Learned About Sailors*. It's the first studio here to wash up the 1933–1934 season. After a week's lull, lot starts on *Judge Priest*, Will Rogers picture, for the new program. This studio, run by Sol Wurtzel and John Stone apart from the Fox Westwood lot, has made 21 features and five Spanish pictures this year.[27]

No doubt the fact that *Judge Priest* turned out to be a smash hit reinforced the Ford-Wurtzel alliance by strengthening Wurtzel's claims on higher budgets in the eyes of Kent and other executives, and opening up the opportunity for Ford to embark upon *Steamboat Round the Bend* on an even more substantial budget at the Western Avenue studio.[28]

Doctor Bull and *Judge Priest*

Doctor Bull concerns an iconoclastic physician who practices in Winston, a small New England town. He is perpetually at odds with the Bannings, a rich and genteel family of old New England stock. His abrupt manner and laissez-faire attitude towards his patients – he tends to let nature take its course – has also alienated him from many of the townsfolk. He attends to the town's poorer inhabitants and scoffs at the scientific trappings of modern medicine as personified by Dr. Verney, a successful young physician from a neighboring city who is preferred by the Bannings. In addition to their doubts about Bull's competence, both the Bannings and the more modest middle-class townsfolk are scandalized by Bull's long-standing affair with the widow Janet Cardmaker. When the town experiences a typhoid epidemic, Dr. Bull, who is also the Health Inspector, is blamed for failing to check the water quality in the reservoir, the source of the infection. The ensuing public censure of the doctor is partly inspired by the long-standing grudges against him, and by moral disapproval of his affair. The novel culmi-

---

24   J. J. Gain, Memo to Wasson and Bagnall, 28 Jul 1933, John Ford Contract File, Twentieth Century-Fox Legal Department, in typescript: "Mr. Ford is to have approval of the subject matter of the second production", and written in pencil: "Mr. Kent phoned approval JJG".
25   Bogdanovich, *John Ford*, 59.
26   Dan Ford, 31; McBride, 148, and see 125n, 131, 138n, 177, 213.
27   "Fox-H'wood Lot Cleans Up '34 Sked of 26 Pix", *Variety* (29 May 1934): 4.
28   *Variety* reports on the performance of Ford's two Wurtzel-produced Rogers films suggest that they did very well, with high box-office returns and several hold-overs. Eyman, *Print the Legend*, 151, reports that *Judge Priest* grossed $1.2 million and *Steamboat Round the Bend* $1.5 million; it is not clear if these numbers include foreign as well as domestic earnings.

nates in a town-hall meeting in which Bull's opponents suggest that he be dismissed from his position as Health Inspector and that one of Dr. Verney's associates be invited to serve as town physician. Bull charges into the meeting late because of work, denounces the assembly for interfering in his personal affairs, thereby further alienating his neighbors, and exits. However, in his absence, the largely Republican town's sole Democratic functionary, a real-estate tycoon, cleverly turns the meeting in Bull's favor as part of a plan to advance his party's interests, and also for his own amusement. The community's change of heart toward the doctor, represented in a cynical and seriocomic mode, forms the high point of Cozzens's novel.

In the film, the town meeting runs concurrently with the doctor's treatment of a patient, Joe, who has lost the use of his legs in an accident and who Verney had advised would never walk again. In the novel, Joe spontaneously recovers well in advance of the town meeting so that his cure has nothing to do with the doctor's political battles. But, in the Fox adaptation, Dr. Bull injects the patient with a homespun remedy developed to treat sick cows, leaves temporarily to repudiate the charges leveled against him at the meeting, and then returns to find Joe has recovered the use of his legs. The idea that Bull should cure Joe by the same method that he applies to cows may have been suggested by Ford or, in any case, to have been influenced by the example of *Arrowsmith*. While certainly more in line with the generally heroic treatment of physicians in the Hollywood cinema, this revision complicates the film's last act since it creates a double climax: the meeting about Bull and the cure of Joe. Moreover, Joe's cure is never fully brought to bear on the problem of the animosity between Bull and the townsfolk, since the emphasis on resolving the romance plot in the final scenes leaves implicit the restoration of the doctor's good standing. It

should be noted that there is no definitive "resolution" of the romance plot in the novel which simply suggests that the doctor's affair with the widow will continue. In the film, after a comic quarrel between the couple and a good dose of cider, the doctor kneels and begins to work up to the question. This is interrupted by his philandering patient Larry Ward (Andy Devine) who is threatened with marriage by his girlfriend's angry relations. Bull calls to schedule an appointment for Larry with a justice of the peace after which he makes his own peace with Janet.

While the changes Ford and his colleagues introduced in the final shooting script made for two scenes – the denunciation of the townsfolk at the meeting and the proposal – which showcased Rogers to great advantage, they had the net result of further sidelining the novel's emphasis on small-town politics. In contrast with *Doctor Bull*, in *Judge Priest* Ford and screenwriters Dudley Nichols and Lamar Trotti dealt extensively with the loyalties and divisions which structured the Judge's community. Indeed, these lie at the heart of the film's stirring finale.

Irvin S. Cobb had begun publishing his stories about Judge Priest in the *Saturday Evening Post* in the 1910s, and by the 1920s they were regularly anthologized and widely known. And, although Cobb is largely forgotten today, in the 1920s and early 1930s he was a popular figure, in great demand as a lecturer and radio performer.[29] Will Rogers had a long association with the writer. The two met while both were living in New York sometime in the 1910s, probably brought together by the humorist and syndicated columnist O. O. McIntyre who was a mutual friend.[30] In 1921, Rogers starred in *Boys Will Be Boys* (Goldwyn, directed by Clarence Badger), adapted from Charles O'Brien Kennedy's play, which derived from Cobb's Judge Priest story of the same name.[31] In 1933, both men were engaged for regular radio broadcasts by the Gulf

29   William E. Ellis, *Irvin S. Cobb: the Rise and Fall of an American Humorist* (Lexington: University of Kentucky Press, 2017), 76–77, 81, 148–149.
30   Anita Lawson, *Irvin S. Cobb* (Bowling Green: Bowling Green State University Popular Press, 1984), 190; Will Rogers, Telegram to O. O. McIntyre [ca. 24 Oct 1931] in Rogers, *The Papers of Will Rogers*, vol. 5: *The Final Years, August 1928–August 1935*, ed. Steven K. Gragert and M. Jane Johansson (Norman, University of Oklahoma Press, 2006), 266.
31   Bryan B. Sterling and Frances N. Sterling, eds., *Will Rogers in Hollywood* (New York: Crown Publishers, 1984), 34. Rogers played Peep O'Day, not Judge Priest, in this feature.

Refining Company – Rogers's program airing over NBC and Cobb's over CBS.[32] Each mentioned the other over the air, and Cobb was in the audience when Rogers paid him tribute.[33] As comedians both men adopted rural personae, one associated with the West and the other with the South. Rogers, sometimes called a "cowboy philosopher", was part Cherokee and hailed from Claremore, Oklahoma, located on what had been a reservation of the Cherokee Nation. He had worked as a cowhand and got his start in vaudeville with a roping act. Cobb came from Paducah, Kentucky, and many of his stories and radio performances glorified the antebellum South. In this context it is worth noting that the Cherokee Nation sided with the South in the Civil War so that despite their regional and national differences both men had paternal relatives who fought for the Confederacy.[34]

The *Hollywood Reporter* first announced Wurtzel's production of *Judge Priest* on February 12, 1934, indicating that Dudley Nichols was about to begin work on the script.[35] By early March, Fox had purchased the rights to three published Cobb stories: "A Treefull of Hoot Owls", "Br'er Fox and the Briar Patch" and "Words and Music".[36] Nichols and Trotti's initial story outline is dated March 16 – presumably they had roughed out the plot in advance of the purchase of the literary properties so that they were able to work with dispatch. It seems likely that Ford was consulted about this outline, but given that production of *The World Moves On* began on February 20 and continued for nine weeks to April 17, he was unlikely to have worked extensively on the story at this point. A script dated April 12, 1934, largely follows the original outline and a surviving copy labeled "John Ford" at the Lilly Library bears his written comments. The Final Shooting Script of April 27, 1934, is divided into scene numbers, presumably the result of Ford's pre-production planning.[37]

The screenwriters used the three stories purchased by Fox to create the situation central to the film's third and final act. "A Treefull of Hoot Owls" is the most important of the three. In it, Judge Priest presides over the trial of Bob Gillis, who has assaulted the town's popular and garrulous barber, Flem Talley.[38] Talley and two friends actually initiated the attack, but they all lie in court, putting the blame on Gillis. The trial does not go well. Gillis, rumored to be a Northerner and a taciturn and isolated man, is not well liked and the lawyer for the defense is inexperienced. The ambitious prosecuting attorney presses Gillis hard but the man refuses to explain the cause of the enmity between himself and the barber – the good name of the young lady Flem slandered is never invoked by either side. The court adjourns after the defense has rested but before the jury can render its verdict, a device taken up in the film. Ashby Brand, the town pastor, then talks privately to Judge Priest, revealing aspects of the accused's past and character. This motivates the Judge to write an anonymous letter to the prosecuting attorney that tricks him into reopening the case the next day. On the witness stand for the defense, Brand explains that when the South was short of men near the end of the war he had conscripted a group of prisoners who had been

32 "Two-Chain Sponsor Signs Rogers, Cobb", *Billboard* (22 Apr 1933): 12; "Rogers' Air Stay Indefinite", *Variety* (18 Apr 1933): 35.
33 Rogers, "Good Gulf Show", NBC broadcast, 30 Apr 1933, transcript in Rogers, *The Writings of Will Rogers*, series vi: *Radio Broadcasts of Will Rogers*, ed. Steven K. Gragert (Stillwater: Oklahoma State University Press, 1983): 71–72; "Radio Reports: Irvin S. Cobb", *Variety* (9 May 1933): 41.
34 Irvin's uncle Major Robert Cobb led his own unit from the beginning of the war and his father enlisted later after finishing college, Ellis, 4. Although the Cherokee Nation was initially divided, the Cherokee owned slaves and eventually sided with the South. Rogers's father Clem enlisted with the regiment of a Cherokee officer, Colonel Stand Watie, "a near-mythical figure in Cherokee history", Ben Yagoda, *Will Rogers: A Biography* (Norman: University of Oklahoma Press, 1993): 8–9.
35 "Wurtzel to Handle Second Rogers Pic", *Hollywood Reporter* (12 Feb 1934): 2.
36 "Words and Music", *Saturday Evening Post* (28 Oct 1911): 9–11, subsequently published in Cobb, *Back Home* (New York: George H. Doran Company, 1912); "A Treefull of Hoot Owls", *Hearst's International-Cosmopolitan Magazine* (Aug 1930): 60–63, 140–142, 144, 146; and "Br'er Rabbit, He Lay Low", *Hearst's International-Cosmopolitan Magazine* (May 1931): 68–71, 200, 202–206, subsequently published as "Br'er Fox and the Briar Patch", both in Cobb, *Down Yonder with Judge Priest and Irvin S. Cobb* (New York: Ray Long & Richard R. Smith, Inc, 1932).
37 The studio files contain the following: *Judge Priest*, Story Outline, 16 Mar 1934; *Old Judge Priest*, First Draft, 12 Apr 1934, by Dudley Nichols and Lamar Trotti; *Judge Priest* (title handwritten over "The Band Plays Dixie", which is crossed out), Final Shooting Script, 27 Apr 1934, all in *Judge Priest* Story File, Twentieth Century-Fox Legal Department.
38 The barber is named "Flem Talley" in the script and film but not in the short story; I use the film name for consistency.

condemned to life imprisonment, promising them their freedom if they survived the fighting. He tells the story of one prisoner who had proven unusually brave and cool-headed under fire – Bob Gillis. The jury, which includes many Confederate veterans and their sons, immediately decides for acquittal. The pastor tells the Judge he is as wise as a "treefull of hoot owls".

The screenwriters embellished this story with elements of "Words and Music", a story similar to "A Treefull of Hoot Owls" but in which the Judge is the witness who rallies the jury's sympathy by recalling the Confederate service of the accused's father. In "Words and Music" the Judge has taken the precaution of adding music to his words. Before the beginning of the trial, he hires a street musician, a one-man band with drums and harmonica, to stand outside the courtroom and play a march on cue during his testimony. The screenwriters added this twist to their trial scene, making two changes to the original: the anonymous street musician (specified only as a Black man in the published text) becomes the Judge's servant Jeff and the march tune becomes "Dixie", the song adopted by secessionists as their anthem in the early 1860s.

In the two preceding stories the Judge was never in jeopardy, rather he came to the aid of others. The screenwriters found a way to put pressure on the Judge himself through a device found in "Br'er Fox and the Briar Patch". In the course of a trial, prosecuting attorney Maydew, an on-going political antagonist of the Judge, maintains that Billy Priest is not impartial and demands that he recuse himself. Priest steps down from the bench but returns as a member of the bar to help the inexperienced lawyer for the defense and of course eventually triumphs over his nemesis. The screenwriters expanded on this plot device as well, since the inexperienced lawyer who is defending Gillis in the film is the Judge's nephew, Rome (Jerome) Priest, newly graduated from law school.

Most of the script's first and second acts are inventions of the screenwriters, but they have been

devised to motivate the third act and enrich its impact. Act one begins in court with Maydew prosecuting Jeff Poindexter (played by Lincoln Theodore Monroe Andrew Perry, stage name Stepin Fetchit) for stealing chickens. Dialogue added during filming makes it clear that Maydew (Berton Churchill) is seeking the Judge's post in an upcoming election. The Judge's affinity with Jeff is also established – both are partial to fishing.[39] The rest of act one establishes the romance plot: Rome (Tom Brown) returns to Kentucky a newly minted lawyer and with the encouragement of the Judge pursues the girl next door, Ellie Mae (Anita Louise). The Judge's status-conscious sister-in-law Callie opposes the match because Ellie Mae is poor and of uncertain parentage; also, she hopes to make a match between Rome and the wealthy Maydew's daughter Virginia. Act two develops the mystery around Bob Gillis's past as well as showing the initiation of his fight with Flem Talley. Talley makes rude jokes to other men in the barber shop about his intentions towards Ellie Mae, and Gillis punches him out. This leads to the attack on Gillis by Flem and his buddies, and Gillis's consequent hiring of Rome in the young lawyer's first case. In addition to the plot thread centered on Gillis, the screenwriters added a lengthy set piece, a church social, which deepened the existing narrative threads: the Judge thwarts Callie's attempts to pair off Rome and Virginia at the party and helps him sneak off with Ellie Mae; Maydew campaigns for the Judge's judicial seat; the assembled Confederate veterans listen to one of Jimmy Bagby's tall tales about his war exploits. The social helps to underline the class differences between Virginia and Ellie Mae, who is serving ice cream alongside the Judge's cook Aunt Dilsey (Hattie McDaniel). At the same time, it highlights the nostalgic attitude towards the Civil War that animates Bagby's fanciful recital. And, as a bonus, it introduces the character of the pastor Ashby Brand (Henry B. Walthall) in preparation for his important part in act three. Another second-act set piece that appeared in all of the written drafts and seems to have been shot

---

39   Although Jeff Poindexter is an on-going character in the Cobb stories, in the film he meets the Judge for the first time in the course of the trial.

5.1

5.2

5.3

5.4

and then excised from the completed film is the attempted lynching of Jeff, to be discussed below.

The ingenuity of act three becomes fully apparent in relation to the narrative threads established in acts one and two. During his testimony Reverend Brand explains the mysteries surrounding Gillis's behavior in act two, revealing him to be not only a Confederate hero but also a father who has been watching incognito over his daughter Ellie Mae. The testimony thus restores father to daughter while elevating the father's social status in the eyes of Confederate sympathizers (i.e., everyone in the court room). It also provides an incontestable victory for the Judge in his pre-election jousting with Maydew. Initially forced by Maydew to abandon the case, the Judge slyly comes back after speaking with Brand, writing the anonymous letter, convincing Jeff to play "Dixie" on cue, and joining Rome as part of Gillis's legal defense team.

The story which exculpates Gillis, though supposedly stage-managed by Judge Priest for the audience within the courtroom, is also given a highly spectacular presentation for us. Brand's narration is accompanied by brief, episodic flashbacks which are superimposed over the shot of the pastor in the witness box (figure 5.1). As Brand begins to narrate the military exploits of the as yet unnamed prisoner, Priest signals a crony at the window who signals to Jeff outside the courtroom on the street. As Jeff begins to play the harmonica he is joined by other Black musicians. The instrumental texture thickens and the music swells over the flashbacks of the men in battle (figures 5.2, 5.3). When Brand completes his narration, he stands and names the prisoner: Gillis. The jury and spectators in the court rise and move toward the defendant, their cheers joining the sound of the music. Maydew tries to speak, to assert himself, but he cannot be heard – he has lost his audience (figure 5.4). Callie sweeps to Ellie Mae's side in a swift resolution of the romance plot.

Looking out the courtroom window, the Judge urges the musicians to keep playing and they begin to march as they continue to perform.

5.5

5.6

Dissolve to the later Confederate Veterans' Day parade with a military band performing (figures 5.5, 5.6). Billy Priest with his comrades are attired in Confederate uniforms as they march at the head of the procession. They stop to pull in Gillis from the sidelines to march beside them. Juror 12, who during the trial has already demonstrated his marksmanship with chewing tobacco, gayly spits into Maydew's upturned top hat. Gallagher calls it one of Ford's "finest finales", and it certainly anticipates the later communal celebrations in films such as *How Green Was My Valley* and, from the post-war period, *The Quiet Man*. But the social unity celebrated at the end of *Judge Priest* is specifically based upon a Confederate anthem and a Confederate past. This raises the question of how, if at all, the film deals with the historical reality of slavery and its ongoing legacy. Does "Dixie" really float all boats? Is the informal, high-steppin' parade of Jeff and his fellow musicians of a piece with the white folks marching down Main Street sporting the Stars and Bars?

Present-day audiences frequently react negatively to the racial stereotypes that are operative in *Judge Priest* at many levels, from the characterizations of Aunt Dilsey and Jeff Poindexter, to the postures and stage business adopted by Hattie McDaniel and Lincoln Perry, to individual lines of dialogue, as when the Judge addresses Jeff as "boy", or chides him: "Come, come, hurry up here! Come on here when I holler at you". It

should be noted however that the film goes out of its way to depict friendly relations between Judge Priest and his servants, and to feature Hattie McDaniel and Lincoln Perry in performance alongside Rogers – as in the scenes in which Rogers improvises blues-like songs with Hattie McDaniel or playfully adopts Lincoln Perry's dialect and intonation. While such interchanges might be taken for granted today, this was not the case in the 1930s. For example, in an infamous letter that was widely circulated to industry executives, Dolph Frantz of the *Shreveport Journal* complained about two films: John Stahl's *Imitation of Life* (Universal, 1934), which featured a business partnership between a white single mother and a Black one, and Raoul Walsh's *Artists and Models* (Paramount 1937), in which Martha Raye performed a specialty number with Louis Armstrong. Frantz wrote:

> I confidently believe that if the practice of mixing the races in pictures continues much longer, the reaction will be very hurtful to the picture industry in this part of the country. I hear the matter commented on frequently. The general feeling hereabouts is the same as my own … . In the South there is a color line and it always will be drawn, and when negroes and white persons act together there will always be a bad reaction. If a picture is entirely of negroes, there is no cause to complain, but when whites are mixed with the negroes, the situation is entirely different.[40]

40 Dolph Frantz, Managing Editor, *Shreveport Journal*, Letter to Adolph Zukor, Paramount Pictures, 25 Aug 1927; and the accompanying letter from E. V. Richards, Jr., Saenger Theatres Corp., New Orleans, to Louis B. Mayer, Y. F. Freeman, Sidney R. Kent, Cecil B. DeMille, Will Hays, 3 Sep 1937, both in the Production Code Administration file for *Imitation of Life*, in *History of Cinema, Series 1, Hollywood and the Production Code*, Selected files from the Motion Picture Association of America

Indeed, in the first film to pair Rogers and Perry, the Sheehan-produced *David Harum* (Fox, 1934, dir. James Cruze), there are no prolonged conversations between the horse trader Harum (Rogers) and the groom Swifty (Perry). It is an unfortunate role for Perry, his character treated as little more than an appendage of his horse. Although he does one brilliant star turn as he watches the horse race in the film's finale, he acts alone, literally talking to himself. In this context *Judge Priest* can be appreciated for the interchanges which allow Rogers to create some great scenes with Perry and with McDaniel. And there is one indication that this aspect of the film pushed against prevailing attitudes in the South. A letter of complaint about the representation of the Black characters in *Judge Priest* addressed to Rogers was quoted in the humorist's syndicated column of November 11, 1934:

> *Judge Priest* is far, very far, from being a true picture of the South of that period … . The Negroes kept, and still do, their places as servants, respectful and obedient, never appearing in public except in caps and aprons (in other words, uniforms); the women with clean dresses, caps and aprons, the men wearing a white coat, all the time keeping a respectful silence.[41]

However stereotyped their roles, Perry and McDaniel are nonetheless powerfully present and important characters in *Judge Priest* – far from respectful and quiet background characters.

The film's employment of racial stereotypes relates to the more general question of how Ford and his screenwriters approached the representation of racial division and inequality in the Judge's Kentucky community. And at this level it seems clear that they tried to do more than now appears on screen. As noted above, act two originally included a sequence in which the Judge faces down a lynch mob that has come after Jeff. This sequence appears in the screenwriters' initial outline and is developed in the two subsequent drafts. It seems to have been inspired by two Irwin S. Cobb stories, "The Mob from Massac" and "The Sun Shines Bright", although Fox did not purchase them in 1934.[42] It is likely that the sequence was filmed since a production still survives.[43] In a 1936 interview Ford recalled: "I remember a few years ago, with the *Judge Priest* picture, putting in an anti-lynching plea that was one of the most scorching things you ever heard. They happened to cut it, purely for reasons of space, but I enjoyed doing that enormously."[44]

In the second act of Nichols and Trotti's Final Shooting Script, Jeff and the Judge have gone fishing, planning to use beef liver as bait (this use of beef liver is established in the script's and the film's first scene). Having forgotten the bait, Jeff is sent for it and is then chased by a group of bloodhounds reacting to the odor of the meat. The dogs are followed by the sheriff and posse on the trail of a murderer and they arrest Jeff. Back in town, a lynch mob forms, egged on by Flem Talley. The mob overpowers the sheriff who is trying to defend the jail but Ellie Mae and Rome have rounded up the Judge and his ex-Confederate cronies in time. The Judge addresses the mob, calling individuals by name, making jokes at their expense, scolding them and eventually dismissing them.

There is no way to verify Ford's recollection that the lynching sequence in *Judge Priest* was excised to reduce the film's length. Existing prints run from seventy-nine to eighty minutes, which is typical for a Rogers film of this period, suggesting that without the excision it would have run a bit long. But industry censors also clearly considered the topic potentially offensive. In spring 1934, at the same time that *Judge Priest* was in

Production Code Administration collection, Filmed from the holdings of the Margaret Herrick Library, Academy of Motion Picture Arts and Sciences, Primary Source Microfilm (Woodbridge, Connecticut: Thomas Gale, 2006), reel 9.
41   Sterling and Sterling, eds., 150–151.
42   "The Mob from Massac", *Saturday Evening Post* (10 Feb 1912): 5–7, 32–33, subsequently published in Cobb, *Back Home* (1912); "The Sun Shines Bright", *Hearst's International-Cosmopolitan* (Apr 1931): 72–74, 130–137, subsequently published in Cobb, *Down Yonder with Judge Priest and Irvin S. Cobb* (1932). In Cobb's story "The Mob from Massac", the Judge talks down a lynch mob composed of white men from Massac county. Some time later, after the real culprit is found, the Massac men all vote for the Judge in gratitude, yielding the winning margin in a tight election. This is the version of the plot that appears in Ford's film *The Sun Shines Bright*. In Cobb's version of "The Sun Shines Bright", it is the Black community that votes for the Judge in gratitude for his stopping a lynching, allowing him to beat the "radical" Republicans and retain his office.
43   It is reproduced in Gallagher, 162.
44   Eisenberg, reprinted in Peary, ed., 13.

preparation, Joseph Breen and James Wingate of the Production Code Administration and their superiors in the Hays office counseled Universal to remove a lynching scene from the script of *Imitation of Life*.[45] Since the PCA file for *Judge Priest* does not survive there is no way to ascertain how this film was evaluated by industry censors. However, given that those censors were at pains to treat scripts from different studios in the same way, it seems unlikely that Fox would have been allowed to include something that Universal could not get away with.

The lynching sequence as written in the *Judge Priest* scripts, and as it appears in *The Sun Shines Bright*, Ford's 1953 remake of *Judge Priest*, is hardly a "scorching" denunciation of racially-motivated violence. It is a rather paternalistic scenario with the Judge protecting the Black characters and acting for them. But the sequence was nonetheless important for the 1934 version because it situated Jeff in a hostile environment as opposed to some edenic vision of the South. In this respect its retention would have helped to clarify an idea that persists in the film, albeit in a more muted form, in relation to the treatment of "Dixie". Jeff does not want to play "Dixie" at the trial. He does so because the Judge offers him a coat and a vest for the performance. Lincoln Perry and Will Rogers improvised the scene as follows:

Judge [referring to Jeff's harmonica]: Can you play "Dixie" on that thing there?

Jeff: For that coon coat? Yes, I play "Dixie", "Marchin' Thru Georgia" … .

Judge: Hey! "Marchin' Thru Georgia!" Yeah. I got you outta one lynchin' … .

Jeff: [Walking away and talking to himself.] Yes, but for that coon coat … . I know that I goin' to get that coat … .

Judge: I catch you playin' "Marchin' Thru Georgia" I'll join the lynchin' … .[46]

"Marching Through Georgia" was written by Henry Clay Work at the end of the Civil War. It refers to U.S. Army General William Tecumseh Sherman's troops who captured Atlanta and then marched to the coast to capture Savannah, burning plantations and other infrastructure in their wake. The chorus is as follows:

> Hurrah! Hurrah! we bring the Jubilee!
> Hurrah! Hurrah! the flag that makes you free!
> So we sang the chorus from Atlanta to the sea
> While we were marching through Georgia.

The improvised dialogue indicates that Jeff would much rather be playing "Marching Through Georgia" than "Dixie", and that the Judge violently dislikes the song that Jeff prefers. Jeff becomes reconciled to "Dixie" because he wants the coat, and also, as the Judge reminds him, because Jeff owes him one for standing up to the lynch mob. As Will Rogers once quipped, "Politics ain't nothin' but reciprocity".[47]

Thus, Ford, Rogers and Perry went out of their way to suggest that Jeff, much more than the Judge himself, uses "Dixie" in an instrumental way and that the halcyon vision of the South evoked in the song at the film's close is not his vision. While it may seem that this analysis places too much weight on a song, or two songs, it is the result of a specifically Fordian emphasis on song as a historical repository, a storehouse of specific national and ethnic and racial identifications. If the lynching scene had been retained in *Judge Priest*, the import of the exchange between Jeff and the Judge over the performance of "Dixie" might be clearer, but even without it the connotations remain. And Ford makes them even clearer in the 1953 remake. After the Judge's shrewdly calculated re-election campaign against Horace Maydew ends in a surprise win, the band breaks into a triumphal rendition of "Dixie". The music continues over a dissolve to the Judge on his front porch as all the political factions of the town march past – the U.S. Army veterans, the men

---

45 Memorandum for the Files, 9 Mar 1934; J. B. Lewis, Inter-Office Memo to Mr. [Joseph] Breen, 10 Mar 1934; Maurice McKenzie, Letter to Joseph Breen, 3 Apr 1934; Will Hays, Letter to Robert H. Cochrane, Universal Pictures, 18 May 1934; and Joseph Breen to Harry Zehner, Universal Studio, 27 Jul 1934, all in the Production Code Administration file for *Imitation of Life*.

46 A comparison with the Final Shooting Script, *Judge Priest* Story File, Twentieth Century-Fox Legal Department, reveals the extent of Lincoln Perry's improvisation. In the script, the interchange is written as follows: "*Judge:* Jeff, how'd you like to have that old coon coat of mine? *Jeff* [stammering with excitement]: Ah-ah-ah-Thanky, Jedge. *Judge:* Hold on. Kin you play 'Dixie' on that harmonicky? *Jeff:* Ah-ah-ah-ummmm".

47 Will Rogers, "Good Gulf Show", NBC broadcast, 2 Jun 1935, transcript in Rogers, *Radio Broadcasts*, 166.

from Massac county whom he talked out of lynching an innocent Black youth, the Confederate veterans and the Women's Temperance League, all marching to "Dixie". After they pass, from the opposite direction, members of the Black community amble by singing the title song, "The sun shines bright … ". The Black community thus shares in this moment of social communion without having to sing the anthem of the Confederacy, their song given preference by the film's title.

Just as Howard Hawks improved on Curtiz's *Casablanca* with *To Have and Have Not*, Ford found one of his most important themes by remaking and improving upon *Doctor Bull*. Like *Doctor Bull*, *Judge Priest* concerns a professional man rooted in a small town who finds himself at odds with his upper-class counterparts. In both films the Rogers character serves as a guardian of the poorer members of the community and stands in opposition to a rich stuffed shirt – the characters Banning in *Doctor Bull* and Maydew in *Judge Priest*, played in both cases by Berton Churchill. But *Judge Priest*, made with Ford's preferred screenwriters and under a producer who trusted him to follow his own preferences, is much more of a comedy than *Doctor Bull*. Maydew's formality is extravagantly ridiculed and contrasted with the freewheeling behavior of a host of eccentric comic characters, not only Jeff Poindexter, but also Jimmy Bagby (Charley Grapewin) and Juror 12 (Francis Ford). Moreover, Ford seems to have learned from what might be seen as a narrative deficit in *Doctor Bull* – the failure to develop fully the social and political dynamic of the story – by his attention to such elements in *Judge Priest*. Two factors, in addition to Ford's personal interest in history and politics, seem to have inspired this approach to his material. The first is Irvin S. Cobb's Judge Priest stories themselves. These stories evoked the antagonisms and loyalties engendered by the Civil War and dealt explicitly and in detail with the machinations of Democratic party politics in the South.[48] The influence of

Cobb's stories was seconded by the example of Will Rogers's newspaper columns and radio broadcasts – funny, improvised accounts of the maneuvers of the President, the Congress and the Supreme Court during the Depression years.[49] Prior to his encounter with these two humorists, Ford had dealt with history in spectacular reconstructions of actual events such as the building of the first transcontinental railroad in *The Iron Horse* and the land rush in the Black Hills of Dakota in *3 Bad Men*. But Cobb and Rogers provided examples of a humorous rather than an epic engagement with history, and one that entailed close attention to divisions within the social fabric: North versus South, Republican versus Democrat. This approach came to predominate in Ford's subsequent films. Major pre-war features such as *Wee Willie Winkie*, *Stagecoach*, *Young Mr. Lincoln*, *The Grapes of Wrath*, *The Long Voyage Home* and *How Green Was My Valley* consistently call attention to differences of class, rank, race, ethnicity or nationality. Many post-War films, including many of his best Westerns, could also be added to this list. This is to say that Ford's use of stereotypes sprang from a lively imaginative engagement with history as expressed in a popular medium, and remained committed to an exploration of the social divisions among men and women in specific times and places, as well as to the identities which bound them.

Steamboat Round the Bend

Ford's second two-picture contract with Fox expired with the completion of *Judge Priest* in July 1934. As described in chapter four, the third Fox contract was signed in late September for four pictures over two years at $45,000 per picture. The success of *Judge Priest*, and the fact that Ford was so clearly in demand at other studios, must have put him in a strong bargaining position. The day after the contract was signed on September 21, 1934, Fox bought the literary rights to the novel *Steamboat Round the Bend* by Ben Lucien

48   The Cobb stories "Judge Priest Comes Back", *Saturday Evening Post* (7 Aug 1915): 3–4, 45–46, 49–51, subsequently published in *Old Judge Priest* (New York: George H. Doran, 1916), "The Mob from Massac", and "The Sun Shines Bright" all deal with Democratic party politics.
49   In addition to Rogers, *Radio Broadcasts*, see, for example, *The Writings of Will Rogers*, series iv: *Will Rogers' Weekly Articles*, 6 volumes, ed. James M. Smallwood and Steven K. Gragert (Stillwater: Oklahoma State University Press, 1980–1982).

Burman from Ford's agent, Harry Wurtzel.[50] Ford had initiated this project with his personal funds before being rehired by his home studio. Moreover, the timing of Fox's purchase of these rights suggests that the company approved this project as part and parcel of the contract negotiations. These circumstances also help to explain the relatively high budget allocated to this Wurtzel production. For the production, Fox rented four sternwheelers for use upon the Sacramento and San Joaquin Rivers. Crew and company were lodged and fed on one of them, the *Port of Stockton*, where they remained on location for over two weeks from May 13 to 30, 1935. Ford cashed in his chips from *Judge Priest* not for much of a raise, but for the grandest of larks.[51]

It is not clear what led Ford to acquire the rights to Burman's novel. A boating enthusiast and from 1934 a yacht owner, Ford had already shot a steamboat race for the silent Fox adaptation of *Cameo Kirby* (1923). Although existing prints of that film are in poor condition, the race does seem to have been photographed on the Sacramento river, or at least a river with similar topography. In addition, Ford may have been inspired by Russell Mack's *Heaven on Earth* (Universal, 1931), an adaptation of Burman's 1929 novel *Mississippi* about the antagonism between steamboat men and shanty-boat men along the river. This ambitious early sound film also had scenes shot on the Sacramento river.[52]

Burman's *Steamboat Round the Bend* is set along a hundred-mile stretch of the Mississippi north of Baton Rouge. It deals with shanty-boat dwellers situated in very small river-side towns and backwoods dwellers situated in even less populous swamp lands. The novel aims to reconstruct the folkways and vernacular speech of the region, and also quotes a Black spiritual, "Eagle's Nest" or "Eagle Builds His Nest So High", which Burman claimed to have heard along the river in the 1920s.[53] In the novel, "Doctor" John Pearly, a shanty-boat dweller and agent for the Little Flower patent medicine company, awaits the arrival of his nephew, Duke, a pilot on a steamboat. They plan to take possession of an old disused steamboat moored nearby. Doctor John has managed to purchase the boat and hopes to restore it for transporting cargo and passengers along the river in partnership with Duke. As in the film, the nephew arrives with Fleety Belle, a girl from the swamps, and confesses that he killed a man who was attacking her. Doctor John convinces Duke to give himself up to the sheriff. At his trial the boy is found guilty. In the course of the highly episodic plot that follows, Doctor John, Fleety Belle and a number of other characters travel the river in two successive derelict steamboats as they try to raise money for Duke's appeal. They also search for the one witness to the fact that the killing was in self-defense – a tramp named Barefoot Charlie. The characters are strange and quaint

50 Ben Lucien Burman, *Steamboat Round the Bend* (New York: Grosset & Dunlap, 1933). The *Steamboat Round the Bend* Legal File, Twentieth Century-Fox Legal Department, contains the following documents relating to the purchase agreement: Agreement between Ben Lucien Burman and Harry L. Wurtzel; "Purchase of Steamboat Round the Bend", 21 September 1934; Assignment of Rights in *Steamboat Round the Bend* from Harry L. Wurtzel to Fox Film Corporation, 22 September 1934; Hazel Delphine, Harry Wurtzel, Inc., "Receipt for $7500 on account for the property entitled *Steamboat Round the Bend*, by Ben Lucien Burman, in accordance with that certain agreement, dated September 22, 1934 between Fox Film Corporation and Harry L. Wurtzel"; George Wasson, Telegram to E. P. Kilroe, 15 September 1934; E. P. Kilroe to George F. Wasson, 2 Apr 1936. Presumably the original deal between Wurtzel and Burman was simply a handshake and an exchange of cash, and the studio required a more formal assignment of rights when it came time for them to buy the intellectual property. Burman describes Ford buying the rights in an interview in Sterling and Sterling, eds., 167.
51 Agreement between Fox Film Corporation and the California Transportation Company and the River Lines, 26 Apr 1935, *Steamboat Round the Bend* Legal File, Twentieth Century-Fox Legal Department. The dates of location work have been established by "Rogers and Cobb Will Skipper River Boats", *Hollywood Reporter* (11 May 1935): 3; "Fox Starts Six on Two Lots This Week", *Hollywood Reporter* (13 May 1935): 2; "Remote Control", *Variety* (29 May 1935): 29. Rogers's radio broadcast of 26 May 1935, transcribed in Rogers, *Radio Broadcasts*, 156, indicates that he and Cobb had finished early and returned to Los Angeles by that date.
52 "*Heaven on Earth* Outside'", *Hollywood Reporter* (14 May 1931): 3; "*Heaven on Earth* Gang Due Back Tomorrow", *Hollywood Reporter* (23 Jun 1931): 4; "*Heaven* Wasn't", *Variety* (30 Jun 1931): 6, 54.
53 Burman describes hearing the spiritual sung "when the *Tennessee Belle* stopped to take on some cattle waiting at the Natchez wharf", in "Music on the Mississippi", part of the liner notes to the album *Steamboat Round the Bend: Songs and stories of the Mississippi*, Smithsonian Folkways Recording, FL 9774 and available at: https://folkways-media.si.edu/docs/folkways/artwork/FW09774.pdf. There has been no independent verification of the authenticity of the spiritual and Fox permitted its use in Ford's film without being able to clear the rights, see James O'Keefe, Memo to George Wasson, 29 Apr 1935, *Steamboat Round the Bend* Legal File, Twentieth Century-Fox Legal Department.

5.7

and sometimes amusing, but the predominant tone of the novel is melancholy. These are desperately poor people who use what little money they can scrape together to make foolish if charming bets on a fading mode of river transport.

Burman's novel provides the melodramatic backbone of Ford's film – the character of Doctor John, the romance between Duke and Fleety Belle, the attempt to exculpate Duke before his scheduled execution. However, the plot was dramatically transformed by Ford, Nichols and Trotti through the incorporation of a variety of other sources – the popular comic song "Steamboat Bill", the writings of Mark Twain, the nineteenth-century iconography of Mississippi steamboats and river boats, as well as their own comic inventions. The film is a prime and early example of what might be called magpie plot construction, a weave of unrelated elements pulled together in what can sometimes seem an offhand way. This becomes one of Ford's favorite strategies for composing plots. *Judge Priest* and *The Sun Shines Bright* are both amalgamations of multiple Cobb short stories. *The Long Voyage Home* creates a continuous narrative out of four of Eugene O'Neill's one-act plays about the crew of the merchant ship *Glencairn*. The post-war calvary

series – *Fort Apache*, *She Wore a Yellow Ribbon*, and *Rio Grande* – draws liberally on James Warner Bellah's short stories about cavalry life in the West, augmented by incidents drawn from military history as well as well-known paintings by Frederic Remington, Charles Marion Russell and Harold von Schmidt (not to mention the songs). This sort of plot construction usually differs markedly from the heavy foreshadowing and inevitable sense of decline found in films such as *The Lost Patrol* and *The Informer*. It tends to be open-ended, digressive and episodic with a more pronounced alternation between comic and dramatic scenes.

There is no steamboat race in the novel *Steamboat Round the Bend*. Instead, Doctor John, dead broke, ill and exhausted by fruitless searching for Barefoot Charlie, comes to rest on his shanty boat and later unexpectedly sees the key witness riding on a coal barge. The two men are driven by automobile to the governor's office to obtain Duke's reprieve. But the steamboat race seems to have been part of Ford's original conception for the film. In a script outline dated January 24, 1935, Nichols and Trotti have Doctor John refer to a plan to fix up a derelict steamboat in order to put her in "the big race".[54] The rescue of Duke

---

54   All script variants are from the *Steamboat Round the Bend* Story File, Twentieth Century-Fox Legal Department. In late January 1935, Nichols and Trotti produced an outline of the story that was still very heavily indebted to the book. The outline contains written comments, which seem to be in Ford's rough hand. Two subsequent drafts of the screenplay dated February 6, 1935, and February 19, 1935, were written while Ford was in production on *The Informer* at RKO. Ford reported back to Fox on April 15, 1935, and the last screenplay draft, with division into master shots, is dated April 22, 1935. This draft contains additions and changes dated May 9, 1935, just before the company left to go on location.

already dovetails with the boat race in that outline. The outline also describes the accidental discovery that Doctor John's remedy (which the screenwriters dub Pocahontas) works as a kind of rocket fuel, thus motivating the old boat's miraculous win.

The source of the steamboat race is the song "Steamboat Bill", with lyrics by Ren Shields and music by the Leighton Bros. In May 1935, Ford actually contemplated changing the film's title to *Steamboat Bill* and the studio acquired the rights to the title as well as the song.[55] A comic song in the American folk "tall tale" tradition, "Steamboat Bill" refers to a well-known race that took place in 1870 between the *Robert E. Lee* and the *Natchez* going from New Orleans to St. Louis, Missouri (figure 5.7, by Currier & Ives, depicts the race). In the song, Steamboat Bill is determined to beat the record of the winner, the *Robert E. Lee*, an attempt which becomes the object of a wager between himself and a Kentucky gambler. During the contest, the boat's furnaces get too hot and explode:

> Billy flashed a roll that surely was a bear,
> The boiler, it exploded, blew them up in the air.
> The gambler said to Billy as they left the
>   wreck,
> "I don't know where we're going but we're
>   neck in neck."
> Says Bill to the gambler, "I'll tell you what I'll do,
> I will bet another thousand I'll go higher than
> you!"[56]

This kind of humorous and fantastic storytelling had been frequently employed in the Rogers films. In *David Harum* (1934, James Cruze), for example, the title character convinces a young friend to bet all his money on a horse that is known to balk but which Harum knows will race fiercely if he sings "Ta Ra Ra Boom De Ay". At the crucial point in the race, the band is persuaded to play the song. In *Life Begins at 40* (1935, George Marshall), Watterson Meriwhether (Slim Summerville) and his many backwoods relatives collectively make their signature hog call, which

mysteriously prompts all of the animals assembled for a hog show to stampede, thereby undermining the political speech planned by Merriwhether's rival. The steamboat race which comprises the last act of *Steamboat Round the Bend* is a variant of this kind of humor.

The bet is present as early as the first, February 6, script draft. As it is worked out in the film, Captain Eli (Cobb) goads Doctor John (Rogers) into putting up the dilapidated *Claremore Queen* (named for Rogers's hometown in Oklahoma) against his top-notch vessel the *Pride of Paducah* (named for Cobb's hometown in Kentucky) pending the outcome of the annual steamboat race. The tag ending in the February 6 and 19 screenplay drafts actually has the steamboat blowing up, as in the song. The final shooting script has Fleety Belle and Duke reunited in the pilot house of the *Pride of Paducah*. Then, Doctor John, fishing off the stern, waves to Captain Eli, passing on the *Bayou Queen*. However, following the death of Will Rogers in August, the studio cut the action of Rogers waving goodbye, as well as any comic bits Rogers and Cobb might have improvised in production, due to concerns about their impact upon grieving audiences.[57] As it stands, the film's ending is a brief epilogue rather than the gag originally envisioned.

In addition to incorporating the race and bet from "Steamboat Bill", the filmmakers altered the source novel to make the New Moses the exculpating witness. In Burman's version, Doctor John knows that Barefoot Charlie is looking for the New Moses in order to be baptized and thus he tracks the preacher's movements up and down the river. The screenwriters simplify this double-search scenario. In the opening scenes of the February 19 draft, the New Moses explains to Doctor John that he plans to travel down river and take passage on the *Memphis Girl*. Doctor John comments that his nephew is a pilot on the steamboat. This sets up the New Moses to witness the fight in which Duke kills a man in self-defense.

55 Edwin Kilroe, Telegram to Sheehan, 20 May 1935, states: "Song Steamboat Bill contains enough of story to make it susceptible of [laws regarding] motion picture adaptation … " and Kilroe, Memo to George Wasson, 7 Jun 1935, confirms that they have acquired rights for the title as well as the song, both in *Steamboat Round the Bend* Legal File, Twentieth Century-Fox Legal Department.
56 Ren Shields and Leighton Bros., "Steamboat Bill" (New York: F.A. Mills, 1910).
57 McBride, 213.

The opening scenes of the film also introduce an invention of the screenwriters: the temperance subplot. From the earliest script draft, the film's Pocahontas remedy, unlike the novel's Little Flower remedy, is identified as alcoholic. The story opens with the New Moses (Berton Churchill) delivering a fiery and rhetorically ornate temperance lecture on the main deck of the *Pride of Paducah*. His oratory convinces the inebriated Efe (Francis Ford) who is in the audience to take the pledge. On another part of the main deck, Doctor John is giving a pitch for the Pocahontas remedy. After joining this audience, Efe finds his new preferred beverage. The comedic possibilities of Efe's passage from the presentation by the temperance lecturer to that by the snake-oil salesman are wonderfully developed in the film through the contrast between Berton Churchill's thunderous, Biblically-inspired exhortation, Will Rogers's informal and relaxed patter, and Francis Ford's inspired silent-comedy drunk act. But the structural brilliance of the opening can only be fully appreciated in relation to the film's third and last act.

Ford's film breaks down into three acts. In act one, Efe takes a job as engineer on board the *Claremore Queen* in order to have ready access to the Pocahontas remedy. Duke returns with Fleety Belle and Doctor John persuades him to give himself up. After an initial period of conflict, Doctor John and Fleety Belle make friends, and face the terrible news of Duke's conviction for murder together. Act two encompasses a long digression concerning Professor Marvel's Wax Museum. The professor has run off and the sheriff reports that the show is in debt. Doctor John offers to take the museum on tour on his boat, hoping to raise money for Duke's appeal as well as paying off the debt. Jonah (Lincoln Perry) emerges out of the mouth of the museum's model whale and is introduced into the *Claremore Queen* group. The team remakes the display to appeal to the people who live along the river and has success until the town of Salt Creek, where they

find themselves threatened by the townsfolk. The act ends with a return to the jail, the news that the appeal has failed, and Duke and Fleety Belle's jailhouse wedding. The sheriff then conducts Duke by rail to the Baton Rouge jail where the execution by hanging is to take place.

Act three begins with the *Claremore Queen* heading down river as the group searches for the New Moses. The search proving fruitless, and with the deadline for the execution approaching, Doctor John and Fleety Belle decide to turn around and head for Baton Rouge in an attempt to persuade the governor to issue a pardon before the hanging. As the boat tries to make speed going up river, three surprising coincidences occur that together lead to the reversal of the group's fortunes. The first coincidence is that the *Claremore Queen* runs into the big race just at the moment that it is starting, thereby conjoining the rescue and the race. A reminder of the upcoming contest was slipped into the badinage between Doctor John and Captain Eli as their boats crossed paths in the middle of act two. However, the wealth of dramatic incident that followed this reminder, especially the threatened attack on the boat in Salt Creek and the dire consequences of the failure of Duke's appeal, effectively took over as the center of attention and interest.[58] Thus the conjuncture between the rescue and the race in act three is both unexpected and transformative as the effort to relieve Duke suddenly becomes a contest of steamboats.

The second and third coincidences are paired, and both entail unexpected reversals. After the race has commenced, Fleety Belle spots the New Moses conducting baptisms on the river's edge. Doctor John lassoes him and pulls him aboard (Rogers performed his signature rope tricks in many films). The most surprising aspect of this reversal is its placement within the plot as a whole. If the New Moses had been discovered when Doctor John and Fleety Belle were searching for him down the river, it would have been a run-of-the-mill dramatic reversal. But Doctor

---

58 For related analyses of surprise in literature see Meir Sternberg, *Expositional Modes and Temporal Ordering in Fiction* (Baltimore: The John Hopkins University Press, 1978), 222–223, which discusses how *Père Goriot* unobtrusively paves the way for the surprise revelation of Vautrin's identity as an arch-criminal, and Vera Tobin, *Elements of Surprise: Our Mental Limits and the Satisfactions of Plot* (Cambridge: Harvard University Press, 2018), 35 and 89.

John and Fleety Belle's apparently definitive abandonment of the search has suggested that this avenue of the rescue has been closed off, while the ensuing excitement of the commencement of the race tends to de-emphasize the whole chain of events relating to the rescue. In this context, the re-appearance of the New Moses is extremely unexpected, a miraculous reversal that is underlined by the improbable rope trick that brings him aboard the steamboat. This second coincidence provides the preparation for the more blatantly fantastic third. The crew having burned the wood they were carrying, the decks, and even the wax museum figures, the *Claremore Queen* runs out of fuel. In despair, Efe takes a swig of Pocahontas remedy. Suspicious, the New Moses tastes the contents of the bottle, identifies the Demon Rum, and then tosses it into the boiler, whereupon it explodes.[59] Thus, having revived the exculpating-witness subplot, the discovery of the New Moses additionally revives the long-buried temperance subplot and thereby solves the problem of the fuel shortage. When we encounter it at the film's opening, the temperance subplot seems only a diversion, a set of funny gags, but when it returns in act three it provides a crucial link in the causal chain of the main plot – the rescue/race. This reversal may not make the cartoonish idea of alcohol-as-fuel plausible in itself, but it does create a motivating logic for it – the preacher's well established horror of drink. The surprise is thus rendered pleasing rather than simply absurd.

The screenwriters' transformation of the opening and ending of Burman's novel pushed *Steamboat Round the Bend* in the direction of a humorous tall tale. However it should be noted that Ford, reacting to Zanuck's editing of the film after the merger of Fox with 20th Century, asserted that this aspect of his work had been lost.[60] He told Bogdanovich: "*Steamboat Round the Bend* should have been a great picture but at that time

they had a change of studio and a new manager came in who wanted to show off, so he recut the picture, and took all the comedy out".[61] A comparison of the final screenplay incorporating the May 9 changes and the completed film indicates that some comic scenes were shortened, some gags eliminated. But, as Ford himself admitted in a later interview, Zanuck was a great editor and it is not at all clear that the cuts made hurt the film.[62] In any case, the producer's changes did not fundamentally alter the comic restructuring of Burman's plot described here.

Mark Twain's *Life on the Mississippi* and *Adventures of Huckleberry Finn* animated Burman's novel, which is similarly organized by journeys up and down the river and which absorbs and to some extent updates Twain's account of the folkways of the inhabitants of the lower Mississippi. In addition to drawing on Burman's work, Nichols and Trotti also drew directly upon Twain's reportage and his famous novel in distinctive ways. *Life on the Mississippi* deals with the author's return to the lower river over twenty years after his youthful apprenticeship as a riverboat pilot in the 1850s. At this point, the steamboat as a mode of transport was in decline and railroads were taking over many of its functions, a change that Twain documents with some regret. By the time of Burman's novel, set in the 1930s, the decline of the steamboat was much further advanced.[63] While his characters seem to share Twain's boyish enthusiasm for the boats and his deep respect for the skills of the pilots, most of the steamboats they encounter are more or less derelict and Doctor John's attempt to make a living ferrying goods and passengers on the river ends in bankruptcy. In contrast, Ford's film posits a lively and robust steamboat trade, although it is set in the 1890s, a point at which riverboat traffic was actually already in decline. The *Claremore Queen* might initially be a wreck, but the *Pride of Paducah* is demonstrated to be part of a

59 A modified form of this gag recurs in later Ford films. In both *Stagecoach* and *The Searchers* a character throws an alcoholic drink into a fire causing a minor explosion which operates as a kind of wordless commentary on the action.
60 The film went into post-production in early July, see "Fox Sets *Steamboat* Ahead of *Kentucky*", *Hollywood Reporter* (5 Jul 1935): 2, which notes that the film was "currently being edited on the Coast" (that is, in Los Angeles).
61 Bogdanovich, *John Ford*, 57. See also, Dan Ford, 94, and Claudine Tavernier, in Peary, ed., 101.
62 Gussow, 162; Gallagher, 198.
63 Interview with Ben Luclen Burman, in Sterling and Sterling, eds., 167.

viable enterprise, unloading goods and passengers in a lively scene in which she docks at the end of the opening segment.

The steamboat race that comprises the film's third act visually evokes Twain's joyous recollection of the commencement of a race in the "flush times" of steamboating.

> Now a number of boats slide backward into the stream, leaving wide gaps in the serried rank of steamers. Citizens crowd the decks of boats that are not to go, in order to see the sight. Steamer after steamer straightens herself up, gathers all her strength, and presently comes swinging by, under a tremendous head of steam, with flag flying, black smoke rolling, and her entire crew of firemen and deck-hands (usually swarthy negroes) massed together on the forecastle, the best "voice" in the lot towering from the midst (being mounted on the capstan), waving his hat or a flag, and all roaring a mighty chorus, while the parting cannons boom and the multitudinous spectators wave their hats and huzza! Steamer after steamer falls into line and the stately procession goes winging its flight up the river.[64]

The race in Ford's film similarly begins with the crowd (figure 5.8 is the establishing shot of the crowd at the starting line). A Southern ritual, it is somewhat anachronistically linked to the Civil War: the band plays "Dixie" as a man decked out in a Confederate uniform gives the signal to fire the cannon that starts the contest (figure 5.9). This is balanced by later shots of the characters of Jonah and Uncle Jeff (John Lester Johnson) feeding the furnace below deck on the *Claremore Queen* (figure 5.10). The film evokes Twain's "stately procession" of steamers with a thirty-two second shot which sedately pans right with the movement of the boats (figures 5.11, 5.12). After cutting around to the back of the boats to show an elongating line of paddle wheels, Ford cuts to a beautiful long shot of the boats stretching out along the river, the crowd walking alongside (figure 5.13).

Adventures of Huckleberry Finn famously assigns a liberatory dimension to life on the river, a thematic epitomized in Huck's narration, following the escape from the feud between the Grangerfords and the Shepardsons: "I was powerful glad to get away from the feuds, and so was Jim to get away from the swamp. We said there warn't no home like a raft, after all. Other places do seem so cramped up and smothery, but a raft don't. You feel mighty free and easy and comfortable on a raft."[65] In contrast, in Burman's novel, the river spawns lives of poverty and despair. The idea of the river as escape from the strictures of shore life informs the film version of *Steamboat Round the Bend* in two principal ways. First, there is a narrative opposition between the "river men" and the people associated with the swamp or the shore, which is developed in the first two acts. Second, there is the cinematographic treatment of the steamboats and the Sacramento river location, which comes to the fore during the race in act three.

The story of Fleety Belle provided in act one mirrors Huck Finn's relationship with his abusive father at the beginning of Twain's novel. Duke describes the beating she received simply for having waved at him on the *Memphis Belle*, and how her father forced her to remain inside. Like Huck, she eventually runs away, her presence on the *Memphis Belle* precipitating the fight which leads Duke to commit murder. Doctor John's initial hostility to the girl (which has no basis in the novel) derives from his identity as a "river man" who despises all those who live in the swamps. After Duke has been incarcerated, however, the *Claremore Queen* is invaded by Fleety Belle's father and other relatives threatening her with violence. The fast-talking Doctor John persuades them that she has married Duke and expels them from the boat. Through the narrative which follows Fleety Belle is converted from swamp girl to river girl, a process that can be traced by her costume changes. At first she wears a skirt made of an old tablecloth, which Doctor John takes as evidence

64   Mark Twain, *Life on the Mississippi* (Harper & Row, 1917), 144–145.
65   Mark Twain, *Adventures of Huckleberry Finn* (Boston: Houghton Mifflin, 1958), 98–99; for further discussion of the thematic import of the river see, for examples, Henry Nash Smith, *Mark Twain: The Development of a Writer* (Cambridge: Harvard University Press, 1962): 113–137; Walter Blair, "When Was *Huckleberry Finn* Written?" *American Literature* 30, no 1 (Mar 1958): 1–25.

5.8

5.9

5.10

5.11

5.12

5.13

of the inferiority of "swamp trash" (figure 5.14). One of the first tangible signs of affection is that he gives her a mid-nineteenth century frock that belonged to Duke's mother (figure 5.15). By act two, however, she is shown at the wheel in the pilot house wearing a dark jacket softened by the lace collar of the dress underneath and a pilot's cap. Doctor John praises her "river talk" when she calls out "steamboat round the bend" and he teases her when she embraces him upon learning

that they will soon be returning home to see Duke: "There ain't nothin' that will run you on a sand bar faster than a lot of huggin' and kissin'". By act three she is wearing denim overalls and a man's shirt as she pilots the *Claremore Queen* through the race (figure 5.16). Fleety Belle finds refuge through becoming one of the river's own.

The confrontation in Salt Creek in act two opposes the steamboat crew to the rural townsfolk. Captain Eli has warned Doctor John to keep the

5.14

5.15

5.16

floating museum away from Salt Creek, since "they lynched one of them hoochie-coochie shows there last week". Doctor John lands there anyway, eager to make the last of the money needed for the appeal. The men of the town approach *en masse* at night, carrying torches, pitch-forks and pick-axes. They begin to dismantle the boat, threatening to burn it and tar and feather Fleety Belle. Jonah runs to warn Efe and Uncle Jeff on an upper deck. His hysterical reaction may be seen as stereotyped but it also confirms his sense that the crew is confronting a lynch mob. Efe and Uncle Jeff push two wax figures of Frank and Jesse James onto the upper deck, their guns pointed down at the crowd. Doctor John immediately makes use of this, begging the outlaws not to shoot, thereby intimidating the mob.

After inviting the pacified mob into the museum, Doctor John then works them around to admiring the wax figures and even spontaneously paying for admittance. This is made possible by the way he and the crew have transformed Pro-

fessor Marvel's wax figures in order to appeal to Southern rural sympathies and prejudices. Professor Marvel's George III, considered too alien to interest their audience, has been transformed into George Washington. Similarly, Queen Elizabeth has become Pocahontas, reinforcing Doctor John's brand. Two bearded Christian prophets were considered too ordinary and have therefore been transformed into Frank and Jesse James. Doctor John and Efe decided that the figure of Ulysses S. Grant that Professor Marvel had displayed would never play in Vicksburg (Rogers quips "No wonder Professor Marvel skipped town") and they have transformed him into Robert E. Lee. Jonah, however, demurred, requesting to keep General Grant's uniform. These figures, along with a model whale rigged so that Efe can pump water out of its blow-hole, fascinate the crowd.

The leader of the mob (the great Roger Imhof) is impressed by the whale and then by the figure of the first president. He pleads with Doctor John to give him a lock of George Washington's hair – as if he is in the presence of the actual man instead of a wax figure. This is followed by the climax of the show – the display of the Confederate general. As Doctor John doffs his hat in tribute, Fleety Belle raises the curtain that hides the wax figure. She activates Lee's arm which has been rigged to salute (figure 5.17). Imhof calls his group to attention and they return the salute (figure 5.18). The whole display is accompanied by "Dixie". Cut to a group of life-sized puppets, Black minstrel musicians apparently performing the music. A pan left reveals Jonah, laboriously

5.17

5.18

5.19

turning a crank to activate the group and singing a conspicuously off-key rendition of the Southern anthem.

The apparently digressive episode of the wax museum draws from the adventures of Twain's hucksters the King and the Duke, who used a religiose patter to defraud their victims. Doctor John is obviously a more sympathetic character, but like them he knows how to appeal to the sentiments of the mob. By this means, he manages the threat of lynching while simultaneously making a tidy profit. The scenes in the museum emphasize the manipulations employed to play upon the crowd's naive belief in the reality of the natural wonders and national heroes paraded before them. Moreover the gag with Jonah and the puppets brings out the difference between Doctor John, who has been revealed to be a Confederate veteran and shares the sympathies of the crowd if not their naive beliefs, and Jonah, who prefers

Grant and contributes to the tribute to Lee only under the threat of lynching.

The wax-museum episode is thus primarily concerned with life on the shore – the antipathies and violence, the exclusions and loyalties that govern society in the rural South. In this sense, the episode also leads logically into the final scenes of the act, the failure of the appeal and the jailhouse wedding between Duke and Fleety Belle. In a more pathetic register than the scenes at Salt Creek, this scene also vivifies the restrictions and difficulties of shore life; it also offers a more genuine if more somber form of performance than Jonah's. The sheriff's young daughter plays the only song she can on the piano, "Listen to the Mocking Bird", which brings on the bride in a comic register. But the sheriff's reading of the vows, mixed with mournful praise of Duke's character, is underscored by a much more apropos hymn from an unexpected source – the jail's Black inmates. A cut calls attention to their release from the segregated cell in which they are usually held (figure 5.19). They sing the spiritual that is quoted in Burman's novel:

Eagle build his nest so high
Cannot hear his young ones cry,
Dark and Cloudy.

He can hardly see the day,
Please O Lord, then show me the way,
Dark and Cloudy.

I'm trying to go where my young ones is,
And my home is hard to find.[66]

---

66   The quotation derives from Burman, *Steamboat Round the Bend*, 271, since the words of the hymn are not fully audible when mixed with the marriage vows in the film.

5.20

5.21

5.22

5.23

5.24

5.25

The despairing tone of act two, which culminates with the sheriff taking Duke away to Baton Rouge to be hanged, abruptly shifts with the beginning of act three, the act of unexpected reversals. From start to finish the cinematography in this act emphasizes the river, and the dynamic presence of the boats. While the movement of the *Pride of Paducah* is featured in a montage at the film's opening, and while the movement of boats and/or views of the river are important during scene transitions in act one, it is only with the search for the New Moses in the opening of act three that the film gives us prolonged sequences that make use of the footage taken on the Sacramento. The search begins with a shot of the *Claremore Queen* sailing laterally across the frame as Doctor John, off, is heard calling out questions about the New Moses to a man fishing from the bank (figure

5.20). The relative fixity of the man in the foreground and the tree front right emphasizes the boat's stately movement. A later shot from behind Fleety Belle at the helm shows the river beyond and barges moored nearby (figure 5.21).[67] As Doctor John toots the whistle to hail the men on the barge, cut to a moving shot from his point of view as the *Claremore Queen* passes them by.

Later, the *Claremore Queen* comes unexpectedly upon a crowd waiting for the race to begin. An irate official charged with keeping the river clear of impediments violently waves a flag to head her off (figure 5.22). As he directs the crew to turn back, he disparages Doctor John's "floating hen house" (figure 5.23). But the boat keeps moving inexorably forward until Efe is brought within spitting distance and takes his revenge (figures 5.24, 5.25). Ford's exploration of ways to display the boats' movements reaches its apex in the race itself. Compositions contrast the boats with still figures watching from the shore, as well as contrasts between boats and people moving at different rates (as in figure 5.13). Of course many shots also highlight the relative movement of the *Pride of Paducah* and the *Claremore Queen*.

When alone on their raft, Huck and Jim are easy and comfortable, but, with the commencement of the race, the crew of the *Claremore Queen* are anything but relaxed. The lasso-induced baptism of the New Moses introduces a Marx-Brothers element, a ferocious and manic energy, into the activity on board the *Claremore Queen* (figure 5.26). The prophet quickly becomes a rescue zealot. As he takes an axe to the ship's furniture, deck and railings in the search for fuel, his blows are punctuated by hosannas. His fervor spreads through the crew. After Doctor John orders them to burn the wax museum, Efe gets so enthusiastic tossing wax figures down the hatch into the boiler room that he attempts to drop the resisting Jonah while Uncle Jeff deposits a headless Napoleon (figure 5.27). Later, as Efe and the New Moses thrust wax figures into the furnace, Jonah admonishes them to speed up as he watches the *Pride of Paducah*'s stern wheel pulling ahead through the

5.26

opening in the lower deck (figure 5.28). After the museum has been entirely consumed, Doctor John joins the group below deck. There is a momentary pause, and quiet, as the New Moses intones, "Nothing can save us now but the power of prayer", at which point he notices Efe taking a swig (figure 5.29). After the preacher disposes of the bottle, the ensuing explosion redoubles the frenetic activity of the crew (figure 5.30). When Efe reveals that he has a hundred jugs of Pocahontas stashed away, the preacher becomes ecstatic, repeating "Down with the demon rum!" and "Hallelujah!" as the crew forms a jug line to feed the fire (figures 5.31, 5.32).

The actual rescue of Duke is de-emphasized in the film to avoid the problem of anti-climax. Doctor John's appeal to the governor is brief, in fast motion, and accompanied by an uptempo version of "There'll Be a Hot Time in the Old Town Tonight", obviating dialogue that might slow up the proceedings. Cut to the jail yard as the governor's trap comes through the gate, Rogers managing the horses. The governor stops the hanging with two sentences and there is a cut to the tag ending. Thus, the rescue is the end but not the point of act three. The emphasis is on getting up the river and on the sometimes uneasy collaborations that make it possible: between a temperance preacher, a drunk and the purveyor of his "medicine", between river men and a swamp-girl-turned-pilot, between a Confederate veteran and Black deck hands. This assortment

---

67 Some shots taken on the boat set make use of back-projected images of the river and the shore (for example figure 5.10), but the sharp focus of the background in this and the following shots suggest it was taken on the Sacramento river.

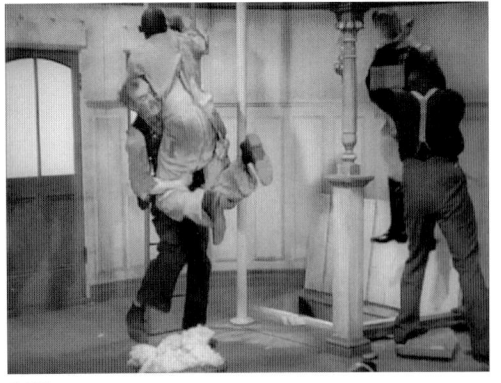

5.27

5.28

5.29

5.30

5.31

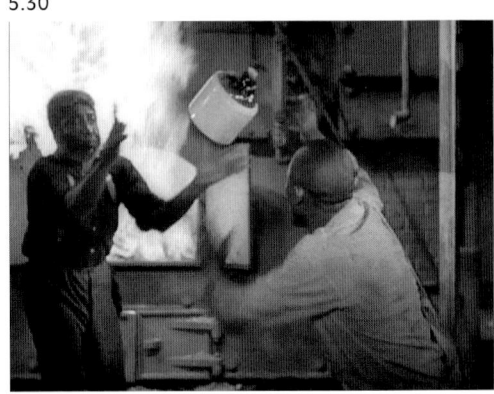

5.32

of social types succeeds in defiance of all expectations, not to mention the laws of physics, enabled by the magical and freeing power of life on the Mississippi.

Steamboat Round the Bend illustrates one of the advantages for Ford of magpie plot construction, of cobbling together a plot from multiple sources. This strategy blocks the anticipation of the ending that is built into the structure of films such as *The Lost Patrol* and *The Informer*. Burman's original story about Doctor John and Fleety Belle and Duke is innocent of any intrinsic connection with gambling on steamboat races or the humorous treatment of temperance. These elements appear to the spectator to have nothing to do with the main storyline because they actually were independent of it. The apparent independence of the plot lines lends itself to the creation of surprise when the connections between them are eventually revealed. The suppression of the causal links between subplots also contributes to the apparent randomness of several plot turns and the impression of Ford's famously slow pacing.[68] Much of the second act may seem to be a digression from the main story thinly motivated by the need to raise money for Duke's appeal. Undue emphasis seems to be placed on the crew's transformation of the museum, which is peppered with sight gags and comic incidents such as the many jokes on the confusion between living beings and waxworks. Racial themes are introduced in the same offhand manner, as in the discussion of how to handle the wax figure of General Grant already noted, and in the introduction of Uncle Jeff, who first appears in a shot holding a wax figure of Little Eva and looking like Uncle Tom. All of these apparently extraneous incidents actually serve as preparation for the confrontation in Salt Creek in which Doctor John and his crew fend off the mob by manipulating their belief in the illusory waxworks. Moreover, the whole episode of the lynching serves by contrast to bring out the more egalitarian and convivial community that is created aboard the *Claremore Queen* in act three. It is no accident that the wax museum is burned during the race but, rather, a buried symbolic connection that only becomes apparent when one realizes that the rescue of Duke may be the end of *Steamboat Round the Bend*, but working together to get up river is the point.

Will Rogers and Ford's Sound Style

Will Rogers's talent for improvisation was honed by many years in vaudeville, the *Ziegfeld Follies*, and an offshoot of the *Follies* called the *Ziegfeld Midnight Frolic*. Rogers biographer Ben Yagoda describes the latter as particularly important for the development of his comic technique. The *Frolic* started after the end of the regular stage show. Customers took elevators up to the roof of

the New Amsterdam theater where they could dance or sit at tables near the dance floor. "It was more intimate than the *Follies*, smaller in scale. The stage wasn't elevated, and the audience was part of the entertainment – they danced between acts, an activity given its own program listing. They participated in the show itself as well. In one number, chorus girls had (male) audience members hold their yarn while they knitted; in another they sat on the runway and dangled fishing lines over the tables."[69] Because the audience for the *Frolic* tended to consist of repeat customers, Rogers needed to change his act nightly. Yagoda suggests that this requirement motivated his well-known practice of drawing material from the daily papers, contributing to the sense of his performances' immediacy and spontaneity. His interplay with the celebrities in attendance also showcased his ability to come up with material on the fly. Apparently it was considered a mark of status to be singled out by Rogers during the show.

Rogers carried his improvisatory techniques over to the sound cinema. David Butler, who directed five films with Rogers, explained: "He had quite a time with his lines. He would branch off. You see, he learned them, but they weren't written in his language. He improved his lines. He was remarkable that way."[70] Ford had the same experience: "Nobody could write for Will … . He'd go away, muttering to himself, getting his lines ready, and when he came back, he'd make his speech in typical Rogers fashion, which was better than any writer could write for him … . We never stuck to the written script. There was nobody that could write for Will. Lamar Trotti, God rest his soul, he could write closer than anybody for Will."[71] A comparison of Rogers's filmed performances with the lines written for the actor by Nichols and Trotti reveals that improvisation served a somewhat different function on set than it did on the rooftop garden of the New Amsterdam. Rogers's comic persona depended heavily upon his distinctive manner of

68 See, for example, Dan Ford, 94.
69 Yagoda, 138–143.
70 Interview with David Butler, in Bryan B. Sterling, ed, *The Will Rogers Scrapbook* (New York: Grosset & Dunlap, 1976), 167.
71 Interview with John Ford, in Sterling, ed., 175.

speaking – a combination of southern and western regionalisms admixed with urban slang, a strategic deployment of markedly "incorrect" grammar and diction punctuated by multiple hesitations and stammers. This idiolect could be readily accommodated when he prepared his own material for the stage or radio but when faced with lines prepared by another writer, the actor needed to rework them in "typical Rogers fashion".

Take, for example, the lively opening of *Judge Priest* in which the Judge holds up Maydew's attempt to prosecute Jeff for chicken stealing by addressing his old Confederate army cronies sitting in the back of the courtroom. They reminisce and bicker about their own attempt to steal chickens following the Battle of Kennesaw Mountain during the Civil War. Overriding Maydew's objection to this patently irrelevant conversation, the Judge explains that Major Ranny, who was their commander as well as Jeff's employer, had appropriated the enlisted men's chickens. The line in the shooting script, addressed to Maydew, reads: "Jest a minute, son. The p'int is that Major Ranny, havin' done his duty like a soldier and a gentleman, seen fit to remove temptation from our path. He et up all the hens – and left us two gristly roosters!" Rogers takes his time, builds to the punch line more slowly and improves its rhythm (italicized words or syllables are those stressed by Rogers). "Now, now, now *senator*, you know now the – now the *p'int is* that a' – that the *Major* eeeh he *acted* the part of a – of a *gent*leman and a *soldier* and he re*moved* the *temptation* from *out* of our *path* by *eatin'* up all the *fat hens* i-i-in the whole bunch and *leav*in' us *nothin'* but a lot o' ole *skin*ny Dominick [Dominique] roosters. You remem*bah* boys?" Note that Rogers's improvisation did not substantially alter the original sense of the line, and that its build-up and delivery actually enhanced the line about chicken thievery by which the screenwriters had slyly put the Black man accused at the bar on a par with the former Confederate soldiers and their superior officer.

Rogers restructured his dialogue much more drastically in the scene which follows Doctor John's expulsion of Fleety Bell's violent kinfolk from the *Claremore Queen* in *Steamboat Round the Bend*. In the scene as written Fleety Belle thanks Doctor John for lying to her father and claiming that she and Duke were married.

> *Fleety Belle*: I'd – I'd mighty like to thank you. [*Brusquely he shakes off her hand, and he tries to hide his emotion towards her as he growls.*]
>
> *Doc*: Never knowed a fella yet tried to lie hisself out of the fryin' pan didn't lie hisself right into the fire! [*As if to repel further advances, too full of emotion to risk any exchange of speech, he gets up gruffly.*]
>
> *Doc*: Derned swamp trash – spoilin' our supper! Bacon's cold as a fightin' fish! [*Goes over to stove grumbling and she watches him with wet eyes as he picks up the skillet and shakes it, frowning at the bacon.*] If they's anything I hate, it's cold bacon. [*Fleety Belle goes to him and takes the skillet right out of his hands.*]
>
> *Doc*: [*Protesting gruffly*] Here, here! You don't know nothin' about bacon!

In the film, Doctor John not only lies to Fleety Belle's father, but also threatens the men with a bread knife that the girl has surreptitiously handed him. Rogers refers to this incident in his improvised dialogue.

> *Shot 110. MS on Fleety Belle and Doctor John at stove. She touches his arm.*
>
> *Fleety Bell*: I'd mighty like to thank you for what you done.
>
> *Doc*: Well a ... You oughta thank me. If it hadn't been for me they'd a got your shoes.
>
> *Fleety Bell*: But – but I mean ... you fixed it ...
>
> *Doc*: Well yes if you hadn't give me the knife they – they might have got 'em anyhow. Comin' in here botherin' us just when we gonna [*pause*] enjoy our supper here. Humph. That's a fine lot of kin folks havin' like that. Swamp people. Look at that bacon! Look at that! It's all burned. Look! Look at that! Humph.
>
> *Fleety Bell*: [*Leans towards stove.*] Let me fix it.
>
> *Doc*: [*Indistinct muttering with the words "swamp people" audibly overlapping "Let me fix it".*] Huh? What do you know about cookin' bacon ... . [*He moves away from the stove and grabs a hand towel.*] You never did cook nothin' but *catfish*.

5.33

5.34

In the script, Doctor John rebuffs Fleety Belle's tender thanks with a rather forced homily: "Never knowed a fella yet tried to lie hisself out of the fryin' pan ... ". In Rogers's improvised dialogue, he does not rebuff her so much as side-step her thanks through two comic non sequiturs. The first makes his action seem trivial – as if he had only prevented the men from taking her shoes. The second calls attention to the fact that she has helped him – by handing him the knife. While taking up the screenwriters' idea of referring to the ruined meal, he also manages to convey his outrage much more simply and vehemently than in the script – "Look at that bacon! Look at that! It's all burned. Look! Look at that! Humph." Moreover, he insults Fleety Belle's swamp origins much more deftly with the final derogatory reference to catfish. However, it should be said in Nichols and Trotti's defense that they probably only rapidly sketched out his lines, since by 1935 they surely expected him to improvise. They handled Lincoln Perry's lines in a similar manner.

While Rogers's improvisations usually respected and improved upon the script, they often effaced the cues that his fellow actors relied on. Lew Ayres told Bryan Sterling that the comedian "sometimes made it difficult on actors who worked with him. It took a particular kind of personality to respond to this loosely arranged manner of carrying on dialogue with him."[72] Sterling Holloway recalled that he "played right along with it", but noted that it was made more difficult

by the fact that Rogers did not like to rehearse the new lines he devised with others: "He wouldn't rehearse them, he didn't like to give them away". Lincoln Perry seems to have returned the favor. Yagoda quotes from an interview that Perry gave after the release of *Judge Priest*, discussing their mutual improvisations: "Paht of the time he suhprises me. Paht of the time I suhprise him. But mos' of the time we suhprises each other." He also admonished the reporter: "If you put anything I says in the papah, it might be wise to kind of transpose it into my dialeck".[73] Other actors also apparently found inspiration in being surprised. Evelyn Venable Mohr explained: "You had to be on your toes. You had to dovetail what you were supposed to say into what he actually had said. You had to do that to make sense and follow the story line. It was fun, because it gave a good deal of freshness to the scenes. But it was a little bit nerve racking, too."[74]

In addition to promoting a "loosely arranged manner of carrying on dialogue", Rogers did not like to repeat takes. Ford told Bryan Sterling: "With Will? We never had any retakes. And he never watched any rushes. When he finished a day's work, he'd get in his car, go home and start roping calves." David Butler recalled that he responded to the situation by shooting with multiple cameras: "We had two cameras, anyway, so when he got too long-winded we'd just cut in. But he never liked retakes. He just wanted to do a scene, and that was that." Rogers's reliance on

72   Interview with Lew Ayres, in Sterling, ed., 137.
73   John C. Moffitt, "Mr. Fetchit in Kansas City", *New York Times* (24 Feb 1935): X5, cited in Yagoda, 312.
74   Interview with Evelyn Venable Mohr and Hal Mohr, in Sterling, ed., 153.

5.35

5.36

5.37

5.38

5.39

improvisation and desire to avoid retakes favored Ford's employment of the long-take strategy analyzed in chapter two in relation to the scene of Sondelius's death in *Arrowsmith*. The director avoided shot-reverse-shot conversation scenes for the star, preferring to set up situations in which Rogers faced off with his interlocutors in real time. For example, the scene from *Judge Priest* discussed above in which Rogers and Perry improvise the

negotiation over playing "Dixie" is filmed in a single forty-six-second take. The scene in which Fleety Belle's kinsfolk invade the *Claremore Queen* demonstrates how Ford's handling of Rogers's dialogue differed from that of Anne Shirley playing Fleety Belle. The initial altercation between Fleety Belle and her relatives is handled in flurry of short reverse shots of no more than seven seconds each (figures 5.33 and 5.34). After Doctor John intercedes for Fleety Bell, the editing shifts into longer takes. Shot 103 (23.5 seconds) begins with them facing off the swamp rats together (figure 5.35), the camera panning right on Fleety Belle's movement to slip Doctor John the knife (figure 5.36). Ford then cuts in for a thirty-four-second shot which maintains the same basic framing from behind Rogers (figure 5.37). Doctor John argues with Fleety Belle's father until he belatedly realizes that he is holding a knife (figure 5.38). Cut back to a long shot for the rout of the swamp rats (figure 5.39). Doctor John's intervention is thus filmed in three long takes from behind the actor. In the absence of reverse shots we do not even see his face for the double-take that reverses the power dynamic of the scene.

The extensive use of the long take to handle Rogers's dialogue drove the films with the comedian to have the highest average shot lengths, that is, the slowest cutting, of any of the middle to late 1930s Ford films. *Doctor Bull* at an ASL of 11.3 and *Judge Priest* at 11.8 are slower than *Young Mr. Lincoln* at 11. While *Steamboat Round the Bend* at 9.7 seconds has a faster average cutting rate than any of these three, this rate is the result of quickly cut sequences in Salt Creek and of the final race. The first act of the film, without these elements, has an average shot length of 12.3 seconds. But the Rogers films do not simply replicate the long-take strategies found in Ford's early sound films, since the bravura camera moves and compositional set pieces of *4 Sons* or *Arrowsmith* have given way to much simpler staging and camerawork. Although a graceful and accomplished athlete, Rogers had neither the interest nor the training to handle complicated, preplanned staging. It seems unlikely that he could have carried off a take such as Coleman's kitchen scene in *Arrowsmith* where the actor had to hit multiple marks, synchronizing gestures and words while shifting position on the set. Compare the carefully engineered compositions within that shot (figures 2.19 to 2.27) with the eighty-three second shot in which Rogers moves around the cabin of the *Claremore Queen* musing over its dilapidated state with Efe. While the dynamic between Rogers and Francis Ford is great fun to watch, the actors move rather freely with respect to each other and without much concern for compositional principles. The scene begins with the two men facing each other (figure 5.40), but Rogers soon crosses in back of Francis Ford and then moves off to the left (figure 5.41). He comes forward briefly to face Ford, then turns away again as Ford also turns, motivated by Rogers's reference to the chickens on the boat (figure 5.42). Towards the end of the shot (figure 5.43) there is a small pay-off for the search – Doctor John comes forward and finds a broom for Efe to use and a captain's cap

for himself. But for most of the shot's duration, the actors simply meander.

Henry King recalled that Rogers loved props and would arrive early on set each morning to check out what was available.[75] In many of Rogers's long takes he adopts a relatively fixed position on the set, animating his performance largely through the manipulation of props. The scene discussed above in which Doctor John gruffly sidesteps Fleety Belle's thanks has Rogers busy at the stove frying bacon in a take of nearly forty seconds, although the close framing cuts off our view of his activities at the stove (figure 5.44). The lovely fifty-second take where Doctor John and Fleety Belle exchange a kiss at the risk of running into a sandbar is dominated by the ship's wheel spinning out of control. This strategy of holding on Rogers while he manipulated a prop worked very well as a device for setting up free improvisation. For example, the ice-cream social in *Judge Priest* has a scene in which Rome, drafted by his mother to pull taffy with Virginia Maydew, is relieved by the Judge to go off with Ellie Mae. Rogers performs the action described in the script but extends the action of pulling taffy in performance, effectively extending the shot into a long take.

> *Shot 172. MS of Virginia (left) and Rome (right) with the Judge far right. Party lights and guests in the background. Band plays, off.*
>
> *Judge*: [*addressing Rome.*] Here. Let me see your hands. You ain't got no butter on there. No wonder. Here, here let me show you. [*Taking Rome's end of the taffy in his own hands and adding in more taffy that he has obtained as part of his plan, he takes Rome's place over the following three lines.*] Put mine in here. Let me show you. There. Go on up there, run on up there and eh put some more stick 'em on your hand, there. Go on right up there. [*Rome gets the idea and thanks the Judge as he departs.*]
>
> *Judge*: [*addressing Virginia.*] That's it, now here [*he stretches the candy and folds it over.*] Put that right over in there now. [*As Virginia turns to look after Rome, the band segues into the chorus of "Dixie" which contains the repeated phrase "look away!"*] Now here, here, here, here, now there's one … . [*Virginia turns to face Judge*]

5.40

5.41

5.42

5.43

that's the thing. Candy pullin' you got to keep your mind right on the – right on the... [*Virginia turns to look after Rome, Judge pushes a wad of candy on her hand.*] That's how you're gettin' it all on your hand. Keep your mind on what you're doin' there now. [*Virginia turns and Judge starts pulling in earnest.*] You're pullin' candy with the champion candy puller of this neighborhood.

The collaboration with Rogers encouraged Ford to take new chances with the long take. In a situation where both rehearsals and retakes were minimized, he tended to devise simple, predominantly static framings and then waited, effectively rolling the dice, to allow his actors the time and space to perform spontaneously. It should be noted that while Rogers was the actor most commonly treated in this manner, he was not the only one. See, for example, the twenty-eight-second shot of Lincoln Perry's funny, improvised description of how to catch fish using liver for bait in *Judge Priest*, or the forty-three-second take of

5.44

Francis Ford drunkenly whitewashing the *Claremore Queen*. In particular, the predilection for unexpected plot turns in *Steamboat Round the Bend* found its analogy in a method of shooting that captured performances before they could become rote, where the lines and the choreography of movement were not perfectly set. As in his plotting, Ford began to allow the acting and staging to take us by surprise.

Part 3
Twentieth
Century-Fox

Chapter 6

Zanuck and Ford

The merger of Fox with 20th Century Pictures in the summer of 1935 occurred just after Ford's preferred screenwriter, Dudley Nichols, had signed a contract with RKO and almost in tandem with the death of Will Rogers in August. These developments left Ford to reconfigure his Fox unit once again. Moreover, he had to do so in the face of a powerful producer who had been given *carte blanche* by Sidney Kent to remake the studio's production sector. As is well known, Ford would eventually make one of the most fruitful alliances of his career with this producer, Darryl F. Zanuck, despite the fact that their relations were never without tension. This chapter considers how the merger affected Ford's on-going contractual negotiations with his home studio, while a production history of *The Prisoner of Shark Island* provides a detailed account of how Ford's approach to filmmaking first began to mesh with Zanuck's.

Zanuck Takes Over

The original spelling of the name of Zanuck's production company, "20th Century Pictures", remains enshrined in the monumental numbers of the Twentieth Century-Fox logo despite the latter company's decision to spell out the name. 20th Century was formed in 1933 when Joseph Schenck, then president of United Artists, partnered with Zanuck, who had recently resigned as production chief at Warners. Schenck had long struggled with the problem that United Artists, a distribution company, was perennially short of films for its annual program and he had already brought in a number of independent producers to augment it. However, with the exception of Samuel Goldwyn, who had been made a partner in 1927, other producers did not share in the profits paid to the producer-owners – D. W. Griffith, Mary Pickford, Douglas Fairbanks and Charlie Chaplin.[1] Schenck recruited Zanuck with the promise that after a year's "trial" he would be permitted to buy stock in UA. In the event, the owners extended the trial to two years, during which Zanuck turned out a roster of unusually successful films. For example, in the spring of 1935, 20th Century opened two roadshows almost simultaneously on Broadway, *Cardinal Richelieu* and *Les Misérables*. Tino Balio highlights 20th Century's contributions to UA in 1934, noting that it delivered nine of the twenty pictures for the year and accounted for well over half the business.[2] Nonetheless, the UA board of directors remained reluctant to open the way to Zanuck's ownership of stock, and hence Zanuck's and Schenck's greater control over the company. So Schenck and Zanuck decided to abandon ship.

If the intransigence of the UA partners made the merger possible, Sidney Kent was its architect. It seems likely that Kent had approached Zanuck about the possibility of taking over production at Fox late in 1934.[3] After several months of secret negotiations, the merger was announced on May 28, 1935.[4] *Variety* reported on a subsequent address Kent delivered to the Fox shareholders

---

1   Tino Balio, *United Artists: The Company Built by the Stars*, i: *1919-1950* (Madison: University of Wisconsin Press, 2009, first published 1976), 60, 69–71.
2   Balio, 120–123.
3   Balio, 125–126 and note 23; Solomon, 215, speculates that Kent, Schenck and Zanuck contemplated the merger as early as August, 1934.
4   "Fox-20th Century Merge", *Hollywood Reporter* (28 May 1935): 1–3; "Fox Film to Merge with 20th Century", *New York Times* (28 May 1935): 31.

explaining why he had sought to recruit Zanuck and Schenck. Reminding them of the dire state of the firm when he was hired in 1932, and that he had brought the Fox companies out of debt,[5] Kent suggested that his next problem was the enhancement of production. This had to be done without "reduplicating" the company's existing assets. Kent explained:

> Fox didn't need a studio, nor did it need any additional distribution facilities. Therefore, any merger which would require Fox Film to assume additional studio property and overhead, was not advisable. Nor was it desirable for Fox Film to consider a merger that would require Fox Film to assume an additional distributing system including exchanges and other property.[6]

Because 20th Century owned minimal real property – it had been utilizing the UA Studios, which were then sold to Samuel Goldwyn – the merger did not entail any sort of reduplication. Moreover, Kent emphasized that the acquisition of 20th Century would fortify Fox Film in the areas in which it was "weak".

By the time of Kent's address, Winfield Sheehan's contract had already been bought out and he had left the company.[7] While Kent did not say, and probably could not have said, that replacing Sheehan with Zanuck was worth considerable expense, he did go out of his way to praise Zanuck's record:

> 20th Century, in two years, has made the finest comparative record he has ever looked at in the 20 years that he has been in the business, Kent told the shareholders, which made that company a very desirable ally with Fox Film … . Kent indicated to the stockholders that at the rate of business which the Zanuck films have been doing, such pictures are estimated to

bring 2½ times the average negative cost. He stated that twice the average negative cost is considered good, but that 2½ is considered outstanding.[8]

In Kent's view, and in the view of others in the industry, the merger definitely capped the fiscal reorganization of Fox Film and its affiliated companies.[9] Fox stock was re-issued as Twentieth Century-Fox stock, and Kent, Schenck and Zanuck took on substantial stock holdings in the new company as well as in Fox-West Coast.[10] While their holdings were dwarfed by those of Chase Bank, still the company's largest creditor, a new period of fiscal independence and administrative stability was inaugurated with the new name.

A comprehensive account of how Zanuck transformed the Fox production sector remains to be written, but even a cursory review of the films released by season suggests that it was not until the 1940s that the studio hit its stride. By the 1940–1941 season, it had several new A-list directors employed – Henry Hathaway, Rouben Mamoulian and Fritz Lang – although not all would stay over the long term. Archie Mayo, formerly at Warners under Zanuck, had also joined the company. Walter Lang and Otto Preminger had been on the payroll for several years and were coming into prominence. Hampered by a limited stable of stars throughout the 1930s, by 1940 the studio finally had several prominent actors under contract, most importantly Henry Fonda, Dana Andrews and Gene Tierney, and Betty Grable and Linda Darnell were in the initial stages of their successful careers. By this point the studio had also hired away two of the UA Studios' most skilled and important department heads – art director Richard Day

5   Fox Metropolitan, the second of the two principal Fox theater subsidiaries, did not emerge from receivership until after the merger in 1935, "Fox Met's Reorganization Plan Approved", *Variety* (3 Jul 1935): 5.
6   "Kent Details the Advantages of 20th Century-Fox Film Merger", *Variety* (21 Aug 1935): 4, 26; "Fox Holders OK Merger", *Hollywood Reporter* (16 Aug 1935): 1, 3.
7   "Sheehan Resigns as Fox Film Chief", *New York Times* (18 Jul 1935): 15; "Sheehan-Fox Settlement Near $450,000", *Variety* (24 Jul 1935): 5.
8   "Kent Details the Advantages of 20th Century-Fox Film Merger", *Variety* (21 Aug 1935): 4, 26; Solomon, 212, 215, supports Kent's assessment of the unusual profitability of Zanuck's company.
9   See, for example, William R. Wilkerson's endorsement of the merger and Kent's business strategy: "Trade Views", *Hollywood Reporter* (22 Jul 1935): 1–2.
10   Solomon, 219; "Chase Bank and G.T.E. Own Most of Fox Film Stock", *Variety* (3 Jul 1935): 4; "Sid Kent's Deal with 20th-Fox Detailed in Statement to S.E.C.", *Variety* (7 Aug 1935): 5; "Fox Merger Voted", *New York Times* (16 Aug 1935): 23; "Fox Film Merger Upheld by Court", *New York Times* (23 Aug 1935): 25; "S.E.C. Reports Reveal 20th-Fox's Stock Shifts", *Variety* (26 Feb 1936): 29.

(hired in 1938) and music director Alfred New-man (hired in 1939).[11]

In the middle 1930s, however, Zanuck had yet to build up these resources. He was in the position of cobbling together the annual program with lower production budgets than he had been able to muster at 20th Century. Moreover, he was required to produce many more films – 20th Century had produced eight or nine films per season while Twentieth Century-Fox had to produce approximately fifty – and thus found his company seriously understaffed. From among the ranks of the Fox producers, Zanuck retained Sol Wurtzel and his associates on the Western Avenue lot for the B half of the program (the feature program was split fairly evenly between A and B, higher and lower, budget ranges). But with producers Sheehan, Jesse Lasky and Al Rockett off the lot, Zanuck needed to install his own associate producers for the A films. In addition to William Goetz and Raymond Griffith, already under contract to 20th Century, he hired Kenneth Macgowan, formerly of RKO. Buddy DeSylva, who had been contributing musicals to the Fox program under Sheehan, was retained for two years.[12] Nonetheless, Zanuck remained so short of senior staff that he announced his intention to hire through the trade press.[13] He promoted screenwriter Nunnally Johnson to the executive ranks with *The Man Who Broke the Bank at Monte Carlo* (1935).[14] Gene Markey, who had worked as a screenwriter at Warners in the early 1930s, was similarly promoted. Producer Harry Joe Brown also joined the company during a crucial time from 1938 to 1941.

Along with the shortage of administrative staff, Zanuck had to cope with Fox's paucity of A-level stars.[15] (It should be noted, however, that Wurtzel had cultivated a very good set of actors

for the studio's B films, most importantly Warner Oland of the Charlie Chan series and Peter Lorre of the Mr. Moto series.) After the death of Will Rogers, Fox's biggest remaining draw was Shirley Temple. Zanuck continued the pre-existing rhythm of two to three Temple films a year, augmenting this aspect of the program with occasional films designed for child actor Freddie Bartholomew, borrowed from MGM. The most prominent 20th Century actress that Zanuck brought to Fox was Loretta Young. She displaced Fox's major female dramatic lead, Janet Gaynor, and remained at Twentieth Century-Fox until 1939. In addition, the producer had recourse to freelancer Barbara Stanwyck, with whom he had worked at Warners. For musical comedy, he sought to develop the career of Alice Faye, who had been hired under the Fox regime. As an addition to the studio's musical offerings he signed Olympic figure-skater Sonja Henie who appeared in two to three films a year in the late 1930s with considerable success. Warner Baxter was probably the most important male lead that Zanuck found under Fox contract. Ronald Colman, who had played in several films for 20th Century, also starred in two following the merger.[16] And, on several occasions Zanuck was able to borrow musical-comedy star Dick Powell from Warners. Zanuck also sought to increase the male leads under contract to the studio by signing actors Tyrone Power, Don Ameche and Cesar Romero soon after the merger. The actors Zanuck decided to cultivate were frequently paired and tripled – the trio of Tyrone Power, Don Ameche and Alice Faye appears perhaps too frequently in the early films of Twentieth Century-Fox.

While the studio did not lack directorial staff, Zanuck did confront a relatively small list of top-flight A directors under contract. As dis-

---

11 "Day Art Department Head for 20th-Fox", *Hollywood Reporter* (16 Sep 1938): 1; Release and Termination for Richard Day, 8 Oct 1938, Samuel Goldwyn papers, folder 4831, Art Department – Richard Day, Special Collections, Herrick Library, AMPAS; "Al Newman to 20th as Musical Director", *Hollywood Reporter* (1 Sep 1939): 3.

12 "Zanuck Picks Up the DeSylva Option", *Hollywood Reporter* (3 Aug 1935): 1.

13 "Zanuck Will Create Producers for 20th", *Hollywood Reporter* (24 Jul 1935): 1; "Ray Griffith Gets Supervision of 8", *Hollywood Reporter* (2 Aug 1935): 6.

14 Tom Stempel, *Recollections of Nunnally Johnson,* oral history transcript (Oral History Program, University of California, Los Angeles: 1969), 47–49.

15 Solomon repeatedly refers to the problematic lack of marquee names at Fox, for example, 152, 167–168, 217.

16 "Selznick Bidding for Ronald Colman", *Hollywood Reporter* (22 Jul 1935): 1, indicates that Colman had a contract with 20th Century-Fox for two films.

cussed in chapter three, during the business down-turn of the early 1930s, Fox had adopted a cost-saving strategy of hiring directors with high salaries on limited-term contracts. By 1934 both Borzage and Walsh had taken advantage of this arrangement to develop freelance deals at other studios and had definitively abandoned Fox. They were soon followed by Frank Lloyd. Lloyd had been at Fox on short-term contracts since 1931 and among other films had directed the Academy Award winner *Cavalcade* under Sheehan. At the time of the merger, Lloyd was at MGM on *Mutiny on the Bounty,* a high-budget spectacular that won the Academy Award for Best Picture in March, 1936. He made one film under Zanuck, reporting to the studio in November 1935 to direct the last on his Fox contract, *Under Two Flags.* After it was completed in March 1936, Lloyd complained publicly about the producer's editing of the film and moved to Paramount on a four-picture deal.[17]

Zanuck thus had few directorial options for his highest-budget films. The dependable Henry King had been at Fox since 1930, often adapting well-known plays or making sound remakes of successful silents. He had worked with the Fox studio's best – Will Rogers, Janet Gaynor and Charles Farrell. Under Zanuck he continued his pattern of making one or two specials a year, and proved instrumental in shaping roles for the actors that Zanuck was attempting to build into stars. For example, between 1937 and 1941 he directed five specials with Power in a lead role, often playing opposite Faye or Nancy Kelly, who Zanuck signed in 1938. Zanuck also made extensive use of Roy Del Ruth, a 20th Century director who had been with the producer since his tenure at Warners. At Twentieth Century-Fox, Del Ruth specialized in musical comedies, making two with Henie, *Happy Landing* and *My Lucky Star,* and

one with Faye, *Tail Spin,* before leaving for MGM in 1940. Zanuck augmented the films of these high-profile contract directors with freelancers Tay Garnett and John Cromwell in the 1935–1936 and 1936–1937 seasons. The producer also assiduously pursued Ford. Indeed, there is a striking contrast between the inept Fox administration that set the director loose in 1931 and the excellent Twentieth Century-Fox administration that did its level best to pin him down in the years following the merger.

The Zanuck-Ford Contract Negotiations

Barring his contractual obligations, Ford might well have left Twentieth Century-Fox alongside Frank Lloyd. As discussed in chapter five, Ford resented Zanuck's editing of *Steamboat Round the Bend.* Moreover, in the context of the founding of the Screen Directors Guild, he joined Lloyd in protesting against the producer's encroachments upon directorial prerogatives, publicly criticizing Zanuck's editing of *The Prisoner of Shark Island.*[18] A quick exit was not possible, however. Zanuck had first moved to secure Ford's services in April, 1935, when the merger negotiations were still secret. At that time, Ford signed a contract to direct *The Man Who Broke the Bank at Monte Carlo* for 20th Century.[19] Following the completion of *Steamboat Round the Bend* in July, Ford injured his back and Stephen Roberts was drafted to direct *Monte Carlo* in his stead.[20] Ford then signed a revised agreement with 20th Century to direct some other unspecified film (eventually, *The Prisoner of Shark Island*) and, as this was well after the merger was finalized, the contract gave 20th Century the right to assign the contract "to any other corporation acquiring all or substantially all of our assets".[21] This effectively added another

---

17   "Frank Lloyd Back", *Hollywood Reporter* (1 Nov 1935): 3, reports Lloyd's return to Twentieth Century-Fox after sixteen months at MGM; "Honor without Peace in Hollywood", *New York Times* (5 Apr 1936): X3.

18   On Ford and Lloyd's protest see "Honor without Peace in Hollywood", *New York Times* (5 Apr 1936): X3. Ford was a founding member of the Screen Director's Guild, see Virginia Wright Wexman, *Hollywood's Artists: The Director's Guild of America and the Construction of Authorship* (New York: Columbia University Press, 2020), 14–17, 41.

19   Draft Letter of Agreement, John Ford and William Goetz, 20th Century Pictures, 8 Apr 1935, John Ford Contract File, Twentieth Century-Fox Legal Department. I have not been able to determine if Ford was privy to the on-going negotiations about the merger when he signed this contract.

20   "Injury Keeps Ford Off *Monte Carlo*", *Hollywood Reporter* (15 Jul 1935): 2.

21   Draft Letter of Agreement, John Ford and William Goetz, 20th Century Pictures, 27 Jul 1935, unsigned, John Ford Contract File, Twentieth Century-Fox Legal Department.

film to Ford's 1934 four-picture Fox contract. He had completed the first of the four with *Steamboat Round the Bend*, but now owed a new one to 20th Century.[22]

In January, 1936, following the completion of *The Prisoner of Shark Island*, Ford took advantage of the clause in his contract that allowed him to refuse work at Fox when he had commitments at RKO. Although not in a position to leave the studio outright, he had been planning to direct both *Mary of Scotland* and *The Plough and the Stars* for RKO since at least April, 1935.[23] After some less than cordial negotiations between his agent, Harry Wurtzel, and Goetz, he took leave for seven months to direct the two films in succession.[24] During his leave, Ford also solicited additional assignments outside his home studio, securing an agreement to make *The Hurricane* for Goldwyn at United Artists. The forging of this deal provides a good example of the director's bold negotiating methods and his lack of commitment to Twentieth Century-Fox.

For much of the year there had been extensive industry trade press coverage of Goldwyn's purchase of the novel by Charles Nordoff and James Norman Hall on which *The Hurricane* was based. It was well known that Goldwyn planned to follow the example of MGM's *Mutiny on the Bounty*, also written by Nordoff and Hall, and shoot on

location in Polynesia.[25] Howard Hawks was originally slated to direct but in late summer he walked off the production of Goldwyn's *Come and Get It*, and Goldwyn embarked on a search for a new director for his South Seas epic.[26] At about the same time, production closed on *The Plough and the Stars* and Twentieth Century-Fox granted Ford's request for a vacation leave. The studio stipulated that he was to return on October 20 and could not work anywhere else in the interim.[27] The Ford family then embarked on the *Araner* for what was described as an extended South Sea voyage.[28] In mid-October, Goldwyn art director Day and production manager Percy Ikerd embarked on the S.S. *Monterey* en route to Samoa, scouting locations for *The Hurricane*.[29] On October 31, over a week past his deadline for reporting back to the Fox lot, Ford sent the following telegram to Samuel Goldwyn: "After reading Hurricane for third time am more than ever convinced I should work with you on it. Wish you could convince Darryl. Entertained Captain Day and party enroute Samoa talked Hurricane great length. Regardless who makes picture positive it will be superb and rebound to your glory."[30] An internal Twentieth Century-Fox memo of November 3 indicates how swiftly Goldwyn managed to secure permission, although Zanuck did make the proviso that Ford first come back to

22 "Ford Will Return in Oct. for Four at 20th", *Hollywood Reporter* (31 Aug 1935): 1.
23 I have not had access to Ford's contracts with RKO, but his engagements for these two films were announced around the same date, "*Mary of Scotland* Bought for Hepburn", *Hollywood Reporter* (25 Apr 1935): 1; "*Plough and Stars* Bought by Radio", *Hollywood Reporter* (29 Apr 1935): 3; and they were soon linked as a pair, "Ford-Nichols H'wood's Hecht and MacArthur", *Variety* (26 Jun 1935): 2, "Making *Mary* First", *Variety* (27 Nov 1935): 3.
24 The Draft Letter of Agreement, 27 Jul 1935, specified that Ford could only take leave in order to make *one* film at another studio, but this position was later reversed, see Draft Letter of Agreement, John Ford and Twentieth Century-Fox, unsigned, 9 December 1935; Harry Wurtzel, Letter to William Goetz, 18 December 1935; all in John Ford Contract File, Twentieth Century-Fox Legal Department.
25 Charles Nordhoff and James Norman Hall, *Mutiny on the Bounty* (Boston: Little, Brown, 1932) and *The Hurricane* (Boston: Little, Brown, 1936).
26 "Goldwyn May Pastel *Hurricane* in Tropics", *Variety* (19 Feb 1936): 5; "*Get It* Halts As Hawks, Goldwyn Call Off Contract", *Hollywood Reporter* (14 Aug 1936): 1; Todd McCarthy, *Howard Hawks: The Grey Fox of Hollywood* (New York: Grove Press, 1997), 238–240; Merritt Hulburd, Telegram to James A. Mulvey, 9 Jun 1936, Samuel Goldwyn Papers, Box 124, Folder 1007, Special Collections, Herrick Library, AMPAS.
27 Letter of Agreement, John Ford and William Goetz, Twentieth Century-Fox, 20 Aug 1936, John Ford Contract File, Twentieth Century-Fox Legal Department.
28 "Shipping News and Activities", *Los Angeles Times* (20 Sep 1936): 21; "Rambling Reporter", *Hollywood Reporter* (22 Sep 1936): 2.
29 "Day, Ikerd on Samoa Call", *Hollywood Reporter* (2 Oct 1936): 3; "Goldwyn Aides to Samoa", *Variety* (7 Oct 1936): 6; "US Navy Co-operation for Goldwyn *Hurricane*", *Hollywood Reporter* (16 Oct 1936): 4.
30 Ford, Telegram to Goldwyn, 31 October 1936, Samuel Goldwyn Papers, folder 1007, Special Collections, Herrick Library, AMPAS. It is possible that Goldwyn, who had been scouting for a director since August, had previously sent Ford a script. However, I found no evidence of this in the Ford or Goldwyn papers.

the Fox lot to direct *Wee Willie Winkie*.[31] In mid-November, Ford was reportedly still away with Day and Ikerd scouting locations.[32] The director thereby flouted both stipulations of his vacation leave since he was six weeks past the agreed-upon deadline for his return and effectively working for another studio.

It seems likely that Zanuck was playing a long game in winking at Ford's South Seas junket and releasing him for another prolonged leave (he was gone for six months on *The Hurricane*). The release of Ford reinforced a mutually profitable and long-standing tradition of sharing staff and facilities with Goldwyn.[33] At the same time, it likely helped the producer to secure favorable terms in the revision of Ford's 1934 Fox contract. The renegotiation of that contract went forward in the summer of 1937 while *The Hurricane* was in production. It bound Ford to Twentieth Century-Fox for a total of ten films, a number that included *Steamboat Round the Bend* and *Wee Willie Winkie*, made under the original agreement, but not *The Prisoner of Shark Island*. It also stepped up Ford's salary to his market rate. Under the terms of the original 1934 Fox contract, Fox paid $45,000 per film for *Steamboat Round the Bend* and *Wee Willie Winkie*, while Goldwyn offered him $100,000 plus profit participation for *The*

Hurricane.[34] Under the revised contract, Zanuck raised the director's salary to a guaranteed $75,000 per film on his next four films, and $85,000 per film on the last four.[35] While a door was left open for Ford to direct for two other producers, to be discussed in chapter eight, the new agreement drastically curtailed Ford's outside activities. Between 1938 and 1941 Ford made seven films for Twentieth Century-Fox and only two outside the studio. This is in striking contrast to the previous six years when Ford had made nine films outside the studio and only eight within it.[36] Zanuck had finally tied the director down, and it would take World War II to shake him loose.

It seems clear why Zanuck brokered the 1937 agreement. He retained a top-flight director, one that could be counted on to handle the studio's prestige pictures, the literary adaptations and biographical films that had dignified 20th Century's output. One imagines that after the March 1936 Academy Awards, when *The Informer* garnered four Oscars to RKO's credit, the famously competitive Zanuck decided that Ford needed to bring some home to Twentieth Century-Fox. And in fact, *The Grapes of Wrath* and *How Green Was My Valley* both won multiple Oscars, the latter providing Zanuck's and Twentieth Century-Fox's first for Best Picture. Ford probably signed

31 W. B. Dover to George Wasson, 3 November 1936, John Ford Contract File, Twentieth Century-Fox Legal Department, discusses whether to loan out Ford to Goldwyn (Harry Wurtzel's preference) or simply to give him unpaid leave (Dover's preference and what was done). Following Ford's return from vacation, he signed a formal agreement with Twentieth Century-Fox which contained the proviso that he direct *Wee Willie Winkie* before proceeding to his assignment with Goldwyn, Letter of Agreement, John Ford and William Goetz, Twentieth Century-Fox, 21 December 1936, John Ford Contract File, Twentieth Century-Fox Legal Department.

32 "Ford Signed to Direct *Hurricane*", *Hollywood Reporter* (16 Nov 1936): 2, noted that Ford was cruising in the South Seas where he "planned" to meet up with Day and Ikerd who were scouting locations in the area, that negotiations had been conducted by wireless, and that Ford planned to return in a month.

33 During the two years that 20th Century distributed through United Artists, it shared the UA Studios and personnel with Goldwyn and such arrangements continued even after the merger – this is clearest in the case of the pooling agreement that the two firms had for sharing Dana Andrews's services, see list of contracts, 13 Jun 1941, showing assignment privileges for Andrews, Samuel Goldwyn papers, folder 4801, Special Collections, Herrick Library, AMPAS; also, "See Goldwyn Veering to 20th", *Variety* (13 Mar 1940): 5.

34 Letter of Agreement, John Ford and Samuel Goldwyn, Inc., Ltd., 14 December 1936, Samuel Goldwyn papers, folder 4942, Special Collections, Herrick Library, AMPAS. The actual salaries are commensurable since the Twentieth Century-Fox contract was for 10 weeks and the contract with Goldwyn was for 25 weeks. However, Ford likely grossed substantially more than his salary given that *The Hurricane* was highly successful and the director was allocated 12 per cent of the profits after UA and Goldwyn had recouped their costs. On the success of *The Hurricane* relative to other Goldwyn releases, see James Mulvey, Memos to Samuel Goldwyn dated 30 Mar 1939, 19 Jun 1939, 14 Jul 1939, Samuel Goldwyn papers, folder 3792, as well as the comparative grosses in folder 3793, Special Collections, Herrick Library, AMPAS. By 1938, Ford's salary was high relative to his colleagues: "Ford Revealed Top Pay Director at NLRB Session", *Hollywood Reporter* (9 Sep 1938): 1.

35 Letter of Agreement, John Ford and William Goetz, Twentieth Century-Fox, dated 28 September 1937 and notarized 28 December 1937; the terms are clarified in F. L. Metzler, Telegram to Sydney Towell, New York Office, 30 September 1937, both in John Ford Contract File, Twentieth Century-Fox Legal Department. In the case of *How Green Was My Valley,* this agreement was suspended and Ford was paid a flat fee of $100,000 to work as long as was necessary, Letter of Agreement, John Ford and William Goetz, Twentieth Century-Fox, 6 Apr 1941, John Ford Contract File, Twentieth Century-Fox Legal Department.

36 See the list of features made by Ford from 1931–1937 in chapter three.

the long-term contract in part because the money was good – $75,000 in 1938 is the equivalent of over $1.7 million in 2025, and he averaged two films a year at that salary. In addition, by the early fall of 1937 it was clear that he needed a stable berth. As discussed in chapter four, Ford had lost important administrative allies with the reorganization of RKO under Samuel Briskin, and he could no longer count on a production base at that studio. It is also possible that, after making two films with Zanuck, Ford had begun to see possibilities for himself, and for a new crew, at Twentieth Century-Fox.

Script Development and Post-production Editing in *The Prisoner of Shark Island*

A hands-on producer, Zanuck remained closely involved with the broad spectrum of A production at the studio. He frequently generated ideas for films. Nunnally Johnson recalled: "He was quite capable of starting at two o'clock in the morning and dictating some sort of outline of a story, roughly, and handing it to a writer or a producer the next day."[37] He kept abreast of script development through meetings with writers and associate producers – Johnson called him "the master of the story conference". His secretary systematically followed up on these meetings by circulating typed copies of her notes, which are an important source of information on his methods.[38] He was well known for his sense of story structure and pacing. Johnson recalled: "I always thought Zanuck had a Geiger counter in his head … . He'd read a script and the minute it got dull, or didn't move, or went off track, tick-tick-tick, he said 'It stopped. Now where did this start?' And he'd go back, two pages, three pages, and then

he'd figure where the movement stopped, or the movement went wrong."[39] In addition to extensive involvement in script development, Zanuck regularly reviewed the dailies, the footage shot for his A films, while they were in production, and evaluated the rough cuts of his films with great attention to problems of clarity and pace. In a well-known memo of 1941 addressed to "All 'A' Directors and Producers", he remarked: "Sitting as I do night after night in the cutting room working on films, I would rank the lack of tempo as public enemy #1".[40] It is unlikely that a major Twentieth Century-Fox film went into release without Zanuck having had multiple meetings about the script, viewed at least some of the raw footage, and re-arranged the rough cut.

The Prisoner of Shark Island provides a prime example of Zanuck's process. A February 4, 1935 piece in *Time* magazine recounted the story of Samuel Mudd, the physician who treated James Wilkes Booth's broken leg after the assassination of President Lincoln and, widely reviled, was sentenced to life imprisonment as a co-conspirator.[41] The article also gave a compelling account of the place where Mudd served his sentence: Fort Jefferson on the Dry Tortugas reef off Key West in the Gulf of Mexico. During the Civil War, the previously abandoned fort had been repurposed as a military prison and surrounded by a shark-filled moat. Zanuck, Raymond Griffith and Johnson worked intensively on creating the film's storyline in February and March 1935, well before the merger and without any anticipation of Ford's participation as director. Zanuck commissioned an analysis of Nettie Mudd's *The Life of Dr. Samuel A. Mudd*, originally published in 1906, largely a collection of her father's prison correspondence.[42] Raymond Griffith made the first attempt at a narrative continuity in a set of notes

37 Stempel, *Recollections of Nunnally Johnson*, 45.
38 Rudy Behlmer, *Memo from Darryl F. Zanuck: The Golden Years at Twentieth Century-Fox* (New York: Grove Press, 1993), xx.
39 Stempel, *Recollections of Nunnally Johnson*, 31, 37; Henry King made similar observations about the producer's talent for managing script development, see Thomas Stempel, "An Oral History Interview with Henry King", Darryl F. Zanuck Research Project (Los Angeles: American Film Institute, 1970–1971), 36–37, 149.
40 Behlmer, *Memo from Darryl F. Zanuck*, 55.
41 "Mudd's Monument", *Time*, 35/5 (4 Feb 1935): 21–22; Stempel, *Recollections of Nunnally Johnson*, 63; "Zanuck to Film Life of Martyred Doctor", *Hollywood Reporter* (11 Feb 1935): 1, refers to a March of Time radio broadcast on the subject (the broadcasts drew from articles in the magazine).
42 Nettie Mudd, *The Life of Dr. Samuel A. Mudd* (New York: Neale Pub. Co., 1906, rpt. Marietta, Georgia: Continental Book Company, 1955).

dated February 21, 1935. A week later, Zanuck responded with two memos that together provided a rough outline of the story as it was eventually filmed. Nunnally Johnson wrote two more detailed treatments, one in April and a lightly revised version in June.[43]

Zanuck had made many bio-pics at Warners and 20th Century, and his attitude toward the historical record was rather cavalier. Johnson recalled that the historian who was advising them during script development for *Cardinal Richelieu* objected to something that Zanuck proposed: "Christ, I think Darryl was going to put the Battle of Waterloo in there or something because it fit … . Darryl thought about it for a few minutes and then he said, 'Aw the hell with you. Nine out of ten people is going to think he's Rasputin anyway.'"[44] Zanuck took similar liberties with history in *The Prisoner of Shark Island*. The film does follow the basic events of the life. Samuel Mudd was tried as a co-conspirator in the plot to assassinate Lincoln, was convicted by a military court and imprisoned in Fort Jefferson. Like several of those convicted by the military court, he aimed to escape from jail, hoping to get arrested in Florida and then employ a writ of habeas corpus to receive a hearing in a civil court. Later, when an epidemic of yellow fever decimated the prison, he took over the hospital, eventually becoming ill himself. But the film freely reworks these events in order to construct a more satisfying narrative. For example, the escape attempt in the film is much more thrilling and affecting than Mudd's written description of the event. In the film, Mudd's wife and father-in-law arrive to rescue him in a schooner and, despite pursuit by soldiers and sharks, the doctor makes his way out of the fort and to the boat in the open sea. The father-in-law is killed in the fight to retake the prisoner,

and Mudd is subjected to a very cruel form of confinement, secured in an underground cellar. Mudd's actual account of the escape is much more mundane.[45] His family was not involved (indeed, they learned of it through his correspondence). He was aided by a sailor who helped him stow away on a mail boat. His absence was immediately noticed, and he was returned to the jail and put in irons.

The film also stretches the historical record when it asserts Mudd's innocence in a very bold and uncomplicated way. Even Nettie Mudd's book, clearly written to restore the family reputation, includes a statement in which Mudd admits to knowing Booth prior to treating him.[46] Lincoln historian Edward Steers, Jr., has argued that while Mudd was not involved in planning the assassination, he was a confederate of the actor's and involved in a prior Booth plot to kidnap Lincoln.[47] Sidney Cook, who was hired by Zanuck to evaluate and summarize Nettie Mudd's book in February 1935, cautioned the producer that the evidence suggested that Mudd was guilty and the sources exonerating him suspect.[48] But Zanuck, in his best damn-the-torpedoes-full-steam-ahead manner, seems to have decided that the film would be more effective if Mudd was positioned as without any previous connection with the assassin, unequivocally innocent, irrevocably wronged.

The adapters struggled with another aspect of their source material, the fact that Mudd complained bitterly about the presence of Black soldiers at Fort Jefferson. He justified his escape attempt on the grounds that the 161st New York Volunteer Infantry regiment who guarded Fort Jefferson were replaced by the 82nd U.S. Colored Troops in September 1865. He wrote to his wife: "It is bad enough to be a prisoner in the hands

---

43 "Notes", by Raymond Griffith, 21 February 1935; Darryl Zanuck, "Notes on Shark Island", 26 February 1935, and "Further Notes on Shark Island", 27 February 1935; Treatment by Nunnally Johnson, 27 Apr 1935; Treatment by Nunnally Johnson (with Mr. Zanuck's Changes), 13 Jun 1935, all in *Prisoner of Shark Island* file, Twentieth Century-Fox Collection, Cinematic Arts Library, Doheny Library, USC.

44 Stempel, *Recollections of Nunnally Johnson*, 33–34.

45 For his account see Samuel A. Mudd, Letter to Jere Dyer, 30 September 1865, reprinted in Nettie Mudd, 123–127.

46 "Sworn Statement of My Father", Nettie Mudd, 42–48.

47 Edward Steers, Jr., *Blood on the Moon: The Assassination of Abraham Lincoln* (Lexington: University Press of Kentucky, 2005), 74–80, 171–173, 234–236; McBride, 256.

48 Sidney Cook, "Report on research on *The Life of Dr. Samuel Mudd, convicted as a conspirator in the plot to assassinate Lincoln*", 9 February 1935, *The Prisoner of Shark Island* file, Twentieth Century-Fox Collection, Cinematic Arts Library, Doheny Library, USC.

of white men, your equals under the Constitution, but to be lorded over by a set of ignorant, prejudiced and irresponsible beings of the unbleached humanity, was more than I could submit to."[49] The adapters seem to have been divided about how to make use of this material. Raymond Griffith was inspired by it:

> As you know, after Lincoln's death, most of the governorships, judges benches and military positions were given to negroes. This was what was known in the North as giving the negro his equality. In THE CLANSMEN [sic] Griffith showed what they did in the legislatures, as Governors, Senators, etc., when they assumed power, which would not interest us here. But when Dr. Mudd arrives at Fort Jefferson – also known as Dry Tartugas [sic] – its command has been taken over by a negro regiment. The inmates were all Southern prisoners of war. The negroes were told when they took command that they were guarding men of whom they were once slaves and to act accordingly. I don't mean that we should rub it in too much, but the mere fact of having a prison with negro guards over their former owners I think will be very arresting dramatically.[50]

Johnson's April treatment follows along the lines of Griffith's notes. For example, Mudd and the other white prisoners build a breakwater in one scene as the guards taunt them. At the end of this scene in the first fully drafted script, Johnson describes Mudd, filthy and exhausted from his labors, standing with the other prisoners at attention at the nightly lowering of the colors, "his eyes are fixed on the flag that is responsible for this tragedy".[51]

From his very first notes on *The Prisoner of Shark Island* in February 1935, Zanuck seems to have been committed to a long-standing Hollywood tradition of minimizing potentially offensive and politically divisive material in the interests of maximizing the potential audience. Throughout the post-production editing process, he repeatedly toned down Johnson's dialogue, limiting the guards' negative use of the words "white man" and Mudd's use of a negative epithet for Blacks. The producer also insisted that Mudd should be the victim of brutality only at the hands of white men (eventually, the character of Rankin played by John Carradine).[52] At the same time he proposed two new subsidiary characters that seem to have been designed to offset the more tendentious elements of the source material. One of these characters, Mudd's father-in-law, "the Colonel", was played entirely for comedy, a sort of irascible Confederate grandpa. He is the only one to voice anti-Yankee sentiments and stands in contrast to the dignified Mudd.

In addition to the Colonel, Zanuck created the character of Buck, a former slave on Mudd's estate who appears in the guise of a Union soldier at Fort Jefferson after Mudd has been imprisoned there.[53] Buck acts as a conduit to the outside, helps to plan a way out of the fort and is eventually punished alongside the doctor. While no doubt intended to counter the racial hostility and prejudice found in *The Life of Samuel A. Mudd*, the character is nonetheless incorporated into the more general, idyllic representation of the antebellum rural South. For instance, Buck is first seen among a group of men that Mudd identifies as "farmhands" listening to a carpetbagger. The Yankee harangues the men to exercise their newly won right to vote, referring to them as former slaves and Mudd as a slave owner. When Mudd orders Buck and the other men to throw the carpetbagger off his land, they oblige in an incident that reveals the carpetbagger's own racial prejudice. While this incident serves briefly to acknowledge that Mudd owned slaves, it does so

---

49   Mudd, Letter to Jere Dyer, 30 September 1865, reprinted in Nettie Mudd, 123–124; see also Mudd, Letter to Sarah Frances [Frank] Mudd, 18 October 1865, reprinted in Nettie Mudd, 131–132, and Mudd, Letter to Jere Dyer, 11 November 1865, reprinted in Nettie Mudd, 139–141.

50   "Notes by Raymond Griffith", 21 Feb 1935, *The Prisoner of Shark Island* file, Twentieth Century-Fox Collection, Cinematic Arts Library, Doheny Library, USC.

51   *Shark Island*, First Draft, 12 August 1935, by Nunnally Johnson, *The Prisoner of Shark Island* Story File, Twentieth Century-Fox Legal Department, 84–86.

52   Darryl Zanuck, Notes on Shark Island, 26 Feb 1935 and Further Notes on Shark Island, 27 Feb 1935, both in *The Prisoner of Shark Island* file, Twentieth Century-Fox Collection, Cinematic Arts Library, Doheny Library, USC.

53   In the film, the motivation for Buck's presence in Fort Jefferson is quite weak. Buck explains that Mrs. Mudd ordered him down to the island and so he went – there is no discussion of the small matter of his enlisting in the Union army and securing an assignment to Fort Jefferson.

under the guise of a highly improbable scenario in which Mudd's relationship with the enslaved is not only presented as cordial, but also completely unaffected by the Emancipation Proclamation or the Union's victory in the Civil War.

There are three fully drafted screenplays in the Twentieth Century-Fox files, one dated August 12, 1935 and two in October 1935 (production ran from November 12, 1935, to early January 1936).[54] By the time of the first script draft in early August, the act structure was set. Act one was comprised of the assassination of Lincoln, Mudd setting Booth's leg and the doctor's arrest. Act two was devoted to Mudd's trial. Act three began with Mudd's arrival at the prison, followed by his escape attempt. Act four dealt with the onset of the yellow fever epidemic, Mudd's efforts to ameliorate it, and subsequent release and return home. In the first October script, Zanuck shortened the August draft. His eliminations strengthened the narrative continuity by removing several major scenes that could be seen as distractions from the dramatic set pieces that defined the act structure.

Two scenes concerning the machinations of the jury as it deliberated Mudd's sentence were eliminated from act two, thereby placing more emphasis on the trial itself and his wife's reaction to it. In act three, the sequence of Mudd's escape was radically cut. In the August draft, Mudd makes his escape and swims to a boat that carries him and the Colonel to a deserted beach. They make their way to a dry clearing in a swamp where Mudd is reunited with his wife, and where they are eventually followed by Rankin and his soldiers. The script also describes the Colonel's ensuing attack on the Yankee soldiers, and his murder at their hands. This whole sequence is eliminated in the October 12 draft. The recapture of Mudd is staged immediately after he swims to the schooner sent to rescue him. Rankin and his men come aboard and kill the Colonel as he attempts to protect Mudd, an act which occurs off-screen while the script (and eventually the film) remain focalized on Mudd and his wife. The shortening

of the escape seems to have been done partly to save time and money (it would have been quite expensive to stage and shoot the scene in the swamp) but Zanuck also seems to have decided to put the emphasis on the doctor's escape from the prison.

The revision of the opening of act four provides a very good example of what Johnson praised as Zanuck's instinct for how to keep a story moving. In this case, changes made during the October revision of the script were followed by additional revisions made in the cutting room during post-production. In the August draft, act four opens with Mrs. Mudd meeting with officials in Washington in an attempt to secure clemency for her husband. The outbreak of yellow fever at Fort Jefferson is introduced in the course of their negotiations. The script then describes a series of what are called "atmospheric shots" of sick and dying men which convey the extent and severity of the epidemic. This segues to the prison doctor, MacIntyre, treating a sick patient and on the verge of collapse himself, a scene that survives in the completed film. By the October 12 draft, the scene of Mrs. Mudd in Washington has been eliminated. The act opens with the captain of a supply vessel deciding to reverse course and put out to sea in reaction to the sight of a quarantine flag flying over the fort. The montage of "atmospheric" shots remain. Little of this rather clunky exposition is left in the completed film, which instead opens with extracts of two scenes that Johnson had placed much later in the narrative sequence. It seems likely that Zanuck brought this material forward during the editing process. In the film, act four begins in the underground isolation cell as Mudd nurses Buck, who suffers from fever, and the men wonder why they have been without food and water for days. Thus, the act begins on a point of acute suspense: Why have Mudd and Buck been left alone without food and water? What is happening outside the confines of the dungeon? Cut abruptly from the dark cell to the middle of an open-air exchange conducted via signals between the fort commander

---

54   The extant drafts, all by Nunnally Johnson, are as follows: *Shark Island*, First Draft, 12 August 1935; *Shark Island*, First Temporary, 20 August 1935 (incomplete); *Shark Island*, Final, 16 October 1935; *Shark Island*, Revised Final, 23 October 1935, all in *The Prisoner of Shark Island* Story File, Twentieth Century-Fox Legal Department.

and the captain of the supply vessel still at sea. Their exchange provides necessary exposition: "Tell the captain of that ship that I have got to have those supplies. Tell him that I got one thousand hospital cases here, and only one doctor …. Tell him he is a filthy yellow coward with my compliments." Zanuck's reordering of the narrative material thus rendered the situation of the main characters in the fort in a much more immediate and compelling form.

In some instances the express train of Zanuck's narrative moves with too much speed and efficiency. For example, following the relatively lengthy and static treatment of the court martial, the pace quickens markedly. Inside the prison, Mudd meets with his family and his lawyer, learning that he has been found guilty and bidding goodbye to his wife and child. In a subsequent brief interchange with the guard outside his cell, Mudd is told he will never be returned there, raising the possibility that he has been condemned to death. Cut back to Mrs. Mudd and the lawyer as they exit into the prison yard where they find a crowd assembled and the gallows already built, again raising the possibility that the doctor's execution is imminent. Mrs. Mudd watches in horror as the prisoners are conducted up to the gallows one by one until she realizes that Mudd has been spared. The surprise revelation of the gallows, and the threat of execution that is dissipated almost as quickly as it is raised, seems underdeveloped, and the dramatic climax of the act a bit forced.

As has often been noted, Zanuck's preference for quick-paced narrative development and short, punchy scenes was at odds with Ford's predilection, strengthened by his collaborations with Will Rogers, for a more relaxed pace and scenes loosely structured around individual performances.[55] This made for on-going tension between the two. Ford's objections to the producer's editing of *The Prisoner of Shark Island* may well have derived

from disagreements regarding pacing, especially the blasts of short shots found in the execution sequence and the presumed re-editing of act four discussed above. Nonetheless, the revisions made by the producer during script development and in post-production made for a much more forceful and character-centered story. Zanuck's laser-focus on plot clearly made him adept at handling sources that, while interesting and potentially marketable film material, did not immediately supply a strong narrative line. This was the case for both *The Prisoner of Shark Island*, where he built a viable script out of a collection of letters, and *Wee Willie Winkie*, in which he developed a feature-length plot from a brief Kipling short story.

Ford's contributions to *The Prisoner of Shark Island*

While Henry King recalled Zanuck as collaborative and supportive,[56] many accounts of the relationship between Ford and Zanuck have emphasized the director's resistance to the producer's executive oversight and his almost fanatical concern to protect his autonomy and control during shooting. Screenwriter Philip Dunne remarked: "When he worked for Zanuck, they had a few clashes, because Ford, after all, was a very temperamental feisty character, he'd flare up over any kind of criticism. That happened with Darryl, but he didn't win any arguments with Zanuck. There was no question who was the boss."[57] Arthur Miller recalled that when a studio executive came on the set of *Wee Willie Winkie* to inquire why the company was "behind", Ford ripped pages out of the script, claiming to have thereby "caught up".[58] McBride reports that Ford did not show up to watch the dailies for *The Prisoner of Shark Island* in the producer's company despite Zanuck's instructions to the contrary.[59] As has been frequently discussed, Ford also consistently

55 Dan Ford, 94; Gallagher, 182; McBride, 253.
56 Stempel, "Oral History Interview with Henry King", 11–12: "I thought Zanuck was the greatest studio head that I had ever seen for the simple reason that he says, 'That's your problem', and he helps you in every way on earth. He never interferes with anything. He never interferes with anything in the world. He wants to stimulate your imagination and for you to go right on, but yet he doesn't want you to throw all the money away."
57 Dunne, quoted in McBride, 247.
58 Fred J. Balshofer and Arthur C. Miller, *One Reel a Week* (Berkeley: University of California Press, 1967), 186.

limited the number of camera positions on a scene as well as the number of takes that he turned over to the studio.[60] A memo from Zanuck to Ford written after viewing the dailies for *How Green Was My Valley* suggests that the producer was indeed nervous that Ford was not planning to give him any close ups:

> I was delighted with the rushes on the daffodil scene. You played this beautifully, and Pidgeon was outstanding. One thing, however, has occurred to me which I think may add something to this particular scene … . I feel the scene would be helped if we had a straight-on close shot of the boy as he tries to walk … . To intercut with this I suggest a straight-on closeup of Pidgeon encouraging the boy and practically holding his breath as he watches to see if the boy will make it. These two close shots can be intercut with the long shot which you now have, and I feel certain it will intensify and build up the emotional value of the scene.[61]

Zanuck got the close ups, but Ford penciled a wry note in the margins of the memo: "Dear Darryl, The sun goes down out here at six-thirty".

While the standard account of the relationship between producer and director is revealing in many ways, it does not do justice to the nature of the collaboration that contributed to the excellence of their films. Ford *did* generally shoot films for Zanuck as scripted, while Zanuck, a gifted producer who was adept at assessing and exploiting the talent available to him, leaned into Ford's strengths. As the example of *The Prisoner*

of Shark Island will suggest, the care and attention that Zanuck devoted to script development was, to some extent, in the service of pitching balls that Ford could hit out of the park.

It is difficult to date precisely when Ford began work on the film, initially titled *Shark Island*.[62] The first full screenplay draft of August 12, 1935, makes reference to *Arrowsmith*, which suggests that Zanuck and Johnson were already contemplating Ford as director.[63] This supposition is borne out by the fact that the director's assignment to the film was first announced in the trade press in early September while he was on vacation in Hawaii.[64] About three weeks later, however, it was announced that he had been reassigned to *Message to Garcia*, apparently to relieve Roy Del Ruth who had initially been assigned to that film but who also hoped to go on his vacation.[65] Ford's definitive assignment to *Shark Island* was first confirmed in an article in the *Los Angeles Times* of October 5.[66] The last two versions of the script, dated October 16 and October 23, were clearly revised after he had come on staff. No story conference notes survive for August or October so there is no direct evidence of Ford's participation in script revision during the six weeks he was on staff prior to the start of production on November 12.[67] But, given that the director often revised scripts by removing pages, and given his fondness for boats, one wonders if Ford suggested the elimination of the August script's extensive land-battle to recapture

---

59 McBride, 250.
60 See the Introduction, n.7; also Bogdanovich, *John Ford*, 9, quoting Robert Parrish on cutting in the camera on *Young Mr. Lincoln*; Michael Killanin, "Poet in an Iron Mask", in Peary, ed., 38–40, originally published in *Films and Filming,* 4/ 5 (Feb 1958); McBride, 251–252.
61 Zanuck, Memo to Ford, 18 Jul 1941, Ford correspondence, Lilly Library, IU.
62 Ford left the port of Los Angeles for Honolulu at the beginning of August, see "Yacht of John Ford, Director, in Hawaii", *Los Angeles Times* (15 Aug 1935): 3; I have not been able to pinpoint the date of his return but he had agreed to do so by September 30, Letter of Agreement, John Ford and J. J. Gain, 23 August 1935, John Ford Contract File, Twentieth Century-Fox Legal Department.
63 *Shark Island*, First Draft, 12 August 1935, by Nunnally Johnson, *The Prisoner of Shark Island* Story File, Twentieth Century-Fox Legal Department, 120.
64 "John Ford Given *Island* at 20ᵗʰ", *Hollywood Reporter* (5 Sep 1935): 3; "*Shark Island* First for Ford Direction at 20-Fox", *Variety* (11 Sep 1935): 7.
65 "John Ford Will Direct *Garcia* After Vacation", *Hollywood Reporter* (27 Sep 1935): 7. In the difficult months immediately following the merger, as Zanuck sought to ramp up production for the 1935–1936 season while his top directors aimed to take their annual vacations, assignments were shifted around quite a bit, see, for example, "Del Ruth's Aim", *Variety* (25 Sep 1935): 6; "Ford Gets *Island*", *Hollywood Reporter* (14 Oct 1935): 1; "Director Switch", *Hollywood Reporter* (22 Oct 1935): 6.
66 Philip Scheuer, "Twentieth Century Directors Switched", *Los Angeles Times* (5 Oct 1935): A7.
67 In this case, the scene numbers do not provide a clue to Ford's participation since Johnson numbered the master scenes in the script from the first draft of 12 August 1935. He did so copiously, providing so many master-scene numbers that Ford could not really be held to them.

6.1

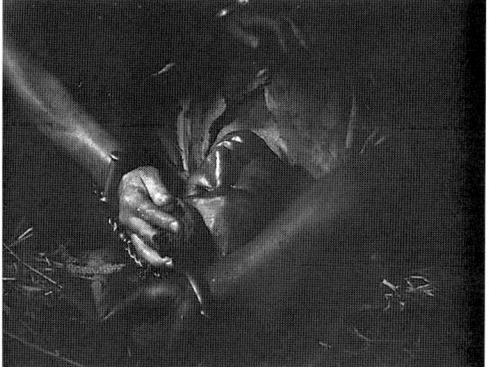

6.2

Mudd. In the film, the shots of the guards embarking in pursuit of the sloop as it picks up Mudd provides a pictorially arresting close to the prison chase (figure 6.1).

Differences between the completed film and the revised final October 23 script can be more readily attributed to Ford, since they were almost certainly made on the sound stage during production. The most notable changes concern the relationship between Mudd and Buck and the interactions between Mudd and the Black soldiers of the fort. Taken together they complicate the racial dynamics of the film's last act. In the scene between Mudd and Buck in the dungeon, Buck suffers from fever and they wonder if they have been abandoned to die. It is possible that Zanuck placed this scene at the beginning of act four because it was so beautifully acted and visually striking. The October 23 script describes Mudd standing and dousing the feverish Buck with water. In the film, the scene is shot in almost total darkness, with spotlights catching details of the men's bodies. Mudd sits on the floor beside Buck repeatedly bathing his face and chest (figure 6.2). The intimacy of the gestures suggests a strong connection between the men at a moment of utter despair.

Ford also expands a later scene between the two men, after Mudd has taken over the hospital. In the October 23 script this interaction merely serves to indicate that Buck has survived the disease. As Mudd stops beside Buck's hospital bed, Buck makes a brief joke about the number of

children he has with Rosabelle back home (Rosabelle's fecundity is a rather unpleasant running gag in scripts and film). Ford develops this into one of his "grace notes", actions or gestures which are not narratively consequential but nonetheless importantly ornament the plot.[68] As the exhausted Mudd sits down to rest beside Buck, the thunder of the storm outside gives way to musical underscoring, "Maryland, My Maryland". Buck reports feeling better and begins to reminisce:

> *Buck*: It sure seems a long way from Maryland.
>
> *Mudd*: [*Pronounced pause as he looks down and sighs.*] Long time. Long ago.
>
> *Buck*: I wonder – I wonder if Rosabelle done forgot me.
>
> *Mudd*: [*Slight chuckle, but still looking down.*] Forget ya after – after twelve children? It's impossible!

The gag about Rosabelle is still there, but the mood is melancholy, evoking the men's shared longing for home and uncertainty about the future. While these changes do not fundamentally alter the master/servant relationship between the men – for example, Buck still calls Mudd "Massa Sam" – they do give it a friendlier tone and more emotional heft.

Somewhat paradoxically, Ford also chose to amplify the conflict between Mudd and the soldiers who guard the jail, going against Zanuck's strategy for minimizing racial conflict within the fort. Following Mudd's release from the dungeon, the Commander gives the doctor authority to

68 McBride, 175, 357, 410.

6.3

6.4

cope with the epidemic and to deal with the soldiers who have barricaded themselves in the mess hall out of fear of infection. In the October 23 script, the opening description of the mess hall is as follows: "The place is jammed with terrified negro soldiers. Some have rifles. All attention is on the negro at the window, who is still sighting down his rifle." And later from the same scene: "As Mudd continues (on the sound track) they glance worriedly toward each other, fear of the fever fighting with fear of threats. Mudd is working on their simple minds, obviously trying to overcome one fear with greater fear."[69] Ford shot the dialogue in this scene largely as Johnson wrote it.[70] But staging and shot composition differ from the script's repeated characterization of the mutineers as superstitious and fearful. The mutineers are shown in highly formalized arrays around the windows, with many rifles in evidence, although, in typical Fordian fashion, the men are given to "individual, whimsical expression" with their uniforms (figures 6.3 and 6.4). As Mudd talks, one soldier is wide-eyed, seemingly terrified, but the others hold their formation, sighting down their weapons and debating courses of action, until the group finally decides it would be better to work for the doctor than face a court martial. It is only at this point that they break ranks.

Ford's treatment of the racial dynamic in act four illustrates the director's capacity to alter components of the script through staging and performance without making substantial changes to plot or written dialogue. Indeed, Zanuck sought out Ford as director partly because he did change things up, improving the script in unexpected ways, as it might be argued the more respectful treatment of the mutineers does. Another important facet of the collaboration was that Zanuck and Johnson seem to have been calling upon what they knew of Ford's previous films, and setting him up to do what he had done before. An analysis of set design, lighting and staging in the prison escape sequence in *The Prisoner of Shark Island* provides a good example of this tendency.

The prison is important, central to the producer's initial inspiration for the film, and evoked in its title. But despite this, Zanuck had no plans to shoot on location. A 1938 memo indicates that at this point in his career he thought extensive location shooting an unwarranted expense.[71] Instead the producer took a very active role in pre-production planning for the prison set. Some time before the composition of the August script, Zanuck had seen *Realm of Ghosts*, a documentary that portrayed the ruins of Fort Jefferson and the island on which it was situated (actually called Garden Key). The studio then acquired permission to use footage from the documentary as stock

69 *Shark Island*, Revised Final, 23 October 1935, by Nunnally Johnson, *The Prisoner of Shark Island* Story File, Twentieth Century-Fox Legal Department, 113–114.
70 A close examination of the actor's lip movements in shot 610 suggests that in post-production Zanuck cut a line from the revised final script: "Put that gun down, nigger."
71 See Zanuck, Memo to Henry King, undated, but circa late September, 1938, in Behlmer, *Memo from Darryl F. Zanuck*, 17–19, in which the producer complains about what he felt were unnecessary expenses King incurred by choosing to shoot *Jesse James* on location in Missouri.

146

shots or reference for set designs.[72] The August and October scripts refer to *Realm of Ghosts* at several points, especially to stills taken from its shots of the ruins which show the old fortress surrounded by ocean, its cloistered or colonnaded walkways, and the great gate opening onto the bridge over the moat. Johnson's viewing of the documentary also seems to have inspired his description of Mudd's escape in act three. For example all of the scripts suggest that Mudd's cell be located on the ground floor of the cell block, and bordered by a colonnaded walkway that gives access to the prison parade ground. The scripts also acknowledge: "The character of the set will govern to a great extent the incidents of Mudd's stay in the enclosed parade grounds of the prison. Use may be made of several small buildings, the incinerator, several terraces, bushes and palm trees, and the constant appearance of the revolving light." In addition to these anticipations of the set design, the script drafts all also carry a suggestion about effects lighting. They call for the production of a miniature of the prison including a lighthouse with a revolving light that then motivates periodic illumination of the grounds during the escape. There is a possibility that the lighthouse effect was suggested by Ford himself in early discussions with the producer, but in any event, the fact that construction of the miniature was called for in the scripts makes clear that screenwriter and producer expected low-key illumination and effects lighting during the escape scene.

There are several indications that Zanuck was cognizant of Ford's experimentation with low-key lighting and atmospheric effects. In an interview near the end of his career, Zanuck praised Ford's visual style generally and *The Informer* specifically: "He won his first Oscar with *The Informer* which was a visual masterpiece almost unparalleled in cinema history."[73] Zanuck gives a much less enthusiastic description of Ford's style in a memo

to Elia Kazan and John Steinbeck written during preparation of *Viva Zapata*: "I am wondering … if it may not seem as if we are trying to make an art or 'mood' picture. The kind of thing John Ford does when he is stuck and has run out of plot. In these cases, somebody always sings and you cut to an extreme long shot with slanting shadows."[74] But despite the retrospective irony, in 1935 Zanuck was apparently looking for a little of that mood magic for the scenes in Fort Jefferson. Ford's own characterization of *The Prisoner of Shark Island* in a January 1936 interview as having "some of the qualities of *The Informer* but more Hollywood", may have reflected his understanding with Zanuck.[75]

Despite Johnson's later claims that Ford "simply" filmed what was in his script, it would be more accurate to say that Ford and his colleagues, set designer William Darling and cinematographer Bert Glennon, used the script as a springboard for further invention.[76] As was typical of the division of labor under the studio system, the script gave a good piecemeal account of the number and character of the required sets. It was then up to the art director in consultation with the director to design a convincing, unified space, one which incorporated the director's ideas about camera placement, shot composition and what would be required of the performers. For *The Prisoner of Shark Island*, art director William Darling who had worked with Ford extensively at Fox from *Hangman's House* to *Steamboat Round the Bend*, was seconded by set decorator Thomas Little. Little joined the Twentieth Century-Fox staff in the fall of 1935, coming from the art department at RKO. It is likely that he had already worked with Ford there on *The Informer*.[77] In any case, he would have been familiar with Polglase's sets for that film. In some ways, the prison sets for *Shark Island* posed problems similar to the Dublin slums of *The Informer*. Both films

72 William Goetz, Letter to Cinelog Corporation, 19 November 1935, *The Prisoner of Shark Island* Legal File, Twentieth Century-Fox Legal Department.

73 Gussow, 163.

74 Zanuck, Memo to John Steinbeck and Elia Kazan, 3 May 1950, in Behlmer, *Memo from Darryl F. Zanuck,* 171–172.

75 Douglas W. Churchill, "John Ford, the Man Behind *The Informer*", *New York Times* (5 Jan 1936): X5, reprinted in Peary, ed., 8.

76 Nunnally Johnson claims authorship of the Ford films that he scripted, see, for example, Stempel, *Recollections of Nunnally Johnson*, 56–60, 66–70.

77 Darling's history with Ford is discussed in chapter one; although Little is not credited for set decoration on *The Informer*, he is credited on *She* and *The Last Days of Pompeii*, which were both made on RKO's Prudential lot immediately following Ford's film.

required architectural structures made at scale – streets or passage-ways lined with buildings and wider playing areas on street corners or parade grounds. Both films also needed to be lit for extended night-time sequences.

Cameraman Glennon had started his career at Paramount in the early feature period. His four films for Josef von Sternberg, *Underworld* (1927), *The Last Command* (1928), *Blonde Venus* (1932), and *The Scarlet Empress* (1934), show great facility with that director's fondness for low-key lighting schemes aptly described by Patrick Keating as "mannerist".[78] After a short stint as a director in the early sound period, Glennon resumed his career as a cameraman at Fox in 1934. Few of the films Glennon shot for Fox are currently available for viewing, but one, *Grand Canary* (1934), directed by Irving Cummings and starring Baxter, would likely have been screened by Zanuck as he was contemplating the casting for *The Prisoner of Shark Island*. The film's plot is clearly indebted to *Arrowsmith*. Baxter plays a doctor who leaves London following a scandal about his use of an experimental serum. He redeems himself in the Canary Islands by using the same serum to quell a yellow fever epidemic. The poor video copies in circulation do not permit close analysis of the lighting, but the opening scenes of a freighter taking on passengers at the London docks are shot without strong overhead illumination, the actors frequently silhouetted as they move amidst heavy shadow and minimal, highly diffused, light. In a similar vein, the gothic mansion used as a hospital near the film's end is enhanced by multiple instances of effects lighting and cast shadows. The very choice of Glennon as cinematographer, a decision that Zanuck was certainly party to, points to the producer's interest in creating spectacular lighting for the prison escape from Shark Island.

For his part, Ford may have turned to Glennon because his preferred cinematographers were not available to him. George Schneiderman, who had shot many of the director's Fox films from *Just Pals* in 1920 to *Steamboat Round the Bend* in

1935, had recently left the studio and was retired by 1940. Joe August had signed a contract at RKO (where he would continue to shoot films for Ford).[79] But even if Ford turned to Glennon out of necessity, the cameraman would shortly become a stellar component of his preferred crew, pushing the director's lighting and staging technique in new directions. *The Prisoner of Shark Island* constitutes a kind of intermediary between August's highly diffused lighting and necessarily restricted use of depth in *The Informer* and the spectacular combination of low-key lighting and deep staging that Ford and Glennon would achieve in *Stagecoach*.

Darling's design of the prison set incorporated architectural features illustrated in the stills prepared from *Realm of Ghosts*. For example, the bridge and moat shown in the documentary (figure 6.5) was replicated in the equivalent set in Ford's film (figure 6.6). Ford's staging on this set evolves over several scenes. In figure 6.6, a straight line of prisoners accompanied by a looser formation of guards creates a perspective leading directly to the gate, formidable in its size and solidity. The two sailors in the left midground are offset from this strong linear composition. Stationed on a beaten earth pathway that runs along the moat, they aimlessly throw rocks into the water. In a composition that is otherwise directed toward the prison and the gate, their movement calls attention to the moat, providing a first, gentle, anticipation of the realm of the sharks. Later, Rankin summons up the sharks to intimidate the new prisoners, throwing meat to the fish from the bridge. This scene is staged in a series of framings which, like figure 6.6, are oriented towards the left of the gate. It seems that Ford decided to "save" the space to the right of the gate, which provides a much longer vista, for the night of the escape. In figure 6.7, the soldiers on the bridge have just opened fire on Mudd who is clinging to the wall in the background, barely visible through the biggest gap in the line.

The prison interior encompassed several sets – the roof top, several colonnaded passage-ways,

---

78   Patrick Keating, *Hollywood Lighting: From the Silent Era to Film Noir* (New York: Columbia Press, 2010), 192–194; the term refers to a tendency to foreground certain lighting conventions, e.g. glamour lighting.
79   On Ford's history with August see chapters two and four.

6.5

6.6

6.7

the dungeon – all built on the sound stages and unified through editing. Figure 6.8 shows one of the largest structures, the parade ground behind the main gate, with illuminated guard houses bordering the entrance. Figure 6.9 is a long shot of the two-story cell block, which, per the description in the script, was fronted by colonnaded walkways similar to ones shown in *Realm of Ghosts*. The turret midground left stands at the junction of two different passage-ways which apparently form a canted angle suggesting the hexagonal perimeter of the actual building. Figure 6.10 shows the rear of the prison, an area distinct from the parade ground behind the gate. In this scene, the feverish Dr. MacIntyre leaves his office in the building on the left and walks toward camera, observed by the group of soldiers in the background. Figure 6.11, shows the same narrow passage between the buildings from the opposite direction, with MacIntyre's office now on the right and Rankin

standing in approximately the same position as the group of soldiers in figure 6.10. The point is not that the casual spectator would necessarily have picked up on these spatial relationships, quite the contrary. As he did with the bridge set, Ford liked to reveal new spaces or transform already familiar ones for dramatic effect. The free-standing buildings establish a perspective across the depth of the set so as to create compositional high points which could be revealed at will. These spaces are not immediately readable in relation to the prison as a whole since they need to be hidden before the reveal, like rabbits in a hat until called forth by the magician. Figure 6.11, for example, derives from the middle of a long take that initially begins with Buck, panning as he leaves Mudd's cell and moves through the archway to exit off left. Without a cut, Rankin then unexpectedly enters from off right. He stares back in the direction of the cell, his suspicions rising and then moves in the direction from which Buck had come. The unexpected spectacular vista punctuates this significant moment – the beginning of the cat-and-mouse game between the officer of the guard and the prisoner.

There are some notable differences between the night lighting of *The Informer* and that of *The Prisoner of Shark Island*. Glennon and August both restricted overhead illumination, relying principally on focused, powerful arcs and multiple effects lights.[80] But Glennon's sets are typically shown in much more detail and greater depth than August's as a comparison of figure 4.31 from

6.8

6.9

6.10

6.11

The Informer and figure 6.11 from *The Prisoner of Shark Island* will clarify. As Gypo stands on a street corner watching Katie walk off into the fog, the sense of distance between them is largely a function of the contrast between his figure in sharp focus in the foreground, and the much softer figures of the girl and the horse and cart across the street. An array of effects lights – street lights and the weaker light spilling out of apartment windows – effectively suggests the surrounding city without defining the outlines of the set beyond the corner. The shot of Rankin on the parade ground in figure 6.11 also relies on the placement of effects lights to render a sense of depth – especially the diminished size of the lighted windows in the background, which are meant to seem farther away than the buildings on either side. But a low level of general illumination allows the contours of the set to remain

visible, and distinctly renders the separation of the overlapping planes of the buildings.

The differences in set lighting between the two films partly derived from Glennon's access to a new, more sensitive film stock, Eastman's Panchro Super X, which was introduced in March 1935, as well as a new focused arc, the Hi-Spot, from Mole Richardson. Super X was 75 per cent faster than Eastman's previous stock, Eastman Super Sensitive Panchro, which had been introduced late in 1931. At the same time, it proved to be very fine-grained.[81] Hal Mohr, who wrote of experimenting with the stock on *Captain Blood*, described it as especially sensitive to the blue of arc light: "In increasing the overall speed of Super X, the blue speed has been considerably increased, so that a beam of the bluer arc light [as compared to the more yellow light of incandescents] will make a surprisingly strong impression on the

81 Emery Huse, A.S.C., and Gordon A. Chambers, "Eastman Super X Panchromatic Negative Motion Picture Film", *American Cinematographer* (May 1935): 186–187, 196; see also, Emery Huse, A.S.C., "The Characteristics of Eastman Motion Picture Negative Films", *American Cinematographer* (May 1936): 190–192, 202–203.

film". He also commented: "Filming some of the night exterior scenes in the set built to represent the town where much of the action takes place, I have had 'Hi-Spots' projecting their beams successfully for more than 150 feet."[82] Similar units were probably used to light the set in the night scenes in *The Prisoner of Shark Island*.

In their article on Panchro Super X in *American Cinematographer* Emery Huse and Gordon Chambers also noted that cameramen had reported success in shooting actual night exteriors with the stock.[83] This was likely important for the open air set of the bridge and moat in *The Prisoner of Shark Island*. In figure 6.7, the bridge set, built on the North lot of the Fox Hills studio, is artificially lit.[84] A bank of arc light from off right softly illuminates the building and makes Mudd's figure dimly visible. Directed arc lights hidden behind the gateway bring out the arch and the men on the bridge. Directed light from off right rounds off the human figures and creates the cast shadows of the light fixtures on either side of the door. The same or a similarly placed light catches the smoke and fire effects as the rifles are discharged at Mudd. Lighting units hidden within the bridge reflect off the water and help to define this architectural feature.

The new stock's increased sensitivity facilitated Glennon's highly differentiated set lighting, permitting subtle variations in the multiple pools of directed light that he typically employed. In figure 6.8, a spotlight picks out the dungeon entrance in the ground foreground left. Strong light spills out of the guardhouse on the left, the interior of which is also decorated with cast shadows and two effects lights. The equivalent door to the right is similar but with a less complicated set up. A light from top right catches the massive archway above the gate and a spotlight mimicking the revolving lamp of the lighthouse passes across this opening as the guards bring in the recaptured Mudd in the background center.

The corridors, arches and pillars of the arcades provided Ford and Glennon with numerous opportunities to experiment with staging and lighting. Many shots feature the perspectives formed by the arcades, as in the case of figure 6.12 in which the receding line of the arches is echoed by the serried guns at the right and the light issuing through the arches from off left. The passageways also made prime locations for hiding and spying. In one of many such episodes, Glennon somehow managed to cast shadows in a primarily dark space. As a patrol marches down the enclosure in front of Mudd's cell, Buck sneaks around one of the pillars of the colonnade into the foreground (figure 6.13). Eventually, as the patrol moves to the left down the corridor, he will circle right around the pillar and take up a position behind the guards. Buck is lit from upper left, so that his shadow is cast on the pillar. Another light source, probably hidden within the colonnade, illuminates the back wall and provides edge-lighting on the marching soldiers. As the patrol moves down the corridor, a strong, directed arc situated farther along the passage casts the looming shadows of the guards on the back wall of the set (figure 6.14).

The play of light and shadow reaches a high point when Mudd makes his way to the front of the prison enclosure and confronts the revolving light of the lighthouse. This segment reveals a hitherto unseen part of the set, at the junction of the great gate and the cell block. Mudd, having traversed the second story of the arcade, spies Rankin hiding in wait for him perched high on a ledge on the far side of the gate (figure 6.15). Not only does this turn of events entail a surprising new perspective on the architecture of the prison, it also initiates a concatenation of lighting effects, rather like fireworks. The revolving light travels rightward across the front wall of the enclosure. Cut in to a closer view of Rankin, who moves further into the shadows to avoid exposure. Cut

---

82   Mohr, "Large Sets Call for Arc Lights", *American Cinematographer* (Nov 1935): 469, 478–479.
83   Huse and Chambers, 196.
84   Revised Shooting Schedule for *Prisoner of Shark Island*, 12 December 1935, *The Prisoner of Shark Island* Legal File, Twentieth Century-Fox Legal Department, indicates that the Exterior Bridge and Gate shots were scheduled to be taken on December 21 on the North Lot, Lower Moat.

6.12

6.13

6.14

back into long shot as the moving light travels towards Mudd's hiding place in the foreground. Cut to a view straight down the arcade with Mudd hiding rear left (figure 6.16). Rays of light from below penetrate two floor-level grates, apparently creating grid patterns on the back wall and the ceiling. As the revolving light hits him, Mudd comes forward and then falls to the floor, looking into the grate where he hears sentries talking below (figure 6.17).

These stills give ample evidence of how Ford's staging of figure movement and Glennon's lighting schemes both informed and took inspiration from Darling's set. Together these filmmakers met the requirements of Johnson's script as written, to the point of respecting his description of the lighthouse light, but they also forcefully reimagined Shark Island as a space of dramatic conflict and a powerful set of images.

A news item published in the *Hollywood Reporter* shortly after Zanuck took over Fox announced:

> Assistant directors on the Twentieth Century-Fox lots become more important as a result of Darryl Zanuck's policy – the same one he had at both Warners and Twentieth Century – the scripts, after final okay, are not be changed by directors during production. The new rule permits assistants to arrange set shooting schedules and details, which cannot be changed by the directors unless sanction is obtained from the front office. Giving the assistants policing powers is to stop the whims and sudden inspirations of directors who are apt to vary from the script or the daily work schedule.[85]

In an April 1935 interview in *Variety*, Johnson took an even more extreme position:

> What most directors contribute is a faithful adherence to the writer's script, besides seeing to it that the actors don't go home at noon. Save in those cases where the director works on the script himself – Capra and Lubitsch are first writers and then directors – the responsibility for a picture may be divided like this: the writer writes the story; the actors are its interpreters; the cutter, its editor.[86]

Despite this attitudinizing, which was probably in part a reaction to the newly organizing Director's Guild and its advocacy of directorial autonomy, it should be clear that from their first film together Zanuck had a collaborative relationship with Ford (and likely with the other A-list directors such as Henry King). Their teamwork developed through three principal avenues. First,

85 "Asst. Directors Get More Power at 20th", *Hollywood Reporter* (29 Aug 1935): 2; it should be noted that Ford's assistant director on *The Prisoner of Shark Island* and *Wee Willie Winkie* was Edward O'Fearna, his brother.
86 "Nunnally Johnson Not Getting That 3 G's", *Variety* (24 Apr 1935): 2.

6.15

6.16

6.17

despite Johnson's claims that Ford had nothing to do with the script, the six-week lag between Ford's start date and the commencement of production on *The Prisoner of Shark Island* suggests that Zanuck consulted Ford on at least the final, shooting, script. This supposition is supported by the examples of the director's later films for Twentieth Century-Fox for which story conference

notes survive.[87] Second, Zanuck knew Ford's films, and he built off what the director had done in the past. Hence the references to *Arrowsmith* and what seems to have been a deliberate reworking of set design and lighting strategies in *The Informer* for the Shark Island prison escape. Third, in his capacity as editor, Zanuck responded sensitively to what he found in the director's footage (which is not to claim that Ford approved of his cuts). This is borne out by the producer's re-editing of act four of *The Prisoner of Shark Island*. In the October script drafts, the interchange between Mudd and Buck in the dungeon is merely a prelude to the Commander's entrance there. Zanuck's decision to isolate the scene as a free-standing unit and place it in a much more prominent position suggests that he responded positively to the arresting combination of tenderness and despair that director, cinematographer and actors achieved.

87   This is especially clear in the memos concerning Johnson's script for *Tobacco Road*, see, for example, Zanuck, Memo to Ford, 24 October 1940, Ford correspondence, Lilly Library, IU.

Chapter 7

Wee Willie Winkie

O f all the films that Ford directed at Twentieth Century-Fox before World War II, the ones written and produced by Nunnally Johnson, *The Prisoner of Shark Island* and *The Grapes of Wrath*, offered the fewest opportunities for the director to tinker with the script. In *The Prisoner of Shark Island*, this was due to the fact that the story originated with Zanuck and the producer took final responsibility for script revision. In *The Grapes of Wrath*, once Zanuck had approved Johnson's highly respectful adaptation of Steinbeck's novel, the script was tamper-proof. In contrast, although *Wee Willie Winkie* started out as a Zanuck project, and one that Ford agreed to make partly in order to get leave to make *The Hurricane* at UA, he ultimately became quite imaginatively invested and intervened directly in plot construction. The film exemplifies a new level of trust and collaboration between the director and the head of the studio.

Script Development

The prolonged script development process for *Wee Willie Winkie* began in late July 1936 at a time when Ford was still at RKO finishing *The* *Plough and the Stars*. Zanuck, associate producer Gene Markey and the screenwriters first assigned to the project, Howard Ellis Smith and Julian Josephson, produced multiple outlines and tentative treatments.[1] The first complete script by Smith and Josephson, dated November 23, 1936, apparently does not survive but was the subject of two story conferences.[2] When Ford returned to the studio on December 2, 1936, he attended the second of these. He was then actively involved in pre-production during December, 1936, and January, 1937, and clearly contributed to the three drafts produced by Ernest Pascal and Julien Josephson at this time.[3]

Zanuck's decision to adapt a Kipling story seems to have been initiated by the publicity attendant upon Rudyard Kipling's death on January 18, 1936. At this time, two adaptations of the author's works by major film companies were already under way. In May 1935, Robert Flaherty had begun location shooting in India for Alexander Korda's *Elephant Boy* (London Films Productions, Robert Flaherty and Zoltan Korda, April 1937), a film based on Kipling's story "Toomai of the Elephants", which launched the career of the young Sabu. At about the same time, MGM began shooting background footage for *Rudyard*

---

1   The script materials for *Wee Willie Winkie* are split between USC and the Fox studio files. The following items may be found in the *Wee Willie Winkie* file in the Twentieth Century-Fox Collection, Cinematic Arts Library, Doheny Library, USC: Treatment-Outline, 25 Jul 1936, Howard Ellis Smith; Conference with Mr. Zanuck, 30 Jul 1936, on Treatment of 25 Jul 1936; Story Outline from Notes, 24 Aug 1936, by Howard Ellis Smith and Julian Josephson; Treatment by Howard Ellis Smith and Julien Josephson, 31 Aug 1936 (in pencil completed 28 Sep 1936); Notes on Conference with Mr. Markey, 8 Sep 1936, by Howard Ellis Smith; Continuity Treatment, 18 Sep 1936, by Howard Ellis Smith and Julien Josephson; Conference with Mr. Zanuck, 27 Nov 1936 on First Draft Continuity of 23 Nov 1936; Conference with Mr. Zanuck, 14 Dec 1936, on First Draft Continuity of 23 Nov 1936; Conference with Mr. Zanuck, 8 Jan 1937, on Temporary Script of 5 Jan 1937. The following scripts, all by Ernest Pascal and Julian Josephson were in the *Wee Willie Winkie* Story File, Twentieth Century-Fox Legal Department: *Wee Willie Winkie*, Temporary, 5 Jan 1937; *Wee Willie Winkie*, Revised Temporary, 14 Jan 1937; *Wee Willie Winkie*, Final Script 18 Jan 1937.
2   Conference with Mr. Zanuck, 27 November 1936, on First Draft Continuity of 23 November 1936; Conference with Mr. Zanuck, 14 December 1936, on First Draft Continuity of 23 November 1936, both in *Wee Willie Winkie* file, Twentieth Century-Fox Collection, Doheny Library, USC.
3   As discussed in chapter six, Ford prolonged his vacation from late August, 1936, until early December in order to accompany art director Richard Day who was scouting locations for *The Hurricane*.

Kipling's Captains Courageous (Victor Fleming, May 1937), with Spencer Tracy and child actor Freddie Bartholomew. Twentieth Century-Fox began efforts to acquire the rights to "Wee Willie Winkie" in July 1936, and studio correspondence indicates that the producer was already planning to change Kipling's boy protagonist to a girl in order to create a role for Shirley Temple.[4]

In the short story, Winkie is the darling of the 195th regiment which his father commands, on the Afghan-Indian border. He has been raised according to military discipline: "When he was good for a week, he drew good-conduct pay; and when he was bad, he was deprived of his good-conduct-strip. Generally he was bad, for India offers so many chances to little six-year-olds of going wrong." Winkie particularly admires the Lieutenant he has nicknamed "Coppy". When he spies Coppy's girlfriend recklessly riding off into the forbidden territory across the river, he follows on his pony. He manages to release the pony just before he and the girl are surrounded by Pashtun tribesmen. The pony returns to the army post, thereby alerting the regiment to mobilize a search for the boy. Meanwhile Winkie enters into negotiations with the tribesmen in Pashto, a language he has learned from a groom in the army stables. When the regiment arrives, the tribesmen disappear into the hills, and Winkie, who Coppy fully expects to be Colonel of the regiment one day, is congratulated on his first successful foray on behalf of the British empire.

There are several reasons why "Wee Willie Winkie" would have appealed to Zanuck. He had already essayed a story which paired a child with a grizzled fighting man: one of the first films he produced at Twentieth Century-Fox was *Professional Soldier* (Tay Garnett, 1936), from a story by Damon Runyon, starring Victor McLaglen opposite Freddie Bartholomew. In addition to allowing the producer to match Temple with

McLaglen, Kipling's "Wee Willie Winkie" offered him an opportunity to rematch the award-winning combination of Ford and McLaglen and to revisit the setting, if not the romance plot, of Ford's *The Black Watch*.

The Black Watch served as a reference in multiple ways during script development. It was likely the source of Zanuck's decision to transform the 195th from an English into a Scottish regiment. At the December, 1936, story conference the producer suggested, or perhaps was prompted to suggest, the musical possibilities inherent in the film, making a clear reference to Ford's previous film: "For our opening title background we will have a formation of Highlanders with their bagpipes, marching directly into camera, six abreast, filling the screen."[5] Indeed, *Wee Willie Winkie* employs the two primary pipe-and-drum marches used in *The Black Watch*: "Wha Saw the Forty Twa", and "Blue Bonnets Over the Border".

The early script drafts of *Wee Willie Winkie* are set in Peshawar and the adjacent Khyber pass, the primary setting of the intrigue in *The Black Watch*. Zanuck advised Ellis Smith and Josephson to read the script of Ford's film for its handling of the political situation on British India's northern border.[6] Although late in the script-development process Zanuck decided to avoid controversy with British censors by setting the film in an unspecified location in northern India rather than explicitly in Peshawar, the scripts continued to invoke the goals of securing a pass which, like the Khyber Pass, is of strategic importance, and preventing the Pashtuns from fomenting revolt in India.[7] In this regard, Zanuck also seems to have borrowed from a film with a similar British colonial setting, *Lives of a Bengal Lancer* (Paramount, Henry Hathaway, 1935).

When Ford returned to the studio in early December, the primary characters had been determined. Unlike Kipling's Winkie, brought up

---

4   Twentieth Century-Fox producer Julian Johnson explained to the legal department that the role was to be adapted for Temple during early discussions about acquiring the film rights, Julian Johnson, Telegram to ? Costain, 6 Jun 1936, *Wee Willie Winkie* Legal File, Twentieth Century-Fox Legal Department; Rudyard Kipling, *Wee Willie Winkie and Other Stories* (New York: Hurst & Co, 1891, first published Allahabad (now Prayagraj, Uttar Pradesh, India): A. M. Wheeler & Co., 1888).

5   Conference with Mr. Zanuck, 14 December 1936, on First Draft Continuity of 23 November 1936, *Wee Willie Winkie* file, Twentieth Century-Fox Collection, Doheny Library, USC; see figure 2.2 from *The Black Watch*.

6   Conference with Mr. Zanuck, 30 Jul 1936, on Treatment of 25 Jul 1936, *Wee Willie Winkie* file, Twentieth Century-Fox Collection, Cinematic Arts Library, Doheny Library, USC.

7   The general region is now in Pakistan but when the script was being written it was part of the British Raj.

in India in a family run according to strict military discipline, Priscilla (later renamed Winkie) is an American, and a newcomer to the regiment and the region. The story revolves to a large extent around her efforts to establish a relationship with her grandfather, the martinet who commands the regiment. In the romance subplot, the young lieutenant nicknamed Coppy courts Priscilla's widowed mother, Joyce. In addition to these transformations of Kipling's original characters, Smith and Josephson invented a part obviously written for McLaglen, a comic Scottish sergeant, MacDuff, who befriends Priscilla. Working from slight references in the Kipling story, Zanuck and the screenwriters also developed two principal Pashtun characters: Khoda Yar (changed to Khoda Khan in the film), a tribal leader involved in a plot to steal rifles from the British, and Din Mohammed (changed to Ramji mid-way through script development and then to Mohammet Dihn), a servant in the Colonel's household who is initially conceived as a mercenary and unscrupulous Pashtun.[8] In addition, the writers introduced Mrs. Allardyce, wife of the chief medical officer, who is antagonistic to both Joyce and Priscilla.

In composing the plot, Zanuck spent a great deal of time imagining different scenarios for the final confrontation between the British and Pashtun forces for which there was no precedent in the short story. He immediately rejected Kipling's motivation for sending Winkie into forbidden territory in the first place, holding it highly unlikely that a six-year-old could saddle a pony quickly enough even to try to follow an adult on a horse.[9] Instead, Priscilla would decide to go into rebel territory in an effort to prevent fighting between the regiment and the Pashtuns. She would be aided by Mohammet Dihn who, having been dismissed, takes the child to Khoda Khan partly out of revenge and partly in hopes of a reward.

In an early story conference Zanuck re-enacted the scene between Priscilla and her grandfather which motivated the child's decision to leave the post and enter Pashtun territory:

> A scene with the Colonel – she asks him why the men are being brought in wounded, cut up – why do they have to go out? Why was the Drummer Boy hurt? Why should they kill somebody they don't even know? She asks him every unexplainable question. Gently, he tries to explain to her that men have to die – that's why they are soldiers. When a man becomes a soldier, if he is a good soldier, that is the way he wants to die – with his boots on. But why? Why is Khoda Yar angry? What did they do to him? He tries to explain – she asks embarrassing questions: "But it's their country, isn't it – they were here first?" He tells her about England – a little island … the English Queen doesn't want fighting – she wishes for peace and happiness, but Khoda Yar cannot be made to understand. The child asks: "Well, why don't they go and tell him that? I bet if they told him, he would stop". The Colonel tells her they *have* tried. She ventures: "I bet if *I* told him, he'd stop … ".[10]

A major contrast between Kipling's Winkie and Zanuck's Winkie was thus in place from the very first discussions of the script. The boy in the short story is conversant with the British officers' attitude toward the Pashtuns, which he adopts: "I am the Colonel Sahib's son, and my order is that you go at once. You black men are frightening the Miss Sahib. One of you must run into cantonments and take the news that the Miss Sahib has hurt herself, and that the Colonel's son is here with her."[11] But Priscilla's questions to her grandfather are "embarrassing" precisely because she hasn't the remotest idea of the political ramifications of England's position as an occupying force. She speaks from a naive perspective, trying to understand what drove the Pashtuns to wage the war that killed her friend – initially the boy Mott (the Drummer Boy referred to above) but later changed to Sergeant MacDuff. It should be noted that Zanuck's sense of the final act's dramatic

---

8   For clarity, I will refer to the characters by the names given in the film, but have preserved the original names in quoting scripts and other studio documents.
9   Conference with Mr. Zanuck, 30 July 1936, on Treatment of 25 July 1936, *Wee Willie Winkie* file, Twentieth Century-Fox Collection, Cinematic Arts Library, Doheny Library, USC.
10 Conference with Mr. Zanuck, 30 July 1936, on Treatment of 25 July 1936, *Wee Willie Winkie* file, Twentieth Century-Fox Collection, Cinematic Arts Library, Doheny Library, USC.
11 Kipling, *Wee Willie Winkie*, 19.

climax entailed a friendship between Priscilla and Khoda Khan, that is, her anticipation of addressing the tribal leader in the scene sketched out above presupposes familiarity between them. In later treatments, the screenwriters created two scenes in which Priscilla defies orders so as to speak to Khoda Khan, who has been imprisoned on the Army post. From an ideological perspective, Priscilla's affinity with the chieftain and her blindness to racial differences are among the most interesting aspects of the plot.

During the December story conference, which Ford attended, Zanuck was still not satisfied with the handling of the stand-off between the British and Pashtun forces. He called for a clearer sense of the impending confrontation that Priscilla eventually helps to ward off: "We want to have a good scene where we find the British force on a hilltop overlooking the headquarters of Khoda Yar. They are assembled – guns, etc. The Colonel tells them he is going down there alone, under a flag of truce – if he is not back in half an hour they are to strike and annihilate the stronghold." Zanuck also proposed to anticipate the final confrontation through building up the subplot relating to the theft of British guns and to transform Mohammet Dihn from a disgruntled former employee into a devious spy. He asked the screenwriters for "a stronger counterplot which would run straight through from beginning to end – so that at all times we are conscious of something impending – something going on behind the story". He described the counterplot as follows:

> Behind our main theme – that of a child winning over the Colonel – is the powerful undercurrent – the natives smuggling guns and starting a revolt. This will be accomplished mainly through the change of character of Mohammet Dihn who will be in Khoda Yar's secret service … . The gun smuggling which we are now only vaguely aware of, should be more important – it should be a strong thread which runs all through – and with a few suggestions to be outlined it will come to life.[12]

The screenwriters were thus advised to improve the scene in which Priscilla sees Khoda Khan arrested for gun smuggling just after her arrival in what the producer decided to call "Raj Pore". In addition, Zanuck suggested new incidents in which Dihn sent and received secret messages and kept an eye on the Khan in prison (only one of these incidents actually survived in the completed film).

In the next story conference, January 8, 1937, further changes were recommended for the film's last act. Up to this point, the producer and screenwriters had accepted Kipling's original assumption of the military superiority of the British. Zanuck had consistently described the British forces as high up in a position from which to ride down and destroy Khoda Khan's stronghold, if at the expense of Priscilla's life. But in the January conference, Zanuck imagined the Pashtuns at the top of the hill. And the fact that he took the unusual step of asking Ford to describe the fort set being built at the Iverson Ranch in Chatsworth suggests that Ford was a party to this revision of the storyline.

> Mr. Ford described the set – the almost impregnable fort built on huge boulders of stone on a hilltop – banners of different tribes flying from it, and the steps leading up to it. We recognize almost instantly that the only means of getting to the fort is through this slope of stone steps – this is where the British will have to charge before they can come to the entrance – which is heavily gated. The entire stronghold is manned with tribesmen.[13]

Ultimately it is not possible to determine if this change originated with Zanuck or Ford (or was taken by one or both from *Lives of a Bengal Lancer* in which the set of the Khan's stronghold was also filmed at the Iverson Ranch and positioned to the disadvantage of the British forces). What seems most important is first, that the change coincided with the process of set construction on location, a process in which Ford was undoubtedly involved, and second, that producer

---

12   Conference with Mr. Zanuck, 14 December 1936, on First Draft Continuity of 23 November 1936, *Wee Willie Winkie* file, Twentieth Century-Fox Collection, Cinematic Arts Library, Doheny Library, USC.
13   Conference with Mr. Zanuck, 8 January 1937 on Temporary Script of 5 January 1937, *Wee Willie Winkie* file, Twentieth Century-Fox Collection, Cinematic Arts Library, Doheny Library, USC.

7.1

7.2

and director worked out the ramifications of this idea together.

A description of the Iverson Ranch appeared in the *Los Angeles Times* in August, 1937, just after shooting was completed on *Wee Willie Winkie*:

> Thirty years ago a middle-aged gentleman named Aaron Iverson bought for practically nothing a ghostly, awesome, high plateau of waterless terrain, cut by deep ravines, peopled with jagged, erupted rocks, eighteen miles from Los Angeles … . This barren strip of land, still designated by its owner the "farm", but known to film producers as Chatsworth ranch, is the most popular of all "locations" and today nets the 70-year-old Iverson a grand total of $40,000 a year.[14]

In preparing *Wee Willie Winkie*, Twentieth Century-Fox built three sets on the ranch site – a suite of buildings which comprised the British army post, the striking open-walled meeting room supposedly within Khoda Khan's fortress and, at a separate ranch site, the heavily guarded stairs bordered by towers and leading to the fort gate.[15] Figure 7.1 shows the completed stair set, built into the rock formations that made the Iverson ranch such a desirable location. Figure 7.2 shows the gate and walled-off area at the top of the steps. Although it is not possible to determine when construction on the fort set began, the first mention of the scene on the stairs in the shooting

schedules is March 9. This date would have allowed ample time for construction following Zanuck's and Ford's revised plan for the final act in early January.[16]

The new-found vulnerability of the British forces seems to have given Zanuck what he was looking for in the film's last act. His revised account of the military stand-off at the January 8, 1937, story conference runs to six typewritten pages. It is quite close to the completed film, anticipating the editing pattern of alternation between the two armies preparing to engage as the Colonel begins to ascend the stairs. The tension escalates until Priscilla breaks away from the Pashtuns and runs down the steps to join her grandfather, a dangerous situation which is resolved when Khoda Khan orders his men to stand down.

With the final act, the character of Khoda Khan seems to have fallen into place for the producer as well. In the January story conference he suggests that "We are going to make Khoda Yar a potential threat of more importance than he is [now]".[17] He revisits an earlier scene in which the chief is questioned, changing what had been an informal interchange to a British attempt at negotiation. The Major General offers to release the chief providing he will guarantee peace. "Khoda Yar doesn't even answer – completely ignores them – finally he tells them he wants nothing –

14 Shelia Graham, "Location Sites Reap Huge Profits", *Los Angeles Times* (22 Aug 1937): C1.
15 The sets are discussed on the Iverson Movie Ranch blog, "A Secret Set Location Where Shirley Temple starred", posted October 17, 2020: https://iversonmovieranch.blogspot.com/2022/01/a-hidden-filming-location-for-john.html.
16 Shooting Schedule, 6 Mar 1937, *Wee Willie Winkie* Legal File, Twentieth Century-Fox Legal Department.
17 Conference with Mr. Zanuck, 8 January 1937, on Temporary Script of 5 January 1937, *Wee Willie Winkie* file, Twentieth Century-Fox Collection, Doheny Library, USC.

they can do what they want with him, etc. Then, when he escapes it promises us something big. This is not just another tribesman from the hills – it is a man of great importance." Zanuck's description of the Khan's bearing during the final conflict on the stairs also clearly suggests that what is at stake for the character goes far beyond the fate of the child. When he receives a missive from the British threatening to attack unless he releases Priscilla, he replies: "Khoda Yar has long waited for the British to climb these steps".

Zanuck's reconsideration of Khoda Khan's character at the January story conference was augmented by Ford's suggestion at the same meeting that the chieftain be largely amused by Priscilla. Zanuck picked up this idea in his description of Priscilla's meeting with Khoda Khan in the fortress. He describes the Khan going into gales of laughter when the child explains that the Queen only wants peace and to help all her people, a laughter that is magnified by the assembled warriors. This is a great improvement on the temporary draft of January 5, 1937, that was under discussion. In that draft, Priscilla met with the Khan's warlike brother in his absence. The brother was impressed with her bravery but paid little attention to her, and treated her largely as a hostage. In the final shooting script and the film, Khoda Khan and his officers actually listen and respond to Priscilla's ideas. Their laughter expresses both Pashtun skepticism towards the claims of the colonial power, and a mocking but, at least in the case of the Khan himself, affectionate stance toward the child – an attitude summed up by his great response when Priscilla complains about being laughed at: "Allah himself would laugh, my child".

Wee Willie Winkie from Script to Film

In the January story conference, Ford made a seemingly casual suggestion that illuminates the changes he made to the plot of *Wee Willie Winkie* in production. He proposed making "a few quick cuts of what Winkie sees when they drive into the Post". In fact, these shots were ultimately placed on the morning after Priscilla and her mother arrive at the outpost. The final shooting script had called for a shot of the daily flag-raising ceremony with a squad in formation and Mott on the drum. This served as a transition between two comic scenes. In the first, the waking of the men in the barracks, the sleeping MacDuff is plagued first by Sneath on the bagpipes and then by Mott who blows a bugle in his ear. In the second, Priscilla, already dressed, attempts to make conversation with a sentry. Ford expanded the single shot of the flag-raising ceremony into a series of shots, establishing a parallel between the rousing of MacDuff and the rousing of the girl.

Shot 167. Long Shot, two turbaned soldiers, presumably Sikhs, ceremonially fire off a cannon.

Shot 168. Medium Shot. Priscilla awakes with a start in response to the sound. A trumpet call begins, off.

Shot 169. Medium Long Shot. Low angle, a soldier in pith helmet playing the reveille. Pan left to pick up the Union Jack being raised.

Shot 170. Long Shot. Priscilla emerges from the mosquito netting around her bed. Reframe right as she runs to the window and peers through the blinds. The reveille continues.

Shot 171. Long Shot. The flag nears the top of the pole.

Shot 172. Medium Shot. Priscilla at the window. As she raises the blinds, light apparently comes through the window, casting a striated pattern on her features.

Shot 173. Very Long Shot. Priscilla's point of view. The parade ground of the army post, bugler mid-center, the flag pole to his right in front of the headquarters (figure 7.3). A pipe-and-drum band stands in formation near the flag pole. After the reveille concludes, the bugler exits right. The band begins to play "All the Blue Bonnets Over the Border". Horses, men and dogs enter from the side and from behind the camera and move swiftly towards the flagpole (figure 7.4).

Shot 174. Medium Long Shot. Highland soldiers in kilts as they quickly come together in formation. The band music continues.

Shot 175, as *Shot 172*. Priscilla moves back from the window and lets the shade fall, presumably eager to dress and explore. The band music continues.

7.3

7.4

Shot 176, as *Shot 174*. The drill sergeant, off, shouts orders to the company, as the men shift the position of their rifles and turn their heads to the right (to face camera). The band music continues until the dissolve to the next scene.

These point-of-view shots stress the excitement and curiosity inspired by the fort as a place and as an institution. The music explicitly recalls the more formal but similarly stirring use of the pipe-and-drum band in the gatherings of the officers in *The Black Watch*, Moreover, as critics have noted, this scene of awakening to the bugle call and the raising of the flag is quoted in *Fort Apache* (Argosy, 1947), made with an adult Shirley Temple, in which shots from her character's point of view similarly dwell on the movements of men and horses in the open space of the parade ground with the rugged landscape visible beyond. In both films, the shots introduce physically isolated and closely populated compounds shortly to be riven by domestic as well as military conflicts, with the flag and the music evoking an initial sense of unity and purpose. To Zanuck, *Wee Willie Winkie* was a story about Temple's character softening a grumpy grandfather, as she had in many previous films, and, less commonly, taming an armed insurgent. But for Ford, this was a story about a little girl who enters into a community and, however improbably, discovers that she wants to be a soldier.

A comparison of the final shooting script and

the completed film reveals that Ford effectively rebalanced the middle section of the story, expanding the sections that dealt with MacDuff and truncating both the subplot concerning Dihn's activities as spy and that concerning Priscilla's problems with Mrs. Allardyce. It is difficult to determine how much Ford and Zanuck collaborated on the changes made by the director on set. There is no correspondence between them relating to this production in the studio files. In addition, new scenes added by Ford were not numbered in the final shooting script and hence cannot easily be traced via the surviving shooting schedules (additional numbers would have been added to the Daily Production Reports, but these were not preserved in the Twentieth-Century Fox Legal files). There is also a conflict between the schedules, which suggest that shooting was to be completed on March 13, and the evidence of the trade press, which indicates that the film was in production for at least another week.[18] The delay was probably the result of unusually inclement weather in February that made it difficult to work on the exterior sets at the Iverson ranch and entailed the multiple postponements recorded in the successive shooting schedules. The most reliable information we have about the end of production is to be found in reports that Ford flew to Honolulu on the China Clipper on March 24, 1937, and that Zanuck wrapped up *Wee Willie Winkie* on March 27.[19] The confluence of these dates

18 "Wyler Tests *Hurricane*: Rolls When Ford Free", *Hollywood Reporter* (12 Mar 1937): 18, reports that Ford was still in production on *Wee Willie Winkie* so that Wyler had to shoot screen tests for *The Hurricane* at Goldwyn; both "Advance Production Chart", *Variety* (17 Mar 1937): 18, and "Majors, Independents...". *Hollywood Reporter* (22 Mar 1937): 10–11, list *Wee Willie Winkie* as still in production.

suggests that director and producer were working together to cope with the production delays necessitated by the weather. In this context it seems likely that they also reached agreement about what scenes in the final shooting script to cut, either before or after shooting, and how to handle the new material that Ford wanted to introduce.

The truncation of the spying subplot helped to make the raid more of a surprise. Ford was partial to surprises, as has been established with regard to the race in *Steamboat Round the Bend*, where the bet on the race is established in act one, briefly recalled in the middle section, but then subsumed by other events only to re-emerge unexpectedly at the close. In contrast, as per Zanuck's instructions, the script drafts after the December, 1936, story conference, built suspense around the brewing Pashtun revolt by having Dihn surreptitiously watch Priscilla's interactions with Khoda Khan, and covertly signal his cohorts in the hills on the night of the dance and subsequent raid. In the film, however, Dihn sends no signals after having tricked Winkie into delivering a secret message to the Khan early in act three. The close of act three in Raj Pore and the preparation for the dance at the British settlement in act four are entirely devoted to the romance plot. Winkie persuades her grandfather to take her mother to the dance while Joyce sneaks out a back window to join Coppy outside the pavilion where the dance is held. By the time the Colonel turns up at the dance looking for Joyce, we are expecting a confrontation between the Colonel, his daughter-in-law and the errant lieutenant who has deserted his post as sentry in order to court her. Concern about the secret message has faded into the background. The raid that interrupts the dance is thus largely unexpected, and thanks to the manipulation of music and effects, provides a rather astonishing tonal contrast.

The truncation of the Allardyce subplot involved more substantial eliminations. In the final shooting script, the scene in which MacDuff renames Priscilla is a brief incident set within the emerging conflict between the girl and her nosy neighbor. After coming up with the name "Wee Willie Winkie", MacDuff orders Mott to drill the new recruit. The disgruntled Mott orders Winkie to march through mud on the parade ground, then directs her through a bed of petunias in Mrs. Allardyce's garden. Mrs. Allardyce appears, Mott flees and Winkie is marched off to the Colonel's where Mrs. Allardyce complains about the girl's behavior and the lack of maternal supervision. Later, Priscilla's new puppy, Archie, not only bites Mrs. Allardyce, as in the film, but pulls off her petticoat. Furious, she puts pressure on her husband, the chief medical officer, to take action against supposedly rabid canines on the post. This subplot originally culminated in an elaborate scene in which all of the dogs on the post are rounded up to be destroyed, at which point Winkie intervenes. The round-up episode was crossed out in the final shooting script and never filmed. Other components of the dog subplot – Archie's removal of Mrs. Allardyce's petticoat, and a scene in which the matron persuades her husband to take action – were either never filmed or cut in post-production.

The presence of Mott and the forced march through Mrs. Allardcyce's petunias having been eliminated, the renaming of Priscilla takes on much greater importance in the completed film. The director retained much of the dialogue for the renaming as written, but mobilized all of the resources of the shot – camera movement, staging in depth, music, and the actors's stellar performances – to create something that went well beyond what the screenwriters had written. In a relaxed and charming eighty-three-second take MacDuff and Winkie walk and talk in the vicinity of the headquarters building. McLaglen and Temple's camaraderie finds expression in their parallel handling of props – he carries a swagger stick under his arm and she carries a small parasol – and the apparently spontaneous way that they walk, pause and resume in tandem. The camera tracks right as the actors move, holding hands (figure 7.5). Priscilla complains: "Who ever heard of a soldier called Priscilla". MacDuff agrees that no one

19   "Around Town with Chatterbox", *Los Angeles Times* (22 Mar 1937): A6, reports that Ford is due to fly from San Francisco on Mar 24; "Zanuck Finishes his '36–'37 Slate", *Hollywood Reporter* (30 Mar 1937): 1.

7.5

7.6

would take her seriously with such a name. The actors then come to a stop for McLaglen's line: "I've got it, I've got it – Wee Willie Winkie!" The line initiates a non-diegetic version of "Wha Saw the Forty Twa", the march heard over the titles and generally associated with MacDuff. The orchestration is much gentler in this instance, the bagpipes having been replaced by the softer timbres of woodwinds and the drums by strummed strings and bells.

The actors resume strolling to the musical accompaniment as they discuss the nursery rhyme from which the name derives. McLaglen's line delivery has an improvised feel.

> *Temple*: Was he [Willie Winkie] a friend of yours?
>
> *McLaglen*: Aye. He was a lad that ran through an old Scotch rhyme. Wee Willie Winkie ran through the town – Wee Willie Winkie ran through the town – ran through the town … . Well, he was a lad that was always getting into difficulties … .

Their talk is interrupted as they pass a line of soldiers at attention in the foreground. MacDuff pauses, takes a pith helmet from the hands of a man at the end of the line, and places it back on the man's head. Winkie echoes her grandfather's previous warning to her: "Sunstroke! Bad!" They then resume walking and discussing the rhyme:

> *Temple*: Was he a sergeant?
>
> *McLaglen*: He would have been, when he grew up.

The gradual accumulation of soldiers drilling

in the background of the long take contrasts with the actors' leisurely stroll in the foreground. In figure 7.5, a single sentry moves at right angles to the direction of their movement. When they stop to salute two officers, a substantial formation of soldiers is visible background right (figure 7.6). By the time of Temple's line: "Then I'd be Private Winkie!" and MacDuff's corresponding salute on the line: "Private Winkie it is – a full-fledged soldier of the Queen", the background group has been expanded even more by the appearance of a line of mounted soldiers in the far rear center.

Ford added other details which stress the affinity between Winkie and MacDuff and show her gradual acclimatization to the Highland unit. After Winkie has been given a uniform (from Mott by way of MacDuff), the sergeant takes her to the barracks. In the script, Winkie is left outside the barracks as MacDuff corrals the men to come outside. In the film, Winkie enters the barracks where the sergeant shows her a photograph of himself as a boy in a Highland uniform, furthering the unlikely parallel between them. Ford and his actors also invented an additional comic drilling scene to celebrate Winkie's initiation into the group. Outside the barracks, she joins the men in formation and McLaglen, doing a parody of a tough-talking sergeant, roughly criticizes her technique, to her evident delight, and gives absurdly precise commands: "Now on the third syllable of the word 'tuuuuurrrnn' ye smartly turn to the right, snapping the left heel against the right heel, with the toes at the angle of forty-five degrees, approximately". Once they begin to march, Temple is shown at the end of the line, gamely stretch-

7.7

7.8

ing her legs to keep up with the group. There is no soft pedaling on this occasion, "Wha Saw the Forty Twa" is done straight, orchestrated for pipes and drums.

Ford further developed the relationship between the girl and the sergeant by enlarging upon a brief scene in the final shooting script in which Winkie, forbidden to drill with the men and confined by the Colonel to her mother's quarters, is given a brief reprieve to go out. She asks to join the Highlanders who are at target practice. In the film, Winkie is shown sewing with her mother, prettily dressed and bored to tears. Seizing on the arrival of visitors to make an exit, she encounters MacDuff leading his men in a boxing lesson. He easily evades his hapless student, Mr. MacTavish, while providing commentary to the assembled group: "You see, the man has no footwork." The scene encompasses several violations of gender expectations, as if to flaunt the Colonel's restriction of Winkie to women's quarters and female-gendered activities. With Winkie looking on, the Highlanders jump from side to side to practice their footwork, their kilts swaying gently from side to side (figure 7.7). But, when prompted to demonstrate "the punch", MacDuff delivers it with such force that the three men who attempt to break the victim's fall, as well as Sneath standing behind them, are sent flying backwards. Boxing gloves on his hips, MacDuff tells the unconscious Mr. MacTavish that he will never make a boxer. Then, seeing Winkie, he joins her, taking her doll on his lap. When she asks to be taught the "manly art of self-defense", he refuses, sadly referring to the Colonel, while correcting her fighting stance

(figure 7.8). He wipes away tears with a gloved hand while Winkie turns away from camera to wipe away hers.

While the boxing lesson might seem like a digression, it is actually less of one than the elaborate dog plot which it partly replaced. First, it anticipates the scene in Khoda Khan's fortress, in which Winkie similarly confronts a hyperbolically male group's rough behavior and aggressive postures, and which similarly gives way to a tender scene between the girl and the group's leader. In addition, the gender reversals of the boxing lesson call attention to the more fundamental gender reversal inherent in Zanuck's decision to make Kipling's Winkie into a girl. This was not simply a matter of her preferring boxing to needlework, but of fundamental narrative structures. Kipling's Winkie follows his upbringing as an English officer and a gentlemen and goes into enemy territory to protect Coppy's girl. Ford and Zanuck's Winkie has no equivalent birthright. Instead she is a girl with a habit of asking questions and a talent for turning up where she is not expected and not supposed to be – making friends with Khoda Khan, marching with the troops and participating in barracks life. When she opts to go into enemy territory, she initially appears to be the spy's dupe, putting her own life as well as the regiment at risk. But the tables are turned when her grandfather faces enemy fire on the stairs to the fortress and she takes a place at his side. The regiment may have mobilized to rescue the girl, but in the end, the rescue worked the other way. Hence the line that Ford has Mott speak at the film's close: "I am forced to admit that you make

7.9

7.10

7.11

a very good soldier. You covered yourself with glory and distinction on the field of battle."

The funeral for MacDuff, killed on a patrol following the raid, clearly formed part of the director's sustained exploration of the relationship between Winkie and the Sergeant. While the director later asserted that this sequence was a spur-of-the-moment decision, he actually signaled his intention to shoot it as early as the story conference of January 8, 1937.[20] In both the final shooting script and the film, the wounded MacDuff dies as Winkie sings him "Auld Lang Syne", at which point she exits, assuring the doctor and the weeping Drum Major Sneath that the Sergeant is "asleep". The script then proceeds to a scene of Winkie crying in her mother's lap after she has realized that the Sergeant is in fact dead. Ford's funeral procession takes the place of the scripted

scene with her mother. The death scene, a one-minute-and-forty-second-long take in which Temple performs "Auld Lang Syne", culminates in Sneath playing the first notes of "Lord Lovat's Lament", a slow march, on his bagpipes. The march is taken up by a full pipe-and-drum corps in the subsequent shots of the men assembled to honor their comrade. It continues over cuts to Winkie in the barracks. A shot of the company marching toward camera with a serried rank of cavalry horses on the right (figure 7.9) cuts to a graphic match of Winkie entering the barracks and walking toward camera against the rows of empty cots on the left (figure 7.10). Cut away to the funeral procession then back to a closer view of Winkie as she looks through MacDuff's trunk and finds the photograph of the young MacDuff he had shown her earlier. She cries: "Sergeant MacDuff ... they are taking you away from me. I want you to come back and play with me some more". Cut back to a very long shot of the funeral procession (figure 7.11). Thus, the funeral actually serves as a vehicle for representing Winkie's realization of MacDuff's death and consequently of the costs of war. Her feelings are expressed in the simple terms appropriate to her age, but the military pageantry of the funeral lends her words much greater solemnity and force. Moreover, the funeral leads directly into Winkie's searching questions to her grandfather about the origins of the animosity and violence between the British

20 In Philip Jenkinson, "John Ford Talks to Philip Jenkinson about Not Being Interested in Movies", *The Listener* (2 Dec 1970), reprinted in Peary, ed., 138, Ford says: "Well, we were out there and I said: 'It's a mistake in the story to kill McLaglen off, because he's one of the leading characters, but at least if we're going to kill him off, let's give him a funeral.' It was in the rain, so I said, 'Let's shoot it in the rain.'"

and the Pashtun tribes. Zanuck, who rejected the motivation for Kipling's Winkie to enter enemy territory as "hokey", could not have asked for better motivation for his heroine.

While the script development process at Twentieth Century-Fox was always firmly controlled by Zanuck and his associate producers, the example of *Wee Willie Winkie* makes it clear that Ford, and presumably other A-list directors, could have input at the level of story structure. First, directors could make suggestions at story conferences, as Ford did when he suggested a "few quick cuts" of Winkie's first view of the fort and the inclusion of a funeral for MacDuff. Even if the screenwriters did not follow up on the director's suggestions (which in these cases they did not), it was thereby possible for Ford to float ideas and signal his intentions prior to the start of production. Once on set, Ford could build up existing scenes, as he did with the renaming of Priscilla, or replace one scene for another, as in the substitution of MacDuff's funeral for the scene of Winkie crying in her mother's lap. One wonders how many of the changes that Ford made to the middle section of *Wee Willie Winkie* were planned, if not shared, during the script development phase: they certainly cohered as a set and pushed the plot in a new direction.

The examples of *The Prisoner of Shark Island* and *Wee Willie Winkie* help to clarify how it was possible for a fiercely independent director such as Ford to collaborate successfully with a hands-on producer such as Zanuck, and why Ford decided to sign on for a ten-picture deal with Twentieth Century-Fox at the close of 1937. First, Zanuck clearly knew Ford's films and sought to build on his strengths. This is indicated by the manifold ways in which *Wee Willie Winkie* takes off from *The Black Watch*. The producer's approach must have been particularly appealing to the director after Sam Briskin at RKO took *The Plough and the Stars* out of his hands, ordering retakes without any understanding of what the director had been trying to accomplish. Second, the increasing stability and prosperity of Twentieth Century-Fox

7.12

in the years following the merger meant not only that Ford received a substantial raise, as noted above, but also that he could essay increasingly elaborate productions. The size and complexity of the prison set in *The Prisoner of Shark Island* and the three exterior sets built at the Iverson Ranch for *Wee Willie Winkie* go well beyond what Ford and Darling had been able to create at Fox in the early 1930s – they are rivaled only by the monumental sets they made (or revamped) for *4 Sons* and *The Black Watch* under William Fox's regime. Third, Twentieth Century-Fox offered Ford access to a greatly enhanced talent pool that drew on the combined resources of Fox, 20th Century and United Artists.

In addition to pairing Ford and Glennon on *The Prisoner of Shark Island* as discussed above, on *Wee Willie Winkie* Zanuck brought Ford together with cinematographer Arthur C. Miller for the first time. Miller had already shot three films with Shirley Temple and was experienced with the challenges of framing and lighting her. In addition, like Glennon, Miller had experimented with Eastman Super X stock early in 1935 when the cameraman found that the smaller and softer lighting units facilitated by the stock were particularly advantageous for lighting children.[21] Ford might have been impressed with Miller's use of light in the Chatsworth location, in which Miller managed to combine gentle artificial light for facial modeling with a landscape flooded by sunlight (figure 7.12).[22] He selected Miller as the

21 Harry Budick, "Don't Show Them Everything … Is Arthur Miller's Policy", *American Cinematographer* (May 1935): 191, 200.
22 Arthur Miller, A.S.C., "Lighting Shirley Temple", *American Cinematographer* (Mar 1937), 94, 100.

second-unit cameraman to shoot the scenes on location on the Sacramento River for *Young Mr. Lincoln*. The cinematographer would also serve as director of photography on *Submarine Patrol*, *Tobacco Road* and *How Green Was My Valley*, the latter winning the Academy Award for best cinematography in 1942.

Zanuck's UA connections were brought to bear when the producer decided to borrow Newman from Goldwyn in order to complete the score for *Wee Willie Winkie*. Although Newman had already scored the director's *Arrowsmith* at UA, that film had a minimal number of cues, and it was only with *Wee Willie Winkie* that his importance as a collaborator in post-production became evident. When Newman took up work sometime in April 1937, the marches "Wha Saw the Forty Twa", "All the Blue Bonnets Over the Border" and "Lord Lovat's Lament", had already been recorded. This was done in February or March, maybe taken on location but more probably in the studio so that the music could be played back during photography.[23] Newman wrote many cues for *Wee Willie Winkie* beyond the pipe-and-drum marches, but his treatment of the marches is of particular interest as it illustrates how much the composer added beyond their direct recording, the strategy employed in *The Black Watch*. He undoubtedly composed and conducted the sweeter version of "Wha Saw the Forty Twa" without bagpipes that underscores the renaming of Priscilla. In the conversation scene between Winkie and MacDuff that precedes Temple's performance of "Auld Lang Syne", he repeatedly modulates between fragments of that folk tune, "God Save the King", and *The Black Watch* march tune played at a very slow tempo and scored for strings, woodwinds and triangle.

Fragments of the march are also played over the full orchestral score associated with the preparations of the Khan's army during the confrontation between Pashtun and British forces. Newman's importance for Ford's œuvre came from his capacity to accept, and value, Ford's interest in historically rooted and recognizable tunes while simultaneously making use of more contemporary methods of cue-based orchestral scoring and introducing more sophisticated harmonies and rhythms than is typical of folk music. He went on to score all of the director's Twentieth Century-Fox films beginning with *Young Mr. Lincoln* and, as a freelance musician, also *The Man Who Shot Liberty Valance*.

Thus, by the end of 1937 Ford was in a good position to build a new production unit at his home studio: his producer was controlling but solicitous of his talent; he could count upon a well-organized process of script development in which he sometimes participated; he could draw upon a greatly enriched set of collaborations in the areas of art direction and set design, cinematography, and music. The only thing he lacked was an actor to anchor the unit, a star on the order of Will Rogers. This would turn out to be a major difficulty, since McLaglen was no longer able to carry a feature on his own and no one, not even Zanuck, thought the director was good for another Shirley Temple vehicle. The problem would not be solved definitively until the *annus mirabilis* of 1939, in which Ford found not only one but two axioms of cinema, the stars that would carry his filmmaking enterprises through the 1930s and beyond: *Stagecoach*, produced in 1938 and released early in 1939, with John Wayne in the leading role, and *Young Mr. Lincoln*, produced and released in 1939, with Henry Fonda.

---

23 The recording of the marches is discussed by James O'Keefe, Memos to George Wasson, dated 25 February and 9 March 1937, *Wee Willie Winkie* Legal File, Twentieth Century-Fox Legal Department; on the loan of Newman see "Newman Tunes *Wee*", *Hollywood Reporter* (29 Apr 1937): 18.

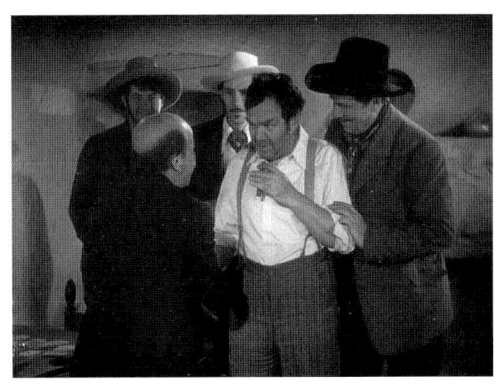

Part 4
Annus Mirabilis

Chapter 8

Stagecoach

Ford made seven films in the three-year stretch from August 1938 to August 1941, five of them undoubted masterworks: *Stagecoach, Young Mr. Lincoln, The Grapes of Wrath, The Long Voyage Home,* and *How Green Was My Valley.* Two of these, *The Grapes of Wrath* and *How Green Was My Valley* were studio projects which originated with Zanuck. In contrast, *The Long Voyage Home* was a full-fledged independent production. This adaptation of Eugene O'Neill's *Glencairn* play cycle was scripted by Ford and Nichols, and produced by Ford and Cooper's newly incorporated Argosy company under a contract with Walter Wanger and United Artists.[1] This section treats two films that may be considered as somewhere in between these two extremes and in different ways and for different reasons constituting initial steps towards the formation of Argosy and its post-war incarnation. The relationship is obvious in the case of *Stagecoach,* the first Wanger film, Ford's first Western with John Wayne in a leading role, and Ford's first use of Monument Valley as a location. While *Young Mr. Lincoln* was made at Twentieth Century-Fox, it was not a Zanuck project but rather a Ford-inspired one inherited from the previous Fox regime. Moreover, Henry Fonda's first collaboration with Ford would prove vital for Ford's transition from Twentieth Century-Fox

contract director to independent producer, a transition one can trace in the actor's post-war roles: *My Darling Clementine,* the last film on Ford's Twentieth Century-Fox contract; *The Fugitive,* the first post-war Argosy film; and *Fort Apache,* where he co-starred with John Wayne and an adult Shirley Temple in a film that inaugurated the series of post-war Argosy westerns starring Wayne.

The United Artists Connection

With the demise of Ford's unit at RKO in the fall of 1936, the director began to explore new venues for independent production, all of them involving companies that distributed through United Artists. Faced with a grave product shortage following the departure of Zanuck and Schenck's 20th Century, UA made new deals with producers Walter Wanger, David O. Selznick, and investor John Hay Whitney's Pioneer Pictures, which employed Merian Cooper. Ford negotiated with all of these prior to signing his revised long-term contract with Twentieth Century-Fox in December, 1937. In January, 1936, he negotiated a two-picture deal with Cooper.[2] At this point, Pioneer had moved off the RKO lot and into UA offices and was slated to release films as part of the UA program.[3] It seems likely

---

1   Argosy was incorporated in May of 1939, Minutes of the First Meeting of the Board of Directors of Argosy Corporation, 13 May 1939, Argosy Pictures Corporation Business Records, MSS 1849, Box 3, Vol II; for Argosy's agreement with Wanger to produce *The Long Voyage Home* see Agreement, 17 February 1940, signed by representatives of Argosy, Wanger and United Artists, Argosy Pictures Corporation Business Records, MSS 1849, Box 10, Folder 8, both in L. Tom Perry Special Collections, Harold B. Lee Library, BYU. Eugene O'Neill originally wrote seven one-act plays about the S. S. *Glencairn* and its crew – see Eugene O'Neill, *The Long Voyage Home: Seven Plays of the Sea* (New York: The Modern Library, 1946) – but the four chosen for adaptation in Ford's film formed a cycle that was presented at the Provincetown Playhouse in 1924 and revived in 1937, see R. Dilworth Rust, "The Unity of O'Neill's *S. S. Glencairn*", *American Literature,* 37/3 (Nov 1965): 280–290.
2   The trade press described it as a four- picture deal, "Ford's 4 Pioneers", *Variety* (15 Jan 1936): 7, but according to Ford's 1937 revision of his contract with Fox, it was a two-picture deal, see note 13.
3   "Pioneer Pictures in 15 U.A. Offices", *Hollywood Reporter* (20 Aug 1935): 2; "Cooper Now Active as Pioneer Head", *Hollywood Reporter* (25 Sep 1935): 2; "Cooper to United", *Hollywood Reporter* (26 Feb 1936): 1.

that the duo were hoping to be able to recreate the free-wheeling partnership that they had enjoyed at RKO when Cooper as president had enabled Ford's productions of *The Lost Patrol* and *The Informer*. The first film announced on Ford's Pioneer contract did not come to fruition, but is of interest for its anticipation of *Fort Apache*. It was to be based on the life of General George Armstrong Custer, and to be shot on location and in what *Variety* called "tint".[4] Later in 1936, shortly after Walter Wanger set up his company at United Artists, Ford reportedly signed a one-picture deal with him to adapt Alfred Batson's novel *African Intrigue*.[5] Zanuck's approval of Ford's backhanded deal to make *The Hurricane* with Goldwyn created another avenue to UA, putting Ford on the studio lot for an extended period in 1937.[6] Moreover, in April, as *The Hurricane* project got under way, the trade press announced that directors Ford and Tay Garnett along with producer Lester Cowan were looking for studio space and planning to release through United Artists. *Variety* reported: "Set up will follow pretty closely the line hewed by Walter Wanger and David Selznick, with Whitney and Giannini money said to be part of their backing".[7] While this deal never materialized, it further corroborates Ford's interest in establishing himself in the United Artists orbit.

Ford was probably acting upon the expectation of going independent when he purchased the rights to Ernest Haycox's story "Stage to Lordsburg" in June of 1937.[8] By this date, Selznick-International had absorbed Pioneer Pictures.[9] Cooper was thus working for Selznick when he and Ford pitched the *Stagecoach* project to the executive. But the deal fell apart due to Selznick's doubts about the story and the proposed casting of John Wayne and Claire Trevor in the leading roles.[10] More fundamentally, the producer was not about to give up control of any project undertaken by his company, even if it had originated with Cooper. His memos on the *Stagecoach* project indicate that he assumed Ford was now under contract to him via Pioneer and he expected to select Ford's assignments.[11] In the event, Cooper resigned from Selznick-International and went to MGM.[12] For his part, Ford renegotiated his contract with Zanuck, doubtless assuming that one talented, ambitious and controlling producer was more than enough. The revised agreement with Twentieth Century-Fox left open the possibility of freelance work outside his home studio, however, specifying outstanding commitments for one picture with Wanger and two pictures with Pioneer.[13]

When negotiating Ford's leave from Twentieth Century-Fox to make *Stagecoach* in June of 1938, Harry Wurtzel justified it as the fulfillment of the director's one-picture deal with Wanger.[14] This suggests that *Stagecoach*, originally pitched to Selznick as a Pioneer project, had replaced the

---

4   "Pioneer's *Custer* in Tint", *Variety* (22 Jan 1936): 5; "M. C. Cooper Due Back to Start on *Custer*", *Variety* (4 Mar 1936): 6; "Cooper Knocks *Custer* Off Pioneer Program", *Hollywood Reporter* (9 Mar 1936): 2. Ford was inspired by a biography, Frederic F. Van de Water's *Glory-hunter; a life of General Custer*, that he first proposed for a film at 20th Century, Zanuck, Memo to Ford, 13 April 1935, Ford correspondence, Lilly Library, IU.

5   "Ford to Direct Wanger Pic", *Hollywood Reporter* (25 Sep 1936): 3; "Wanger's Meggers", *Variety* (30 Sep 1936): 3; "Cromwell, John Ford to Wanger on Singles", *Variety* (26 May 1937): 7.

6   Ford's deal with Goldwyn is discussed in chapter six.

7   "Ford, Garnett and Cowan Talking Indie Prod. Deal for Quality Pix", *Variety* (14 Apr 1937): 3.

8   "Ford Buys *Stage*", *Hollywood Reporter* (17 Jun 1937): 1; "Story Buys", *Variety* (23 Jun 1937): 23; Ernest Haycox, "Stage to Lordsburg", *Collier's Weekly* (10 Apr 1937): 18–19, 68–69.

9   "See Merger of Selznick, Pioneer by Jock Whitney for Economy", *Variety* (10 Jun 1936): 5; "Selznick Heads Prod'n in Full Pioneer Absorption", *Hollywood Reporter* (20 Jun 1936): 1; "Selznick Prez of Merged Film Co.'s", *Variety* (24 Jun 1936): 5.

10   For Cooper's account of his negotiations with Selznick over *Stagecoach* see Ron Haver, *David O. Selznick's Hollywood* (New York: Knopf, 1980), 224, 226; and Rudy Behlmer, *America's Favorite Movies: Behind the Scenes* (New York: Frederick Ungar Publishing Co., 1982), 107–108.

11   Selznick, Memo to [John Hay] Whitney and [John] Wharton, 29 June 1937 and Selznick, Memo to [Daniel T.] O'Shea, 16 July 1937, both in Behlmer, *Memo from David O. Selznick*, 116–118. Eyman, *Print the Legend*, 190–194, discusses Selznick's efforts to get Ford to direct another project for him.

12   "Cooper, North as M-G Prods"., *Variety* (21 Jul 1937): 5.

13   Letter of Agreement, John Ford and William Goetz, Twentieth Century-Fox, 28 Sep 1937, John Ford Contract File, Twentieth Century-Fox Legal Department.

14   Harry Wurtzel, Letter to Goetz, 1 June 1938; Harry Wurtzel and Ford, Letter to Wasson, 17 August 1938, both in John Ford Contract File, Twentieth Century-Fox Legal Department.

Batson project originally intended for Wanger. Indeed, a letter from Nichols to Ford written after the release of *Stagecoach* suggests that the director had even contemplated remaining at UA to direct an adaptation of the Batson novel after completing the Western.[15] Presumably that project was put on hold when Ford had to return to Twentieth Century-Fox to direct *Young Mr. Lincoln*. And, by the time of the Argosy deal with Wanger in 1940, the Batson project had morphed into *The Long Voyage Home*. Writing to Goetz to justify the director's leave for this UA project, Harry Wurtzel argued that Ford's two-picture deal with Pioneer had been absorbed by Argosy.[16] Given that Selznick-International had actually taken over Pioneer, it is not at all clear that this claim would have held up in a court of law. But, it probably did represent how Ford and Cooper viewed the Argosy venture – as a reboot of the production arrangement the partners had hoped to put in place at Pioneer.

If Ford was moving towards independent-producer status when he made *Stagecoach*, it was not only because of his relationship with Cooper, but also, and perhaps primarily, due to the expansion and solidification of his professional network. When the director had made *The Lost Patrol* and *The Informer* at RKO, he had had to expend considerable time and effort to make a place for his star, his screenwriter and his cinematographer at that studio. But in the case of *Stagecoach* and the great films that followed, Ford was able to move readily across studios with his preferred cast and crew, taking advantage of long-standing labor-sharing agreements between Zanuck and Goldwyn, and Goldwyn and other UA producers such as Wanger.[17] For example, after Glennon shot *The Prisoner of Shark Island* at Twentieth Century-Fox, Ford convinced Goldwyn to bor-

row him for *The Hurricane*. Wanger also borrowed Glennon for *Stagecoach* before director and cinematographer ducked back into Twentieth Century-Fox for *Young Mr. Lincoln*. Similarly, after Zanuck borrowed cinematographer Gregg Toland from Goldwyn for *The Grapes of Wrath*, Wanger also made a deal to get the cinematographer for *The Long Voyage Home*.[18] In addition to the inevitable Ford stock company players such as Francis Ford and Harry Tenbrook, major actors also migrated with Ford from studio to studio. John Carradine had played for Zanuck in several 20th Century productions and followed the producer to Twentieth Century-Fox. But, after his role in *The Prisoner of Shark Island*, he appeared in *Mary of Scotland* at RKO, *The Hurricane* for Goldwyn and *Stagecoach* for Wanger, before returning to his home studio for *Drums Along the Mohawk* and *The Grapes of Wrath*. Berton Churchill and Claire Trevor, both Fox stalwarts, took major roles in *Stagecoach*. Although Thomas Mitchell was not contracted to Twentieth Century-Fox, he was engaged by both Goldwyn and Wanger for the director's UA productions: *The Hurricane*, *Stagecoach* and *The Long Voyage Home*. Donald Meek, a freelancer often cast as timorous characters, first worked for Ford at Columbia in *The Whole Town's Talking*, appeared in *The Informer* at RKO, moved to UA for *Stagecoach*, and ended up cast against his usual type in *Young Mr. Lincoln*. Thus, there is much greater continuity of cast and crew between Ford's Twentieth Century-Fox and UA films than there had been between the RKO and Fox films he made before the merger. By the end of the decade Ford was moving smoothly and seamlessly between studio contract work and his freelance productions, taking the skills and contacts developed in one context and applying them to the other.

---

15 Nichols, letter to Ford, 26 Mar 1939, Ford correspondence, Lilly Library, IU; the possibility of Ford remaining at UA to direct another film following *Stagecoach* is mentioned in Harry Wurtzel and Ford, Letter to Wasson, 17 August 1938, John Ford Contract File, Twentieth Century-Fox Legal Department.

16 Harry Wurtzel to William Goetz, 11 Jan 1940, John Ford Contract File, Twentieth Century-Fox Legal Department.

17 "See Goldwyn Veering to 20th", *Variety* (13 Mar 1940): 5; "Champ Talent Lender", *Variety* (5 Jun 1940): 4; Berg, *Goldwyn*, 327–328, 337–339, 348–349, argues that as Goldwyn's relationship with UA deteriorated in the late 1930s, he produced fewer films and increasingly resorted to loan-outs to support his studio and his staff.

18 Wanger made two agreements securing the loan of Toland and his camera crew, see the two letters, both Reeves Espy, Samuel Goldwyn Inc., Letter of Agreement with C. E. Ericksen, Walter Wanger Productions, 26 February 1940, United Artists Corporation Records, Series 4G, Walter Wanger Preproduction, Box 2, Folder 1, Wisconsin Center for Film and Theater Research, Madison, Wisconsin (hereafter WCFTR).

Story Structure

Ford and Nichols's plot is extremely complicated, drawing on three other sources in addition to Haycox's short story about a prostitute and a gunman traveling by stagecoach through hostile Apache territory. Maupassant's "Boule de suif", which seems to have inspired the Haycox story, and which Ford acknowledged as an influence, deals with a carriage primarily occupied by respectable citizens fleeing Rouen during the Franco-Prussian war.[19] Maupassant dwells on the fine distinctions between mercantile, haut-bourgeois and aristocratic couples, as well as the different ways in which the men and their wives react to the presence of a prostitute in the coach. But all of them, as well as the two nuns who are also traveling, eventually pressure her to sleep with the Prussian officer who obstructs their passage. This story probably contributed to Ford and Nichols's emphasis on class differences in *Stagecoach*, a theme that is not particularly salient in Haycox's story.

The filmmakers also borrowed the initial situation of Bret Harte's "The Outcasts of Poker Flat", in which several louche characters are forced out of town by the local populace, which has been temporarily energized by "the loss of several thousand dollars, two valuable horses, and a prominent citizen".[20] In *Stagecoach*, Doc Boone (Mitchell) and Dallas (Trevor) are forced out by what Ford and Nichols identify as the organized, respectable middle-class women of the town, the Ladies League. Although the satire is heavy-handed in comparison with Harte's, their version of this situation sets up the distinctions between more and less respectable characters that are perpetuated within the stagecoach itself.[21] At the top of the hierarchy of passengers is the unimpeachable Lucy Mallory (Louise Platt), the pregnant wife of an army officer traveling to join her husband. While Hatfield (Carradine), the elegant town gambler, is initially represented as suspect, his bad reputation averred by both Curly, the sheriff (George Bancroft), and one of Lucy's female friends, he is soon revealed as having been a gentleman and officer in Lucy's father's Confederate regiment. Peacock (Meek), although a whiskey drummer, is a married man with five children and a mysterious air of sanctity. The ostensibly respectable town banker Gatewood (Churchill), whose wife is one of the leaders of the Ladies League, has gone on the lam with money he has embezzled from his bank. Ringo (Wayne), encountered on the road newly escaped from jail, joins Dallas and Doc at the bottom of the coach hierarchy. Buck (Andy Devine), the driver, remains somewhat outside this hierarchy, although as a friend of Ringo and a working man with a large family from Chihuahua, he is on the lower end of the spectrum. Curly, riding shotgun on the stage in the hopes of garnering the reward for the capture of Ringo, eventually takes on the role of expedition leader, partly because it is his job to protect people and maintain order, and partly because he wants to get his prisoner safely to the authorities in Lordsburg.

Edmund Goulding's *Grand Hotel* (MGM, 1932), famously an ensemble plot, comprised a third influence on the story structure. In a 1939 interview, Ford and Nichols explained that their story was "conceived in the *Boule de Suif-Grand Hotel* tradition", and indeed, at the time of the film's release, it was dubbed "*Grand Hotel* on wheels".[22] Both films depend upon the unexpected contrasts and convergences that develop from a group of randomly assembled protagonists each pursuing their own goals, a form David Bordwell has described as "network narratives".[23] But the ensemble of characters in *Stagecoach* does not remain as motley as it at first appears. The

19 Guy de Maupassant, "Boule de Suif", in *Contes et nouvelles*, 1, Bibliothèque de la Pléiade (Paris: Gallimard, 1974), 83–121, first published in *Les Soirées de Médan* (Paris: Charpentier, 1880).
20 Bret Harte, "The Outcasts of Poker Flat", in *The Luck of Roaring Camp and Other Stories* (New York: Penguin Books, 2001), 27–37 (originally published in the *Overland Monthly* in January 1869). Ford directed what seems to have been a rather free adaptation with this title starring Harry Carey for Universal in 1919, unfortunately a lost film.
21 The ramifications of this scene are analyzed in Gaylyn Studlar, "Be a Proud, Glorified Dreg: Class, Gender and Frontier Democracy in *Stagecoach*", in Barry Keith Grant, ed., *John Ford's Stagecoach* (New York: Cambridge University Press, 2003), 132–157.
22 Mok, in Peary, ed., 21–23; Review of *Stagecoach*, *Variety* (8 Feb 1939): 17.
23 David Bordwell, "Mutual Friends and Chronologies of Chance", in *Poetics of Cinema* (New York: Routledge, 2008), 191.

journey itself enfolds them in an over-arching, goal-driven logic, one emphasized by Devine's frequent sing-song recital of the stations along the way: Tonto, Dry Fork, Apache Wells, Lee's Ferry, Lordsburg. Moreover, the threat of attack by militant Apaches under Geronimo that is immediately established in the film's prologue provides a highly unifying narrative squeeze, especially as it intensifies from act to act.[24] In act one, in which the passengers are gradually assembled, Lieutenant Blanchard warns the group that they travel at their own risk but leads the armed escort that mitigates this risk during the first stage of the journey. Act two begins with the arrival in Dry Fork. The passengers decide to proceed despite the fact that the soldiers they expected to accompany them on the next stage, including Mrs. Mallory's husband, have moved on. Buck takes an alternate route through the high mountains in the hopes of avoiding Apache war parties, the first of a series of hardships that passengers and driver endure. Act three begins with the stage's arrival in Apache Wells, where they encounter a much more dangerous situation than at Dry Fork. Not only have the soldiers moved on ahead of them, but Captain Mallory has been injured in a skirmish, and, after dark, some of the horses are stolen. The birth of Lucy's baby further increases the vulnerability of the group, and occasions another discussion about whether or not to proceed.

Act four begins as the stage departs from Apache Wells after smoke signals are sighted, a threat that quashes all debate. But Lee's Ferry proves to be an even more dangerous place than Apache Wells. This time the travelers find no help or refuge, only the remains of buildings in flames and a woman's corpse.[25] The men must improvise a means of floating their vehicle across the river, and after accomplishing this task, briefly suppose they have reached safety on the opposite shore of the river. But after a short respite, an Apache ambush forces them off the trail and onto an open plain, instigating a fast-moving and spectacular

battle. It concludes with the last-minute arrival of the cavalry that the travelers have been seeking throughout their passage. That is, by the end of act four, there is a very strong sense of closure; the threat of Apache attack has been overcome and the stage brought safely into Lordsburg.

As act five begins, several of the other subplots subtended by the journey are also resolved. Hatfield has already died in battle. After the Army medical wagons pull in to Lordsburg, Dallas says goodbye to Lucy and her baby, and to the injured Peacock. Gatewood is arrested for theft directly after descending from the stage. The bulk of act five is thus comprised of the plots that are "left": the revenge plot involving Ringo, Curly's related attempt to bring Ringo back to jail, and the romance involving Ringo and Dallas. While Hollywood narrative and genre conventions might certainly lead us to identify these as central, the film nonetheless risks anti-climax given the multiple endings which occur in succession at the end of act four and the beginning of act five. Thus, it is worth considering how the various subplots were interwoven to foreground the intertwined stories of Ringo and Dallas and maintain our interest through to the film's final point of closure.

Ringo's vendetta is set up in the first scene between Buck and Curly in Tonto, and is reinforced in their conversation along the route. There is also a weighty pause when Doc Boone asks Ringo about his brother, whose broken arm he once fixed, and Wayne responds with a brief sentence dripping with menace: "He was murdered." This plot is given a new twist from the perspective of Dallas after Ringo proposes. She does not want him to risk his life dueling in Lordsburg, and she also does not want him to discover her profession there. She manages to persuade him to run away, but at the very last minute her plan is derailed through its intersection with two of the other subplots: Curly, on the alert for his prisoner, retains Ringo just at the point that the latter has stopped in his tracks after spot-

---

24 Robin Wood points out that the way stations get progressively "more primitive" in "Shall We Gather at the River? The Late Films of John Ford", *Film Comment*, 7/3 (Fall 1971): 12.

25 This scene has a basis in the Haycox story, in which the travelers find the ranch house initially described to them as marking the "safe" zone burned to the ground. Ford returned to this scenario with the arrival of Captain Brittles's unit at Sudro's Wells in *She Wore a Yellow Ribbon*. In *The Searchers*, Ethan describes wrapping Lucy in his coat before burying her, a repetition of Hatfield's gesture of covering the dead woman with his.

8.1

8.2

ting the smoke signals in the hills. This particular configuration of subplots arouses great sympathy for Dallas and generates suspense about what will happen to her when the coach reaches Lordsburg, if its reaches Lordsburg.

Bordwell argues that ensemble plots tend to link stories through parallelism as well as causal logic. *Stagecoach* has several ongoing parallels which give rise to clear-cut symbolic associations or oppositions. Hatfield and Lucy, a couple established by their shared history, and by the use of Stephen Foster's "I Dream of Jeanie with the Light Brown Hair" in association with the gambler, provide a strong contrast to Ringo and Dallas. While the scene in the lunch room at Dry Fork is often discussed in terms of its emphasis on Lucy's optical point of view, and, in moral terms, her disapproval of Dallas,[26] it also importantly sets up an implied contrast between the couples: southerners versus westerners, aristocratic versus humble origins, propriety and decorum versus directness and informality. These oppositions are reinforced by the later episode of the proffered drink, in which Hatfield offers Lucy water in a collapsible silver cup engraved with his family crest while leaving Dallas to drink directly from the stage's canteen. Ringo jokes: "No silver cup!"

An additional, partially comic, parallelism connects Doc to Dallas – both cast out of Tonto but rehabilitated through service to Lucy. The scripts specifically call for a major change in Dallas after assisting at the birth: "Dallas stands there, the little bundle of wailing life wrapped in a bigger bundle of blanket. The last of hardness has vanished from Dallas as she holds the infant in her arms." In the case of Doc, the scripts indicate his weariness as he returns to the bar for the bottle he had corked before sobering up. In the film, Ford and Mitchell play this in a mock heroic mode. The men gather as Peacock circles round to shake his hand saying simply, "Doctor Boone" (figure 8.1). Then, with a slight shift of the eyeline, Mitchell looks toward the bar and moves right anticipating his first swig (figure 8.2). But Doc's character *is* actually transformed in the succeeding scenes. Dallas goes to him for advice about Ringo's marriage proposal and he counsels her and facilitates their meeting in the kitchen. Whereas he took a jocular and devil-may-care attitude during the company's first discussion about whether or not to proceed from Dry Fork, in Apache Wells he speaks seriously and modestly, recommending that mother and baby be allowed to rest in place for a day. He even makes up with Hatfield, who had previously despised Boone but now demands respect for the doctor's "professional opinion". His heroism during the battle – tending to Peacock's wound while punching out the hysterical Gatewood – culminates in Lordsburg when Doc backs up Ringo by going face to face with Luke Plummer in the bar. After Plummer passes him by, he quips: "Never let me do that again." But, while not quite a Western hero by the story's

---

26   Nick Browne, "The Spectator-in-the-Text: The Rhetoric of *Stagecoach*", *Film Quarterly* 29/2 (Winter 1975–1976): 26–38; Gallagher, 231–236.

close, his trajectory nonetheless runs parallel to Ringo's as well as Dallas's.

In its assimilation of the stories by Haycox, Maupassant and Harte with the ensemble plotting of *Grand Hotel*, *Stagecoach* resembles the magpie plot construction of Ford and Nichols's scripts for *Judge Priest* and *Steamboat Round the Bend*, which were also assembled from disparate sources. But in its sense of predetermination – of gradual and inevitable progress towards ends that are foreseen from the start – it is much closer to their first two RKO scripts. The steady escalation of the threat of Apache attack over the course of the journey recalls the steady attrition of the British unit under siege in *The Lost Patrol* and the persistent accounting for Gypo's dwindling resources as he spends and drinks his way to execution in *The Informer*. All of these stories predictably proceed from bad to worse, with only minimal respite and no surprises. In the case of *Stagecoach*, the progression is eventually relieved by two last-minute reversals – the arrival of the calvary in act four, and Ringo's victory over the Plummers in act five, with the latter reversal supported by Curly's change of heart. While quite welcome, these reversals are both deeply embedded in genre conventions and foreshadowed within the film itself, given that the passengers have been trailing behind the cavalry throughout their journey, and that the build-up to the moment of the duel has been accompanied by an emphasis on Ringo's superior marksmanship. Even the birth of the baby in *Stagecoach*, which surprises Buck, is not unexpected by audience members familiar with 1930s circumlocutions such as "You shouldn't be traveling in your condition". And, while ensemble plots typically play off chance encounters and accidental congruences, Ford and Nichols's close co-ordination of the subplots in *Stagecoach* subsumes every character within the tight compass of the film's grand design. Drunkard is paired with whiskey drummer. Union veteran is pitted against Confederate officer. The high-minded respectable army wife is warned against traveling with the very outcasts she must ultimately depend upon when giving birth. Thus, while *Stagecoach*

certainly looks forward to the post-war Westerns, it just as surely looks back towards a method of plot construction that Ford and Nichols essayed in the middle 1930s and that the director would eventually jettison.

Even a cursory comparison of *Stagecoach* with *Wagon Master*, the 1950 Western that is also organized around a journey, reveals the latter's reliance on happenstance and surprise. Like the prologue in *Stagecoach* that establishes the threat of Geronimo, the pre-credit sequence in *Wagon Master* introduces the major antagonists: the Cleggs are shown committing murder in the course of a robbery. These characters are immediately set aside, however, as the narrative picks up the horse traders Sandy and Travis who eventually sign on to guide a Mormon wagon train headed west. At the beginning of the second act, a chance meeting with a group of traveling players stranded in the desert makes for a socially incongruent addition to the group. Differences between the Mormons, cowboys and worldly actors come to the fore as they make their way across the desert. But about halfway through the film they reach a river and come together in a celebratory dance. This ritual is interrupted by a most unwelcome surprise, the arrival of the Cleggs, which puts the newly constituted alliances under stress. Ford described *Wagon Master* as coming "closest to being what I wanted to achieve".[27] It is structured to produce the unexpected plot turns of a film like *Steamboat Round the Bend* rather than the intricate and high unified network of *Stagecoach*.

Script Revisions and Songs

Given that Ford was in charge of script development from the start, he was not in the position of remaking someone else's scenes or sequences in production. Nonetheless, it is instructive to note the changes he opted for in production and post-production. In particular, the score had to be rewritten late in the production process to remove a song that had been integral to it. This necessitated the addition of a new scene and had

27 Bogdanovich, *John Ford*, 88.

important consequences for dialogue and characterization. It is a mark of the importance of songs to Fords' films that changes to the score entailed changes to the story as well.

Nichols signed with Wanger for the *Stagecoach* project in August, 1938, about two-and-a-half months before production began.[28] Wayne recalled what was presumably an early stage of script development in which Ford would "make Nichols write a scene five or six times till Nichols was just about drenched. And then he'd find three lines out of three scenes that Dudley had written and use them for that particular speech."[29] The publicly available versions of the script are undated but derive from much later in the development process. The earlier one, a copy of which is in both the Nichols and the Ford papers, contains inserts of three new pages dated November 4 or 5, 1938. The later one, in the Wanger papers, has over twenty new pages dated November 11 or 14, 1938 (both versions are entitled "Final Continuity").[30] But even the earlier version reflects advanced production planning: all of the principal cast members are identified, the script includes diagrams of the seating arrangements inside the coach, and there are references to shooting in Monument Valley. Most of the differences between the initial and final version are quite minor. One of the most consequential, on new pages dated November 11, 1938, transforms the characterization of Billy Pickett, manager of the station at Dry Fork, to create a comic role for Francis Ford.[31] Another change was made in the scene in which Lucy and the baby are carried away after arriving in Lordsburg. In the earlier version there is no communication between Lucy and Dallas, who is left without a word of thanks. This version of the scene may be an inheritance from "Boule de Suif", where, after the prostitute

has rescued the other passengers from the Prussian officer, they revert to their original contemptuous treatment of her. In pages dated November 11, 1938, there is a note: "Mr. Ford wishes to cover above scene by shooting it a second way." The new pages contain the dialogue as it exists in the film, in which Lucy gratefully tells Dallas to be in touch if she ever needs anything and then pauses, embarrassed, as she recollects her own snobbish refusals of Dallas's offers of help prior to the baby's birth.[32]

The gag in which Peacock is repeatedly misrecognized as a clergyman is motivated in all the script versions. In the lunch-room scene at Dry Fork, the salesman explains that he inherited a whiskey business from his wife's family and abandoned his plans to become a clergyman as a result. These lines were eliminated during production. The director may have decided that the gag would be funnier if he simply relied upon Donald Meek to convey an air of sanctity without explicit motivation, or he may have decided to focus on the relationship between Doc Boone and the Francis Ford character for comic relief in the Dry Fork scenes.

All of the scripts are much more explicit about Ringo's sexual naïveté than the completed film. For example, in the scripted versions of the scene at the lunch table in Dry Fork, Ringo's response after Hatfield, Lucy and Gatewood move away from Dallas at the lunch table reads as follows:

> *Ringo*: Well, I guess you can't break out of prison and into society in the same week. [*She (Dallas) doesn't lift her face from her plate and he rises apologetically.*] I'm pretty dumb for sittin' down with a lady like you. Thanks for not movin' away like they did.

In the film, the last two sentences are cut.

28   "Dudley Nichols Signed by Wanger on Ford Yarn", *Hollywood Reporter* (23 Aug 1938): 3; "Wanger's Wider Prod. Activity Via UA Setup", *Variety* (24 Aug 1938): 3.
29   Scott Eyman, "Looking Back: John Wayne Talking to Scott Eyman", *Focus on Film* (Spring 1975): 17–23, cited in Behlmer, *America's Favorite Movies*, 108. Wayne's recollection is supported by Nichols's comment: "*Stagecoach* made quite a roar as it rumbled through New York. If there was ever a picture that was the director's picture it was that one", Letter to Ford, 26 March 1939 [archivist's date], Ford correspondence, Lilly Library, IU.
30   *Stagecoach*, Final Continuity, n.d., Dudley Nichols papers, Box 8, UCLA Library Special Collections; *Stagecoach*, Final Continuity, n.d., Ford mss., Scripts and Production Materials, Box 4, folders 9–10, Lilly Library, IU; *Stagecoach*, Final Continuity, n.d., Walter F. Wanger papers, Box 93, folders 7–8, WCFTR; Nicola Hayden's notes comparing script and film in *Stagecoach: a film by John Ford and Dudley Nichols* (New York: Simon and Schuster, 1971), 144–152, refers to the version in the Nichols papers.
31   The relevant pages in the version of the script in the Wanger papers are: 36, 36A, 37–41.
32   Compare the script in the Nichols papers, 106, with that in the Wanger papers, 106.

Similarly, the scripted interchange between Ringo and Dallas following his proposal in Apache Wells is as follows.

> *Dallas*: You don't know me! You don't know who I am!

> *Ringo*: I know all I want to know. You're the kind of girl a man wants to marry.

In the film, the last sentence of Ringo's speech has been cut. These cuts create ambiguity about how much Ringo knows or suspects about Dallas's occupation. When, during the discussion about whether or not to proceed from Dry Fork, he urges Curly to solicit a vote from "the other lady", putting her on the same level as Lucy, we may think of him as naïve, or correct in his estimation of Dallas, or both.

Stagecoach was scored by the music department at Paramount where Wanger had been a unit producer and had connections. In all probability Paramount's involvement was due to the fact that Newman was no longer available, having resigned his position as music director at the United Artists Studio in December 1938.[33] In addition to being outsourced, the scoring process for *Stagecoach* was rushed. Ford did not complete shooting until early January at which point the film went to Otho Lovering and Spencer for editing.[34] The team of composers at Paramount, who, unusually, were all named in the credits, had only a few weeks to prepare the film for its February 2, 1939 preview and February 22 release.[35] The process was rendered more difficult when all uses of the song "Ten Thousand Cattle Straying", which was both performed on-camera and the source of multiple non-diegetic cues in the first score recorded, had to be removed.

A Ford favorite eventually included in *My Darling Clementine*, "Ten Thousand Cattle Straying" was written, or at least copyrighted, by Owen Wister for the stage production based upon his novel *The Virginian*.[36] In the *Stagecoach* scripts, the song is placed just after Ringo is picked up on the roadside. As the stage continues on the way to Dry Fork, a dispute between Doc and Hatfield threatens. Both Ringo and Gatewood try to make peace (in the film only Ringo's dialogue remains). Peacock then attempts to promote unity by suggesting they all sing a hymn, appealing to Ringo to start them off.

> *Ringo*: Not me. [*Sees Dallas looking at him and he smiles.*] I'll bet you know plenty of 'em, ma'am.

> *Dallas is speechless. She can only look at Ringo. Lucy looks out the window self-consciously. Hatfield regards the boy with faint derision in his eyes. Peacock looks at Dallas appealingly, as if expecting her to start a hymn. A dry smile curls about Gatewood's mouth.*

Doc Boone then saves the situation by launching into a song that the script entitles "Ten Thousand Cattle Gone Astray". Eventually all the other passengers join in.

It is not immediately clear why the director called for this particular song in the scripts. Its later use in *My Darling Clementine*, in which Chihuahua mockingly sings it to Wyatt Earp after the Clantons have stolen the Earps' cattle, seems much more apropos. Indeed, Ford may have been motivated to take the unusual step of making Earp a cowboy in order to motivate the song. The introduction of "Ten Thousand Cattle" in *Stagecoach* seems to have been occasioned by the fact that Ringo has lost his horse, thereby forcing

33   Berg, *Goldwyn*, 327, reports that Newman resigned from his position at Goldwyn, which had required him to score the films of all the UA producers, in December 1938. The relevant clause of Newman's original contract with Goldwyn described the United Artists Studio as a "facility" for UA producers and required Newman to "render services for any and/or all of them", Alfred Newman Contract File, Goldwyn papers, folder 5082, Herrick Library, AMPAS. Newman's credits indicate that he did not begin working exclusively for Twentieth Century-Fox until September 1939; see also chapter six, note 11.

34   The undated Negative Cost Report in the Wanger papers lists the production period as 31 October 1938–23 December 1938, Walter F. Wanger papers, Box 93, Folder 7, WCFTR, but trade press evidence suggests that Ford shot additional scenes in late December and early January, see "One Day Left for *Coach*", *Hollywood Reporter* (28 Dec 1938): 4; "Spencer Editing *Coach* for Feb. 22 Release Date", *Hollywood Reporter* (9 Jan 1939): 7.

35   Review of *Stagecoach*, *Variety* (8 Feb 1939): 17, gives the date of the preview as 2 February at the Westwood Village theater.

36   "Ten Thousand Cattle Straying (Dead Broke)", words and music by Owen Wister (New York: M. Witmark & Sons, 1904); the play, based on Owen Wister's 1902 novel *The Virginian: A Horseman of the Plains* (New York: Macmillan, 1902) , was adapted by Kirke La Shelle and the author, and opened on Broadway on 5 January 1904. There is some debate about whether or not the song actually originated with Wister, see Kathryn Kalinak, *How the West Was Sung: Music in the Westerns of John Ford* (Berkeley: University of California Press, 2007), 212, note 41.

him to have recourse to the public conveyance. Given the focus on Dallas in the dialogue leading up to Doc's performance, it is possible that Ford was also interested in Wister's second verse, which concerns a sweetheart who has departed in addition to the cows: "My girl she has went straying; She quit me too and traveled away." Thus, "Ten Thousand Cattle Straying", which Wister had subtitled "Dead Broke", becomes the anthem of the outcasts, an association strengthened by the fact that Doc chooses it in place of the hymn.

Sometime during production, Ford changed the placement of the song from the moment when Ringo joins the group to the Apache Wells segment, where it was sung by the men awaiting the birth of Lucy's baby. It seems likely that the song was moved for several reasons. First, the dialogue that motivates its introduction in the scripts is patently weak – Peacock's suggestion that they sing a hymn is absurd, even for his character. Second, the lead-in emphasizes Ringo's idealization of Dallas to a risible extent, and its elimination follows the logic of the other cuts in his dialogue described above. Third, the scripted version of the Apache Wells segment transitioned too quickly from the scene in which Doc enters Lucy's room prior to the birth to the scene in which Buck comments that what he assumes is a coyote howling sounds like a baby. That is, the song stands in for and covers the time of Lucy's labor.

The displacement of the song from the end of the first act to the Apache Wells segment is evident from the cue sheets for the first version of the score. A relatively long visual-vocal (i.e., sung on-camera) cue for "Ten Thousand Cattle" is listed in proximity to another visual-vocal cue

from the same song that remains in the film. It consists of Doc singing "My horse has gone ...." to the opening notes of the verse in order to tease Chris whose wife has stolen his horse.[37] A second cue sheet, prepared at Paramount, is less detailed but indicates that "Ten Thousand Cattle" was sung after a cue entitled "Birth of Baby" and before a cue entitled "The Baby is Born".[38] It is difficult to imagine how the motivation and staging of the song was handled after its placement in the Apache Wells segment, but it is clear the director considered it important since the theme was repeated eight times throughout the course of the non-diegetic score in addition to the two times it was sung. However, all of these cues except the snippet of Doc singing were eventually removed, and the score altered to its final form. Kalinak suggests that the filmmakers and the studio had assumed "Ten Thousand Cattle" was a folk song in the public domain and it was only relatively late in the process that they determined it was in copyright and deemed the cost of its use prohibitive.[39]

Another ballad assumed the place of "Ten Thousand Cattle Straying" in the Apache Wells segment. The final cue sheet for *Stagecoach* notes the addition of a "Spanish song" with the name Elvira Ríos penciled in.[40] Although the connection between Ford and Ríos remains to be elucidated, it seems likely that the director initially cast her as the innkeeper Chris's Apache wife Yakima on the basis of her striking appearance (figure 8.3). She may have been recommended for the part by Chris-Pin Martin, who played the character Chris in Ford's Western and who had previously acted alongside Ríos in the Paramount

---

37   Music Cue Sheet, *Stagecoach*, Recorded at United Artists Studio, n.d., Walter Wanger Productions, in United Artists Corporate Records, Series 2H, Music Cue Sheets, Box 2, Folder 1, this cue sheet lists 75 cues.

38   *Stagecoach*, 30 January 1939, Walter Wanger Productions, in Paramount Pictures music cue sheets, File 862, Special Collections, Herrick Library, AMPAS. This cue sheet seems to have been prepared to assign responsibility for the music to the relevant member of the composing team. It does not list distinct cues in any comprehensive way, dividing the film into only 32 segments. The six-second cue from "Ten Thousand Cattle", which we know from the film was placed in the Apache Wells segment, was assigned to the lunch room at Dry Fork, a discrepancy I can only explain as a result of human error during a rushed job.

39   Kalinak, *How the West Was Sung*, 70; Behlmer, *America's Favorite Movies*, 117–118, implies that preview audiences disliked the song, but if that had been the case, it would not have been necessary to remove the non-diegetic cues and go to the trouble of remaking the score. It should also be noted that John Wayne recalls the 2 February 1939 preview as overwhelmingly successful, see "The Company Remembers *Stagecoach*", in *Action: Directors Guild of America*, 6/5 (Sep–Oct 1971): 25.

40   Music Cue Sheet, *Stagecoach*, n.d., typescript with penciled annotations, in Paramount Pictures music cue sheets, File 862, Special Collections, Herrick Library, AMPAS; we know this cue sheet postdates the others because of its reference to a "Spanish Song" and naming of Ríos; it seems to have been prepared to assign responsibility for rewriting the score in the wake of the decision to remove the "Ten Thousand Cattle" cues.

8.3

film *Tropic Holiday* (1938, Theodore Reed).[41] But Ríos was also a cabaret performer and was best known for her interpretations of songs in the bolero genre. She had come to Hollywood for her role in *Tropic Holiday* in which she sang the Spanish-language lyrics of several well-known hits by Agustín Lara prior to their performance by others in English translation.[42] When problems developed with the use of "Ten Thousand Cattle", it is likely that she offered or was invited to fill in the gap. Her song is sometimes referred to as "En mi soledad" or "Al pensar en ti" or "Yakima's song". The melody consists of bars 9–17 of Wister's "Ten Thousand Cattle", although with slight variations to allow for the structure of the new lyrics.[43] One suspects Ford liked the melody and found a way to retain it under the radar of the studio lawyers. This hypothesis would explain why Ríos was never credited for her performance.

The scripts have Peacock scream "Savages!" when Yakima first appears inside the Apache Wells inn. His subsequent conversation with Chris sets up a contrast between the white man's hysteria and the Mexican innkeeper's practical, and somewhat cynical, attitude towards the Indians: "Sure. She's one of Geronimo's people. I think, maybe not so bad to have Apache wife,

eh? Apaches don't bother me, I think." But the script has additional dialogue that has been eliminated from the film: Chris goes on to explain that he bought his wife in exchange for two horses, and that she doesn't like him much and would prefer a "big Apache buck". This conversation is followed by a short scene set later that night in which Yakima, alone in the kitchen, observes three vaqueros making away with the horses. She remains silent, listening, while "a curious smile glints in her black eyes". It is not clear what to make of the script's description here. Perhaps Yakima is supposed to be inspired by the vaqueros' example, or to take malicious pleasure in their theft of the white men's animals. In any case, the film replaces the scene in the kitchen with a scene in a studio-constructed exterior. A fire burns in a rough lean-to where the three vaqueros are gathered, one strumming a guitar (the sole accompaniment to the song, which seems to have been recorded on set with the vocal performance). Yakima stands beside the adjacent corral containing the horses. She sings the first verse of "En mi soledad", which expresses longing for her native land: "Al pensar en ti/Tierra en que nací/Que nostalgia siente mi corazón".[44] She then urges the vaqueros to go: "Ahora, muchachos, vayanse!" As they mount the horses off screen, she sings a second verse about an absent lover.

The song provides a much more compelling dramatization of Yakima's motivations for running away than Chris's scripted dialogue. She directly expresses her loneliness and her longing to return home, emotions rendered especially vibrant by Ríos's performance. Moreover, her alliance with the vaqueros is underlined by her Apache character's use of Spanish. Taken together the characters of Chris and Yakima open up what Charles Ramirez Berg has termed a "multicultural dynamic".[45] While Chris may not respect his wife

41 Ford had previously cast Chris-Pin Martin for a bit part in *Four Men and a Prayer*, and doubtless knew him from his role as Warner Baxter's comic sidekick in the Fox films *The Cisco Kid* (1931) and *Under the Pampas Moon* (1935); Martin was scheduled to appear in another Cisco Kid sequel while *Stagecoach* was in production: *The Return of the Cisco Kid* (1939).
42 "The Lamp on the Corner/Farolita", sung by Ríos and Tito Guízar; "My First Love/Mi primer amor", sung by Ríos and Dorothy Lamour; "Tonight Will Live/Oración caribe", sung by Ríos, Lamour, Guízar, all three songs with music by Lara.
43 I have not been able to ascertain the author of the Spanish-language lyrics.
44 When I think of you/Land where I was born/Nostalgia fills my heart.
45 Charles Ramirez Berg, "The Margin as Center: The Multicultural Dynamics of John Ford's Westerns", in Gaylyn Studlar and Matthew Bernstein, eds., *John Ford Made Westerns: Filming the Legend in the Sound Era* (Bloomington: Indiana University Press, 2001), 75–101.

very much, their relationship indicates that he is at ease with the Apaches and co-exists peaceably with the tribe, an attitude that contrasts starkly with the travelers' fear and horror of the "savages". And the converse is true of his wife. Even as she steals her husband's horse and hightails it back to her people, Yakima's song creates a diversion to help the vaqueros get out of harm's way. Thus, this episode opens up a vision of cross-cultural and cross-racial exchange that is generally at odds with the conventions of the Western, and with most of the other depictions of the Apaches in *Stagecoach*. However, unlike Chris, whose acquaintance with Buck and friendly warning to Ringo about the Plummers allies him with the travelers, Yakima seems to be conspiring with the vaqueros against the white invaders. The point is emphasized by the urgency and furtive quality of her address to the men, by the fact that Ringo, Buck and Curly bolt into the exterior and react with dismay to the theft of the horses, and, importantly, by the fact that she is not singing in English. Which is not to argue that she is an unattractive character but, rather, a mysterious one. Her emotions and intentions are largely opaque to the travelers, to her husband, and to the non-Spanish speaking members of the audience. She is a woman who takes her own counsel and follows her own star. Despite the circumstances which mitigated against the use of "Ten Thousand Cattle", Ford's storied good luck seems to have held. With one brief but unforgettable scene, he was able to retain the melody, at one remove but much improved, and replace the anthem of the outcasts with the mournful anthem of the soon-to-be dispossessed.

Ford and Glennon on Location

Ford and Glennon's use of location footage in *Stagecoach* was indebted to the model of Goldwyn's *The Hurricane* on which they had collaborated in 1937. Goldwyn had originally planned to shoot his entire film in the South Seas but abandoned the plan due to logistical challenges. Instead, second-unit director Stuart Heisler, cinematographer Archie Stout and a camera crew were sent to Pago Pago where Ford briefly joined them to select locations. After his return to Los Angeles, the unit remained for over two weeks shooting footage of a schooner, important to the plot, in different locations and at different times of day. They also shot the inhabitants of the island performing as stand-ins for principal actors Dorothy Lamour, Jon Hall and Al Kikume – climbing trees, sailing small boats, swimming and diving in long shot. Glennon meanwhile shot principal photography on a spectacular open-air lagoon set built at the UA studio and on the studio sound stages. Following Heisler's return with the footage from Pago Pago, Ford and James Basevi, in charge of special effects for the film, supervised the process shots that incorporated the principal actors and the second unit's backgrounds. Additional scenes requiring skilled stunt men were shot in the waters off Catalina Island by Heisler and Stout.[46]

Within the limits of its more modest production budget, location shooting in *Stagecoach* was similarly dispersed. Ford's first foray into Monument Valley, in Navajo territory spanning the Utah-Arizona border, saved the cost of a spectacular open-air set, since the director found one ready-made.[47] As in the case of *The Hurricane*, the backgrounds in Monument Valley and the desert adjacent to Mesa, Arizona, were shot first. However, there was no second unit as such. Ford and Glennon went to Arizona with assistant-directors Wingate Smith and Lowell Farrell, and Glennon's camera crew.[48] The only actors to accompany the crew were Tim Holt, who played Lieutenant Blanchard, and extras for the cavalry unit that was shot riding with the stage. It is not clear if the stagecoach that they shot in the vicinity of Monument Valley was transported to the site by train, or if another coach was rented on loca-

---

46 *Hurricane* Daily Production Reports, Samuel Goldwyn papers, folder 1009, Herrick library, AMPAS; Basevi's special-effects unit also handled the photography of the miniatures that conveyed the damage wrought by the storm.

47 Behlmer, *America's Favorite Movies*, 110–112, summarizes the various accounts of how Ford discovered this location, so important for the post-war Westerns.

48 Unsigned Memo to Daniel Keefe, copies to John Ford, Wingate Smith, Lowell Farrell, Jack Kirston, 28 October 1938, John Ford correspondence, Lilly Library, IU; "Glennon on Location", *Hollywood Reporter* (29 Oct 1938): 2.

8.4

8.5

8.6

8.7

tion. In the first of many such deals between the director and the tribe, the Navajo inhabitants of the region were hired to provide and handle horses and as extras to play the Apaches. The stunt work for *Stagecoach*, done under the direction of Yakima Canutt and with the active participation of John Wayne, took place in various locations in Southern California.[49] The attack on the stage was shot near Victorville at Lucerne Dry Lake, and the crossing at Lee's Ferry was taken on the Kern river near Kernville. As had been the case with *The Hurricane*, principal photography was frequently conjoined with the location footage by back-projection. For example, figure 8.4, from the shot of the stage leaving Tonto, showcases Agathla Peak on the horizon line. The next shot, figure 8.5, is a process shot of Curly and Buck at the reins against a back-projected image of the same peak. Figure 8.6, of the stage during the attack sequence, was photographed during stunt work at Lucerne

Dry Lake, as indicated by the pronounced shadows visible on the sand. Figure 8.7, from earlier in the sequence, is a process shot with the stage lit and photographed in the studio in front of a projected background. The framing eliminates the ground and any shadows which might have called attention to the change to artificial light.

It should be clear that Ford's use of locations in *Stagecoach* differed markedly both from his earlier practice, as described in the cases of *The Iron Horse*, *The Lost Patrol*, and *Wee Willie Winkie*, and from his post-war practice in which company, cast and crew all went on location for extended periods. *Stagecoach* should also be distinguished from *Air Mail*, the director's first use of back-projection, discussed in chapter three. In *Air Mail*, process shots most frequently evoke the exterior space of the airfield as viewed through the windows of the interior set of the control room, that is, as an extension of the apparent depth of the

49   Yamika Canutt, *Stunt Man: the autobiography of Yakima Canutt with Oliver Drake* (New York: Walker and Company, 1979), 107 112.

8.8

8.9

8.10

8.11

8.12

In figure 8.9, from the next shot, the stage climbs a dune in an undetermined desert location. In figure 8.10, from a shot of the stage driving full-tilt towards camera and taken in what looks like the vicinity of the Iverson Ranch in Chatsworth, the vehicle approaches the meeting place. Cut to the soldiers fording a shallow stream, figure 8.11, in still another locale, perhaps adjacent to the Kern river, a shot establishing that the stage is now unaccompanied. This kind of editing is similar to a sequence such as the horse race in *Hangman's House*, in which the continuity of the horses' movement enabled Ford to shuffle from one great landscape shot to another. But in the case of *Stagecoach*, the intercutting of locales gives rise to surprising discontinuities in the treatment of the Monument Valley rock formations. As Edward Buscombe notes, these formations recur throughout the stage's journey.[50] For example, despite the sequence described above, which suggests that the stage leaves the area of the buttes as it approaches the meeting with Ringo, Ford's favorite triumvi-

set. But in *Stagecoach*, as in *The Hurricane*, back-projection used in tandem with editing together shots from widely separated actual locales combined to create a full-blown imaginary landscape.

The piecemeal use of location footage can be seen in the shots which lead to the first encounter with Ringo on the roadside. Figure 8.8, a slow pan following the progress of the stage caravan across the desert floor of Monument Valley culminates in a view of Mitchell Butte on the left.

8.13

8.14

8.15

8.16

rate of West and East Mittens and Merrick Butte appear well after this point. The director cuts to a view of the stage climbing a hill with these formations in the background after the pause which follows Ringo's revelation to Doc that his brother was murdered. At the conclusion of act one, just prior to the arrival in Dry Fork, a pan of the stage traveling on the valley floor begins with the view of East Mitten and Merrick Butte and moves left (figure 8.12). In act four, just prior to the attack on the stage, two similar pans show the stage in the same valley, dwarfed by the same rock formations, but now observed by an Apache war party on a high cliff overlooking the vehicle. Ford seems to have used these shots as a means of punctuation, marking off the beginning or ending of important sequences, as well as a way of reminding us of the hostile surroundings which threaten the travelers.

While Ford's piecemeal approach to location footage survives in the post-war films made in Monument Valley, the consistent use of back-projection was limited to *Stagecoach*. And the difficulty of reconciling the technique with Ford and Glennon's approach to location shooting becomes clear in the confrontation between Ringo and Curly at their first meeting. Cut from the soldiers fording the stream, figure 8.11, to the stagecoach on the road as it makes an abrupt stop very close to camera. Cut to the famous first shot of the star in character, resting his saddle on one arm and with the other, single-handedly cocking his rifle as the camera tracks in to close up (figure 8.13). This process shot combines Wayne in the studio with a back-projection of the Stagecoach Formation, a configuration of buttes in Monument Valley.[51] Cut to a two-shot of Buck and Curly as the sheriff leans forward and raises his shotgun,

50   Edward Buscombe, *Stagecoach*, BFI Film Classics (London: BFI Publishing, 1992), 45.
51   Booth Wilson, in his illuminating study "How John Ford's West Was Framed: Landscape and Geography in the Monument Valley Films", *Journal of Cinema and Media Studies*, 59/3 (Spring 2020): 98, explains that the Stagecoach Formation includes three distinct buttes, Stagecoach, Castle Rock, and Bear and Rabbit (the first of these is not named after the film).

8.17

8.18

8.19

8.20

smiling at his prize (figure 8.14). Not much of the landscape is visible behind them, but back-projection is likely, to match other shots in the shot-reverse-shot series. As they talk, cut back to a medium shot of Ringo with the Monument Valley buttes in the background. Eventually Ringo approaches the stage in long shot. Like all of the long shots in the scene, this takes place on the Chatsworth location (figure 8.15). Curly demands he cede his Winchester. Cut in to a medium shot of Ringo with a new projected background – now that he has approached the stage the rock formations are less spectacular (figure 8.16). Ringo resists Curly's request: "You may need me and this Winchester." The sheriff gets tough, informing Ringo he is under arrest and pointing his gun in a threatening manner (figure 8.17). The use of back-projection is more prominent in this framing than the previous two-shot of Buck and Curly. The filmmakers evidently decided to match the background to the medium shots of Wayne as opposed to the long shot of

the stage. Cut back to the medium shot framing of Ringo who starts to object but breaks off when an off-screen whinny motivates the actor's turn to the left (figure 8.18). Return to the long-shot framing, as Lieutenant Blanchard appears in the background and rides toward camera followed by his unit (figures 8.19 and 8.20). In the foreground Ringo gives up his gun, then his saddle.

The nicely understated contest between the two men is defused when Ringo realizes he has been outflanked. And the spatial integrity of the long shot, established in the very first shots of the stagecoach coming down the road to camera, is integral to the maneuver which depends upon the juxtaposition between foreground and background action. This kind of staging is hard to reconcile with the back-projection found in the shot of Ringo cocking his rifle and the medium shots that followed suit. While it is clear why Ford was tempted to use it in this case – the buttes connect Ringo with wild places and the frontier – it nonetheless committed him to a very different

186

construction of space – the location rendered as inert wallpaper behind the principals. The common studio practice of having a second unit shoot what were called "backgrounds" or "atmosphere" did not sit well with a director whose staging and editing routinely mobilized the depths of the shot. The solution, a return to his early practice of staging all the relevant action in wild places evoking the old west, was resumed with location shooting in Utah for *Drums Along the Mohawk* in 1939 and eventually became one of his trademarks.

Ford and Glennon on Set

The acclaimed interior cinematography of *Stagecoach* was not *sui generis* but rather the product of the director's years of experimentation with low-key lighting, and in particular his prior collaboration with Bert Glennon on *The Prisoner of Shark Island*. As discussed in chapter six, in that film director and cinematographer experimented with what was a new stock in 1935, Panchromatic Super X. The negative's increased sensitivity, especially to the blue color of arc light, facilitated the elimination of overhead illumination for the nighttime prison escape and Glennon's highly selective set lighting. The stock also provided greater depth of field and separation of planes than had been available to Ford and August shooting under similar circumstances in *The Informer*. For *Stagecoach*, director and cinematographer had access to a new round of black-and-white film stocks released by Eastman Kodak in the fall of 1938. Plus X, a high-speed, fine-grained panchromatic negative was twice as fast as the previous Super X. Super XX, described as a "special purpose" panchromatic negative was four times as fast as Super X at about the same level of grain.[52] These innovations led director and cinematographer to devise new techniques of lighting, composition and staging.

Judging from accounts published in *American Cinematographer*, the new stocks first went into general use in the studios in the fall of 1938, at the same time that *Stagecoach* began production.[53] While some cinematographers praised the greater depth of field that could be achieved with their enhanced sensitivity, there was even more discussion about the opportunity to use less powerful lighting units. Victor Milner commented: "It makes it possible for us to run the scale between extremely soft, naturalesque low-level lightings (50 foot-candles or less), shot with full lens apertures, or to the opposite extreme of higher-level illumination (perhaps as high as 200 foot-candles or more) exposed at greatly reduced apertures for a new and greater depth and crispness." Tony Gaudio also saw lower light levels as more naturalistic: "You can do what all of us have for years wanted to do: you can come down to almost natural lighting levels." In a 1940 report on lamp use, there was wide-spread enthusiasm for small incandescent units, particularly one made by Bardwell-McAlister, the so-called Dinky Inky, with 500-watt and 750-watt lamps that could be readily concealed on set.[54] In the same article, Joseph Valentine noted that the fast films in combination with the new lighting units led to a decisive change in lighting strategy: "Six years ago most of us began with an overall spread of flat foundation-light, with the highlights and modeling lighting built up from this. Today almost everyone employs the so-called precision lighting method, in which virtually the entire scene is lit with spotlights and the old floodlighting units are vanishing." In his 1939 description of shooting *Juarez*, Gaudio had already reached the same conclusion: "With the old film, I'd use, say, a Junior for my keylight, and fill in with Baby Juniors. Now I use Baby Juniors for my keylight! Those lamps and the new film were just made for each other! … On low-roofed stages I've had to turn

52   William Stull, A.S.C., "Technical Progress in the Past Year", *American Cinematographer* (Jan 1939): 8–10, 46; Stull notes that equivalent Agfa stocks were released earlier in 1938.
53   In "Lighting the New Fast Films", *American Cinematographer* (Feb 1939): 69–70, Ted Tetzlaff discussed the use of the stocks in *Cafe Society* (Paramount, Edward H. Griffith), in production mid-October to early December 1938; Tony Gaudio, in *Juarez* (Warner Brothers, William Dieterle), in production late November 1938 to early February 1939; Victor Milner, in *Union Pacific* (Paramount, Cecil B. DeMille), in production October 1938 to February 1939. On the start date for *Stagecoach* see note 34.
54   William Stull, A.S.C., "How Small Lamps Are Being Used on Major Sets", *American Cinematographer* (May 1940): 202–203; Arthur Miller, A.S.C., "Putting Naturalness into Modern Interior Lightings", *American Cinematographer* (Mar 1941): 104–105, 138.

8.21

8.22

8.23

out the ceiling work lamps when I was shooting ... Using these smaller units it's easier to put the light just where you want it. Doing it with baby spotlights you can get your lamps into places where they'll do the most good – even in cramped quarters where you could never put a bigger lamp."

While neither Ford nor Glennon discussed their use of the new stock, there are many shots in *Stagecoach* which attest to their experimentation with its increased sensitivity and depth of field. For example, the relatively high light levels of the inn at Dry Fork permitted them to show Hatfield seated at table in medium shot with the patterns on the tablecloth and his ace of spades razor sharp (figure 8.21). Peacock and Gatewood standing well behind the table appear somewhat soft, but this may have been a deliberate choice to throw attention on the foreground detail. Later, when Hatfield asks Lucy if she would prefer to change her seat in order to move her away from Dallas, Doc and fellow drinker Billy Pickett seated behind

them at the bar are in perfect focus as they look askance at Hatfield's subterfuge (figure 8.22). And, in the next shot, the only one in the Dry Fork inn which does not favor a corner of the table, the placement of the camera slightly higher than table height and directly down its central axis emphasizes the physical distance that has been established between Lucy and Dallas (figure 8.23).

Clearly, the move away from massive banks of arcs or floodlights described by cinematographers as a consequence of the new negative stock would have been welcomed by Ford, who had sought to reduce overhead illumination in favor of a limited number of directed light sources as early as *The Informer*. In the Apache Wells segment, which takes place at night and early the following morning, director and cinematographer achieved astonishing depth effects in low-key lighting schemes. Figure 8.24, taken on a dark exterior set, maintains focus over the distance between Ringo and Dallas, an expanse emphasized by the wall that stretches between them, and the tangle of corral fencing on the right. Mist is present, as in the dark Dublin streets of *The Informer*, but here it used only for decorative purposes, for the way it catches the light, not to obscure the background. Note, too, how the light, from top right, picks out the texture of the wall and the tracery of branches on it. This level of detail is maintained in the next shot, a medium framing of Wayne against a fairly bright background (figure 8.25). This study in opalescent grays is enlivened by dim light off right which, given the sensitivity of the negative, is enough to prevent him from being silhouetted.

8.24

8.25

8.26

8.27

After Yakima runs off and Chris awakens the men sleeping in the main room of the inn, a complex lighting scheme suggests the morning light (figure 8.26). Light from off right is projected on the back wall, as if coming from windows in the unseen "fourth" wall of the set. This light picks out Ringo in front of the fireplace. An intense light outside the front door catches Curly's right side and provides back light on Chris. Doc, seated on the bar, and Buck, on the floor in front of him, are primarily lit from off left. Despite the generally low light levels, Buck's check shirt and Chris's plaid remain quite distinct and, as in the exterior set, there is a wide range of grays and excellent rendition of detail. After Ford cuts in, Peacock, in the darkest corner of the room behind the door, and Buck, standing in the brightest light in the doorway, are both rendered in as much detail as Doc, more evenly lit foreground right, and already the center of attention (figure 8.27).

The sense of enclosure on the interior sets of the inn was reinforced by Ford's renowned decision to have them built with ceilings. In an interview conducted during the production of *Stagecoach*, Glennon explained the use of ceilings as a result of his intention to utilize a wide-angle (25mm) lens which would have revealed the upper scaffolding of the sound stage if left uncovered.[55] But the director also seems to have welcomed the control over lighting that could be exercised in cramped, tight places with the new, malleable lighting units. Consider the shots that introduce the scene of Ringo's marriage proposal. In the first, twenty-second, shot he watches Dallas walk down a dark narrow hallway leading to an exterior door. Wayne stands foreground left illuminated from top right, while a lower and softer light reflects off of Trevor's dress (figure 8.28). The door at the end of the hall is open, and a powerful light source is directed toward camera. As Trevor approaches it, the pattern on her dress fades to a black silhouette while her cast shadow

55   John Castle, "Bert Glennon Introducing New Method of Interior Photography", *American Cinematographer* (Feb 1939). 82–83.

8.28

8.29

8.30

8.31

8.32

set. He is carrying one of the oil lamps which are omnipresent throughout the setting (figure 8.31). In this case it seems to conceal an effects light which illuminates Ringo's face after Ford cuts in (figure 8.32). As Chris quietly informs Ringo that all three Plummers are in Lordsburg, the low-key illumination and their somewhat furtive air recall the fact that the young man about to go a-courting is also an ex-convict planning a potentially fatal act of violence. The change of tone as the revenge plot impinges on the romance plot is facilitated by the cut to medium-shot framing and by the shift in the lighting scheme which has a pronounced effect in the restricted compass of the space.

Ford's staging in the Apache Wells sequence frequently employs deep space compositions which play off the contrast between foreground and background, as in the shot that mobilizes depth for Trevor's spectacular entrance immediately following the birth of the baby. The set itself is certainly not spectacular in the way that the

becomes prominent (figure 8.29). After she crosses the threshold, the pattern on her dress becomes visible once again, crystal clear despite her distance from the camera (figure 8.30). In this deceptively simple movement, Dallas's newly exalted character is celebrated by her passage through gradations of light. But the shot is not over. Ringo sets off after Dallas and as he reaches the mid-point of the hall, Chris emerges from off left through a hitherto concealed opening in the

190

8.33

8.34

Shark Island prison was. It is an ill-defined and awkward intersection of the main room and the hallway with a bedroom tucked out of view. But it creates a quasi-cinematic arrangement in which all eyes are focused on a blank wall in the background, as the men listen, and imagine the activity in the unseen space. Ford prepares the spectator for this viewpoint by an earlier set of point-of-view shots in which the travelers watch Curly carry Lucy into the bedroom after she has fainted, his shadow projected on the opposite wall (figures 8.33 and 8.34). Later, the moment of the birth is presaged by a shot of a coyote, apparently in the wild. The sound of its howling is briefly imitated by a flute on the music track. Cut inside to a close shot of Wayne, leaning forward to light a cigarette by means of an oil lamp, as the howling continues. Cut back to reveal Curly, seated with a pipe, and Hatfield with an array of cards. The sound of a baby crying joins the mix, Wayne pulls back from the lamp and the other men look off right in response (figure 8.35). Cut further back

for the initiation of a forty-second shot. The table, formerly well inside the main room, has been moved forward to a position just outside the hallway, creating a clear sightline to the hall (figure 8.36). Devine enters from the right and pauses in front of the others, effectively blocking their view, while noting that the coyote sounds "just like a baby" (figure 8.37). He then proceeds to stand against the wall on the left, his remarks calling the men's attention to Hatfield's cards. They all shift the direction of their looks down towards the table (figure 8.38). As the bedroom door opens illuminating the wall in the hallway, Wayne shifts his gaze to the right, creating a narrow aperture through which Trevor's shadow, and then Trevor herself, become visible (figure 8.39). Wayne leans back, opening up the sightline, as she comes forward with the baby (figure 8.40).

The compelling deep space composition of Dallas and baby is capped by a terrific cut, a 180-degree reversal. At the end of the long take,

8.35

8.36

8.37

8.38

8.39

8.40

8.41

8.42

the men gather around to see the new-born, obscuring our view (figure 8.41). Cut to a camera position from within the hallway looking out (figure 8.42). The new framing neatly sets up the shot-reverse-shot exchange between Ringo and Dallas that is to follow. Their exchange of looks in this long shot is emphasized by their placement within the composition – on opposite sides of the doorway and closest to camera. But, in addition, the receding line of men's heads, with the short

and hatless Peacock at the furthest remove, is both formally pleasing in itself and powerfully suggestive of Dallas's new status within the group. She is viewed with attention and respect by all, not just by Ringo.

In many ways, the interior cinematography of *Stagecoach* represents a culmination of the director's stylistic experiments across the 1930s – the low-key lighting, longer takes, and atmospheric effects that began with the transition to sound. By this point in his career one imagines Ford moving characters and camera around the set like chess pieces on a board, thinking about how to advance the story (Dallas transformed by maternal feeling, Ringo in love), establish a mood (watchful waiting, the male camaraderie of smoking and cards), establish important symbolic contrasts (the space of waiting versus the space of labor), generate the time and space for the actors to perform (first Devine, then Trevor, and always Wayne), set up the cut to the next shot or shots (the reverse angle, the consequent shot-reverse-shot editing), and, of course, make beautiful pictures (the embedded aperture framings, the realistic motivation of a composition complete with halo that derives from centuries of painting the Madonna). The duration of the shot is a factor as well. Buck's entrance may seem digressive, a frivolous introduction of comic relief, but the universal change in the direction of the eyelines as the men look at the table and the slight relaxation of tension gives Trevor's entrance an extra frisson of surprise. All these considerations coalesce, then, in a single shot of long duration, and what superficially appears to be a relatively straightforward narrative rendering.

One of the central paradoxes of *Stagecoach* is that just at the point when Ford gets access to extra sensitive film stock and extremely malleable lighting units, innovations that enable him to move his characters with ever greater facility into and around a set, and control tone and atmosphere more precisely, he opts for a story that locks them down in a four-square position inside a stagecoach, or on top of it, for most of the time. But the juxtaposition of plots and contrasts between characters develop in a much more relaxed manner in the segments outside the stage, in which the director can freely indulge his gift for staging, when Doc can just happen to overlook Hatfield, giving him the evil eye from his position at the bar, or Dallas brush past Ringo who runs into Chris in the hallway where their fates converge.

Chapter 9

Young Mr. Lincoln

If concepts of freedom and democracy could be expressed by hieroglyphs, in the style of Chinese script, then the eccentrically bent silhouette of this tall stooping man, in frock coat and topper, with huge hands and disjointed movements, would be this hieroglyph.

Sergei Mikhailovich Eisenstein[1]

The year spent at Twentieth Century-Fox between October 1937, when Ford completed production on *The Hurricane* for Goldwyn, and October 1938, when Ford went on leave to direct *Stagecoach* for Wanger, was not a particularly productive one for the Ford-Zanuck collaboration. Script development for *Four Men and a Prayer*, from a novel Zanuck had acquired in 1936, proved unusually disorganized, involving six writers and two associate producers.[2] In January 1938, the *Hollywood Reporter* announced that Zanuck had increased the budget to "road-show scale" and assigned Ford.[3] Production started on January 20, about a week before Richard Greene, the relatively unknown British stage actor hired to play opposite Loretta Young, flew into Los Angeles.[4] Zanuck was still at work on the script in February, well after shooting had commenced.[5] In later interviews, Ford dismissed the film due to its weak storyline.[6]

While *Four Men and a Prayer* was in production, Zanuck and Ford negotiated about his next project. Their correspondence indicates that neither one had a clear plan for how best to employ the director's talents. In February, Zanuck sent Ford the script for *Suez*, written by two of the studios best screenwriters, Julian Josephson and Philip Dunne, with Tyrone Power already announced for the lead role.[7] In March, Ford responded to Zanuck's offer of the *Suez* script by loaning his boss a print of Renoir's *La grande illusion*, which he proposed remaking in an English setting with contract players McLaglen, Joseph Bromberg and David Niven in the principal roles.[8] After Zanuck demurred, they settled on a Navy story that associate producer Gene Markey had had in development since 1936, a project of many names that was eventually entitled *Submarine Patrol*. Ford again utilized Richard Greene, although the film was actually structured around the secondary parts carried by such Ford regulars as Preston Foster, Slim Summerville, John Carradine, Warren Hymer, and J. Farrell MacDonald. Both Markey and Ford having been well-connected members of the Naval reserve, they managed to secure the loan of four surviving World War I submarine chasers held at Annapolis.[9] A charming lark that was well reviewed in

---

1   Sergei Eisenstein, "Mr. Lincoln by Mr. Ford", in *Selected Works* iii: *Writings, 1934–1947*, trans. William Powell, ed. Richard Taylor (London: I.B. Tauris & Co, 2010), 279.

2   David Garth, *Four Men and a Prayer* (New York: H. C. Kinsey & Co., 1937). Associate producer Kenneth Macgowan initially supervised the adaptation by writers Sonya Levien, Wallace Sullivan and Richard Sherman. Harry Joe Brown took over as associate producer in September of 1937 with a new writing team. By January of 1938, however, Macgowan had resumed his supervisory role and another writer, Walter Ferris, had been brought in. The principal writers and their supervising producers are listed in the entry for *Four Men and a Prayer*, Kenneth Macgowan Scrapbooks, Cinematic Arts Library, Doheny Library, USC.

3   "Zanuck Tilts Ante …", *Hollywood Reporter* (8 Jan 1938): 1.

4   "Greene in for *Prayer*", *Hollywood Reporter* (28 Jan 1938): 2.

5   Zanuck, Memo to Ford, 3 February 1938, Ford correspondence, Lilly Library, IU.

6   Bogdanovich, *John Ford*, 69.

7   Zanuck, Memo to Ford, 10 February 1938, Ford correspondence, Lilly Library, IU; "Power in Line for *Suez*", *Hollywood Reporter* (7 Dec 1937): 1.

8   Ford, Memo to Zanuck, 1 March 1938, referring to *Suez* and *La grande illusion*; for Zanuck's polite but definitive refusal see his memo to Ford, 2 March 1938, both in Ford correspondence, Lilly Library, IU.

the trade press, *Submarine Patrol* was neither a major film nor a major success, but it was surely much more fun for the director to make than *Suez* would have been. Nonetheless, it is clear in retrospect that Ford was working below his pay grade. *Suez*, directed by Allan Dwan, was reportedly allocated a budget of two million dollars, and became one of Fox's biggest films of the season.[10] Given his salary and expertise, Twentieth Century-Fox needed Ford to be making films of this order, big-budget spectaculars that advanced the careers of the stars the studio had under contract.

The pairing of Ford and Henry Fonda for *Young Mr. Lincoln* effectively opened up a new avenue for Ford at Fox, providing the director, who seems to have been reluctant to work with Tyrone Power, with a much more congenial and versatile actor. Zanuck also gained enormously from their relationship, which helped convince Fonda to sign a long-term contract, greatly enhancing Twentieth Century-Fox's star roster. But despite the value that the studio head eventually came to place on the Ford-Fonda collaboration, Zanuck initially opposed the Lincoln project, probably because he had not been involved with it from the start. Early in 1935, Winfield Sheehan had produced two films with Fonda, then a stage actor under contract to Wanger and loaned to Fox for his first films. *The Farmer Takes a Wife* (Victor Fleming, 1935) was based on Fonda's success in the play of the same name.[11] It was followed by a sound remake of *Way Down East* (Henry King, 1935), which, like *The Farmer Takes a Wife*, made use of Fonda's boyish demeanor in a *jeune premier* role. Having secured an option for an additional film, Sheehan hired Howard Estabrook, one of the screenwriters on *Way Down East*, to draft a script about Lincoln for the star.[12] Sheehan envisioned the film as having comedic elements but culminating in a big dramatic trial scene following the model of *Judge Priest*. He instructed George Marshall, one of two directors with whom he corresponded about the script: "I see the picture treated and developed very much along the lines of *Judge Priest*, and I would suggest you take a look at *Judge Priest* before we have a talk."[13] Estabrook's treatment, dated July 22, 1935, was tentatively entitled "The Young Lincoln". It concluded with a trial scene loosely based on accounts of Lincoln's successful defense of William "Duff" Armstrong, which hinged upon evidence drawn from a farmer's almanac.[14] The treatment was shelved following Sheehan's departure, when Zanuck chose not to pursue the option for a third film with Fonda.[15]

At the beginning of 1938, Lamar Trotti, co-writer of *Judge Priest* with Dudley Nichols, wrote a treatment entitled "Lincoln Trial Story". It is possible that Trotti, an amateur historian, was involved in the Lincoln project as early as 1935, or, more plausibly, that he pitched the original story idea to Sheehan, who was fully capable of turning around and assigning it to Estabrook. In any event, the screenwriter went out of his way to present his 1938 treatment as a newly conceived proposal. It began with a preface:

> This story is based in part on a murder trial which I covered as a newspaper man. The idea of putting it back in time with Lincoln as a lawyer, conducting his first case, came when I discovered that Lincoln was involved, as lawyer, in a famous murder trial which he solved successfully by the introduction of an almanac

---

9   Review of *Submarine Patrol, Variety* (2 Nov 1938): 15: "The four [boats] left at Annapolis were used in the filming of the picture, location shots on which were taken here [i.e., in Maryland]."

10 "$2,000,000 Budget for 20th's *Suez*", *Hollywood Reporter* (12 Mar 1938): 3.

11 Frank B. Elser and Marc Connelly, *The Farmer Takes a Wife*, based on the novel *Rome Haul*, by Walter D. Edmonds (Boston: Little, Brown and company, 1929).

12 "Henry Fonda to Play *Young Lincoln* at Fox", *Hollywood Reporter* (8 Jun 1935): 4; "Cummings May Direct *The Young Lincoln*", *Hollywood Reporter* (20 Jul 1935): 3.

13 Sheehan, Memo to George Marshall, 21 June 1935, cc to Julian Johnson, *Young Mr. Lincoln* Legal File, Twentieth Century-Fox Legal Department.

14 Howard Estabrook, "The Young Lincoln", Story Adaptation, 22 Jul 1935, *Young Mr. Lincoln* Story File, Twentieth Century-Fox Legal Department.

15 "20th Drops its Option on Fonda for Picture", *Hollywood Reporter* (16 Nov 1935): 1; after taking over at Fox, Zanuck dropped many scripts that had been planned for production, for example, see "Zanuck Tosses Out Four More Yarns", *Hollywood Reporter* (31 Jul 1935): 1.

showing the position of the moon on the night of the crime, thus trapping the chief eye-witness, and proving he was lying.[16]

While Trotti's experience as a journalist may well have informed his treatment, it is highly improbable that he developed a story about the young Lincoln ending in a trial reminiscent of the Duff Armstrong murder case independently of Estabrook's draft. A likely explanation for his introductory note is that both the screenwriter and associate producer Macgowan who submitted the script to Zanuck were concerned that the studio head would reject the project out of hand if Sheehan's involvement were acknowledged.

Zanuck's initial rejection of the proposal reveals the amusingly byzantine nature of studio-system politics. He wired Macgowan's colleagues, the producers William Goetz and Harry Joe Brown, and asked them to tell Macgowan that he thought the script would make a great subject for Shirley Temple (presumably an allusion to *The Littlest Rebel* of 1935, in which the character played by Temple appeals to Lincoln to save her father).[17] Nothing more happened with the project for almost a year, until October, 1938, when Robert Sherwood's play *Abe Lincoln in Illinois* opened to acclaim and an extended run at the Plymouth Theatre in New York. In that month, producer Julian Johnson wrote a summary of the play and suggested that Zanuck might want to make a film adaptation with Raymond Massey,

who was playing Sherwood's Lincoln.[18] At about the same time, production closed on Twentieth Century-Fox's *Jesse James*, in which Henry Fonda, again on loan from Wanger, gave what was generally agreed to be a show-stealing performance as Frank James opposite Tyrone Power's Jesse.[19] Together these events seem to have motivated Zanuck's about-face. On November 10, he wrote to Macgowan that the Lincoln story would be temporarily titled "Lawyer in the West", and that he had already wired Trotti directly to assign him the script. On November 11, Zanuck instructed Macgowan to proceed with tests of Fonda for "Lawyer in the West".[20] On November 14, Johnson carefully brought up the topic of the Estabrook treatment. He claimed to have re-discovered it in the files and, by a "curious" coincidence, found that Estabrook (not Sheehan) had envisioned Fonda in the role of Lincoln.[21] By this ruse, Estabrook's treatment, as well as Sheehan's proposed casting of the lead role, were duly shorn of any association with the former studio head.

Ford's participation in the project seems to have been anticipated before the completion of the first script draft of January 13, 1939.[22] A letter from Zanuck addressed to the director at Walter Wanger Productions in early December begins: "Happy you are pleased with the Lincoln assignment. We have got a great story and, of course, you know Trotti is practically an authority on

---

16   Lamar Trotti, "Lincoln Trial Story", 17 January 1938, *Young Mr. Lincoln* Story File, Twentieth Century-Fox Legal Department.

17   Zanuck, Excerpt of Telegram to Bill Goetz or Harry Joe Brown, 30 May 1938, *Young Mr. Lincoln* Legal File, Twentieth Century-Fox Legal Department.

18   Julian Johnson, Memo on *Abe Lincoln in Illinois*, 21 October 1938, *Young Mr. Lincoln* Legal File, Twentieth Century-Fox Legal Department; RKO's adaptation of Sherwood's play, directed by John Cromwell with Raymond Massey reprising his stage role, was released in January 1940, about seven months after *Young Mr. Lincoln*. Sherwood and the Playwrights Producing Company unsuccessfully sued Twentieth Century-Fox for trying to capitalize on the success of Sherwood's play.

19   For example, from the review of *Jesse James*, *Hollywood Reporter* (10 Jan 1939): 3: "Tyrone Power couldn't be a more attractive Jesse James, but he's not quite the type, except if you're talking pictures. However, Jesse isn't the only bandit in the crowd. There's Henry Fonda giving one of the best performances of his career as brother Frank, and doing a right smart job of being a slow-talking fast-on-the-trigger character." See, also, the slyer digs at Power in the review in the *New York Times* (14 Jan 1939): 13, and "Mr. Power: a Beau Jesse", *New York Times* (8 Jan 1939): 126.

20   Zanuck, Memo to Dover and Macgowan, 10 November 1938, assigning Macgowan and Trotti to "Lawyer in the West"; Zanuck, Memo to Macgowan, 11 November 1938, requesting tests of Fonda for "Lawyer in the West"; Requisition for Artists, Casting Office, 19 November 1938, Call for Henry Fonda to report for make-up tests for "Lawyer in the West", all in *Young Mr. Lincoln* Legal File, Twentieth Century-Fox Legal Department.

21   Julian Johnson, Memo to Zanuck, 14 November 1938, *Young Mr. Lincoln* Story File, Twentieth Century-Fox Legal Department.

22   The Twentieth Century-Fox files contain three script drafts, all by Lamar Trotti, and notes from two story conferences: Temporary Script, 13 January 1939; Conference with Mr. Zanuck, 23 January 1939; Final, 27 January 1939; Conference with Mr. Zanuck, 20 February 1939 (with Ford's participation); and Revised Final, 27 February 1939, all in *Young Mr. Lincoln* Story File, Twentieth Century-Fox Legal Department.

Lincoln."[23] In January, however, Ford had his agent inform the studio that he did not want to do the story.[24] The director again reversed himself in early February, just after the *Hollywood Reporter* announced that production on *Young Mr. Lincoln* was about to commence under Irving Cummings.[25] But despite Ford's initial reluctance to take on the Lincoln project, it is clear that his films were a palpable influence on it as early as 1935, given Sheehan's borrowings from *Judge Priest* and Trotti's later involvement as screenwriter.

The well-known story of Ford shaming Fonda for being too intimidated to take on the role of Lincoln[26] needs to be reconciled with the fact that Fonda had been slated for the part of Lincoln in 1935 and had done screen tests for Zanuck in November 1938. The actor recalled feeling anxiety about impersonating Lincoln after viewing the screen tests and having second thoughts about taking the part at that time.[27] In November, Ford seems to have been looking forward to directing *Young Mr. Lincoln*, a point confirmed by Zanuck's letter of December 3, 1938. Thus, the director may well have roughly reassured Fonda by telling him that the film dealt with Lincoln as a "jack-legged lawyer" not as his revered hero. In contrast, by mid-January, when Ford had Wurtzel wire Goetz that he did not want to direct *Young Mr. Lincoln*, Fonda was clearly committed – the trade press announced that the actor had signed a term contract giving Fox the option for up to two films a year for five years in order to get the part.[28] Ford may have demurred because he wanted to make *African Intrigue* as per his original agreement with Wanger, as discussed in chapter eight. He may also have had his own anxieties about the Lincoln project.

Story Sources and Structure

Trotti consulted multiple sources during script development for *Young Mr. Lincoln*. He refers to a book of "White House stories", probably Francis B. Carpenter's *Six Months at the White House with Abraham Lincoln*, while Zanuck mentions a "new book of Lincoln anecdotes", unfortunately without giving its title, but probably Emanuel Hertz, *Lincoln Talks*, published in early February.[29] But the single most important source for *Young Mr. Lincoln* was undoubtedly Carl Sandburg's *Abraham Lincoln: The Prairie Years*.[30] Sandburg's biography was first published by Harcourt Brace in 1926 in two volumes which together ran over one thousand pages. It sold more than ten thousand sets in advance of publication and went through four printings in the first month.[31] Highly acclaimed and much discussed, the book renewed attention to the Midwestern setting which shaped Lincoln as a man and as a politician. The preface delineates Sandburg's intended scope:

> For thirty years and more I have planned to make a certain portrait of Abraham Lincoln. It would sketch the country lawyer and prairie politician who was intimate with the settlers of

---

23 Zanuck, Letter to Ford, 3 December 1938, Ford correspondence, Lilly Library, IU.

24 William Goetz, telegram to Harry Wurtzel, 24 Jan 1939, John Ford Contract File, Twentieth Century-Fox Legal Department.

25 "20th Schedules *Lincoln* for March 6 Production", *Hollywood Reporter* (2 Feb 1939): 5; see also "Fonda as Young Abe", *Variety* (8 Feb 1939): 2; in early February, Wurtzel wired Goetz that Ford was prepared to take on the film some time in June, Harry Wurtzel to Wasson or Goetz, 6 February 1939, John Ford Contract File, but the director reported to the studio in mid-February, William Koenig, to All Department Heads, 20 February 1939, *Young Mr. Lincoln* Legal File, Twentieth Century-Fox Legal Department.

26 See, for example, Howard Teichmann, *Fonda: My Life* (New York: New American Library, 1981), 125–127; Henry Fonda interview in Anderson, 221–222; Dan Ford, 138.

27 Anderson, 221.

28 "Fonda Gets *Lincoln* Lead as First on 20th Ticket", *Hollywood Reporter* (17 Jan 1939): 1; "Fonda's Kudos", *Variety* (18 Jan 1939): 5; "20th Tags Henry Fonda for Two Features Yearly", *Hollywood Reporter* (6 Feb 1939): 1.

29 Francis B. Carpenter, *Six Months at the White House with Abraham Lincoln: The Story of a Picture* (New York: Herd & Houghton, 1866); Emanuel Hertz, *Lincoln Talks: A Biography in Anecdote* (New York: Viking Press, 1939). Trotti's reference occurs in his January 1938 treatment, page 11; Zanuck's mention, in the story conference of 20 February 1939.

30 Carl Sandburg, *Abraham Lincoln: The Prairie Years*, 2 vols (New York: Harcourt, Brace and Company, 1926); Robert Sherwood acknowledged the importance of this source in "The Substance of *Abe Lincoln in Illinois*", in Sherwood, *Abe Lincoln in Illinois* (New York: Charles Scribner's Sons, 1939), 191: "It was not until I had read Carl Sandburg's *The Prairie Years* that I began to feel the curious quality of the complex man."

31 Penelope Niven, *Carl Sandburg: A Biography* (New York: Charles Scribner's Sons, 1991), 432–433.

the Knox County neighborhood where I grew up as a boy and where I heard the talk of men and women who had eaten with Lincoln, given him a bed overnight, heard his jokes and his lingo, remembered his silences and his mobile face.[32]

The book strikes a balance between history proper and the stuff of legend. The author pored over documentary evidence including period newspapers and legal records as well as Lincoln's writings, what he called the "high document".[33] At the same time, he drew liberally on anecdotes drawn from reminiscences and interviews. These were freely interspersed with evocations of Lincoln's cultural milieu – sermons, school texts, reading lists, doggerel, superstitions, tall tales, jokes. In addition, Sandburg's 1927 collection of folk music *The American Songbag* included a section entitled "The Lincolns and Hankses" devoted to the hymns, dances, and ballads that he argued would have been heard and played by those families as well as by Ann Rutledge's.[34] The very drive to make a film about the young Lincoln drew not only data points but inspiration from Sandburg's monumental account of Lincoln's cultural origins and personal and professional development.

While Sandburg was an important source for all of the young Lincoln stories discussed here – for Sherwood's play and Estabrook's treatment as well as Trotti's – the depth and scope of the biography created a number of problems of narrative structure and temporal organization for all of them. It is instructive to begin with Sherwood's *Abe Lincoln in Illinois*, which, although written after both the Estabrook and the Trotti versions, was the most straightforward temporal rendering of Lincoln's life before taking up the presidency. Sherwood's play was divided into twelve discrete episodes presented in chronological order. It began with the first campaign for the state legislature and the courtship of Ann Rutledge in New Salem

in the 1830s and built to the late 1850s, the Lincoln-Douglas debates and the presidential campaign.[35]

Unlike Sherwood, Estabrook's treatment took liberties with the chronology of the life, thereby restricting the plot to the 1830s and earlier. The screenwriter drew on Sandburg's descriptions of Lincoln laboring on his father's homestead, his facility with an axe and skill as a wrestler, his first jobs ferrying goods to New Orleans via flatboat and keeping store for Denton Offut. Many episodes were set in New Salem during the years 1831 to 1835. In addition to the courtship of Ann Rutledge, and Lincoln's burgeoning political alliances with Whig politicians, Estabrook developed several comic incidents involving the backwoodsmen Jack Kelso and Jack Armstrong. Although actual friends of Lincoln in New Salem, Estabrook's fictional account of their exploits was designed as preparation for his version of the Armstrong trial, which he moved from 1858 back to the late 1830s, during the years in which Lincoln commenced his career as a lawyer in Springfield.[36] Given this shift in chronology, the identity of the defendant was moved back a generation: from Duff Armstrong to his father Jack. Estabrook also made the trial contemporaneous with Lincoln running for election to the US House of Representatives, a campaign which actually took place in 1847, and the Lincoln-Douglas debates, which took place about a decade later.

The length of Estabrook's treatment, and the variety of incidents recounted, characters introduced, and sets required, would have rendered it unworkable as a script. Indeed it may have been intended as a compilation of likely incidents to be considered for inclusion rather than a definitive iteration of the story. In contrast, Trotti's January 1938 treatment was much more temporally restricted and narratively unified. A brief first act set in New Salem was largely devoted to Lincoln's

32   Sandburg, *Prairie Years*, 1:vii.
33   Sandburg, *Prairie Years*, 1:viii.
34   Carl Sandburg, *The American Songbag* (New York: Harcourt, Brace and Company, 1927), 152–168, also Sandburg, *Prairie Years* 1:181.
35   In contrast, RKO's film version included material on Lincoln's life before he settled in New Salem and began his campaign for the legislature.
36   In his preface, the author called attention to "a major condensation and transposition of events" in the Springfield section of the story: that is, he moved the 1858 Armstrong trial to the late 1830s.

decision to study law. His relationship with Ann Rutledge and her death were both presented in the context of her encouraging him to become a lawyer. The subsequent action was set in Springfield. A slight prolepsis overlaid the events of 1836, the beginning of Lincoln's law career in partnership with John T. Stuart, with events of 1840, when Mary Todd moved to Illinois to live with her married sister, Elizabeth Todd Edwards, and entertained both Lincoln and Stephen Douglas as prospective suitors.

In contrast with Estabrook, the trial that Trotti set in Springfield in the 1830s was not connected with the Armstrongs but peopled with fictional characters: the Clay family, mother Abigail and her grown sons Adam and Matt who were accused of the murder; John Cass, the lying eye-witness; and Scrub White, the murder victim. The prosecuting attorney John Felder and the presiding Judge Bell were likewise fictional constructs. Trotti retained selected elements of the Duff Armstrong trial for his rendering of the trial of the Clay boys, principally the use of the almanac to undermine the lying witness and the questioning of Bill Killian, a prospective juror.[37] He also retained Estabrook's fictional plot twist in which Lincoln successfully trapped the eye-witness into admitting that he was the murderer (in the actual trial, the evidence of the almanac simply undermined the veracity of the witness's testimony). This made for a much neater resolution of the murder plot.

Imaginatively freed from any extensive connection with the Armstrong trial, Trotti was able to develop the crime story in much greater depth than Estabrook, establishing the characters involved in advance of the commission of the crime and showing the murder from Abigail Clay's point of view. The screenwriter built suspense about the trial's outcome in ways that borrowed from major sequences in *Judge Priest*. In both films, the court case is divided into two parts separated by an evening recess. In the initial session, the respective prosecuting attorneys examine witnesses with

great rodomontade. It seems certain that the accused will be convicted. During the quiet evening hiatus, the protagonists receive an offer of help: Judge Priest accepts the help proffered by the Reverend Brand, while Lincoln rejects the help proffered by Judge Bell. In court the next day, the arguments introduced by the wily defending attorneys overturn the cases for the prosecution restoring the reputations of the accused to the general acclaim of the assembled spectators.

In another borrowing from *Judge Priest*, the scene in which Lincoln defends the Clay brothers from a lynch mob is structured like the scene in which the Judge similarly defends Jeff Poindexter (as discussed in chapter five, this scene was shot but excised by the studio). In both films, the protagonists disarm the crowd through their ready wit, calling out their neighbors by name. In the Lincoln story, the attempted lynching bears more directly on the set piece of the trial than the one in the *Judge Priest* script, since it is directed towards the accused, and establishes the general hostility their lawyer must counteract in the courtroom. Trotti also took the scene in which Judge Priest visits the grave of his deceased wife to talk over his troubles as a model for the scene in which Lincoln overcomes his hesitation to take up law in a conversation addressed to Ann at her graveside.[38]

Despite the fact that the core of his story is fictional, Trotti makes more extensive use of Sandburg than Estabrook did. He seems to have known chapter and verse of *The Prairie Years* and wove small, telling details into his narrative with great skill. A paragraph becomes the inspiration for a scene, a turn of phrase the inspiration for a line of dialogue. For example, Sandburg briefly recounts the way that Lincoln acquired Blackstone's *Commentaries*: "A mover came by, heading west in a covered wagon. He sold Lincoln a barrel. Lincoln afterward explained: 'I did not want it, but to oblige him I bought it, and paid him half a dollar for it.' Later, emptying rubbish out of the barrel, he found books at the bottom, Blackstone's

---

37   Sandburg, *Prairie Years,* 2:55.
38   Rogers's actions and gestures are repeated again by John Wayne as Captain Brittles at his deceased wife's grave in *She Wore a Yellow Ribbon.*

9.1

9.2

Commentaries on the Laws of England."[39] Trotti took this anecdote, highly appropriate for a screenplay about Lincoln as lawyer, as the gist of his first scene. The first, January 13, 1939, script opened with an anonymous family traveling west by covered wagon who trade the barrel containing the book for goods from the Lincoln store. Sandburg also describes Lincoln reading Blackstone, resting "on the flat of his back on the grocery-store counter, or under the shade of a tree with his feet up the side of the tree". Trotti used this brief description of Lincoln reading as the commencement of the next scene, the conversation between Lincoln and Ann Rutledge: "A summer's day. Camera pans down to reveal him in his favorite reading posture, lying on his back, his face in the shade, with his feet high in the air."[40] For Ford's staging, see figure 9.1.

Like many other scenes from the film, Trotti's description of Lincoln's arrival in Springfield is informed by a dense network of references to *The Prairie Years*. Sandburg describes it as a momentous occasion and a major turning point in Lincoln's life.

> Carriages held men riding in top-boots and ruffled silk shirts, and women in silks and laces. It was civilization which Abraham Lincoln, twenty-eight years old, saw as he rode into Springfield that March day in 1837 – to be a lawyer … . The centre of the town was a public square, with the courthouse, jail, stores, churches, banks, harness-makers, and black-

smiths lined about the square. The streets and sidewalks were plain black Illinois soil underfoot.[41]

The biographer also characterized Lincoln as faintly comic and anomalous in this general scene: "As he rode with his long legs straddling a borrowed horse that day in March, 1837, toward Springfield … he had seven dollars in cash in his pockets, and he was more than a thousand dollars in debt." Trotti's first script draft cites Sandburg in order to explain the significance of Lincoln's move to the city and to give inspiration to the art director and set and costume designers:

> Like most small towns of the period, the heart of the town is a public square with the courthouse in the center; the jail, stores, churches, banks and blacksmith shops lining the square. The streets and sidewalks are plain black Illinois soil. There is a "society" here, however, and smart carriages move through the streets, the men in ruffled silk shirts, the women in silks and laces … . Into such a town, one fine day in March, 1837, rides Abraham Lincoln, astride a borrowed pony, coming to Springfield to be a lawyer.[42]

In the scripted version of Lincoln's arrival in Springfield, he is characterized as "comical indeed, with his long legs reaching almost to the ground. He has on a coat, but his pantaloons are still too short for him. He has on a hat, too – a high hat, a relic of his legislator's wardrobe." In the film, Fonda is riding a mule, which not only emphasizes the length of his legs, but also Lincoln's humble

39 Sandburg, *Prairie Years*, 1:163.
40 *Young Mr. Lincoln*, Temporary Script, 13 January 1939.
41 Sandburg, *Prairie Years*, 1:215–216.
42 *Young Mr. Lincoln*, Temporary Script, 13 January 1939.

origins and straitened circumstances (figure 9.2). Nonetheless, he is wearing a high hat, which the actor emphasizes by doffing it to salute the flag that flies from the courthouse. The hat motif, which is prominent in the film, is also indebted to Sandburg. Among many references to the topper, the biography traces Lincoln's transition from coonskin cap to top hat.[43] Similarly, in the film, Lincoln wears a coonskin cap in the winter scene at Ann's grave before donning his signature headgear in Springfield.

A few of many possible examples will illustrate the lines Trotti ingeniously derived from Sandburg's book. In the script drafts, and the film, Lincoln is brought to the verge of a proposal by Ann's sorrowful comment "Some folks I know don't like red hair!" The line reworks Sandburg's reference to one Parthenia Hill "who had married a man who once wanted to marry Ann, saying, 'Ann isn't beautiful – to begin with she has red hair'".[44] During the trial scene, Lincoln makes fun of the lying witness, J. Palmer Cass, by asking him why he "parts his name in the middle". Sandburg describes Lincoln making fun of a witness named J. Parker Green in the same manner, although the joke develops somewhat differently in that case.[45] *The Prairie Years* recounts the adolescent Lincoln intervening in a fight between two men, proclaiming: "I'm the big buck of this lick. If any of you want to try it, come on and whet your horns."[46] Trotti improvises on this threat, splitting it between the characters of Buck and Lincoln during the lynching scene:

> *Lincoln*: Now gentlemen, I'm not up here to make any speeches. All I got to say is I can lick any man here hands down … . Hold on Buck! I thought I'd find that big mouth of yours around here telling people what to do.

> *Buck*: I'm big Buck alright. I'm the biggest Buck in this lick!

> *Lincoln*: Well, come on up and whet your horns!

With *The Prairie Years* as principal text and frame of reference, Trotti drew on a powerful storehouse of documentary evidence, jokes and songs, lore and legend. This source helped to characterize his protagonist with what tradition had consecrated as Lincoln's words and deeds. It also helped to render many lines of dialogue in Sandburg's carefully contrived nineteenth-century Midwestern dialect, which lent even purely fictional scenes and sequences a period gloss.

Problems of Exposition and Emphasis

As one might expect from one of the screenwriters of *Judge Priest* and *Steamboat Round the Bend*, the plot of *Young Mr. Lincoln* did not lend itself to the brisk and linear exposition that Zanuck preferred. Like the scripts for the Will Rogers films, the Lincoln script builds in a roundabout way to the final set piece of the trial. The characters and major conflicts are introduced piecemeal, and it is not until the commencement of the trial that the relationships among the characters are fully clarified and their import revealed. The first act, in New Salem, depicts Lincoln in search of a calling: his attraction to the law comes into conflict with his inherent modesty and uncertainty about his own prospects. He tentatively imagines studying law in Jacksonville while Ann Rutledge (Pauline Moore) attends a ladies academy there, but their mutual plans are cruelly closed off by her death.

The second act, which begins with the move to Springfield, shows a much stronger, more assertive side of Lincoln's character. He trades jokes with the loafers who inhabit the front porch of the general store on the day of his arrival. He masterfully deals with two quarreling farmers who appeal to him for advice. But then the story seems to drift, as Lincoln leaves his office to join in a local fête. The nature of these festivities shifted across the script drafts – from circus parade and midway to Independence Day parade and fair – but the primary function remained the same.

43   Sandburg, *Prairie Years*, 1:302.
44   Sandburg, *Prairie Years*, 1:187.
45   Sandburg, *Prairie Years*, 2:44. This joke is also reported in Frederick Trevor Hill, *Lincoln the Lawyer* (New York: Century Co., 1906), 219–220.
46   Sandburg, *Prairie Years*, 1:52.

They were an excuse to introduce the main characters and initiate the important subplots. Lincoln runs into Stephen Douglas (Milburn Stone) in the company of Ninian Edwards and his wife, and is introduced to Mary Todd (Marjorie Weaver). The Clays travel into town from their homestead in the country for the show. While watching the attractions, Sarah, Matt's wife, is accosted by the inebriated White and Cass (Ward Bond). Later, during the evening festivities, the Clay brothers get into a fight with White and, after Cass's intervention, are accused of his murder. It is only when the boys are faced with lynching by the outraged men of the town that Lincoln enters into association with the Clays, a pact that is sealed in conversation with Mrs. Clay (Alice Brady) at the end of act two.

But there is more exposition yet to come. Stephen Douglas and Mary Todd, the most important historical personages in the film aside from Lincoln, only appear briefly at the fête and are not extensively developed until the dance sequence in act three. At this function, Mary Todd's flirtation with Douglas and simultaneous interest in Lincoln are made manifest. On the next day, Lincoln rides out to the Clay homestead, tries unsuccessfully to get Mrs. Clay to reveal which of her sons killed White, and incidentally receives the almanac from Sarah Clay. Thus, by the start of the trial in act four, Trotti has established the popular sentiment against the Clay boys, Lincoln's fealty to the Clays despite his worry over Mrs. Clay's refusal to choose one son over another, and his personal rivalry with Douglas. Lincoln has also acquired the almanac that will turn out to be his ace in the hole. This disposition of the characters takes over half of the film's one-hundred-minute running time.

Zanuck, never a fan of dilatory exposition, worried about the lack of clear narrative direction, particularly in the opening segment and the second act. At the January 23 story conference, he suggested that the anonymous pioneer family that provides Lincoln with Blackstone be changed to the Clays: "Seeing her [Abigail] in the opening episode will serve to tie her up with the story and will help the transition to the murder and what follows. Too … what he learns in the book which he originally got from her enables him to serve her and her boys later on." Zanuck's suggestion built on two other scenes from Trotti's original draft, both involving Lincoln and Mrs. Clay and set beside that family's covered wagon: in the first, Lincoln agrees to defend the boys following the lynching attempt, in the second they say goodbye following the conclusion of the trial. By making the anonymous pioneers of the first act the Clays, Zanuck not only set up Lincoln's ensuing advocacy on behalf of the family, but created three parallel scenes between Lincoln and Abigail Clay, thereby unifying the plot more tightly.

Zanuck made another change to the opening that brought forward the association between Mrs. Clay and Lincoln's mother, Nancy Hanks. Trotti's first script draft introduced this association at the end of the second act, when Lincoln tells Mrs. Clay that she reminds him of his mother. Zanuck probably added the excerpt from the poem "Nancy Hanks" by Rosemary and Stephen Vincent Benét that appears directly after the credits in the film. It was not mentioned in any of the script drafts and appears to have been added in post-production. Written in the voice of Lincoln's mother, the poem asks how Lincoln turned out, if he grew tall, if he ever learned to read, if he got on. The poem's reference to reading resonates with Zanuck's idea of making Mrs. Clay the source of the book in the first scene. The producer thus made the mother theme already present in Trotti's first draft more prominent as a means of tightening up and streamlining the plot.[47]

Zanuck's revisions and additions personalized a first scene which was originally calculated to bring out Lincoln's affinities with pioneers, or what Sandburg called "movers", as a group. The initial title of the film, "Lawyer of the West", a phrase taken from Trotti's 1938 treatment, derives from this impetus in the writer's work. It is worth tracing out how Sandburg's more general empha-

---

47   This promotion of the role of the mother was very important for the famous reading of *Young Mr. Lincoln* by the editors of *Cahiers du Cinéma*, "John Ford's *Young Mr. Lincoln*", translated in *Screen* 13/3 (Autumn, 1972): 5–44, originally published in *Cahiers du cinéma*, 223 (Aug, 1970): 29–47, although at the time of writing the authors were not aware of Zanuck's intervention.

sis on Lincoln's prairie origins, of which Nancy Hanks was only a part, influenced Trotti's plot, Ford's treatment of it and Fonda's performance of the character.

New Salem: The River

The New Salem section of the film reveals Ford's extraordinarily careful attention to mood or atmosphere, the deliberate pacing that gave the actors time to develop their characters through movement or gesture, and his deep investment in landscape. These concerns inspired his subtle changes to the first scene of the revised final shooting script, the political meeting in which Stuart and Lincoln are running for election. The February 27 script described the audience gathered in front of the Lincoln-Berry store as "good-natured, but rough, backwoods people … . Here and there buckskin breeches and Indian moccasins are in evidence, indicating how really close New Salem is to the wilderness." In an incident presumably indicative of New Salem's rough but good-natured populace, Efe helps himself to a whiskey barrel set up in front of the store during Stuart's oration, becoming so unruly that Lincoln must dunk his friend in a nearby rain barrel before the aspiring politician can deliver his first speech. Zanuck seems to have approved of this rough-housing, since in the February story conference he instructed screenwriter and director to end the first scene with some sort of gag about Efe, still wet from the rain barrel. In the completed film, however, Efe is not present in the opening scene. He does not appear until the celebrations in Springfield, and his friendship with Lincoln is never explained.[48] Analysis suggests Ford eliminated Efe from the opening in order to alter its tone.

As it appears in the completed film, the scene in front of the Lincoln-Berry store does not evoke the Wild West of Trotti's description but a pastoral image of early American democracy. The Clays' wagon pulls up to a clearing bordered by tall trees. The Lincoln-Berry store is a small build-ing midground left, nestled in the forest (figure 9.3). Men are grouped around the porch while women picnic in the left foreground and two girls stand off to their right. The perspective is emphasized by a foreground object, felled logs resting on a cart that point down the road towards the group in the clearing. As the scene progresses, emphasis is placed on the informality but also the seriousness of the proceedings. Although a more polished speaker than Lincoln will prove to be, Stuart is shown hatless, speaking from a porch that barely raises him above the level of the assembled citizenry. This male group is orderly and attentive, some smoking pipes as they listen. They wear store-bought hats, not coonskin caps, many sport vests and jackets, and they stand in a neat array (figure 9.4). The atmosphere is festive but subdued, akin to a church social. After Stuart introduces Lincoln, cut to reveal Fonda in character for the first time. He is sitting off to the right, his legs resting on a barrel (figure 9.5). He rises slowly, the camera tilting up to emphasize his height and panning left to follow his movement. As he assumes Stuart's position at the top of the porch steps, his thin and angular form is echoed by an upright rough-hewn log that supports the porch roof, as well as by the trees in the background (figure 9.6). He rests his hand on the lintel briefly, then fumbles nervously before putting his hands in his pockets. A cut away to Efe at the whiskey barrel would have distracted from Fonda's hesitant movements and from the continuity of the pan that emphasizes Lincoln's height in multiple ways, giving him a heroic visual treatment despite the brevity and modesty of his speech, "short and sweet as the old woman's dance". Ford was inclined to rough humor, and particularly to gags involving whiskey, but clearly he was aiming for a different effect in this scene. Rough-housing belonged to the Springfield streets during the fête, where it was prominent in the contests such as the tug-of-war. But Ford's New Salem opening focused instead on the first, quiet stirrings of Lincoln's political career in a small community on the edge of the wilderness.

---

48   The shooting schedule indicates that Eddie Collins, who played Efe, was among the actors to be called for the Lincoln-Berry store scene, so it is possible that footage involving the whiskey barrel episode was shot, see Shooting Schedule, 1 April 1939, for the days April 8 and April 10, *Young Mr. Lincoln* Legal File, Twentieth Century-Fox Legal Department.

9.3

9.4

9.5

9.6

It is clear that the strong pictorial integration of the people and landscape in figure 9.3, as well as the gentle joke comparing Fonda's figure to that of the porch pole in figure 9.6, were deliberate components of the director's staging and cinematography. However, it should be noted that Ford had to argue for the location shooting which enabled him to exploit natural surroundings in this way. At the February story conference, Zanuck instructed Ford to shoot any necessary location footage in long shots with doubles, and to make process plates for back-projection, emphasizing that "the principals" were not to leave the studio.[49] Ford resisted this directive, perhaps as a result of dissatisfaction with the shots made

with process plates in *Stagecoach*. While he did use back-projection for the river background during the winter scene at Ann's grave and for the later shot in which Efe and Lincoln ride beside the river, he seems to have convinced the producer to let Fonda go on location for other strategically important shots and scenes in the New Salem section of the film. An early shooting schedule indicates that the initial plan was to shoot the scene at the Lincoln-Berry store on the golf course on the Fox lot. In later schedules the location was upgraded to the Sherwood Lake area in the Santa Monica mountains, which is where parts of the first scene were eventually filmed.[50] Similarly, a mid-April trade press report, dated after produc-

---

49   Conference with Mr. Zanuck, 20 February 1939, on *Young Mr. Lincoln*, Final, 27 January 1939, *Young Mr. Lincoln* Story File, Twentieth Century-Fox Legal Department.

50   The shooting schedule dated 14 March 1939 shows the golf course location, while a shooting schedule dated 1 April 1939 shows "Sherwood Forest", and one dated 8 April 1939 shows retakes in the same area. The forest adjacent to Lake Sherwood was then owned by William Randolph Hearst, who frequently rented it out to the studios, see "The History of Lake Sherwood", https://calreinfo.com/the-history-of-lake-sherwood/. There is a set reference photograph of the Lincoln-Berry store without trees and with the road and split-rail fence used in the last scene of the film in the background, suggesting it was initially built on the Fox backlot, Twentieth Century-Fox Film Corporation set reference photographs, *Young Mr. Lincoln* file, Photograph Archive, Herrick Library, AMPAS.

9.7

9.8

9.9

9.10

tion on *Young Mr. Lincoln* had closed at the studio, almost triumphantly confirmed the departure of Ford and "the principals" for Sacramento to film a river scene.[51]

The first scene between Lincoln and Ann is one of the stylistic highlights of *Young Mr. Lincoln*, and one which reverberates throughout the subsequent film. A comparison of the revised final shooting script and the film reveals the remarkable way that the director and actors transformed the valence of the written dialogue. In the scene as filmed, Lincoln comes much closer to an accepted proposal, a change conveyed through the performances and the staging. These elements were augmented by the radiantly backlit trees and softly-lit facial features achieved by Miller, the second unit cinematographer. The later addition

of Newman's "Ann Rutledge" cue, which was re-recorded at an unusually high volume relative to the dialogue, increased the lyrical undertow of the scene.[52]

Ford eliminated portions of Trotti's original scene in production. He cut a brief comic dialogue that precedes Ann's entrance in which Squire Godbey, another comic backwoods type, derides the young man for wasting his time by reading law. He also cut Trotti's final section, in which the couple sit beneath a tree and Lincoln almost proposes, but fails to carry through. The dialogue that remained after these cuts consisted largely of Ann urging Lincoln to have confidence in himself and follow his ambition to study the law, advice he parries with self-deprecating jokes. Ann calls from off frame to arrest Lincoln's reading.

51 "*Lincoln* River Clip", *Hollywood Reporter* (18 Apr 1939): 12, reported that Ford and the principals were about to go on location near Sacramento; L. Metzler, Treasurer, Twentieth Century-Fox, Letter to B. B. Chamberlain, Natomas Company, 17 March 1939, *Young Mr. Lincoln* Legal File, Twentieth Century-Fox Legal Department, asks to utilize the Smith Mound Grove located near Sacramento for *Young Mr. Lincoln,* but at this point the location may have been intended only for backgrounds for the scenes between Lincoln and Ann Rutledge.
52 *Young Mr. Lincoln* bound score, Alfred Newman Papers, Box 1, Cinematic Arts Library, Doheny Library, USC.

9.11

9.12

9.13

Lincoln, law book in hand, steps over the split-rail fence that lines the path to join her. While chatting about other matters, he takes a flower from the basket she is carrying, sniffs it, then takes her basket to carry (figure 9.7). They set off down the path together, turning away from camera. In a brief establishing shot, the couple promenade toward the camera framed by bent tree branches which form a distinct arch, a spontaneously occurring wedding arbor (figure 9.8). The first complete iteration of the "Ann Rutledge" theme begins on this shot. Cut to a medium-long-shot framing, an eighty-second leftward track along the river path, the camera remaining behind the fence at a discrete distance (figure 9.9). A parallax effect is created as we see fence posts, trees and other elements of the terrain pass more quickly in the foreground than the actors in the midground. The contrast in the speeds of movement underscores the grace and ease of their joint amble.

About half-way through the shot they stop at a gap in the fence, Lincoln left and Ann right, a strongly curved tree trunk behind them with the river beyond. As she urges her point about his talents, Fonda indicates Lincoln's embarrassment by looking down (figure 9.10). Over her line "I just had my heart set on your goin' over to Jacksonville to college when I go to the seminary there ...." Fonda snaps into one of his characteristic Lincoln poses, a penetrating stare, the direction of his gaze at Ann echoed by the shape of the tree trunk behind him (figure 9.11). Moore, who has been facing the camera, turns to look at him and lets her line die out as she perceives his stare. An eleven-second silence ensues before Fonda resumes speech: "You're mighty pretty Ann." The long take ends at this point. Cut in to a medium shot of Ann, who speaks after another pronounced pause: "Some folks I know don't like red hair." Cut to a low-angle medium shot of Fonda, with a background of tree branches (figure 9.12): "I do." Cut back to Ann, after a shorter pause, eagerly: "Do ya Abe?" Resume the two-shot framing with only a slight pause as Lincoln says: "I love red hair." This is followed by a thirteen-second pause as they continue to look at one another, and a new iteration of the "Ann Rutledge" theme commences. She shyly retakes the basket and turns to depart. Cut into long shot as Moore moves off left, backlight illuminating the tree and Fonda looking after her in the midground (figure 9.13). The wedding-arbor effect is again pronounced. Cut to a position closer to the river, as Fonda walks towards it with several glances off left in Ann's direction. He picks up a stone and gracefully pitches it into the water. Ford added this last bit of business to make the transition to the following montage of river shots which takes us to the winter scene at Ann's grave. But considered in the context of the prior conversation, it also seems a discrete expression of joy, and a tribute to the river's beauty. In the courtship scene as filmed, the emphasis is not on Lincoln's timidity so much as the joint movement through a locale which renders complete verbalization of the couple's mutual understanding unnecessary. When they arrive at the gap in the fence, the conversation slows down and the film shifts into shot-reverse-shot as both Lincoln and Ann pause, hesitate, and speak volumes in small phrases.

In his script drafts, Trotti had deliberately developed a theme about the inarticulateness of common people, a theme climaxing in the contrast between Mrs. Clay's refusal to identify which of her sons killed Scrub White and the verbal acuity of the lawyers involved in the trial. Lincoln defends Mrs. Clay when she is harassed to speak on the witness stand, describing her as one of many country women who "say little and do much". When empaneling jurors, he chooses Sam Boone (Francis Ford) who is praised as "honest", even though the backwoodsman, in a manner reminiscent of Harpo Marx, responds to his questions only with bashful nods of the head.[53] Trotti had also planned to have the whole Clay family sit in silence during the scene in which they gather together in the jail after the disastrous end of the first day in court. In production, Ford eventually opted to have them quietly hum the hymn "Leaning on the Everlasting Arms", a hymn Newman later made the basis of the musical cue "The Clays". Nonetheless, the Clays' reticence is still highlighted. And, while Lincoln proves himself a master of oratory in the course of the trial, he starts out in the New Salem sequences as one of the quiet people.

Springfield: the Mob and the Dance

In the final story conference on *Young Mr. Lincoln*, Zanuck criticized the circus scenes in the January 27 script, which he considered dull and lacking focus on Lincoln. He liked one episode, in which Lincoln bested a circus performer in a contest of strength, but charged Ford and Trotti with changing the circus to a country fair, and coming up with additional contests for the hero. He also directed them to shorten the sequence.[54] In the event, Ford and Trotti decided to make the fair an Independence Day celebration inaugurated by a parade honoring the veterans of American wars. Despite Zanuck's instructions, they effectively lengthened the sequence and largely preserved its open-ended quality. However, they did remake the episodes of the day to better illuminate Lincoln's character. During the parade, Lincoln observes a panorama of American history, culminating with the veterans of the revolution of 1776, for whom he removes his hat. During the fair, the pie contest is a comic anticipation of Mrs. Clay's later dire predicament of being asked to choose between her sons. In Fonda's brilliant performance of Lincoln as judge, he manages both to eat voraciously and to discourse eloquently on the virtues of peach and apple pie in turn, unable to make a choice.[55] He can be seen still munching on pie at the beginning of the tug-of-war episode. In this later event, where he serves as anchor to Efe's team, Lincoln surreptitiously takes advantage of an adjacent donkey cart to give his side an advantage when they prove unable to resist the superior force of the opposing Hog Wallow Boys. The incident anticipates many later wily moves on Lincoln's part such as the calculated use of jokes told during the trial and, ultimately, the clever resort to the almanac as evidence in court.

But the parade and fairground proved to be much more than a device for bringing together the major characters of the story and featuring

---

53. It is not clear if Trotti envisioned Francis Ford in the part of the silent witness when he wrote this episode, which appears in the first, 13 January 1939, script.
54. Conference with Mr. Zanuck, 20 February 1939, on *Young Mr. Lincoln*, Final, 27 January 1939, *Young Mr. Lincoln* Story File, Twentieth Century-Fox Legal Department.
55. *Young Mr. Lincoln* bound score, Box 1, Alfred Newman Papers, Doheny Library, USC, contains a cue for a hog-calling competition that Ford, or Zanuck, later removed in favor of the more generic rail-splitting competition that follows the pie contest in the film.

9.14

Lincoln's strength and crafty nature. It also set up two very different social groups that would eventually be allied against Lincoln and the Clays in the course of the trial – a rough male group which included Scrub White and Palmer Cass, and the upper-class Springfield elite. The sequence begins on the sidelines of the parade route with a crowd that is characterized as lower-class and mildly unruly. Lincoln and Efe stand with a group who initially chant a comic rhyme in time with the marching soldiers. At Lincoln's instigation, they quiet down to show respect for the veterans of the revolution. As a young woman dressed as Miss Liberty rides by in a pony cart, two older women call out vociferously. Miss Liberty breaks her pose to greet her mother and the ensuing shouted remarks reveal that she serves flapjacks at a local establishment. Two unattended boys with a slingshot disrupt the parade by shooting at a mounted officer who loses control of his horse, causing havoc on the sidelines. Ford also seeds the friendly but rambunctious crowd with men who will later make up the lynch mob. Sam Boone makes his first appearance wearing his coonskin cap and carrying a jug while marching at the head of the veterans of the war of 1812. He appears later at the forefront of the lynch mob that tries to break into the jail. Buck (Jack Pennick), who Lincoln calls out during the lynching attempt, is first introduced by the fairground barker as the head of the Hog Wallow Boys at the commencement of the tug-of-war.

The staging of Lincoln's meeting with the Edwardses, Todd and Douglas puts them at a remove from the street crowd. Lincoln wanders up into the grandstand where the foursome are seated in the front row.[56] A group of genteel ladies standing to the left of Douglas indicates the lack of additional seats, and also perhaps his self-absorption, while Lincoln calmly seats himself on the floor of the platform (figure 9.14). The fête thus provides a panorama of Springfield social classes and types, from the highest reaches of the social elite to backwoodsmen such as Efe and Sam Boone, and the friendly Lady Liberty who in reality waits tables. In his essay on the film, Eisenstein praised the "frantic, frantic movement of the merriment of a provincial fair",[57] but it should be noted that this sense of movement and merriment is rooted in the crowd on the street and not the elite in the grandstand. Moreover, Ford masterfully depicts how the energy of this crowd is transformed as night falls, the tar barrels are lit and the somewhat rowdy men, drunk and overcharged by the festivities, become hostile when confronted with the murder of one of their own, supposedly by strangers. He establishes the popular origins of the lynch mob by having the men break off from the festive crowd in the town square to gather at the crime scene after the killing, and then race from the crime scene to the jail following the arrest of the Clay brothers.

The dance sequence that initiates the third act of *Young Mr. Lincoln* focuses on the upper echelons of Springfield society and further develops the Todd-Douglas subplot introduced at the parade grandstand. In the 1938 treatment, Trotti forthrightly spells out its inner logic: "Douglas is Lincoln's rival for Mary's affection, just as he will be Lincoln's rival for the Senate, on the stump in the greatest debates ever held in this country, and for the Presidency itself." In all of the script drafts the romantic rivalry between Lincoln and Douglas is more overt than in the film. In the version of the dance sequence from the second draft, Douglas and Lincoln have a somewhat prickly conversation in which his plan to support Felder

---

56 Ford seems to have devised this staging during production; in the revised final script draft, this encounter took place on the street, with Lincoln simply moving away from the company of loafers.
57 Eisenstein, 275.

9.15

9.16

9.17

9.18

9.19

in court is revealed. In the same draft, Mary Todd explicitly frames the upcoming trial as a contest for her favor:

> *Mary Todd*: I'm not looking for flattery in men, but intelligence – and the courage to seize from life all that it has to offer. Something in me – my woman's intuition, perhaps – tells me you can be that kind of man if you wish to be – that you can go on – and on –

Lincoln [*a quizzical smile on his lips*]: You haven't by any chance got me mixed up with Mr. Douglas, have you? *My name's Lincoln.*

Mary Todd: Mr. Douglas is that kind of man, too. Perhaps *he will be the – stronger.*[58]

In the film, however, the romantic rivalry between the men, and Mary's somewhat mischievous way of pitting them against each other, is only suggested visually, as in figure 9.15, in which Douglas stands in the background, watching Todd invite Lincoln to invite her to dance. Ford effectively subdues this subplot in favor of an emphasis on the class difference between Lincoln on the one hand and both his rival and his intended on the other.

The dance sequence is dominated by the strains of "The Cuckoo Waltz", a choice Trotti specified as early as the first complete script of January 13, 1939. The "waltz", in duple time despite its name, derives from the "Lincolns and Hankses" chapter of *The American Songbag*. The

58 *Young Mr. Lincoln*, Final, 27 January 1939, this is the second of the three drafts.

210

song's lyrics, which are sung in the course of the dance, refer to a "charming girl", Miss Susan Brown, "with golden slippers on".[59] Trotti was probably drawn to this piece because the lyrics could be associated with Mary Todd. But if Trotti found it, Ford made it his own. The tune became a staple of the square dances in the post-war films. In the famous sequence from *My Darling Clementine*, Wyatt Earp and Clementine Carter dance to it on the floorboards of the unfinished church. In *Fort Apache* it is played at the non-commissioned officers' dance, temporarily suspending the dispute between Colonel Thursday and Sergeant Major O'Rourke. In *The Sun Shines Bright* the dance occurs at the Strawberry and Lemonade Festival that brings together all of the factions of the town on the eve of Judge Priest's fight for re-election. In Ford's works taken as a whole, then, "The Cuckoo Waltz" is a song of social communion. It has a similar function in *Young Mr. Lincoln*, but the communion is limited to the Springfield elite and operates to the exclusion of Lincoln.

The sequence begins with an instrumental version of "The Cuckoo Waltz" heard over a montage composed of Mary Todd's written invitation and Lincoln's humble preparations for the event – he cuts his own hair and polishes his own shoes. The dance music continues as a liveried butler carrying Lincoln's top hat walks through a spacious entrance hall, followed by Lincoln himself. Pan left with Lincoln as he walks further into the house and track back as he turns toward camera, in the apparent direction of the music. The track back continues through a doorway revealing the presence of dancers in the foreground, all holding hands as they circle around the room (figure 9.16). Lincoln's separation from the group is emphasized by the doorway as well as the closed circle of hands. He is approached by a group of elderly gentlemen who claim his attention.

The cut to shot 250 reveals the palatial drawing room in which the dance is taking place (figure

9.17). Although a caller intones the steps and even sings the lyrics, this square dance is exceedingly refined. The ladies are outfitted in white gowns, the gentlemen wear white gloves, coats and tails. In shot 252, the camera, now moving among the dancers, tracks in on the Todd-Douglas pair who join with another couple to form a quadrille-like group. Hold on Todd-Douglas as they separate off (figure 9.18). Cut to a close shot of the spinet player who is as far from the typical square-dance fiddler as possible (figure 9.19). He is a wearing an elaborately ruffled shirt front that recalls Sandburg's description of the elegance of Springfield's inhabitants. His music rests on a beautiful wood scroll and a candle, housed in glass, burns to his right.

Near the conclusion of the waltz, the camera tracks through the moving dancers to close in on Lincoln, still in his position outside the door, talking with the older men. As the dancers disperse, Mary Todd seats herself in a corner of the drawing room. Douglas stands at her side, carefully removing one of his gloves. He compliments Todd's graceful dancing and, referring to the male group on the other side of the door, opines: "Mr. Lincoln is a great storyteller. Like all such actors he revels in boisterous applause." And later: "He has ability in handling an unthinking mob. Not even his enemies deny he has a certain political talent." Cut to Lincoln and the older men, now standing in the richly appointed reception room. In response to an inquiry about whether he belongs to the well-known Lincoln family of Massachusetts, Lincoln replies (Fonda playing up the vernacular diction): "Then I say the evidence is all against us belongin' to it. No Lincoln I ever knew amounted t' a hill of beans."[60] Both Douglas's unabashed condescension and Lincoln's joking deflection of the older gentleman's inquiry imply that Lincoln is in some sense out of his element within this upper-class gathering.

Lincoln and Todd begin dancing to a slow waltz in triple time with an exaggerated oompah accompaniment. Although Newman jokingly

59   The tune is an old one, sometimes titled "Golden Slippers", and has had different lyrics set to it. The film employs the lyrics in Sandburg, *American Song Bag*, 160; a legal memo references the Sandburg song collection, James O'Keefe, Memo to George Wasson, 25 January 1939, Twentieth Century-Fox Legal Files.
60   This retort has a basis in an incident recounted in Carpenter, 122.

entitled the cue "Lincoln's Revenge",[61] it seems clear that Lincoln is the one discomfited in the course of the dance. Fonda's stiff-backed posture, in contrast to his character's usual relaxed and lounging stances, suggests that Lincoln is less than at ease. The camera starts in close and tracks back, then pans back and forth to follow the couple as they circle round, surrounded by the other dancers. Lincoln seems to be managing well enough until the music cadences and resumes with "The Cuckoo Waltz", at a faster tempo and in duple time. While the other dancers smoothly adjust to this rhythmic shift and continue dancing, Lincoln stops in confusion. Douglas can be seen in the background, observing his embarrassment. With Todd's help Lincoln eventually takes up the rhythm, even giving a little hop on the upbeats as they continue. However, Todd breaks it off, with a flirtatious laugh: "Mr. Lincoln, at least you're a man of honor. You said you want to dance with me the worst way and I must say you kept your word. This is the worst way I've ever seen." Todd then invites Lincoln to talk instead of dance, leading the way through the now almost empty reception area through which the strains of "The Cuckoo Waltz" continue to resonate.

There is an abrupt change of mood as they pass from the well-lit interior to the dark front porch, illuminated principally by light spilling out of the door and windows. On the sound track, the dance music fades, and the "Ann Rutledge" theme takes over. Cut to a view of the river from the front porch, then to a low-angle shot of Todd and Lincoln in which he appears transfixed by the view (figure 9.20). She gives him a backwards glance as she moves off toward the house and settles herself on a settee, expecting him to follow. Cut to Lincoln still standing, looking at the river, and fade to black. This striking scene evolved slowly over the course of production. In the second script of January 27, written before Ford's involvement, Lincoln and Todd exit the house and pass onto the front lawn where several guests

9.20

are gathered. As they walk through the garden, Todd, as quoted above, makes clear that she is looking for a successful husband. Set reference photographs for the film demonstrate that a series of garden sets were constructed to stage this walk, suggesting that it was planned this way even after the start of production.[62] However, the pages for the scene in the third script of February 27, 1939, were removed in favor of new pages dated April 11, 1939, when production was well advanced. In this modified version, Lincoln and Todd exit onto the porch, not the lawn, and Lincoln becomes absorbed in the view of the river.[63] At the same date that the scene with Todd was modified, the director added the subsequent scene in which Lincoln rides by the river with Efe, and in which the backwoodsman states: "I never saw a man in my life look at a river like you do. Folks'd think it was a pretty woman or something." Thus, Ford added two references to the river, and indirectly Ann Rutledge, in early April. At this date, he likely anticipated being able to take Fonda and Moore to Sacramento to shoot the scene with Anne Rutledge by an actual river (as noted, their departure was announced in the trade press on April 18). And, he adjusted the scene with Mary Todd in anticipation of the scene with Ann that he was about to shoot. Nonetheless, even the pages dated April 11 included a brief exchange about Lincoln's prospects for winning the trial as

61 *Young Mr. Lincoln* bound score, Box 1, Alfred Newman Papers, Doheny Library, USC.
62 Twentieth Century-Fox Film Corporation set reference photographs, *Young Mr. Lincoln* file, Set #42, #43, #46, Photograph Archive, Margaret Herrick Library, AMPAS.
63 These changes appear in the third script of 27 February 1939, in new pages marked as revised on 11 April 1939, *Young Mr. Lincoln* Story File, Twentieth Century-Fox Legal Department.

well as Lincoln eventually joining Todd on the settee. The remaining dialogue and action were likely cut in post-production after the decision was made to use the "Ann Rutledge" cue as underscore.

The scene on the porch as filmed may be readily assimilated to the legend that holds that Rutledge was Lincoln's true love as opposed to Todd, with whom he reputedly had an unhappy marriage. But Ford amplifies the traditional contrast between the women by inviting a comparison between the tenor of the scenes – the relaxed and companionable walk versus the strict formality of the dance with its unexpected rhythmic shifts, natural vistas versus an opulent constructed setting. And this contrast becomes poignant in the context of the dialogue and staging of the dance sequence, which has clearly positioned Lincoln as outside his class. The river speaks, not only of Ann, but of New Salem – the beauty of the tree-lined waterway, the egalitarian community, the lack of pretension. Sandburg evoked Lincoln's prairie origins by describing the round of tasks on the farm, the young Lincoln plying his ax alone in the woods, the Indiana clay oozing between his bare toes,[64] but Ford made these origins palpable by summoning up the memory of a landscape.

In the later sequence in which Lincoln visits the Clay homestead, Lincoln's rural origins are more explicitly, perhaps too explicitly, evoked in dialogue. On the way to the farm, Lincoln and Efe ride and talk beside a back-projected river. In conversation with the Clay women, Lincoln recalls the apple trees that grew outside his own family's log cabin while Mrs. Clay recalls her husband's death and raising her family on the farm. But this evocation of rural life, almost entirely a matter of the dialogue and voiced in studio-constructed exteriors, suffers in comparison with the earlier scenes.[65] In compensation, Newman pulled out all of the stops for the underscore which, as was typical, was mixed at a high volume relative to the speech. All the predominant cues

derive from the New Salem scenes: "Mr. Lincoln", "the Clays", and, of course, "Ann Rutledge".

The Trial

Trotti's decision to restrict his story to the 1830s bypassed the most consequential events of Lincoln's political career and represented a significant departure from precedent, and from his most important source. The second volume of *The Prairie Years* begins with the passage of Douglas's Kansas-Nebraska Act, which opened the territories of the Louisiana purchase to additional settlement and to the extension of slavery. It becomes the moral and intellectual thread which organizes the second half of Sandburg's biography.[66] The process of Lincoln finding a cause and an antagonist in Douglas also provides a very satisfactory narrative arc, one that culminates in the campaigns against Douglas for the Senate and the Presidency. The last act of Sherwood's play follows a trajectory similar to Sandburg's second volume. Even Estabrook, charged with closing on the centerpiece of the trial, squeezed what promised to be a highly anachronistic version of a Lincoln-Douglas debate into his plan for the trial sequence set sometime in the 1830s.

The denouement of Trotti's 1938 treatment for the Lincoln story remained somewhat indebted to these sources. In the treatment, Douglas himself prosecuted the case against the Clays, so that the two lawyers faced off directly as they would in the debates. The introduction of Felder as prosecuting attorney in the January 13 draft, which permitted Trotti to remake the prosecutor along the lines of Maydew in *Judge Priest*, sidelined Douglas to some extent. Nonetheless, all of the script drafts contained dialogue scenes in which Douglas advised and supported Felder and conferred with Judge Bell. None of this dialogue survived in the completed film. While Ford shows Douglas in conversation with Felder, thereby implying his support for the prosecution, the conversations are never audible to the spectator. With

---

64   Sandburg, *Prairie Years*, 1:49.
65   There are three establishing shots as Efe and Lincoln approach the Clay homestead that look like real landscapes and, according to the shooting schedule, were shot on location in Sherwood Forest.
66   See, for example, Sandburg, *Prairie Years*, 2:5–18.

9.21

9.22

the addition of the character of Felder, and the progressive reduction of Douglas's role in assisting the prosecution, the legal proceeding came to seem much less like a dry-run for the Lincoln-Douglas debates. Instead, the resolution of the trial provided its own morally and dramatically satisfying ending, independent of Lincoln's political "future".

The denouement in the completed film, similar to that of *Judge Priest*, is structured through the time-honored devices of reversal and recognition. In the Rogers film, the Reverend Brand slowly but spectacularly reveals the defendant's true identity as a Confederate hero and protective father of Ellie Mae, justifying his altercation with the plaintiff. This recognition brings about a triple reversal of fortunes – the defendant is vindicated, the way is cleared for Rome's marriage to Ellie Mae, and Judge Priest is assured of re-election in his campaign against the prosecuting attorney. The trial in *Young Mr. Lincoln* concludes with a double reversal: of the unjust accusation against the Clays, and of Lincoln's imminent loss of his first case. The reversals are produced by the proof of Cass's guilt, and entail a further acknowledgement of Lincoln's superior juridical craft and acumen. Douglas plays a particularly important part in the general recognition of Lincoln's sterling qualities. Having first dismissed Lincoln as a storyteller, a man effective at handling an unthinking mob but hardly up to the challenge of a thinking one, he is finally brought round to promising the young Lincoln that he will never underestimate him again.

While Trotti's scripting of the trial scene in

Young Mr. Lincoln drew heavily from the one in *Judge Priest*, Ford's direction differed markedly between the two films. The denouement of the Rogers film depended upon extensive superimpositions that portrayed the accused's exploits during the Civil War, heroic images of battle that surround the narrating witness as if projected behind him (see figures 5.1 to 5.3). Of course, it also depended upon the music, on "Dixie", for which the Judge had shrewdly bargained and on which he, and the film, relied. In contrast, there are no special effects in the trial of the Clay boys and no music, apart from the rhythms of the actors' speech. Rather, Ford utilized shot composition and staging to play Fonda's elegant and understated performance against Donald Meek's calculatedly over-the-top histrionics and Ward Bond's bad-boy antics on the witness stand. In both close shots and deep-space compositions, he set off Fonda's slightest words and gestures, and celebrated the character of Lincoln. It was a mise-en-scène bonanza.

The staging began with the set. While we do not have direct evidence of Ford's collaboration with Day, it seems unlikely that he did not communicate with the art director about his basic requirements, especially since he had already staged a similar courtroom scene. Day packed the area adjacent to the judge's bench and the witness box much more tightly than art director Darling had in *Judge Priest*. In figure 9.21, from the Rogers film, the elevated judge's bench and witness box are isolated within an alcove and fenced off by a railing, well removed from the jury box midground right. Moreover, the seating arrange-

9.23

9.24

9.25

ments place the legal antagonists at opposite ends of the set. Horace Maydew, visible back to camera beyond the witnesses in the foreground, directly faces the judge, while the table utilized by the defense is off left. In Day's set the jury box is squeezed into the right rear corner, directly adjacent to the witness box (figure 9.22). Moreover, the lawyers, accused, and principal interested parties are crammed around a single central table in the foreground in much greater proximity to the judge. While the frontal view of the Springfield courthouse audience illustrated in figure 9.23 accommodates many rows of spectators and a great apparent distance to the back wall, it should be noted that the foreground group remains tightly packed, with the line of Clay women pancaked behind the brothers, and the whole group flanked by the lawyers's seats, indicated in this shot by their respective top hats.

Despite the close quarters, Day's set design provided for a clear spatial distinction between the respectable citizenry, seated in the central aisles of the courtroom, and the rowdy male group familiar from the fête and the lynching, accommodated in the standing room along the sides. In figure 9.24 Mary Todd and her sister sit amongst the crowd in the center with Douglas behind them on the right (the women remain visible in the long shot framing of figure 9.23 thanks in part to their wide-brimmed bonnets). In figure 9.25, Sam Boone, jug in hand, emerges from the bay of standees adjacent to the prosecutor's side of the table. The sheriff, standing behind the gate at the railing, is typically posted near this group to assist the judge's efforts to maintain order. Buck, a virulent Clay opponent, stands on the right and is usually prominent in the shots of this area.

The tight configuration of the playing area permitted the director to exercise his ingenuity in creating alternatives to shot-reverse-shot for the examination of witnesses (rapid-fire shot-reverse-shot is reserved for Felder's harassment of Mrs. Clay during her testimony). Fonda as Lincoln assumes a series of spectacularly unconventional poses in the course of the trial. For example, during the empaneling of Bill Killian, Lincoln is stretched out across the bottom third of the frame, feet propped on the corner of the clerk's desk, while Killian stands in the midground with the prospective jurors rear right (figure 9.26). In a touch that suggests the close collaboration between actor and director, Fonda marks Lincoln's final acceptance of Killian by lowering one leg and rocking back and forth in his chair, a comic point emphasized by a tilt down (figure 9.27). On several occasions, when Lincoln interrupts

9.26

9.27

9.28

9.29

9.30

9.31

Felder's witnesses, the director cuts to a long shot of the actor looming in the foreground, seated beside his hat, witness and jury in the background (figure 9.28).

Many of Ford's shots play off of the L-shaped space composed of clerk, judge, and witness along the back wall, and the jury to their right. For example, in figure 9.29, during the examination of the sheriff, Meek as Felder shows the murder weapon to the witness, while also triumphantly displaying it to the jurymen. Figure 9.30 is from the almost thirty-second shot in which Lincoln, building the case for self-defense, tells the joke about the farmer's dog.[67] While Fonda as Lincoln

67 Although not cited in Sandburg, this joke, which appears in Trotti's earliest draft, as well as some other ripostes made during the trial, are part of the Lincoln canon, see Henry S. Cohn, "Abraham Lincoln at the Bar", *The Federal Lawyer* (May 2012): 55, citing Hill, 217–218.

9.32

9.33

9.34

9.35

9.36

judge has ordered the clerk to strike the joke from the record, Fonda, with only a slight change in position, moves to address the off-screen jury: "Don't remember about that dog" (figure 9.31). The tight configuration of the central playing area permits this clever use of off-screen space.

The proximity of the lawyers, the accused and the rowdy spectators allowed for direct confrontations which sometimes intimate a renewal of the crowd's violence. This threat is played up in the course of Felder's opening argument, which involves a bravura series of movements across and around the set. Meek as Felder begins speaking directly to the jury. In the course of describing the struggle between Scrub and the accused, the prosecutor refers to Scrub as a "peace-loving servant of the law". Cut to Fonda, who has already been established as browsing through a bookcase on the other side of the courtroom, incongruously perched on the railing with book in hand (figure 9.32). Fonda parodies Meek's phrase: "From all I hear Scrub was doin' some mighty fancy fightin'

looks at the witness, ostensibly addressing him alone, his joke is actually intended for a much wider audience. The composition permits us to observe the judge, midground top right, and the clerk of the court, background lower left, waiting for the punchline. As these officials break into laughter, Ford cuts to a medium long shot of Todd laughing, with Stone as Douglas seeming less than pleased (figure 9.24). Later, after the

9.37

9.38

for a 'peace-loving man'". Meek turns his back on the jury and advances toward his antagonist, moving directly toward the camera (figure 9.33). He responds with a cliched encomium for the deceased: "True Mr. Lincoln! True! For Scrub White was a man. An American! In whose veins flowed the blood of pioneers who braved the wilderness to make this great state what it is." Cut to the judge who has fallen asleep. Cut to Meek who continues, eventually returning to his position facing the jury. His oration builds to a climax: "Scrub White loved life. He loved the blue of God's heaven, the soft caress of the south wind. He loved life, but, he is dead." Over these lines, Fonda, now standing in front of the bookcase, glances in the direction of the sleeping judge. Cut back to Meek after the word "dead" (figure 9.34). He points off right and moves toward the table, the camera panning to follow him (figure 9.35). "And there, gentlemen, there sit his murderers!" The shot continues as Meek pivots to the left and reaches out to the standees: "I tell you, gentlemen..." cut away to the Clay women, then back to Meek, "they must be wiped out as a man wipeth a plate!" The standees go wild, potentially threatening the stoical defendants who sit directly to their right (figure 9.36). The noise awakens the judge who pulls out a six-gun with one hand while pounding with his gavel for order with the other.

The scene thus shifts the axes of conversation and regard at multiple points. Meek reverses his position 180 degrees to make his retort to Lincoln on the wall opposite the jury box. He later shifts his address from the jury to the standees by way of the accused. Moreover, following the judge's intervention, another perspective on the space is activated as Lincoln is abruptly manifested in the center of the playing area viewed from the perspective of the Clays (figures 9.37 and 9.38). These movements around the set effectively contrast the social groups and competing legal interests that are in conflict during the trial. Moreover, they provide a canvas on which Fonda can enact Lincoln's irony and self-possession. In "Mr. Lincoln by Mr. Ford", Eisenstein praised the unity of concept and purpose in Ford's style.[68] This is particularly evident in this section of the trial, in which the set design beautifully facilitated the director's staging and framing strategies, which in turn released Fonda to make the most of every posture and every reaction shot.

But, as one might expect, Ford saved his biggest effects for the reversal. During the initial questioning of Cass on the second day of the trial, Fonda as Lincoln plays possum, feigning uncertainty and insecurity as he leads the unsuspecting witness to repeat his assertion about the moonlight that illuminated the crime scene. Then, abruptly changing tack, he pulls the almanac from his hat and lets loose the lightning of his terrible swift sword – a flurry of questions that harry Cass to the point of confession. In contrast with Felder's oration, which is heavily dependent on editing, Lincoln's attack is filmed in a three-minute take interrupted only by two short cut-ins near the

9.39

9.40

9.41

9.42

close. With each question or assertion, Lincoln's words gradually reconfigure the space, as the company is mobilized in response to them.

Bond has stepped down from the witness box and is on his way out of a heretofore little-used gate, opposite to the jury's side of the room (figure 9.39). Presumably Ford established this exit with its relatively more open sight lines so that he could move people around in the background over the course of this long take. Lincoln "recalls" that he has another question and asks several. On the question "What did you kill him for?" both judge and prosecutor stand, and Stone as Douglas turns in his seat to face camera, looking up at Lincoln (figure 9.40). In this framing, the almanac is just visible in the hat that rests on the table, in what Ford has established as its usual place, now directly in front of Douglas, who has taken Lincoln's usual seat. The hat motif is further emphasized by the hats of the jurymen which hang from pegs in the right rear corner of the room. Fonda picks up the almanac while moving forward toward Bond,

who has turned to face him (figure 9.41). As he directs the witness to "look at page twelve", some of the jurymen stand rear right, and the sheriff (Cliff Clark), vacating his usual post near the jury box, circles around to appear on Lincoln's left. In this configuration, Fonda blocks our view of the seated Stone, but Meek remains visible in the aperture between Fonda and Bond. The actors remain in these positions for over a minute and a half with slight, but significant variations as Lincoln's dialogue slowly builds to his conclusion that Cass stabbed White in the back. For example, a slight reconfiguration of the staging in figure 9.41 emphasizes Fonda's line: "You see what it says about the moon? That the moon was only in its first quarter that night, and set at 10:21, *forty minutes before the killing took place*." Over the course of this dialogue, additional members of the jury stand. At the final phrase Bond looks up at Lincoln and drops the almanac to the floor, and the murmuring of the crowd increases. Eddie Quillan, playing Adam, is briefly visible as he

9.43

9.44

9.45

9.46

9.47

stands, looking back towards Lincoln, before he is blocked by Bond in the foreground. "So you see it couldn't have been moon bright, could it? You lied, didn't you Cass? And you weren't tryin' to save these boys' necks, were you? You were trying to save your own! Weren't ya! Well come, weren't you!"

As Bond begins to deny the evidence, the interrogation gets quite heated, with Fonda raising his voice and running over the other actor's lines. As they argue about the reason for Cass's admitted quarrel with Scrub, the sheriff moves forward to stand beside Lincoln at the gate, as if providing him with backup. Lincoln begins to hypothesize about the real reason for the quarrel: "Maybe it was money. Maybe you owed him money or maybe he owed you some. Maybe he was getting a little graft here and there and you wanted to get in on it." On this last line of Fonda's, Bond goes through the gate, definitively revealing Quillan (figure 9.42). Fonda then steps to the right on the phrase: "Well I'll tell you what happened … ", closing the gate and leaning aggressively towards Bond (figure 9.43). His new position blocks our view of Meek in the midground, and isolates Quillan, thereby highlighting the victim of Cass's lie. The actors hold this blocking configuration for the duration of the lines: "You heard a row and you saw the fight start. And you come runnin'. And you saw that Scrub was still livin'. And right there on the ground you saw the knife

220

that Matt had dropped. And you bent over him and you picked up the knife. And your body hid what you were doin'. And you stabbed him. You stabbed him in the back and killed him."

There is a decisive reconfiguration of the blocking following the completion of Lincoln's accusation. Fonda moves back on the line "And these two boys, Matt and Adam", to look at his clients while explaining their motivations for remaining silent. At the same time, Clark comes through the gate to stand opposite Bond (figure 9.44). The attorney for the defense and the sheriff are now clearly working together. Moreover, they have friends. On Fonda's line "They each knew he didn't do it", Ford begins to track back revealing the standees gathering in the foreground in silent disapproval of Cass (figure 9.45). The camera movement is slight but important, demonstrating that Lincoln has won over the popular, rowdy crowd. This vivid illustration of the change in the group's allegiance actually dwarfs the lines that explain the conduct of Lincoln's clients. Hence the necessity of the cut to a close up of Alice Brady as Lincoln explains that Mrs. Clay saw the knife in Matt's hand but "couldn't say so without puttin' a rope around his neck". Fonda then returns to his position at the now open gate, to resume his address to Bond: "And you. You killed him. And ya lied. And your lie tripped you up." Over the course of these words, Stone appears in the background, approaching the judge at the bench (figure 9.46). Cut in to a close up of the judge waving off Douglas in order to listen to Lincoln's words. Return to the long shot framing as Lincoln forces a confession from Cass and the crowd, including Buck, close in on the murderer (figure 9.47). It is clear that Lincoln has won over the room.

The staging of this shot is perfectly pitched to the dialogue, and to Fonda's performance of the relentless barrage of questions. The actor re-mains largely in the midground, his movements small but powerful: leaning to the right to accuse the lying witness, turning away from the camera and walking back a few steps and then coming forward to renew the attack. And, unlike Will Rogers, charming in his refusal to hit marks or memorize lines, Fonda's rigorous control opened the way to more complicated deep-space compositions. His slight movements, along with Bond's, hide and reveal characters standing directly behind them on cue. Without apparent artifice, Fonda holds his position, as in figure 9.43, for the duration of highly emotional and important lines. Ford could also confidently track back to extend the foreground, or have Stone pop into background (figure 9.46) while counting on Fonda to hold our attention in the midground. The final effect is of an electrifying attack which ramifies throughout the space.

The importance of *Young Mr. Lincoln* needs to be assessed both in terms of its immediate impact on the situation at Twentieth Century-Fox and in terms of the long arc of Ford's career. Although Zanuck had resisted the project in 1938, he began to benefit from it as early as January 1939 when he optioned the actor to two films a year on the basis of getting the part.[69] While *Young Mr. Lincoln* was still in production, he moved quickly and efficiently to capitalize on this contract, getting two more projects underway for Fonda and Ford. The first of these was *Drums along the Mohawk*. The studio had acquired the rights to the novel by Walter D. Edmonds in September 1936 and invested in two treatments, one by Bess Meredyth and one by William Faulkner, before putting the project on hold.[70] In October, 1938, Zanuck made a third attempt, assigning scriptwriter Sonia Levien, and planning for Randolph Scott and Nancy Kelly in the principal roles.[71] Seeing the rushes for *Young Mr. Lincoln* apparently led him to rethink the film

---

69 See note 28.
70 Walter D. Edmonds, *Drums along the Mohawk* (Boston: Little, Brown, and company, 1936). Treatment, 9 January 1937, Bess Meredyth, *Drums along the Mohawk* file, Twentieth Century-Fox Collection, Doheny Library, USC; Treatment, William Faulkner, 15 March 1937, *Drums along the Mohawk* Story File, Twentieth-Century Fox Legal Department.
71 Story Conference, 30 December 1938, on First Draft Continuity, 2 December 1938, by Sonia Levien, *Drums along the Mohawk* file, Twentieth-Century Fox Collection, Doheny Library, USC. I have not been able to find the subject of the conference, the First Draft Continuity by Levien.

and to put Trotti on the project.[72] After reading and severely critiquing Trotti's first, March 11, draft, he wrote to Ford offering him a story "exactly for you", with a "magnificent" script by Trotti and the opportunity to shoot in Technicolor.[73] Ford's and Fonda's participation on *Drums along the Mohawk* were separately announced in late April.[74] Perhaps partly due to the decision to shoot in three-strip Technicolor, which in this period was often utilized for shooting outdoors in natural surroundings, the project, in contrast with *Young Mr. Lincoln*, involved extensive work on location. Sets were built in the upper end of Sidney Valley in the Dixie Forest Reserve in Utah and the studio arranged for food and lodging for a cast and crew of 250.[75] Thus, by this point, it seems clear that Zanuck considered director and star a team worth the highest level of investment.

The Grapes of Wrath is the third and last of what has come to be considered Ford's and Zanuck's trilogy of American history films (under the assumption that *The Grapes of Wrath* counts as contemporary history).[76] Zanuck's negotiations with John Steinbeck for the rights culminated in a contract dated April 24, 1939, and thus, like *Drums along the Mohawk*, this project was in the works prior to the close of production on *Young Mr. Lincoln*.[77] There is some evidence that it was planned for Ford and Fonda from the earliest stages of script development, if not from the outset. The July 19 story conference on Nunnally

Johnson's first complete script draft included a provisional cast list with Henry Fonda as Tom Joad.[78] The subsequent rumor published in the trade press that Spencer Tracy was being considered for the part instead of Fonda was likely leaked by the studio as part of an effort to put pressure on Fonda, who recalled being persuaded to sign an exclusive contract with Twentieth Century-Fox in order to get the part.[79] The completion of Johnson's first script also prompted Zanuck to pressure the famously recalcitrant Ford to commit quickly to the new project. A mid-July letter drafted by the director from his company's Utah location attempted to bargain for more time to complete *Drums along the Mohawk* as well as a month off before starting *The Grapes of Wrath*.[80] In the event, Ford closed on the former on September 5 and started on the latter on September 28, at less than a month, one of his shortest vacations on record.[81]

Drums along the Mohawk and *The Grapes of Wrath* should be considered first and foremost Zanuck projects, planned to take advantage of the talent he had on contract or wanted to secure under contract. Along with *The Return of Frank James* (Fritz Lang, 1940), these projects were engineered to show Fonda off to best advantage (which was no doubt why the actor bound himself to the studio). They were also designed to interest Ford and keep him employed at his home studio on high-budget projects that redounded to the credit of Twentieth Century-Fox – no more

72 The extant drafts by Trotti and related story conferences are as follows: Temporary Script, 11 March 1939, by Lamar Trotti, *Drums along the Mohawk* file, Twentieth-Century Fox Collection, Doheny Library, USC; Story Conference, 4 or 5 April 1939 on script of 11 March 1939; Story Conference, 3 May 1939, on Final Script of 24 April 1939 by Lamar Trotti; Shooting Final, 18 May 1939, by Lamar Trotti, all in *Drums along the Mohawk* Story File, Twentieth-Century-Fox Legal Department.
73 Zanuck, Memo to Ford, 18 April 1939, Ford correspondence, Lilly Library, IU.
74 "Ford Directs *Mohawk*", *Hollywood Reporter* (25 Apr 1939): 1; "*Mohawk* Leads Set", *Hollywood Reporter* (26 Apr 1939): 1. At this point Fonda and Kelly were announced for the film; Claudette Colbert did not replace Kelly until May.
75 J. N. Smith, Cedar City, Utah, to Twentieth Century-Fox Film Corporation, 24 June 1939; Twentieth Century-Fox Film Corporation, Letter to Anderson Boarding and Supply Company, 28 June 1939, both in *Drums along the Mohawk* Legal File, Twentieth Century-Fox Legal Department.
76 See, for example, McBride, 267, 309.
77 John Steinbeck, *The Grapes of Wrath* (New York: The Viking Press, 1939). Agreement for *Grapes of Wrath*, Viking Press, Inc., John Steinbeck and Twentieth Century-Fox Film Corporation, 24 April 1939, *The Grapes of Wrath* Legal File, Twentieth Century-Fox Legal Department.
78 Screenplay, 13 July 1939, by Nunnally Johnson; Story Conference, 19 July 1939, on the screen play, 13 July 1939, by Nunnally Johnson, both in *The Grapes of Wrath* Story File, Twentieth Century-Fox Legal Department; Behlmer, *America's Favorite Movies*, 125–127.
79 "Century-Fox Bids Tracy for Fonda *Grapes* Role", *Hollywood Reporter* (5 Sep 1939): 1; Teichmann, 128–129.
80 Ford, unsigned carbon of Letter to Zanuck, 17 July 1939, and Ford, drafted Memos to Zanuck and Koenig, ? July 1939 [archivist's date], Ford correspondence, Lilly Library, IU.
81 Employee Closing Notice, 5 September 1939 and Employee Starting Card, 28 September 1939, both in John Ford Contract File, Twentieth Century Fox Legal Department.

Hurricanes, no more *Submarine Patrols*. This is not to say that Ford suffered from making *Drums along the Mohawk* and *The Grapes of Wrath*. Advantages were conferred – shooting on location in Technicolor on *Drums along the Mohawk*, his first collaboration with cinematographer Gregg Toland on *The Grapes of Wrath*, continuing his collaborations with Fonda – but it seems clear that he had little to say about the choice of story or script development. His role in the production process on both *Drums along the Mohawk* and *The Grapes of Wrath* was thus closer to the one he had on *The Prisoner of Shark Island*, where he elaborated upon Zanuck's and Johnson's script, than to the one he had on *Wee Willie Winkie*, where he played an active role in developing character and story.

Young Mr. Lincoln occupies a unique position among the films Ford made at Twentieth Century-Fox before the War in that Trotti had worked with Ford under Wurtzel and had deep knowledge of the Rogers films. From its very conception the film was Ford's, in the sense that it consolidated and refined prior films by the director. This included not only the components of the *Judge Priest* script discussed above, but also the method of magpie plot construction discussed in relation to *Steamboat Round the Bend* in chapter five. In that film, the storyline drawn from Burman's novel was augmented by the tall tale evoked in the song "Steamboat Bill". The bet on the boat race which derived from the song was so removed from the other concerns of the plot that the filmmakers could successfully bury it until the culminating rescue of Duke, the moment that called for reversals. Ford's and Trotti's interest in creating surprises operated slightly differently in *Young Mr. Lincoln* than in *Steamboat Round the Bend*. Thanks to its inclusion in the popular canon of Lincoln stories and anecdotes, it was possible that many spectators would have picked up on the significance of the farmer's almanac for the upcoming trial upon its first appearance at the Clay homestead. Nonetheless, like the punchline of a familiar joke in which the structure of the delivery remains unaltered, the almanac was initially downplayed, and then magically produced, as if it were a surprise. At the Clays, Lincoln casually asks for something to write upon and is handed the only paper in the house, his subsequent doodling with a pencil more prominent in the frame than the pamphlet itself. Later, the young lawyer just happens to be perusing a pamphlet when Judge Bell visits Lincoln to propose a plea bargain. As Lincoln dismisses the judge, the actor reveals the pamphlet's title to camera before lightly tossing it aside. Then, in the midst of a courtroom where hats adorn the walls and seem to multiply on the central table, the almanac emerges from Lincoln's fabled topper to undermine Cass's story and initiate the reversals.

Not only is *Young Mr. Lincoln* structured around a more or less expected surprise, but, like *Steamboat Round the Bend*, it is composed in a roundabout manner, drawing on heterogeneous sources and encompassing apparent digressions. It is clear that Zanuck was discomfited by the loose-jointed narrative structure, assimilating the pioneers of the first act to the subplot concerning the Clays, and directing Ford and Trotti to truncate the episodes of the fair and to focus them more tightly on Lincoln. Analysis demonstrates the writer's and director's quiet resistance to the second directive, their persistent use of the fair episodes to explore the town, and to set up the social distinctions between the backwoodsmen, the rowdy urban-dwellers and the Springfield elite. These "digressions" eventually paid off in the trial scene, in which the different social strata could be distinguished in the audience, and were eventually joined in admiration of the veracity and morality of the young lawyer's arguments.

Young Mr. Lincoln can thus be situated at the crossroads of two different production situations; it was both a Fox film and a Twentieth Century-Fox film. While the story was indebted to the old Rogers unit, Zanuck's influence is most evident at the level of the film's style, which was enabled by the talented crew that Ford had access to following the merger: Glennon and Miller, Day and Newman. One other quality of the film distinguishes it from *Drums along the Mohawk* and *The Grapes of Wrath* and helps to explain its unique position within his œuvre: the conception of the hero, which Ford inherited from Sandburg, via Trotti.

He looked like a farmer, it was often said; he seemed to have come from prairies and barns rather than city streets and barber shops … . The very words that came off his lips in tangled important discussions among lawyers had a wilderness air and a log-cabin smack … . As he strode or shambled into a gathering of men, he stood out as a special figure for men to look at; it was a little as though he had come farther on harder roads and therefore had longer legs for traveling; and a little as though he had been where life is stripped to its naked facts and it would be useless for him to try to put on certain pretenses of civilization.[82]

This conception operated at many levels in the film, informing Trotti's characterization of Lincoln as the "Lawyer of the West", the contrast Ford established between Lincoln and the Springfield elite at the dance, and Fonda's quasi-heroic and quasi-comic performance of Lincoln's speech, gait and postures. But, in addition, the hero's wilderness air, his palpable difference from the common run of city men, pointed a way forward to the post-war films. Such a characterization may also be applied to Wyatt Earp as acted by Fonda in *My Darling Clementine*, and to Captain York as acted by John Wayne in *Fort Apache*, a film in which Fonda gamely took up the Felder-Douglas position as the representative of civilization's pretenses. Thus, in the *annus mirabilis* of 1939, Ford not only consolidated the stylistic techniques and storytelling strategies which had preoccupied him since the coming of sound, but laid down some chits for the future.

82 Sandburg, *Prairie Years*, 1:303.

Afterword

The Director's Share

He just photographed him [Victor Mature] – he just photographed all of us. Where Ford was great was knowing where to put his camera and he hated if it wasn't on a tripod. He was old-fashioned, so he hated dolly shots – he'd do them, reluctantly – but he loved it if the camera was on a tripod. The guy slung the tripod over his shoulder and Ford said "Put it right down here".

Henry Fonda, interviewed by Lindsay Anderson[1]

With the completion of *Young Mr. Lincoln* in April 1939, Ford still had five films left on his contract with Twentieth Century-Fox and he remained fully ensconced as a contract director. By the end of 1940, however, this phase of his career was obviously coming to a close. With multiple Navy connections but no official sanction, Ford had taken it upon himself to create a filmmaking unit for active duty in World War II, recruiting and training men for what would become the Field Photographic Branch of the Office of Strategic Services.[2] Between June of 1939 and December of 1940 he had also completed three of the remaining five films owed to Zanuck – *Drums Along the Mohawk*, *The Grapes of Wrath* and *Tobacco Road* – and would fit in one more, *How Green Was My Valley*, before the War. In addition, having completed *The Long Voyage Home* in the spring of 1940, he had begun planning for a second Argosy production. In a May 1941 letter to Bolton Mallory,

Ford referred to a pending adaptation of Graham Greene's *The Power and the Glory*,[3] eventually released as *The Fugitive*. At that point the director was hoping to film in Mexico with Gregg Toland as cinematographer and Thomas Mitchell in the lead role. But, as Ford informed Mallory, the project had to be postponed since Merian Cooper had been called up for service in the Army, and the director and proposed cinematographer had been notified that their mobilization in the Navy was pending. Ford's military career and the definitive move into independent production would be transformative for his production process and his films, topics slated for future research. Here, it seems appropriate to look back at Ford's work in the studio system in the 1930s, and to consider what he left behind.

Ford was doubly lucky during the 1930s phase of his career. The first stroke of luck was that Fox fired him in 1931. With Harry Wurtzel's help, he rapidly began to take advantage of the fact that he had the whole sandbox to play in, and for the rest of the decade would be negotiating deals outside his home studio, and pushing against the restrictions of his subsequent contracts. His temerity is particularly evident in the years immediately following the merger of Fox with 20th Century, in which he followed up a six-month leave to make the last two films on his RKO contract with a request, via Goldwyn, for another six-month leave for *The Hurricane*. The second stroke of luck was Zanuck's labor-sharing arrange-

---

1   Anderson, 222.
2   Ford's correspondence, Lilly Library, IU, includes letters to personnel of the 11th Naval District in 1939–1940 seeking recruits and proposing a photography unit in the Navy. By January, 1941, Ford was shooting *Sex Hygiene* for the US Army in partnership with Zanuck. Ford and over 100 members of his unit enlisted in September 1941. See Lea Jacobs, "*December 7th, The Battle of Midway*, and John Ford's career in the OSS", *Film History* 32/1 (2020): 3–4.
3   Graham Greene, *The Power and the Glory* (London: Heinemann, 1940), published in the U.S. as *The Labyrinthine Ways* (New York· Viking Press, 1940). Ford refers to it by the American title in his May 1941 letter to Mallory, Ford correspondence, Lilly Library, IU.

ment with Goldwyn (again, the brilliance of the bid to make *The Hurricane*). Even as Zanuck rewrote the director's contract in 1937 and sought to enforce an agreement that limited the director's outside activities, the United Artists connection opened new doors, enabling Ford to move with Fox colleagues to make films with Goldwyn and Wanger at the same time that new resources flowed into Twentieth Century-Fox. These were the preconditions of the *annus mirabilis* of 1939. It is hard to imagine the director making *Stagecoach* in the form it assumed without his prior experience with Glennon making *The Prisoner of Shark Island* and *The Hurricane*. It is also hard to imagine *Young Mr. Lincoln* without the contributions of Glennon, Day and Newman.

Thus, in a period when many filmmakers were locked into exclusive contracts with a single studio, Ford ranged more widely. For a director of his reputation and experience, he also made a very large number of films, typically three or four a year as against two, at most, for an A-list director such as Henry King. He was able to do so not only because he worked quickly but because he seemed happy to accept projects outside the highest budget range. Thus, he did not miss a beat when film budgets were cut at Fox in the early years of the Depression, readily switching from the large casts, more leisurely production schedules and elaborate settings that he enjoyed on *4 Sons* and *The Black Watch* to what amounted to B-production methods on *Salute* and the early sound films that followed. On *Salute*, he cut costs by repurposing Movietone footage and shooting on location at Annapolis. In *Men Without Women* and *Seas Beneath* he continued to make use of Navy equipment and facilities, and shot major scenes on location off the southern California coast. At RKO, he opted for modest projects in order to secure his own choice of story or casting, famously deferring salary in order to make *The Informer* and *The Plough and The Stars* on a very moderate scale. He also bartered a high-budget prestige project for a smaller one when he agreed to make *Mary of Scotland* in exchange for *The Plough and the Stars*. Ford's flexibility in terms of

budget ranges, and his idiosyncratic sense of what kinds of project would be fun to pursue are fully in evidence in his decision to turn down Zanuck's offer of *Suez*, with a multi-million dollar budget and bona-fide stars, in favor of *Submarine Patrol*, with a B-plus budget, no-name actors and a script based on a technical military history of the splinter fleet.[4]

Ford's ability to move from studio to studio and the large number of projects he undertook extended his professional networks and enhanced his ability to build, and rebuild, his preferred casts and crews. Following the ouster of William Fox, he had taken advantage of the lapse in centralized authority at Fox to build a semi-autonomous unit with James McGuinness and William Collier. One of his greatest coups was to reunite key members of this group at RKO in the mid-thirties, although it is not quite clear how he managed to insinuate Victor McLaglen into the lead role on *The Lost Patrol*, nor how he managed to shake Joseph August loose from Columbia for *The Informer*. When the director resumed work at Fox in 1933, his short-term contracts allowed him to exchange one assigned film for one of his choice – *Doctor Bull* for *Pilgrimage*; *The World Moves on* for *Judge Priest*. In the case of *Doctor Bull*, an assigned Will Rogers film, Winfield Sheehan chose the screenwriters and Ford had nothing to do with the choice of story or script development. But, for *Judge Priest*, the director was able take control of script development, utilizing Dudley Nichols and Lamar Trotti who already reported to Sol Wurtzel at the Western Avenue lot where Ford chose to make the film. With *Judge Priest*, Rogers also became important to Ford's crew, not simply in his capacity as star but also in his capacity as humorist. Ford's decision to utilize the stories of Irvin S. Cobb for subject matter likely derived from Rogers himself, given the star's previous connections with Cobb, and their common interest in dialect comedy and the regional setting of the rural South. And, given his talent for improvised dialect humor, Lincoln Perry should also be considered a member of the team. That is, the director effectively created a loosely knit group

---

4   Ray Millholland, *The Splinter Fleet of the Otranto Barrage* (New York: Bobbs-Merrill, 1936).

around Rogers that could feed the star material to his taste and match his performance style. Team-building in this sense was part of every competent director's remit, but it was a clearly a task at which Ford excelled.

While Ford entirely deserves his reputation as a capricious, secretive and dictatorial boss, we need to attend to more than anecdotes about the interpersonal dynamics on set to understand his methods of direction. His techniques evolved in the early sound period as a consequence of three experiences: first, the constraints of multiple-camera shooting during the transition to sound; second, the specific problems of filming Will Rogers; and third, his advocacy of directorial autonomy in connection with the formation of the Director's Guild, and confrontations with Zanuck about changes made to his films in post-production.

Following the transition, the difficulty of synchronization, and of cutting sound on film meant that sound and image had to be taken at the same time. Ford avoided the flattening effects of the multiple-camera method by abjuring typical shot-reverse-shot staging and editing. Instead he opted for shooting conversation scenes with a single camera in a long take, as in the case of the interaction between Ronald Colman and Helen Hayes in the kitchen scene in *Arrowsmith*, or by focusing multiple cameras on a single actor, as he did with Richard Bennett during the scene of Sondelius's death in the same film. These solutions restored depth to his compositions while maintaining the synchronization of sound and image and giving his actors the ability to move freely about the set, punctuating the dialogue with gestures and the manipulation of props (as Colman did) and to improvise their lines and react to the sound effects simultaneously recorded on set (as Bennett did).

Will Rogers, a true vaudevillian and too important to be bossed around, regularly improvised his lines, gestures and movements. He could not be expected to make or keep his marks. He also refused to do retakes. Filming Rogers thus posed problems analogous to dialogue scenes in the early sound period – the director had to capture the performance in real time. And, since Ford avoided the use of multiple cameras at this point, there could be no cutting in for close ups. One can

observe the director resorting to longer takes to deal with these constraints in the scene in *Steamboat Round the Bend* in which Fleety Belle's relatives invade the *Claremore Queen*. Ford shot Ann Shirley's interaction with Charles Middleton, playing her abusive father, in a shot-reverse-shot segment, but for Rogers's confrontation with the same character used a single framing, from behind the star.

Zanuck's recutting of *Steamboat Round the Bend* does not seem to have been extensive. In addition, the producer's cuts and displacement of footage in the last act of *The Prisoner of Shark Island* were clearly justified in the sense that they provided a much more compelling introduction to the yellow-fever epidemic than that given in the shooting script (although it would be interesting to know what was destroyed, that is, the entire scene in solitary confinement as originally paced and staged). But the director's perceived loss of control over these films, shortly followed by Briskin's remaking of *The Plough and the Stars* at RKO, must have reinforced his desire to minimize the possibility of re-editing by studio executives. While cutting in the camera may have been his practice even prior to the conflicts with Zanuck and Briskin in 1935 and 1936, afterwards it became a matter of principle, a means of asserting his authority. With the exception of fast-cut action sequences, such as the Apache attack in *Stagecoach*, Ford most frequently divided his scenes into long-shot framings for establishing shots and group interactions, and medium-long-shot framings for interactions between two characters. These were carefully interleaved with singular medium shots or close ups with unmistakable cues as to their placement due to matches on action, point-of-view relationships and/or lines of dialogue. As Zanuck's favorite editor, Barbara McLean, told Thomas Stempel, the cutting was implicit in the footage: "You couldn't hurt a Ford picture, you know."

Ford's experiences dealing with the constraints of shooting with early sound technology as well as his concern to limit options for tampering with his work in post-production reinforced his existing predilection for deep-space compositions and actively discouraged him from some of the most common forms of classical Hollywood scene dissection. For example, in the trial scene in *Young Mr. Lincoln*, the questioning of witnesses rarely takes the form of alternating shots of single characters, with the exception already noted of Felder's aggressive questioning of Mrs. Clay, which contains very rapid cutting between the interlocutors. When Lincoln questions witnesses he is frequently included in the frame (as in figure 9.26 in which Fonda is stretched out on the bottom of the frame while Robert Lowery, playing Bill Killian, stands in the background). The director did sometimes cut away to indicate the reactions of the crowd, and of the Clay women as a group (and some of the discontinuities in the configurations of the seated Clay women suggest that Zanuck changed up the reaction shots). But many of the most dramatically salient interactions between Lincoln and his audience occur in a single framing, as in figure 9.30, during the questioning of the sheriff, when Lincoln recounts the joke about the farmer's dog to the off-screen jury while being observed by the court clerk and judge who are wedged into the corners of the frame. The long take in which Lincoln forces Spig to confess is the ultimate extension of this strategy, as Fonda advances towards Bond in the midground, as the whole social machinery of jury, judge, opposing attorneys and even the audience circle round.

Even before the development of more sensitive film stocks made it relatively easy to activate backgrounds through deep-space compositions in the style of *Stagecoach* and *Young Mr. Lincoln*, we find Ford's actors interacting side by side rather than in tightly edited single shots. In *Steamboat Round the Bend*, Shirley and Rogers frequently stand facing camera at the wheel of the *Claremore Queen*, with the river back-projected behind them. In *The Informer*, McLaglen and Margot Grahame are shown reflected in the travel agency window as they contemplate the impossibility of reaching America. Ford did not dislike cutting per se, indeed, we find brilliant examples of scene dissection as early 1917, as demonstrated in the example of *Straight Shooting*. Moreover, the av-

erage shot lengths of his films of the 1930s are only slightly longer than the norm.[5] But his framings tend to be highly differentiated with much less frequent repetitions of setups than the norm. This was partly due to his desire to prevent meddling in post-production – repeated setups are an invitation to an editor to change things up – but also an effect of his powers of invention – even where a repetition might have made sense, he liked to fiddle with the subsequent iterations of a potential series to reflect changes in mood or the dramatic situation. One example, from *Stagecoach*, is the eye-line matches as the passengers at the entrance to the Apache Wells inn watch Curly carry Lucy into the bedroom (figures 8.33 and 8.34). One might expect that the long shot which culminates with Curly entering the bedroom, and his shadow projected on the wall of the hallway, would be capped by a return to the previous shot of the onlookers. Instead, Ford cuts to a new setup, a frontal medium shot of Trevor and Mitchell, who had already been established as part of the group. They look off left in the direction of the bedroom as a spotlight catches the left side of Mitchell's face, emphasizing his expression of trepidation. The change of setup emphasizes their joint realization of the task ahead of them, as the ones who are specifically called upon to help, giving greater emotional resonance to Trevor's line, "Come on, Doc".

The director's decisions about camera placement followed from his preference for allowing action to play out within the parameter of the shot. While Fonda recalled these decisions as occurring spontaneously on set, "Put it right down here", and no doubt they sometimes did, the evidence of the films themselves points to a great deal of forethought. This is obvious in the case of the elaborate choreography of a long take such as the denouement of *Young Mr. Lincoln*. It is also apparent in the close co-ordination of set design and framing throughout Ford's films of the 1930s. Sets were built to accommodate key camera positions. The distinctive architecture of the inn at Apache Welles permitted scenes organ-

---

5   According to Salt, 236, the mean ASL for American sound films between 1928 and 1933 was 10 seconds and for the period 1934 to 1939 fell to 8.6 seconds. The average ASL for Ford's films in the same periods start at 12.3 seconds and fall to 9.4 seconds.

ized around the three doorways – the front entrance, the portal leading to the bedroom and the other exterior door, and the door to the kitchen where Doc is sobered up. Similarly, as noted, the courtroom in *Young Mr. Lincoln* clearly distinguished the distinct social groups interested in the proceedings and allowed the director to frame the interactions between lawyers and witnesses with judge, court clerk and jury in the background of the shots. In *The Prisoner of Shark Island,* the prison sets may have been modeled on the actual ruins of Fort Jefferson, but they were engineered to accommodate multiple camera positions and used to provide surprising revelations of space: three different perspectives defined by the buildings within the walls (figures 6.9, 6.10 and 6.11); the ground view of the main gate contrasted with one from the second story arcade (figures 6.8 and 6.15) and, on the open-air set of the prison exterior, a contrast between the initial views of the bridge favoring the area to the left (figure 6.6) versus the long perspective on the right revealed on the night of the escape (figure 6.7). A similar level of forethought is evident in the planning for shooting on location in *Wee Willie Winkie*, with Ford reporting back to Zanuck and the screenwriters about his vision of the confrontation between the British and Pashtun forces on the steps leading up to Khoda Khan's stronghold (figures 7.1 and 7.2).

Ford's experiences in the early sound period had important consequences for his subsequent treatment of actors. In a departure from industry practice in the middle 1930s and after, his cast members were not expected to repeat lines multiple times as scenes were filmed from multiple angles. While he did not generally expect actors to improvise their lines as Rogers had, he seems to have wanted to replicate the effect that the comedian's improvisation had on other cast members. As already described, some actors complained about not receiving the cues they expected from Rogers, but others enjoyed the challenge of having to instantaneously reformulate their lines

in relation to the star's performance, and Lincoln Perry recalled that he and Rogers sought to surprise each other. These sorts of interactions on set seem to have motivated or reinforced Ford's concern to keep the performances in his films alive and fresh. He limited rehearsal, as Fonda recalled in the case of his scene with Jane Darwell in *The Grapes of Wrath*. Moreover, experienced actors generally found Ford uncommunicative about their parts although Harry Carey, Jr., recollects that he gave explicit instructions to neophytes.[6] Sometimes the director introduced new bits of business or dialogue just prior to shooting, improvements on the scene, certainly, but also changing things up for the cast.[7] His general approach was to ensure that actors understood the mechanics of the scene in advance – where they needed to be in relation to each other, the direction of their glances, the camera movements if any. He also seems to have employed more or less devious stratagems for setting the mood, through rituals such as having Danny Borzage play music on set, and possibly through personal interactions such as picking on a cast member. But Ford ultimately gave his actors a great gift – the uninterrupted time of his takes. Colman could pace up and down the kitchen set in *Arrowsmith* at will, Perry and Rogers could trade barbs as they negotiated the Black man's performance of "Dixie", Fonda as Lincoln faced with his first political address could drag out his approach to the crowd and fumble with his hands. When the lights went on and the cameras rolled, Ford's actors knew that this might be their only chance to make their points, that they had to expect the unexpected from other cast members, and that they were correspondingly free to follow their instincts and emotions. The shot compositions had been foreseen and very closely controlled, but the stage was theirs.

Authorship criticism has too often been concerned with parsing the director's individual contributions to a film, as opposed to those of others,

---

6   Carey in Anderson, 212–213, described Ford demonstrating to Ben Johnson and himself what was wanted in the course of scenes in their early films together.
7   Fonda in Anderson, 222: "It [*Young Mr. Lincoln*] was a beautiful script, but like in *Clementine* there were things that he'd put in at the moment, just little pieces of business, sometimes little pieces of dialogue, that were so right on."

especially screenwriters – Hawks versus Furthman in *To Have and Have Not*, Welles versus Mankiewicz in *Citizen Kane*. Such analyses become particularly tendentious when screenwriters attempt to counter what they experience as an over-emphasis on the director's art by asserting their own claims to authorship. In Ford's case, this occurred with both Nunnally Johnson, who disparaged Ford's contributions to *The Prisoner of Shark Island* while claiming primary credit for script and story, and Philip Dunne, who suggested that Ford merely "faithfully and brilliantly" shot *How Green Was My Valley* while claiming that the primary credit for the film belonged to Zanuck, Wyler, who worked on the project in pre-production, and himself.[8] But even more fair-minded attempts to isolate a single or primary creative source for the films of the 1930s run counter to the conditions of production in the Hollywood cinema. In the highly specialized labor system of the studios every film was touched by many hands as a relatively small number of people generated relatively large numbers of movies under strict budget and time constraints. They also closely watched each others' films, and more or less creative borrowings were the norm. Sometimes borrowing occurred via shared genre conventions or story material – Hawks and Wead reworking Van Every and Wead's script for Ford's *Air Mail* in *Ceiling Zero*, for example. On other occasions borrowing occurred through the accumulated experiences of the crew. Zanuck wanted mood lighting in *The Prisoner of Shark Island*. Perhaps at Zanuck's suggestion, Ford took up with Bert Glennon, a veteran of von Sternberg's famously stylized lighting in films such as *Underworld* (1927) and *The Scarlet Empress* (1934), and who had also shot *Grand Canary* (1934), about a pandemic and with low-key lighting effects, in

Lasky's Fox unit. Shooting in 1935, director and cinematographer had access to more sensitive film stocks than had previously been available. Under these conditions, their partnership gave rise to path-breaking innovations in low-key cinematography in *The Prisoner of Shark Island* and *Stagecoach*. That is, very distinctive and apparently personal stylistic choices were made possible through a network of affiliations and shared expertise which included the duo's work with multiple producers and directors not to mention their reliance on advances made by the chemical engineers at Eastman Kodak.

Above all, Ford was a wily and pragmatic director who had come of age in Hollywood as the studio system was being formed. His survival strategy, apart from the *Araner* and frequent drinking binges, was to mine the system for what it could best provide – craft. The most productive years of his career were marked by sustained, purposeful and highly creative collaborations. Following the release of *Stagecoach* in 1939, Nichols wrote to Ford from the east coast:

> If there was ever a picture that was the director's picture it was that one, and I tried to make that clear to everyone who complimented me in New York … . I feel I was a very happy collaborator and tried to do my best as did Bert Glennon, Tolubov [set designer Alexander Toluboff], Lovey [editor Otho Lovering] and the rest. That is one thing you invariably do, inspire your whole crew including the writer to pitch in and do their best. I don't believe you will ever have a bad crew.[9]

Taking our cue from Nichols, our object should not be to separate Ford's work from his writers, casts and crews, but rather to understand the magic he wrought with the sometimes merry bands he managed to bring together.

---

8   Philip Dunne, *Take Two: A Life in Movies and Politics*, updated edition (New York: Limelight Editions, 1992), 98.
9   Nichols, Letter to Ford, 26 Mar 1939 [archivist's date], Ford correspondence, Lilly Library, IU.

Bibliography

Primary Document Collections

Argosy Pictures Corporation Business Records, MSS 1849, L. Tom Perry Special Collections, Harold B. Lee Library, Brigham Young University, Provo, Utah.

Cooper, Merian C., papers, L. Tom Perry Special Collections, Harold B. Lee Library, Brigham Young University, Provo, Utah.

Ford, John, papers, Lilly Library, Indiana University, Bloomington, Indiana.

Fox Movietone News, Moving Image Research Collections, University Libraries, University of South Carolina, Columbia, South Carolina.

Goldwyn, Samuel, papers, Special Collections, Margaret Herrick Library, Academy of Motion Picture Arts and Sciences, Beverly Hills, California.

Macgowan, Kenneth, Scrapbooks, Cinematic Arts Library, Doheny Library, University of Southern California, Los Angeles, California.

Newman, Alfred, papers, Cinematic Arts Library, Doheny Library, University of Southern California, Los Angeles, California.

Nichols, Dudley, papers, UCLA Library, Department of Special Collections, Manuscripts Division, Charles E. Young Research Library, Los Angeles, California.

RKO Radio Pictures records, UCLA Library, Department of Special Collections, Manuscripts Division, Charles E. Young Research Library, Los Angeles, California.

RKO Radio Pictures research collection compiled by Richard Jewell, Special Collections, Margaret Herrick Library, Academy of Motion Pictures Arts and Sciences, Beverly Hills, California.

Twentieth Century-Fox Collection, Cinematic Arts Library, Doheny Library, University of Southern California, Los Angeles, California.

Twentieth Century-Fox Film Corporation set reference photographs, Photographic Archive, Margaret Herrick Library, Academy of Motion Picture Arts and Sciences, Beverly Hills, California.

Twentieth Century-Fox Contract Files, Twentieth Century-Fox Legal Department, 10201 West Pico Boulevard, Los Angeles, California. These files were viewed during two trips to the studio in March and June 2018 prior to its acquisition by Disney. Readers wishing to verify the primary sources should address inquiries to the author.

Twentieth Century-Fox Legal Files, Twentieth Century-Fox Legal Department, 10201 West Pico Boulevard, Los Angeles, California. These files were viewed during two trips to the studio in March and June 2018 prior to its acquisition by Disney. Readers wishing to verify the primary sources should address inquiries to the author.

Twentieth Century-Fox Story Files, Twentieth Century-Fox Legal Department, 10201 West Pico Boulevard, Los Angeles, California. These files were viewed during two trips to the studio in March and June 2018 prior to its acquisition by Disney. Readers wishing to verify the primary sources should address inquiries to the author.

United Artists Corporation Records, Series 2H, Music Cue Sheets, Wisconsin Center for Film and Theater Reseach, Wisconsin Historical Society, Madison, Wisconsin.

United Artists Corporation Records, Series 4G, Walter Wanger Preproduction, Wisconsin Center for Film and Theater Research, Wisconsin Historical Society, Madison, Wisconsin.

Wanger, Walter F., papers, Wisconsin Center for Film and Theater Research, Wisconsin Historical Society, Madison, Wisconsin.

World-Wide-Web Sources

All these sites were accessible as of May 3, 2025

American Film Institute Catalog of Feature Films, https://aficatalog.afi.com/.

"Blue Bonnets over the Border (1)", *The Traditional Tune Archive*, https://tunearch.org/wiki/Blue_Bonnets_Over_the_Border_(1).

Bocquel, Joe, *Harold E.Morehouse Flying Pioneers Biographies collection*, National Air and Space Museum Archives, Smithsonian Institution, https://sova.si.edu/record/nasm.xxxx.0450/ref49?t=W\&q=bocquel.

Darling, William S., *Art Directors Guild Hall of Fame*, https://adg.org/awards/hall-of-fame/william-s-darling/.

"Drill, Ye Tarriers, Drill", *The Traditional Ballad Index*, http://balladindex.org/Ballads/LoF217.html/.

Fox Studios Historical Timeline, Century City Chamber of Commerce website, https://centurycitycc.com/fox-studios-historical-timeline/.

History of Lake Sherwood, The, California Real Estate Consultant Groups website, https://calreinfo.com/the-history-of-lake-sherwood/.

Internet Broadway Database, https://www.ibdb.com.

Internet Movie Database, https://www.imdb.com.

Motion Picture Association of America, Production Code Administration Records, Margaret Herrick Library Digital Collections, https://digitalcollections.oscars.org/digital/collection/p15759coll30.

Santa Clarita Valley history website, https://scvhistory.com/scvhistory/lw2142c.htm.

"Secret Set Location Where Shirley Temple starred, A"', Iverson Movie Ranch blog, https://iversonmovieranch.blogspot.com/2022/01/a-hidden-filming-location-for-john.html.

"Steamboat Round the Bend: Songs and Stories of the Mississippi", Smithsonian Institution Folkways Records website, https://folkways-media.si.edu/docs/folkways/artwork/FW09774.pdf.

Steiner, Max, cues for *The Informer*, Max Steiner Digital Thematic Catalog, maintained by the Max Steiner Institute, https://maxsteinerinstitute.org/film.php?id=88.

"Wha Saw the Forty Twa", *The Traditional Tune Archive*, https://tunearch.org/wiki/Wha_Saw_the_Forty_Twa.

"Wha Wad'na Fecht for Charlie", *The Traditional Tune Archive*, https://tunearch.org/wiki/Wha_Wad'na_Fecht_for_Charlie.

Magazines and Newspapers Consulted

American Cinematographer

Billboard, The

Bookman, The

Exhibitors Daily Review

Exhibitors Herald-World

Film Daily

Film Spectator

Film Weekly

Hollywood Reporter

International Photographer

Irish Times

Kinematograph Weekly

Listener, The

Los Angeles Times

Motion Picture Herald

Motion Picture News

Moving Picture World

New Theatre

New York Herald Tribune

New York Post

New York Times

Time

Variety

Published Sources

Anderson, Lindsay, *About John Ford* (London: Plexus, 1981).

Anderson, Maxwell, and Laurence Stallings, *What Price Glory*, in *Three American Plays* (New York: Harcourt, Brace and Company, 1926), 1–89.

Balio, Tino, *United Artists: The Company Built by the Stars*, i: *1919–1950* (Madison: University of Wisconsin Press, 2009, first edition 1976).

Balshofer, Fred J., and Arthur C. Miller, *One Reel a Week* (Berkeley: University of California Press, 1967).

Batson, Alfred, *African Intrigue*, Beacon Library 4 (London: Jarrolds, 1937).

Behlmer, Rudy, *America's Favorite Movies: Behind the Scenes* (New York: Frederick Ungar Publishing Co., 1982).

Behlmer, Rudy, *Memo from Darryl F. Zanuck: The Golden Years at Twentieth Century-Fox* (New York: Grove Press, 1993).

Behlmer, Rudy, *Memo from David O. Selznick: The Creation of Gone with the Wind and Other Motion-Picture Classics, as Revealed in the Producer's Private Letters, Telegrams, Memorandums and Autobiographical Remarks* (New York: Viking Press, 1972).

Bellour, Raymond, "To Segment/To Analyse (on *Gigi*)", in *The Analysis of Film*, ed. Constance Penley (Bloomington, Indiana: Indiana University Press, 2000), 193–215; first published as "Segmenter/Analyser", in Bellour, *L'Analyse du film* (Paris: Éditions Albatros, 1979), 247–270.

Berg, A. Scott, *Goldwyn: A Biography* (New York: Alfred A. Knopf, 1989).

Berg, Charles Ramirez, "The Margin as Center: The Multicultural Dynamics of John Ford's Westerns", in Gaylyn Studlar and Matthew Bernstein, eds., *John Ford Made Westerns: Filming the Legend in the Sound Era* (Bloomington, Indiana: Indiana University Press, 2001), 75–101.

Bergstrom, Janet, "Murnau in America: Chronicle of Lost Films", *Film History*, 14/3–4 (2002): 430–460.

Bergstrom, Janet, "Murnau's *Sunrise*: In-Camera Effects and Effects Specialists", in Martin Lefebvre and Mark Furstenau, eds., *Special Effects on the Screen: Faking the View from Méliès to Motion Capture* (Amsterdam: Amsterdam University Press, 2022), 347–351.

Bernstein, Matthew, *Walter Wanger: Hollywood Independent* (Berkeley: University of California Press, 1994).

Blair, Walter, "When Was *Huckleberry Finn* Written?", *American Literature*, 30/1 (March, 1958): 1–25.

Bogdanovich, Peter, *John Ford* (new, revised and enlarged edition, Berkeley: University of California Press, 1978).

Bogdanovich, Peter, "The Autumn of John Ford", in Gerald Peary, ed., *John Ford Interviews* (Jackson, Mississippi: University Press of Mississippi, 2001), 58–60, first published *Esquire* (April, 1964): 106–107.

Bordwell, David, *Figures Traced in Light: On Cinematic Staging* (Berkeley: University of California Press, 2005).

Bordwell, David, "Mutual Friends and Chronologies of Chance", in *Poetics of Cinema* (New York: Routledge, 2008), 189–250.

Bordwell, David, "The Introduction of Sound", in David Bordwell, Janet Staiger and Kristin Thompson, *The Classical Hollywood Cinema: Film Style and Mode of Production to 1960* (London: Routledge & Kegan Paul, 1985), 298–308.

Brosnan, John, *Movie Magic* (New York: St. Martin's Press, 1974).

Browne, Nick, "The Spectator-in-the-Text: The Rhetoric of *Stagecoach*", *Film Quarterly*, 29/2 (Winter 1975–1976): 26–38.

Burman, Ben Lucien, *Mississippi* (New York: J. Day & Co., 1929).

Burman, Ben Lucien, *Steamboat Round the Bend* (New York: Grosset & Dunlap, 1933).

Buscombe, Edward, *Stagecoach*, BFI Film Classics (London: BFI Publishing, 1992).

Byrne, Donn, *Blind Raftery and his wife, Hilaria* (New York: The Century Co., 1924).

Canutt, Yakima, *Stunt Man: the Autobiography of Yakima Canutt with Oliver Drake* (New York: Walker and Company, 1979).

Carpenter, Francis B., *Six Months at the White House with Abraham Lincoln: The Story of a Picture* (New York: Herd & Houghton, 1866).

Clarke, Donald Henderson, *Louis Beretti: A Novel* (New York: Grosset & Dunlap, 1929).

Cobb, Irvin S., "A Treefull of Hoot Owls", in *Down Yonder with Judge Priest and Irvin S. Cobb* (New York: Ray Long & Richard R. Smith, Inc., 1932), 54–84, first published *Hearst's International-Cosmopolitan Magazine* (August, 1930): 60–63, 140–142, 144, 146.

Cobb, Irvin S., "Br'er Rabbit, He Lay Low", in *Down Yonder with Judge Priest and Irvin S. Cobb* (New York:

Ray Long & Richard R. Smith, Inc., 1932), 109–142, first published as "Br'er Fox and the Briar Patch" *Hearst's International-Cosmopolitan Magazine* (May, 1931): 68–71, 200, 202–206.

Cobb, Irvin S., "Judge Priest Comes Back", in *Old Judge Priest* (New York: George H. Doran, 1916), 92–140, first published *Saturday Evening Post* (August 7, 1915): 3–4, 45–46, 49–51.

Cobb, Irvin S., "The Mob from Massac", in *Back Home* (New York: George H. Doran Company, 1912), 246–283, first published *Saturday Evening Post* (February 10, 1912): 5–7, 32–33.

Cobb, Irvin S., "The Sun Shines Bright", in *Down Yonder with Judge Priest and Irvin S. Cobb* (New York: Ray Long & Richard R. Smith, Inc., 1932), 27–53, first published *Hearst's International-Cosmopolitan Magazine* (April, 1931): 72–74, 130–137.

Cobb, Irvin S., "Words and Music", in *Back Home* (New York: George H. Doran Company, 1912), 3–37, first published *Saturday Evening Post* (October 28, 1911): 9–11.

Cohn, Henry S., "Abraham Lincoln at the Bar", *The Federal Lawyer* (May, 2012): 52–55.

"Company Remembers *Stagecoach*, The", *Action: Directors Guild of America*, 6/5 (September–October, 1971): 24–29.

Cozzens, James Gould, *The Last Adam* (New York: Harcourt, Brace, 1933).

Dumont, Hervé, *Frank Borzage: Sarastro à Hollywood* (Paris: Cahiers du cinéma/Milan: Edizioni Gabriele Mazzotti, 1993).

Dunne, Philip, *Take Two: A Life in Movies and Politics*, updated edition (New York: Limelight Editions, 1992).

Edmonds, Walter D., *Drums along the Mohawk* (Boston: Little, Brown, and company, 1936).

Edmonds, Walter D., *Rome Haul* (Boston: Little, Brown, and company, 1929).

Eisenberg, Emanuel, "John Ford: Fighting Irish", in Gerald Peary, ed., *John Ford Interviews* (Jackson, Mississippi: University Press of Mississippi, 2001), 10–14, first published *New Theatre* (April, 1936): 7, 42.

Eisenstein, Sergei Mikhailovich, "Mr. Lincoln by Mr. Ford", in *Selected Works*, iii: *Writings, 1934–1947*, trans. William Powell, ed. Richard Taylor (London: I. B. Tauris & Co., 2010), 274–283.

Eisner, Lotte H., *The Haunted Screen: Expressionism in the German Cinema and the Influence of Max Reinhardt*, trans. Roger Greaves (London: Thames and Hudson, 1969), first published as *L'Écran démoniaque* (Paris: Le Terrain vague, 1965).

Ellis, William E., *Irvin S. Cobb: the Rise and Fall of an American Humorist* (Lexington, Kentucky: University of Kentucky Press, 2017).

Eyman, Scott, "Looking Back: John Wayne Talking to Scott Eyman", *Focus on Film* (Spring, 1975): 17–23.

Eyman, Scott, *Print the Legend: The Life and Times of John Ford* (New York: Simon & Schuster, 1999).

Ford, Dan, *Pappy: The Life of John Ford* (Englewood Cliffs, New Jersey: Prentice-Hall, 1979).

Frazier, Adrian, *The Hollywood Irish: John Ford, Abbey Actors and the Irish Revival in Hollywood* (Dublin: Lilliput Press, 2011).

Fulton, Maude, *The Brat: A Comedy in Three Acts* (New York: Longmans, Green & Co., 1926).

Gad, Urban, *Der Film: seine Mittel seine Ziele*, trans. Julia Koppel (Berlin: Schuster & Loeffler, 1921), first published as *Filmen, dens midler og maal* (Copenhagen: Gyldendalske Boghandel/Nordisk Forlag, 1919).

Gallagher, Tag, *John Ford: Himself and His Films* (Apple Books, 2020).

Gallagher, Tag, *John Ford: The Man and His Films* (Berkeley: University of California Press, 1986).

Garth, David, *Four Men and a Prayer* (New York: H. C. Kinsey & Co., 1937).

Gomery, Douglas, *The Coming of Sound: A History* (New York: Routledge, 2005).

Gomery, Douglas, *The Hollywood Studio System* (London: MacMillan, 1986).

Greene, Graham, *The Power and the Glory* (London: Heinemann, 1940), published in the U.S. as *The Labyrinthine Ways* (New York: Viking Press, 1940).

Gussow, Mel, *Don't Say Yes Until I Finish Talking: A Biography of Darryl F. Zanuck* (New York: Doubleday and Company, 1971).

Harte, F. Bret, "The Outcasts of Poker Flat", in *The Luck of Roaring Camp and Other Stories* (New York: Penguin Books, 2001), 27–37, first published in the *Overland Monthly and Out West Magazine*, 2/1 (January, 1869): 41–47.

Haver, Ron, *David O. Selznick's Hollywood* (New York: Knopf, 1980).

Haycox, Ernest, "Stage to Lordsburg", *Collier's Weekly* (April 10, 1937): 18–19, 68–69.

Hertz, Emanuel, *Lincoln Talks: A Biography in Anecdote* (New York: Viking Press, 1939).

Hill, Frederick Trevor, *Lincoln the Lawyer* (New York: Century Co., 1906).

Hirschhorn, Clive, *The Universal Story* (New York: Crown Publishers, 1983).

History of Cinema, Series 1, Hollywood and the Production Code, Selected files from the Motion Picture Association of America Production Code Administration collection, Filmed from the holdings of the Margaret Herrick Library, Academy of Motion Picture Arts and Sciences, Primary Source Microfilm (Woodbridge, Connecticut: Thomas Gale, 2006).

Jacobs, Lea, "*December 7th, The Battle of Midway*, and John Ford's career in the OSS", *Film History* 32/1 (2020): 1–39.

Jacobs, Lea, "Dialogue Scenes in the Period of Multiple-Camera Shooting: the Example of *Arrowsmith*", in Daniel Wiegand, ed., *Aesthetics of Early Sound Film: Media Change around 1930* (Amsterdam: Amsterdam University Press, 2023), 29–48.

Jacobs, Lea, *Film Rhythm after Sound: Technology, Music, and Performance* (Oakland, California: University of California Press, 2015).

Jacobs, Lea, "Making John Ford's *How Green Was My Valley*", *Film History*, 28/2 (2016): 32–80.

Jacobs, Lea, "Men without Women: The Avatars of *What Price Glory*", *Film History*, 17/2–3 (2005): 307–333.

Jacobs, Lea, "The Innovation of Re-recording in the Hollywood Studios", *Film History*, 24/1 (2012): 5–35.

Jewell, Richard B., *RKO Radio Pictures: A Titan is Born* (Berkeley: University of California Press, 2012).

Jewell, Richard B., with Vernon Harbin, *The RKO Story* (New York: Crown Books, 1982).

"John Ford's *Young Mr. Lincoln*" by the editors of *Cahiers du cinéma*, *Screen*, 13/3 (Autumn, 1972): 5–44, first published in *Cahiers du cinéma*, 223 (August, 1970): 29–47.

Kalinak, Kathryn, *How the West Was Sung: Music in the Westerns of John Ford* (Berkeley: University of California Press, 2007).

Kalinak, Kathryn, "Max Steiner and the Classical Hollywood Film Score: An Analysis of *The Informer*", in Clifford McCarty, ed., *Film Music 1*, Garland Reference Library of the Humanities, 966 (New York: Garland Publishing, 1989), 123–142.

Keating, Patrick, *Hollywood Lighting: From the Silent Era to Film Noir* (New York: Columbia University Press, 2010).

Keating, Patrick, *The Dynamic Frame: Camera Movement in Classical Hollywood* (New York: Columbia University Press, 2019).

Kelly, Angeline A., ed., *The Letters of Liam O'Flaherty* (Dublin: Wolfhound Press, 1996).

Killanin, Michael, "Poet in an Iron Mask", in Gerald Peary, ed., *John Ford Interviews* (Jackson, Mississippi: University Press of Mississippi, 2001), 38–40, first published *Films and Filming*, 4/5 (February, 1958): 9, 28.

Kipling, Rudyard, "*Captains Courageous*": *A Story of the Grand Banks* (New York: Macmillan, 1897), first published *McClure's Magazine*, 8 (November, 1896–April, 1897): 17–31, 165–175, 222–235, 341–355, 424–431, 521–529, and 9 (May, 1897): 611–618.

Kipling, Rudyard, "Toomai of the Elephants", *The Jungle Book* (New York: The Century Co., 1894), 217–261, first published *St. Nicholas Magazine*, 21/2 (December, 1893): 99–111.

Kipling, Rudyard, *Wee Willie Winkie and Other Stories* (New York: Hurst & Co, 1891, first published Allahabad, now Prayagraj, Uttar Pradesh, India: A. M. Wheeler, 1888).

Koszarski, Richard, *An Evening's Entertainment: The Age of the Silent Feature Picture, 1915–1928* (New York: Charles Scribner's Sons, 1990).

Krefft, Vanda, *The Man Who Made the Movies: The Meteoric Rise and Tragic Fall of William Fox* (New York: Harper Collins, 2017).

La Farge, Oliver, *Laughing Boy* (Boston: Houghton, Mifflin, 1929).

Lawson, Anita, *Irvin S. Cobb* (Bowling Green, Ohio: Bowling Green State University Popular Press, 1984).

Leguèbe, Éric, "John Ford", trans. Jenny Lefcourt, in Gerald Peary, ed., *John Ford Interviews* (Jackson,

Mississippi: University Press of Mississippi, 2001), 70–74, first published in Leguèbe, *Confessions 2: un siècle de cinéma américain par ceux qui l'ont fait* (Paris: Ifrane éd., 1995), 37–41.

Lewis, Sinclair, *Arrowsmith* (New York: Harcourt, Brace & Co., 1925).

Llewellyn, Richard, *How Green Was My Valley* (London: M. Joseph, Ltd., 1939).

Lockwood, Lewis, *Beethoven's Lives: The Biographical Tradition* (Woodbridge, Suffolk: The Boydell Press, 2020).

Loew, Katharina, *Special Effects and German Silent Film* (Amsterdam: Amsterdam University Press, 2021).

Long, Derek, "Reprogramming the Movies: Distribution Strategy and Production Planning in the Early Studio System, 1915–1924" (PhD diss., University of Wisconsin-Madison, 2017).

McBride, Joseph, *Searching for John Ford: A Life* (New York: St. Martin's Griffin, 2003).

McCarthy, Todd, *Howard Hawks: The Grey Fox of Hollywood* (New York: Grove Press, 1997).

MacDonald, Philip, *Patrol* (New York: A. L. Burt Company, 1928).

Macgowan, Kenneth, "Introduction", in Macgowan, ed., *Famous American Plays of the 1920s* (New York: Dell, 1959), 7–28.

Madsen, Axel, "Ford on Ford 1", Interview of March 14, 1966, translated from Danish by Jan Lumholdt (except for Ford's own original English replies), in Gerald Peary, ed., *John Ford Interviews* (Jackson, Mississippi: University Press of Mississippi, 2001), 81–92, first published in Per Calum, ed., *John Ford: En Dokumentation* (Copenhagen: Det Danske Filmmuseum, 1968), 17–33.

Madsen, Axel, "Ford on Ford 2", Interview of April 4, 1967, translated from Danish by Jan Lumholdt (except for Ford's own original English replies), in Gerald Peary, ed., *John Ford Interviews* (Jackson, Mississippi: University Press of Mississippi, 2001), 113–117, first published in Per Calum, ed., *John Ford: En Dokumentation* (Copenhagen: Det Danske Filmmuseum, 1968), 35–43.

Madsen, Axel, *William Wyler: The Authorized Biography* (New York: Thomas Y. Crowell, 1973).

Marzola, Luci, "Better Pictures through Chemistry: DuPont and the Fight for the Hollywood Film Stock Market", *Velvet Light Trap*, 76 (Fall, 2015): 3–18.

Maupassant, Guy de, "Boule de Suif", in *Contes et Nouvelles*, 1, ed. Louis Forestier, Bibliothèque de la Pléiade (Paris: Gallimard, 1974), 83–121, first published in *Les Soirées de Médan* (Paris: G. Charpentier, 1880), 51–105.

Millholland, Ray, *The Splinter Fleet of the Otranto Barrage* (New York: Bobbs-Merrill, 1936).

Mitchell, George J., "Ford on Ford", in Gerald Peary, ed., *John Ford Interviews* (Jackson, Mississippi: University Press of Mississippi, 2001), 61–69, first published *Films in Review*, 15/6 (June–July, 1964): 321–332.

Mok, Michel, "The Rebels, If They Stay Up This Time, Won't Be Sorry for Hollywood's Trouble", in Gerald Peary, ed., *John Ford Interviews* (Jackson, Mississippi: University Press of Mississippi, 2001), 21–23, first published *New York Post* (January 24, 1939).

Mudd, Nettie, *The Life of Dr. Samuel A. Mudd* (New York: Neale Publishing Co., 1906, rpt. Marietta, Georgia: Continental Book Company, 1955).

Mundy, Talbot, *King of the Khyber Rifles* (Indianapolis, Indiana: Bobbs-Merrill, 1916).

Nelson, Bruce, *Workers on the Waterfront: Seamen, Longshoremen, and Unionism in the 1930s* (Urbana and Chicago, Illinois: University of Illinois Press, 1988).

Niven, Penelope, *Carl Sandburg: A Biography* (New York: C. Scribner's Sons, 1991).

Nordhoff, Charles, and James Norman Hall, *Mutiny on the Bounty* (Boston: Little, Brown, 1932).

Nordhoff, Charles, and James Norman Hall, *The Hurricane* (Boston: Little, Brown, 1936).

Nottebohm, Gustav, *Zweite Beethoveniana*, ed. Eusebius Mandycewski (Leipzig: Peters, 1887).

O'Flaherty, Liam, *The Informer* (London: Jonathan Cape, 1925, rpt. 1964).

O'Neill, Eugene, *The Long Voyage Home: Seven Plays of the Sea* (New York: The Modern Library, 1946).

Parrish, Robert, *Growing Up in Hollywood* (New York: Harcourt Brace Jovanovich, 1976).

Paul Ivano: an American Film Institute Seminar on his Work, held April 20, 1974, *The American Film Institute Seminars*, 1/91, *New York Times* oral history program (Glen Rock, New Jersey: Microfilming Corporation of American, 1977).

Rieupeyrout, Jean-Louis, "A Meeting with John Ford", trans. Jenny Lefcourt, in Gerald Peary, ed., *John

Ford Interviews (Jackson, Mississippi: University Press of Mississippi, 2001), 44–45, first published *Cinéma 61*, 53 (February, 1961): 8–10.

Roberts, Randy, and James S. Olson, *John Wayne: American* (New York: Simon & Schuster, 1995).

Rogers, Will, *The Papers of Will Rogers*, v: *The Final Years, August 1928–August 1935*, ed. Steven K. Gragert and M. Jane Johansson (Norman, Oklahoma: University of Oklahoma Press, 2006).

Rogers, Will, *The Writings of Will Rogers*, series iv: *Will Rogers' Weekly Articles*, ed. James M. Smallwood and Steven K. Gragert, six vols (Stillwater, Oklahoma: Oklahoma State University Press, 1980–1982).

Rogers, Will, *The Writings of Will Rogers*, series vi: *Radio Broadcasts of Will Rogers*, ed. Steven K. Gragert (Stillwater, Oklahoma: Oklahoma State University Press, 1983).

Rohmer, Éric, *L'organisation de l'espace dans le* Faust *de Murnau* (Paris: Union générale d'éditions, 1977).

Rust, R. Dilworth, "The Unity of O'Neill's *S. S. Glencairn*", *American Literature*, 37/3 (November, 1965): 280–290.

Salt, Barry, *Film Style and Technology: History and Analysis* (London: Starword, 3rd edition, 2009).

Sandburg, Carl, *Abraham Lincoln: The Prairie Years*, 2 vols (New York: Harcourt, Brace & Co., 1926).

Sandburg, Carl, *The American Songbag* (New York: Harcourt, Brace & Co., 1927).

Sarris, Andrew, *The American Cinema* (New York: E. P. Dutton, 1968).

Scott, Sir Walter, *The Monastery: A Romance* (Edinburgh: Constable, 1820).

Selvin, David F., *A Terrible Anger: The 1934 Waterfront and General Strikes in San Francisco* (Detroit, Michigan: Wayne State University Press, 1996).

Semenov, Lillian Wurtzel, and Carla Winter, eds., *William Fox, Sol M. Wurtzel and the Early Fox Film Corporation: Letters, 1917–1923* (Jefferson, North Carolina: McFarland & Company, 2001).

Sharpe, Howard, "The Star Creators of Hollywood", in Gerald Peary, ed., *John Ford Interviews* (Jackson, Mississippi: University Press of Mississippi, 2001), 15–20, first published *Photoplay*, 50/41 (1936): 14–15, 98–100.

Sheeran, Patrick F., *The Informer* (Cork: Cork University Press in association with the Film Institute of Ireland, 2002).

Sheeran, Patrick F., *The Novels of Liam O'Flaherty: A Study in Romantic Realism* (Dublin: Wolfhound Press, 1976).

Sherwood, Robert, *Abe Lincoln in Illinois* (New York: Charles Scribner's Sons, 1939).

Shields, Ren, and Leighton Bros., "Steamboat Bill" (New York: F. A. Mills, 1910).

Smith, Henry Nash, *Mark Twain: The Development of a Writer* (Cambridge, Massachusetts: Harvard University Press, 1962).

Solomon, Aubrey, *The Fox Film Corporation, 1915–1935: A History and Filmography* (Jefferson, North Carolina: McFarland & Company, 2011).

Spring, Katherine, *Saying It with Songs: Popular Music and the Coming of Sound to Hollywood Cinema* (New York: Oxford University Press, 2013).

Stagecoach: a film by John Ford and Dudley Nichols, Classic Film Scripts (New York: Simon and Schuster, 1971).

Steers, Edward, Jr., *Blood on the Moon: The Assassination of Abraham Lincoln* (Lexington, Kentucky: University Press of Kentucky, 2005).

Steinbeck, John, *The Grapes of Wrath* (New York: The Viking Press, 1939).

Stempel, Thomas, "An Oral History Interview with Barbara McLean", Darryl F. Zanuck Research Project (Los Angeles: American Film Institute, 1970–1971).

Stempel, Thomas, "An Oral History Interview with Henry King", Darryl F. Zanuck Research Project (Los Angeles: American Film Institute, 1970–1971).

Stempel, Thomas, *Recollections of Nunnally Johnson*, oral history transcript (Oral History Program, University of California, Los Angeles: 1969).

Stephens, Michael L., *Art Directors in Cinema: A Worldwide Biographical Dictionary* (Jefferson, North Carolina: McFarland, 1998).

Sterling, Bryan B., ed., *The Will Rogers Scrapbook* (New York: Grosset & Dunlap, 1976).

Sterling, Bryan B., and Frances N. Sterling, eds., *Will Rogers in Hollywood* (New York: Crown Publishers, 1984).

Sternberg, Meir, *Expositional Modes and Temporal Ordering in Fiction* (Baltimore, Maryland: The Johns Hopkins University Press, 1978).

Studlar, Gaylyn, "Be a Proud, Glorified Dreg: Class, Gender and Frontier Democracy in *Stagecoach*", in Barry Keith Grant, ed., *John Ford's Stagecoach* (New York: Cambridge University Press, 2003), 132–157.

Tavernier, Bertrand, "Notes of a Press Attaché: John Ford in Paris, 1966", trans. Jean-Pierre Coursodon, in Gerald Peary, ed., *John Ford Interviews* (Jackson, Mississippi: University Press of Mississippi, 2001), 104–112, first published *Positif*, 82 (March, 1967): 7–22, this translation first published *Film Comment*, 30/4 (July–August, 1994): 66–73, 75.

Tavernier, Claudine, "The Fourth Dimension of Old Age", trans. Jenny Lefcourt, in Gerald Peary, ed., *John Ford Interviews* (Jackson, Mississippi: University Press of Mississippi, 2001), 98–103, first published *Cinéma*, 137 (June, 1969).

Teichmann, Howard, *Fonda: My Life, as Told to Howard Teichmann* (New York and Scarborough, Ontario: The New American Library, 1981).

Thompson, Kristin, "The Formulation of the Classical Style, 1909–1928", in David Bordwell, Janet Staiger and Kristin Thompson, *The Classical Hollywood Cinema: Film Style and Mode of Production to 1960* (London: Routledge & Kegan Paul, 1985), 155–240.

Tobin, Vera, *Elements of Surprise: Our Mental Limits and the Satisfactions of Plot* (Cambridge, Massachusetts: Harvard University Press, 2018).

Troy, William, "The Position of Liam O'Flaherty", *The Bookman* (March, 1929): 7–11.

Tuska, Jon, *Encounters with Filmmakers: Eight Career Studies* (New York: Greenwood Press, 1991).

Twain, Mark, *Adventures of Huckleberry Finn* (Boston: Houghton Mifflin, 1958, first published London: Chatto & Windus, 1884).

Twain, Mark, *Life on the Mississippi* (New York: Harper & Row, 1917, first published Boston: James R. Osgood & Co., 1883).

Van de Water, Frederic, *Glory-hunter: A Life of General Custer* (New York: The Bobbs-Merrill Company, 1934).

Vaz, Mark Cotta, *Living Dangerously: The Adventures of Merian C. Cooper, Creator of King Kong* (New York: Villard, 2005).

Wagner, Walter, *You Must Remember This* (New York: Putnam, 1975).

Wexman, Virginia Wright, *Hollywood's Artists: The Directors Guild of America and the Construction of Authorship* (New York: Columbia University Press, 2020).

Wilson, Booth, "How John Ford's West Was Framed: Landscape and Geography in the Monument Valley Films", *Journal of Cinema and Media Studies*, 59/3 (Spring, 2020): 90–113.

Wister, Owen (words and music), "Ten Thousand Cattle Straying (Dead Broke)" (New York: M. Witmark & Sons, 1904).

Wister, Owen, *The Virginian: A Horseman of the Plains* (New York: The Macmillan Publishing Company, 1902).

Wood, Robin, "Shall We Gather at the River? The Late Films of John Ford", *Film Comment*, 7/3 (Fall, 1971): 8–17.

Wylie, Ida Alexa Ross, "Grandmother Bernle Learns Her Letters", *Saturday Evening Post* (September 11, 1926): 8–9, 136, 139–140, 145–146, 150.

Wylie, Ida Alexa Ross, "Pilgrimage", *American Magazine* (November, 1932): 44–47, 90–96.

Yagoda, Ben, *Will Rogers: A Biography* (Norman, Oklahoma: University of Oklahoma Press, 1993).

Index